GRAMMATICALIZATION AND LANGUAGE CHANGE IN CHINESE

This innovative study of grammaticalization in Chinese offers a highly accessible and comprehensive overview of both the diachronic development and current syntactic status of a wide variety of grammatical morphemes in Chinese. Approaching the issue of grammaticalization from a formal, theoretical point of view, but also making use of traditional insights into language change, Xiu-Zhi Zoe Wu shows how a range of syntactic mechanisms have conspired to result in the grammatical constructions and functional morphemes of modern Chinese. Patterns from Chinese and an in-depth analysis of the development of functional categories in the language are also used to argue for more general, cross-linguistic principles of language change, and provide valuable insights into the principled ways that grammatical words evolve across languages.

Grammaticalization and Language Change in Chinese is a bold and inspired attempt to apply formal, Chomskyean syntactic theory to the traditional area of the study of language change. Although the analyses of the book are cast within such a theoretical approach to language, the data and generalizations brought to light should be of considerable interest to linguists from quite different backgrounds, and the central ideas and intuitions of the various chapters are presented in a way that makes them accessible to a wide and varied readership. The book is not only a highly informative and useful resource on Chinese but also clearly indicates what Chinese is able to show about language change and the phenomena of grammaticalization in general.

Xiu-Zhi Zoe Wu is a Lecturer in the Chinese Program, Department of East Asian Languages and Cultures at the University of Southern California.

ROUTLEDGECURZON ASIAN LINGUISTICS SERIES

Editor-in-Chief: Walter Bisang, *Mainz University*

Associate Editors: R. V. Dhongde, *Deccan College Pune* and Masayoshi Shibatani, *Rice University, Texas*

Asia is the world's largest continent, comprising an enormous wealth of languages, both in its present as well as in its eventful past. The series contributes to the understanding of this linguistic variety by publishing books from different theoretical backgrounds and different methodological approaches, dealing with at least one Asian language. By adopting a maximally integrative policy, the editors of the series hope to promote theoretical discussions whose solutions may, in turn, help to overcome the theoretical lean towards West European languages and thus provide a deeper understanding of Asian linguistic structures and of human language in general.

VIETNAMESE–ENGLISH BILINGUALISM
Patterns of code-switching
Ho-Dac Tuc

LINGUISTIC EPIDEMIOLOGY
Semantics and grammar of language contact in mainland Southeast Asia
Nick J. Enfield

A GRAMMAR OF MANGGHUER
A Mongolic language of China's Qinghai-Gansu Sprachbund
Keith W. Slater

FUNCTIONAL STRUCTURE(S), FORM AND INTERPRETATION
Perspectives from East Asian languages
Edited by Yen-hui Audrey Li and Andrew Simpson

FOCUS AND BACKGROUND MARKING IN MANDARIN CHINESE
System and theory behind *cai, jiu, dou* and *ye*
Daniel Hole

GRAMMATICALIZATION AND LANGUAGE CHANGE IN CHINESE
A formal view
Xiu-Zhi Zoe Wu

GRAMMATICALIZATION AND LANGUAGE CHANGE IN CHINESE

A formal view

Xiu-Zhi Zoe Wu

First published 2004 by RoutledgeCurzon
2 Park Square, Milton Park, Abingdon, Oxfordshire OX14 4RN

Simultaneously published in the USA and Canada
by RoutledgeCurzon
29 West 35th Street, New York, NY 10001

RoutledgeCurzon is an imprint of the Taylor & Francis Group

Publisher's Note
This book has been prepared from camera-ready copy provided by the author.

© 2004 Xiu-Zhi Zoe Wu

Printed and bound in Great Britain by TJ International, Padstow, Cornwall

All rights reserved. No part of this book may be reprinted or reproduced or utilised in any form or by any electronic, mechanical, or other means, now known or hereafter invented, including photocopying and recording, or in any information storage or retrieval system, without permission in writing from the publishers.

British Library Cataloguing in Publication Data
A catalogue record for this book is available from the British Library

Library of Congress Cataloging in Publication Data
A catalog record for this book has been requested

ISBN 0-415-33603-1

CONTENTS

ACKNOWLEDGMENTS	ix
1. INTRODUCTION	1
1.0 Overview	1
1.1 Background: Grammaticalization as an Area of Study	2
1.2 A Formal Approach to Grammaticalization	5
1.3 Patterns to Be Examined in the Work	8
2. THE CLASSIFIER *GE*: MOVEMENT AND REANALYSIS	13
2.0 Introduction	13
2.1 *Ge* as a General Classifier for Nouns	13
2.2 *Ge* as a Classifier for Events Denoted by the Predicates	14
2.2.1 *Occurrence Between a Verb and Its Cognate Object 14*	
2.2.2 *Occurrence Between a Verb and an Indefinite Object 15*	
2.2.3 *Ge Introducing a Simple Resultative/Descriptive Adjective 18*	
2.2.4 *Ge Introducing an Idiom or Fixed Expression 21*	
2.2.5 *Ge with Perfective but not Imperfective Aspect 21*	
2.2.6 *Apparent Constraints on Verb Selection 22*	
2.3 Syntactic Properties	23
2.3.1 *Event Ge Introducing a Non-predicational Adjective 23*	
2.3.2 *Event Ge Licensing an Extra Argument 26*	
2.3.3 *Ge Licensing the Expletive 'It' 29*	
2.4 The Proposal—*Ge* as a Weak Unselective Determiner in D^0	30
2.4.1 *Ge as a Nominalizer 30*	
2.4.2 *Ge as a D^0 32*	
2.4.3 *Further Evidence 33*	
2.5 Grammaticalization, Reanalysis and *Ge*	37

2.6 Concluding Remarks	45
Notes	45

3. RELATIVE CLAUSE *DE*: DIRECTIONALITY, CLAUSAL RAISING AND SENTENCE-FINAL PARTICLES — 51

3.0 Introduction — 51

3.1 Relative Clauses in Government and Binding Theory — 52
3.1.1 Chiu (1993/1995) and SuoP; Ning (1993) 53
3.1.2 DE as a Complementizer 56

3.2 Directionality and C-selection—a Theoretical Problem for Standard Analyses — 58

3.3 Kayne (1994) and a Uniform Theory of Relativization — 61
3.3.1 Determiners, Demonstratives and Definiteness Agreement 65
3.3.2 Further Evidence for the NP-raising Analysis: (1) Language Acquisition: Chiu (1998); (2) Connectivity and Idiom-chunks 69
3.3.3 Relativization in Japanese, Murasugi (1991/1998) 72
3.3.4 Process Nominals and the Structure of Noun-Complement Clause CNPs 77
3.3.5 Other Noun-Complement Clause CNPs 80

3.4 Taiwanese Tone Sandhi and the Clausal Raising Hypothesis — 84
3.4.1 Tone Sandhi Patterns in Taiwanese 84
3.4.2 Tone Sandhi in Taiwanese Relative Clauses 87

3.5 Extensions: Grammaticalized Complementizers in Taiwanese — 90
3.5.1 Tone Sandhi Patterns with Kong *93*
3.5.2 Grammaticalization of Kong *and Motivations for IP-movement 98*
3.5.3 Evidence for PF Movement? 101
3.5.4 An Alternative—Cyclic Spell-Out 103

3.6 Concluding Remarks	107
Notes	108

4. *DE* IN FOCUS SENTENCES: FROM D TO T — 120

4.0 Introduction — 120
4.1 Object-*De* Repositioning in the *Shi-de* Construction — 122
4.2 Post-object *De* — 128
4.3 The Syntax of Reanalysis in *Shi-de* Sentences — 138
4.4 Summary: D-to-T and Paths of Grammaticalization — 149
4.5 Appendix: on the Focus Interpretation of *Shi-de* Forms — 153

Notes 156

5. Resultative Constructions: Directionality and Reanalysis 161

5.0 Introduction 161

5.1 Previous Analyses 163

5.1.1 Resultative Verb Constructions: an introduction 163
5.1.2 The Lexical Approach—Yafei Li (1990) 165
5.1.3 The Syntactic Approach—Zou (1994) 167
5.1.4 Sybesma (1999), Hoekstra (1992) 170
5.1.5 Objections to the Syntactic Approach 173

5.2 An Alternative Analysis: V_2 as Aspect 180

5.2.1 Telicity and Non-predication 180
5.2.2 The Historical Re-positioning of V_2 in RVCs: Reanalysis and Aspect 182
5.2.3 Literal V_2 and Reanalysis 190
5.2.4 Responses to Apparent Objections 194

5.3 V_2 Re-positioning and Directionality 200

5.3.1 Arguments Against a Phonological Explanation 201
5.3.2 V_2 Elements as Verbal Suffixes 204
5.3.3 V_2 Elements Do Not Undergo Raising to V_1 205

5.4 Consequences Related to Other Structures 216

5.5 English Resultatives: a Speculation 219

5.6 Summary 225

Notes 226

6. Verbal *Le* : Aspect and Tense 234

6.0 Introduction 234

6.1 The Re-positioning of *Le/Liao* 234

6.1.1 The Current Status of Verbal Le and Completive Aspect 236
6.1.2 Smith (1997): Two Different Types of Aspect 239
6.1.3 Verbal Le and Perfectivity 244
6.1.4 Grammaticalization and the Dual Status of Verbal Le 250
 6.1.4.1 Parallel grammaticalization of independent X^0-heads and affixes 250
 6.1.4.2 Current distinctions between completive and perfective le: evidence for diachronic development 259

6.2 Verbal *Le* and Tense 267

6.2.1 Tense, Aspect and Perfectivity 270

  6.2.2 Possible Objections to an Analysis of Le *as Tense 275*
  6.2.3 Arguments against the Objections 277
   6.2.3.1 Optionality of *le* 277
   6.2.3.2 Lack of generality I: non-occurrence with simple verbs of cognition or communication 280
   6.2.3.3 Lack of generality II: *le* with statives 281
   6.2.3.4 Subordinate clauses 288
   6.2.3.5 Imperatives 293
   6.2.3.6 Matrix *jiu* sentences 294

6.3 Summary	**298**
Notes	**299**
7. POST-WORD	**303**
BIBLIOGRAPHY	**310**
INDEX	**320**

ACKNOWLEDGMENTS

Many people have played an important role in the conception, development and refinement of this book, which is a rewritten and reworked version of the doctoral dissertation I completed at the University of Southern California in 2000. As before, I would like to thank a range of different people for their help and inspiration both during the time I spent in the Linguistics Department in USC, and during the last three years when I have continued to work on the topic of grammaticalization. Among the very many at USC who I owe much gratitude to are the following: Joseph Aoun, Hagit Borer, Hajime Hoji, Audrey Li, Jean-Roger Vergnaud, and Maria-Luisa Zubizarreta. They and others taught me so much about language and linguistics and continually inspired me in my research. I would also like to thank my friends and colleagues in the department of East Asian Languages and Cultures at USC for their great support and friendship over the last ten years, in particular Yi-chia Hsu, Grace Li and Li Yan, as well as Lina Choueiri my fellow student in Linguistics. Outside of USC, many, many thanks are due to all those brothers and sisters I have regularly met with in the Church of Los Angeles over the past ten years. Their endless support, friendship and prayers have helped me through many trying years. Finally, I would like to thank my family, for the love and support I have often taken for granted - my parents, who do not understand what linguistics is but believe it is a great and worthy subject to study because of their beloved child; my two brothers and their wives, who have always supported me morally and financially whenever I needed help, and also their dear children who remind me of the kind of role model I should be. I thank all of you from the bottom of my heart. Without the love, security, optimism and support that you have constantly given me over the years, this book would never have come into existence. Last but not least, I would also like to thank Andrew Simpson, my dear friend and colleague from SOAS, London. Without Andrew's great help and encouragement, and inspiration from the joint work we have carried out together over the past few years, the writing of this book would have been so much harder, and I thank you very sincerely for all the good things you have regularly brought to my research.

1

INTRODUCTION

1.0 Overview

This book is an investigation of the phenomenon of grammaticalization and its manifestation in the development and synchronic status of a range of grammatical morphemes and functional categories in Chinese. There are two primary aims in the investigation: first to see how a study of various functional paradigms in Chinese may shed further light on the mechanisms of language change and grammaticalization that are generally available cross-linguistically, and secondly to examine how the use of diachronic information may help in the analysis of certain otherwise problematic synchronic phenomena in Chinese.

The book is divided into five main chapters, each of which attempts to address the above-stated dual aims of: (a) providing a synchronic analysis of a certain functional paradigms in Chinese assisted by considerations of how functional categories may develop over time, and (b) investigating the nature of general processes of grammaticalization. Concerning the latter goal, each chapter will argue for and attempt to illustrate a different process of grammaticalization at work in Chinese, and will show how grammaticalization may have important effects on aspects of surface linear word-order, frequently causing significant distortions of the underlying syntactic structure.

General conclusions of the investigation are provided chapter by chapter and also outlined below in a brief preview of the various phenomena to be considered. Prior to this however, the chapter provides a short background introduction to certain general ideas relating to grammaticalization and explains the rationale for applying a formal theoretical approach to the study of grammaticalization phenomena in Chinese. Concerning the technical framework and theoretical assumptions adopted in the book, analysis is carried out in a broad Minimalist/Chomskyean approach which assumes a transformational component (i.e., movement) and two interface levels, PF and LF. As in Chomsky (1993, 1995), the combination of lexical items via Merge into initial syntactic structures is assumed to lead first to a point of Spell-Out feeding PF and phonetic interpretation, and then derivationally continue on to a level of LF and semantic interpretation. Various other assumptions relating more specifically to language change and the phenomenon of grammaticalization will be introduced as the chapters proceed and as such notions become particularly relevant.

1.1 Background: Grammaticalization as an Area of Study

Grammaticalization as a term was first used by the French linguist Antione Meillet in a paper written in 1912. Commenting on Meillet's paper, Ramat (1998; p.108) observes that gramaticalization is assumed to have two rather different functions:

(a) to create new forms that replace old forms in existing grammatical structures, which remain essentially the same from the point of view of function,
(b) to introduce into grammar new categories, i.e., new units of form/function.

Most commonly, grammaticalization is assumed to involve some kind of *reanalysis,* involving the development of a word/morpheme into a grammatical marker of some type. In many cases this may involve the development of a word which has descriptive, referential content (e.g., a noun, adjective, verb, etc.) into a grammatical morpheme/word which has a predominantly *functional* role (e.g., a complementizer, tense-mood marker, determiner, etc.), as schematized in (1). The term "grammaticalization" here is sometimes used to refer to the *results* of such a categorical conversion (e.g., the creation of a new tense-marker from a descriptive verb), and also to the *mechanisms* and *processes* which actually give rise to the reanalysis.

(1) Common shift in category type in grammaticalization
lexical word → grammatical word/morpheme
(e.g., verb → complementizer, noun → agreement-marker)

In all occurrences of grammaticalization there is some change in the *meaning* of the grammaticalizing element. Characteristically this is described as involving changes from more referential meanings to increasingly more abstract meanings. Hence, for example, a word with clear descriptive, "referential" content such as (a person/animal's) 'back' denoting the tangible part of a physical body might become re-employed as a more abstract temporal relational term with the meaning 'X-ago (X=point in time)', and syntactically come to function/grammaticalize as an adposition in some languages.

(2) Typical shift in meaning accompanying grammaticalization:
more descriptive/referential → more abstract

INTRODUCTION

Much of the work that has been carried out in the study of grammaticalization in the last century has focused on trying to understand and explain how the shifts of meaning which occur in instances of grammaticalization can be viewed as natural paths of evolution, with a range of *cognitive* and *pragmatic* explanations being given for the variety of changes attested (e.g., Heine, Claudi and Hünnemeyer 1991). Such work frequently describes changes in terms of "grammaticalization chains", in which one link (stage) in a path of development naturally leads to a following link/stage via processes of pragmatic enrichment and inferencing. Expansion and development of meaning here is sometimes suggested to be due to the cognitive mechanism of (permitting) *metaphor*, as for example in the common creation of future auxiliary verbs/expressions from verbs denoting motion to some distant point (English 'going to': I am going to leave, French *aller*: *Je vais partir*), the mental image of motion towards an entity allowing for itself to be re-interpreted metaphorically as 'motion' of the subject towards a future point in time. Growth in the strength of *pragmatic implicatures* made when linguistic expressions are used has similarly been noted to be a cause of meaning change which can over time result in grammaticalization, with secondary inferred meanings coming to be more and more automatically associated with the use of a word/expression (see in particular König 1988, Traugott and König 1991). Two examples of abstract grammaticalization chains are given in (3) and (4) from Bybee, Perkins and Pagliuca (1994, chapter 7). These represent common routes of development in which verbs with the meanings given in small capitals on the left have been noted to frequently develop/grammaticalize into verbs with meanings on their right. Hence in (3), a verb encoding the meaning of DESIRE (e.g., 'want') may develop the meaning of WILLINGNESS, and then INTENTION before finally becoming used as a verb of prediction/a future tense verb.

(3)　DESIRE > WILLINGNESS > INTENTION > PREDICTION

(4)　MENTAL/PHYSICAL ABILITY > ROOT POSSIBILITY > EPISTEMIC POSSIBILITY

In addition to comprising a series of two or more links corresponding to different but relatable meanings, grammaticalization chains are regularly taken to have three further properties. The first of these is that the process of grammaticalization frequently results in increased phonetic reduction and phonological dependency on some other host word. It has been observed that independent descriptive words may first develop into syntactically independent grammatical words, and then with increased use often undergo phonetic reduction and begin to display semi-dependent clitic-like status. Finally such elements may become fully dependent on a restricted lexical host and so evolve into bound morphology. Such a chain of development is indicated in (5), and reflects Givón's (1979) oft-quoted statement concerning the potential effects of grammaticalization: 'Today's morphology is yesterday's syntax'.

(5) Route of development for elements grammaticalizing as bound morphemes:
lexical word → grammatical word → grammatical clitic → bound morpheme

A second property commonly assumed to constrain the development of one meaning of a word/morpheme in a grammaticalization chain into a second, different meaning is the occurrence of *periods of overlapping variation*. If a certain word/morpheme has an original meaning A, and this over time develops into a different meaning B, it is argued that there will always be some intermediate period where the relevant word/morpheme can potentially encode either the meaning A or the meaning B (Hopper and Traugott 1993). In such a period of variation before the (frequent) disappearance of the original meaning A, there will hence be a stage in the grammaticalization chain in which a single morpheme is ambiguous between the newly emerging meaning and the earlier original meaning. In this sense, grammaticalization is often taken to be a *gradual* process of change with no sudden and abrupt changes in meaning:

(6) A → A/B → B

The third property argued to characterize grammaticalization chains with very limited exception is the property of *unidirectionality* of development. This is a claim, resulting from much observation of patterns of grammaticalization, that any development of a word/morpheme down the path of a grammaticalization chain is irreversible, and there can be no undoing of any change and regression of a morpheme to an earlier stage in the grammaticalization chain once a change has been properly effected. The only way for a word/morpheme to develop over time is therefore always forwards to new stages in a grammaticalization chain, and not back to earlier/prior stages. This constraint is assumed to affect both the development of meaning from more referential to less referential (2), and the progression of increasing phonological dependency schematized in (5). Consequently, with regard to meaning, if a morpheme following the path in (3) has developed the meaning of INTENTION and fully lost the earlier interpretation of DESIRE, it is argued that it will never re-develop the interpretation of DESIRE (or WILLINGNESS) from a loss of the meaning INTENTION. Rather, the only way for such a morpheme to develop is to a new, less subject-centered meaning such as PREDICTION. Similarly, concerning the developmental pattern indicated in (5), if an element has developed into a bound morpheme, it is assumed that it will never later redevelop its phonological independence and revert to one of the earlier (leftward) stages in the sequence of development.

INTRODUCTION

Summarizing briefly now, most work which has been (and still is) carried out on grammaticalization phenomena is primarily concerned with (a) charting the development of descriptive words into increasingly more grammatical forms, and (b) attempting to find plausible cognitive and pragmatic explanations for the changes of meaning which occur during the course of grammaticalization. Such work has led to the important discovery of a whole range of developmental patterns and the suggestion that grammaticalization often conforms to many typical routes of development referred to as grammaticalization chains.

1.2 A Formal Approach to Grammaticalization

Although the majority of research into grammaticalization has been developed within functionalist and cognitive grammar-type frameworks, the current study of Chinese makes use of a formal theoretical framework to approach grammaticalization phenomena, and specifically the set of theoretical assumptions made in recent Chomskyean-Minimalist approaches to language (in particular those in Chomsky 1993, 1995). There are a number of reasons for selecting a formalist approach here, and I outline the rationale for this below.

One important reason for making use of a formal syntactic framework for the present study relates to the nature of the data examined in the work. In much previous work on grammaticalization it has often been fairly clear what the identity of a grammaticalizing morpheme is both prior to and after its reanalysis, hence (for example) a descriptive/referential verb such as 'want' may develop into an auxiliary verb expressing future tense, or a verb such as 'get/receive' may develop into a modal verb expressing obligation (both such cases incidentally having occurred in Chinese). In such instances where the beginning and end-points of the change seem to be clear and identifiable, the analytic focus is generally on explaining how the meaning change might be explained in cognitively plausible ways. In many of the cases examined in the present work, however, the categorical identity, meaning and sometimes even the function of the grammaticalized morphemes is often far from clear, in some instances both before and after grammaticalization (i.e., the source of the grammaticalized morpheme may be quite obscure, as well as its synchronic syntactic status). These are therefore cases of genuine syntactic puzzles and challenges for any mode of analysis. Because of this, the present work turns first to a formal theoretical model of syntactic analysis in the belief that such an approach and the way that it requires one to approach data can be useful in narrowing down what the synchronic analysis of a particular data set should be, and so lead one on to a diachronic analysis and then to conclusions about the kind of grammaticalization that has actually taken place. Formal syntax is therefore used as an effective tool to unravel puzzling aspects of surface syntax, and to provide clues to the underlying origin and grammaticalization of current functional morphemes in cases where synchronic and diachronic analyses are not immediately straightforward or obvious.

A second reason for adopting a formal syntactic approach here relates to the amount and scope of the data that the present work believes it is important and necessary to examine in each case of grammaticalization. In more traditional approaches to grammaticalization, there is a tendency to focus rather narrowly on just the morpheme/word which is undergoing reanalysis, and not to consider wider aspects of the construction/structure that the morpheme/word is embedded in. Grammaticalization chains such as (3) and (4) consequently isolate the relevant morpheme from its surrounding syntactic environment and describe the change which the morpheme appears to be undergoing largely without reference to other potential changes which may be taking place within a construction. However, a careful study of individual cases of grammaticalization shows that there may frequently be *secondary syntactic effects* of the changes affecting a grammaticalizing morpheme, which provide important clues to the structural and categorical reanalysis taking place and lead to a broader picture of the process of grammaticalization. In order to understand more about the consequences of grammaticalization for elements other than the grammaticalizing morpheme, and to probe the effects of reanalysis throughout a construction, a detailed syntactic analysis is often called for, and this can be well-effected within a formal syntactic approach such as the Minimalist Program. The present study therefore uses formalist methods to analyze more of the background construction in which grammaticalization is taking place in each instance, and rather than simply describing the 'label' change of an element from (for example) verb of completion to perfective marker, the emphasis will be more on how this change is syntactically encoded and how the changes interact with other aspects of syntax (and sometimes phonology). In this sense, the approach of the book and its choice of a formal syntactic framework has the goal of taking traditional descriptions of grammaticalization in a rather different direction, arriving at more detailed description of the syntactic structures and processes which accompany grammaticalization.

Quite generally, a further reason for using a formal theoretic framework to consider grammaticalization phenomena is that the use of a different, (primarily) non-functionalist approach naturally leads to different kinds of questions being asked about the subject matter, and in so doing, raises the potential for different, (hopefully) interesting new insights and information about the mechanisms at work in grammaticalization.

Finally, for those reading this introduction who are already working within Chomskyean/Minimalist approaches to language, there is clearly much less need for arguments as to why it may be interesting and appropriate to use a specifically formalist approach to study grammaticalization. However, it is worth pointing out why the study of grammaticalization phenomena is itself highly interesting and relevant for Minimalism. Grammaticalization construed in Minimalist terms is essentially the study of functional categories and functional projections and how these may come to be created and instantiated in different ways by overt morphemes. Given the significant attention accorded functional projections in current Minimalism (their universality, arrangement, etc.), and the widespread belief (within Chomskyean linguistics) that cross-linguistic surface variation in language is largely due to variation in the lexical elements which instantiate functional projections (and their properties), it is clear that studies of the way such elements come into existence can be extremely informative and revealing for our understanding of the mechanisms at work in synchronic syntax. In addition to this, the nature of the analysis of diachronic syntax results in it being an extremely rigorous testing-ground for theories commonly applied just to synchronic syntax. If one has to provide an account of a synchronic language state B which is not only internally consistent but also consistent with a separate account of a prior language state A, *and* show how state B could have developed from state A via the same basic principles governing A and B, this obviously provides and ensures more checks on the validity and consistency of a theory than the consideration of only synchronic state grammars. The formal study of grammaticalization therefore has the potential to test quite effectively ideas which have been developed about functional categories from predominantly synchronic paradigms. In this regard, much of the present book is an attempt to solve puzzles relating to the present syntactic status of functional elements in Chinese precisely from a consideration of their development.

All in all then, it can be suggested that there is much to be potentially gained from examining instances of grammaticalization from a formal perspective. Having said this, and having given a clear rationale for using a formal syntactic framework approach in the upcoming work, I would also like to point out and stress that it is *not* the intention of the current work to attempt to replace the valuable insights and ideas of traditional grammaticalization simply with formal theoretical machinery. Rather the intention is to *supplement* earlier ideas and insights with a formal approach that will allow the study to proceed in a different direction and consider more closely the structural aspects of grammaticalization, the aim being to uncover further syntactic mechanisms at work in grammaticalization and arrive at explanations of the range of surface changes attested. To some extent then, the present book represents more of an attempted partnership between formal Chomskyean linguistics and more traditional grammaticalization, and in the chapters to come it will be seen that various insights and ideas from earlier, functionalist-oriented studies are appealed to during the course of the analysis. In what follows now, in section (4), I provide a brief preview of the kinds of phenomenon which will be investigated, and certain of the notions that will be used to analyze them.

CHAPTER 1

1.3 Patterns to Be Examined in the Work

The main part of the book begins in chapter 2 with an investigation of the general classifier *ge* in its full present-day distribution. Like other classifiers, *ge* frequently occurs with a numeral and an NP as in (7). However, *ge* is now also found in additional environments such as in (8) and (9) where other classifiers may not occur. The aim of the chapter is therefore to reach an understanding of the underlying synchronic syntax of this functional element and to see how it may have grammaticalized into a functional type different from ordinary classifiers:

(7) ta chi-le liang ge pingguo.
     he eat-LE two GE apple
     'He ate three apples.'

(8) wo yao chi ge bao.
     I want eat GE full
     'I want to do a satisfying eating.'

(9) ta yi-kouqi   he-le ge san-ping jiu.
     he one-breath drink-LE GE three-CL wine
     'He drank three bottles of beer in one breath.'

In order to capture the full range of patterns found with this special use of *ge*, the chapter argues that *ge* has undergone grammaticalization from being a regular classifier base-generated in the CL⁰ position in DPs to become a new unselective weak determiner inserted in the D⁰ position.

This development of *ge* is suggested to be an example of grammaticalization which involves a three-stage sequence of movement and reanalysis in the functional super-structure dominating a lexical category (here the noun). In such a process of 'vertical' grammaticalization, an element is originally base-generated in a lower position A and then raised higher to a second functional-head position B, before eventually being reanalyzed as base-generated directly in B. During intermediate stages of the process, the element will instantiate both categories A and B, and in the final stage only B, allowing for A to be occupied by new overt elements. This is the stage assumed to characterize *ge* in modern Mandarin examples such as (9) where *ge* in D⁰ co-occurs with a distinct numeral and classifier in Num⁰ and Cl⁰.

Chapter 2 thus introduces and illustrates a first type of grammaticalization process which results in categorial reanalysis critically via movement upwards in a functional structure and subsequent reanalysis ('vertical grammaticalization').

Chapter 3 has two major parts. The first focuses on the syntactic status of the functional morpheme *de* which occurs in relative clauses such as in (10):

(10) [wo zuotian mai] de shu.
    I yesterday buy DE book
    'the book(s) I bought yesterday'

Early Chomskyean analyses assume that *de* in such structures is a complementizer/C^0. However, following ideas in Simpson (2002), the chapter argues for an analysis of *de* as a bleached determiner in the end stages of grammaticalization, developed from an earlier demonstrative source. The chapter both draws on existing observations in Simpson (2002) and provides a range of new arguments for such an analysis, including patterns from language acquisition and tone sandhi phenomena in relative clauses in Taiwanese.

Tone sandhi also provides the link into the second main part of chapter 3 which focuses on the grammaticalization of a new sentence-final particle in Taiwanese, the element *kong*, as illustrated in (11):

(11) Ahui m   lai kong.
    Ahui NEG come KONG
    'Ahui is not coming.'

In contrast with older S-final particles whose origin is often unknown, the source of Taiwanese *kong* in the verb to 'say' is still clear, and the syntax underlying its development is also largely transparent due to patterns of tone change which occur when *kong* is used. The combination of information available with *kong* is argued to suggest that its sentence-final position in fact results from a clausal topicalization operation in which the S/IP to the left of *kong* is raised to its surface position from an underlying position to the right of *kong*, and has diachronically resulted from the collapse of a bi-clausal structure into a mono-clausal form with the verb in the higher clause grammaticalizing as a functional head in the new single clause structure. The active grammaticalization pattern found with *kong* provides new insights into the debate about whether Chinese is exceptionally head-final in its CP constituents, and reveals a significant route of grammaticalization, not previously discussed in the literature, by means of which head-initial languages can apparently develop S-final particles.

Chapter 4 continues to investigate the categorial status of the element *de* as it occurs in clause-final position in cleft-like sentences such as (12), and attempts to account for the alternation where the object of the verb optionally appears positioned after *de* as in (13):

(12) ta shi zuotian mai piao de.
    he BE yesterday buy ticket DE
    'It was yesterday that he bought the ticket.'

(13) ta shi zuotian mai de piao.
 he BE yesterday buy DE ticket
 'It was yesterday that he bought the ticket.'

Most research on the *shi-de* construction has concentrated on offering accounts of how the focus interpretation of such forms may be syntactically encoded, and this has led to interest being firmly centered on the copula element *shi*. Comparatively little attention has however been given to the role and status of the element *de*, and there is almost no discussion of the alternation in (12) and (13) in the current literature. The chapter suggests that a study of the role played by *de* and the alternation in (12) and (13) leads to the conclusion that *de* is currently undergoing a significant reanalysis and re-grammaticalization. Due to the strengthening of a past time conversational implicature present in *shi-de* sentences, it is argued that the D^0 determiner *de* has now become reanalyzed as an instantiation of (past) Tense/T^0, this accounting for a range of its synchronic behavior and interpretation. Such reanalysis is suggested to be an example of 'lateral grammaticalization', where a functional head in one domain (here the nominal domain) is reanalyzed as a corresponding functional head in another domain (in this case the clausal domain). In contrast to the 'vertical grammaticalization' process outlined in chapter 2, where an element undergoes movement and reanalysis within the functional structure of a single domain, lateral grammaticalization is not derived via any movement operation, and the relevant element is simply reanalyzed as instantiating a related functional head in a different but parallel domain. With *de*, it is suggested that the reanalysis of a D^0 element as a T^0 morpheme can be seen to be a natural developmental shift. Noting that D^0 and T^0 are both functional heads which serve to provide reference to their respective (NP and VP) complements, in the D-to-T reanalysis it is argued that the definite reference-fixing property of the D^0-element simply becomes re-interpreted in the locus of temporal reference, the T^0 position. Finally, the chapter re-considers non-past interpretations in *shi-de* sentences and argues that speakers actually maintain a dual analysis of *de* as both a T^0 and a D^0 element in different structures, this having direct effects on a number of syntactic phenomena.

Chapter 5 considers resultative verb constructions/RVCs in Chinese, which synchronically consist in two adjacent verbal elements V_1 and V_2, the latter V_2 element encoding the result or completion of the action represented by V_1, as in (14) and (15):

(14) ta xi-ganjing yifu le.
 he wash clean clothes LE
 'He washed the clothes clean.'

INTRODUCTION

(15) wo kan-wan shu le.
 I look-finish book LE
 'I have finished reading the book.'

The chapter investigates the grammaticalization of the V_2 element in RVCs and attempts to understand why such elements repositioned themselves right-adjacent to the verb from an original position following the object of the V_1 as in (16):

(16) V_1 Object V_2 → V_1 V_2 Object

It is suggested that this and other changes relating to the V_2 occurred as the result of a significant increase in focus on the telic aspectual contribution of V_2 elements in the construction, this resulting in the reanalysis and grammaticalization of such elements as *primarily* aspect markers synchronically *suffixed* to the V_1 in RVCs. The chapter makes important use of Minimalist assumptions concerning the syntactic licensing of morphology interacting with pressures for a uniform direction of selection/headedness to account for the word order change in (16), and suggests that the grammaticalization of V_2 elements in RVCs has resulted in a new functional projection/grammatical category in Chinese, completive aspect. The chapter also offers a formal account of how it may be that suffixation arises in head-initial languages, as typologically this is a property which is much more expected of head-final languages (Greenberg 1978, Dryer 1992).

The last of the man chapters of the book, chapter 6, turns to examine the verbal suffix *le* illustrated in (17):

(17) ta mai-le san-ben shu.
 he buy-LE three-CL book
 'He bought three books.'

Largely because of the completive meaning that *le* originally had, and because it underwent the same re-positioning shown in (16) as other resultative verbs (and at the same historical time), it is concluded that *le* initially grammaticalized as a marker of completive aspect similar to other V_2 elements in RVCs. Further synchronic evidence however indicates that *le* has developed further and has a modern function different from simple completive aspect, as *le* is now able co-occur with a separate marker of completive aspect. In order to account for the patterns found, the paper adopts Smith's (1997) two-tiered approach to aspect and suggests that since its initial grammaticalization, verbal *le* has developed from being a completive *situation* aspect marker to instantiate structurally higher perfective *viewpoint* aspect, a view in line with common synchronic perceptions of *le*.

The chapter then attempts to provide a formal modeling of this change and argues for a development of the movement-based approach to grammaticalization introduced in chapter 2. Whereas this approach was initially intended to account for the reanalysis of free-standing morphemes, chapter 6 suggests that suffixes are also subject to further reanalysis in a highly similar way, and that the model of grammaticalization initiated for free morphemes can be naturally developed to account for this.

Following this, the chapter attempts to account for other aspects of the interpretation of modern verbal *le* and makes the more contentious claim that *le* has now grammaticalized further to instantiate *past tense* as well as perfective aspect. Such a possibility has been explicitly rejected in the literature (e.g., in Li and Thompson 1981). However, the chapter shows that there is in fact much evidence in support of such a reanalysis and that the arguments standardly given against such a hypothesis can all be given effective counter-explanations. Generally, the chapter confronts the difficult problem of modeling the apparent gradualness of change and develops a formal, tree-based and movement-based alternative to the notion of developmental 'clines', showing how the different interpretations of modern-day *le* are in fact not random but quite predictable from the syntactic structure which is projected in various clausal environments.

Finally the book is closed with a brief post-word, picking up on various themes which have surfaced through the main chapters and identifying a potential research agenda for the future. The post-word highlights certain broad issues and questions which still critically require answers for formalist approaches to language, and attempts to indicate how further research into the rich area of grammaticalization has the potential to provide the relevant empirical data which can lead to realistic and plausible answers.

2

THE CLASSIFIER *GE*
MOVEMENT AND REANALYSIS

2.0 Introduction

This chapter is an examination of the status of the classifier *ge* in nominal and verbal environments. There are two types of (related) elements pronounced as *ge* in Mandarin Chinese. One is a general classifier which is commonly used to "type" or individuate a noun which follows it for purposes of counting. The other *ge* will be shown to be used to count the event denoted by the predicate (in which *ge* occurs) as a *single event*. While the first use of *ge* has long been known as the most general classifier in Mandarin, the second type of *ge* has not been investigated thoroughly in the literature. The discussion in this chapter will be focused on the second type of *ge*. Section 2.1 presents *ge* as the most general classifier for count nouns. Section 2.2 discusses the distribution and the semantic contribution of the event classifier *ge*. Section 2.3 presents the syntactic properties of the event classifier *ge*. Section 2.4 makes a proposal to structurally encode *ge* within the DP in a way which mirrors its central syntactic properties. Section 2.5 then argues for the grammaticalization of *ge* from a classifier to a determiner. Section 2.6 is a brief conclusion.

2.1 *Ge* as a General Classifier for Nouns

The most frequent use of *ge* is to serve as a classifier for its following noun. Mandarin nouns all behave like mass nouns in English in the respect that a classifier (or a measure word) is needed in counting. For example, to count 'glasses' or 'water', one could use 'a pair of glasses' and 'two drops of water' in English. *Ge* is found to be the most general classifier for nouns. When *ge* occurs as a general noun classifier, it is preceded by a numeral and directly followed by a noun, as in (1):

(1) a. wo you liang ge pingguo.
    I have two GE apple
    'I have two apples.'
  b. zuotian   si-le   san ge ren.
    yesterday die-ASP three GE person
    'Three people died yesterday.'

When the numeral preceding a classifier is 'one', it is well-noted that this numeral can in fact be deleted, as shown in example (2):

(2) wo chi-le (yi) ge juzi.
    I eat-ASP (one) GE tangerine
    'I ate a tangerine.'

Ge as a noun classifier is defined as "individual classifier" by Chao 1968. The noun following *ge* is a count noun denoting an object which usually does not have big volume and has to be a separable entity in the physical world. That is, the entity is physically "bounded" in Allen's 1966 sense. The verbs that can occur with the noun classifier *ge* are diverse. Stative verbs (as in 1a), activity verbs (as in 2) and achievement verbs (as in 1b) are all possible.

2.2 *Ge* as a Classifier for Events Denoted by the Predicates

The second use of *ge*, which constitutes the main focus of this chapter, is where it occurs preceded by a verb and followed by a bare noun, a classifier-measure string, an adjective, or a clause-like idiom. In what follows, this second *ge* will be shown to contribute to the aspectuality of the predicate and makes the denoted action counted as a single event.

2.2.1 Occurrence Between a Verb and Its Cognate Object

Although in its most common use *ge* follows a numeral and introduces regular concrete count nouns, it may also occur between certain V-O *compounds*. In (3a), the object part of the compound is only licensed to occur when together with the verbal part of the compound. In (3b), the verbal part 'jump' can mean 'dance' only when it occurs with the object part. When *ge* occurs separating the verb and its object, the *ge*-O sequence functions like an "individuated" cognate object of the verb:

(3) a. women qu you ge yong ba!
　　　 we　　 go swim GE swim PRT
　　　 'Let's go for a swim (do a swimming)!'
　　b. women zuotian qu na-jia wuting tiao-le ge wu.
　　　 we yesterday go that-CL club jump-ASP GE dance
　　　 'We went to that club and did an activity of dancing.'

Some speakers even accept examples such as (4), in which *ge* intervenes between the verbal members of a V-V compound:

(4)　xue　ge　xi
　　　study GE study
　　　'do an activity of studying'

In these cases, it can be argued that *ge* is used to help count out a single event and cause the action to be interpreted as being telically bounded. For example, if *ge* is omitted in (3a), the interpretation of the verb *youyong* is as a simple unbounded action of 'swimming'. However, when *ge* occurs between the two syllables of 'swim', (3a) rather means to 'do a swimming' (and there is a single swimming event). Similarly in (3b), *ge* allows in the interpretation of one dancing event. This event may consist of one dance or more than one dance; the main point is that *ge* helps count out the event as a whole.

Above in example (2) with nominal classifier *ge* it has been observed that the classifier is optionally able to appear *without* a preceding numeral, and that when this happens, the numeral 'one' is implied. Consequently here where these V-O and V-V sequences occur with a 'bare' *ge* intervening, it can similarly be suggested that the numeral one is implied and that the occurrence of *ge* makes the activity verb countable--as *one* event. Indeed, it is possible to insert the element *yi* 'one' in examples (3) and (4):

(5)　you　yi　ge　yong
　　　swim one GE swim
　　　'do a swimming'

(6)　xue　yi　ge　xi
　　　study one GE study
　　　'do an activity of studying'

2.2.2 Occurrence Between a Verb and an Indefinite Object

Ge can also directly occur between a verb and a regular non-cognate object nominal. This post-verbal nominal is usually indefinite and is often a bare noun, as in (7). The appropriate classifiers are *tiao* 'strip' for 'fish' and *gen* 'stick' for 'rope', as in (8). As in the examples in (3), it can be suggested that when *ge* comes in between the V-N sequence it functions to quantify over the predicate/event and results in a single buying event. Note that in (7a) there could be a single buying event of several pieces of rope, whereas in (8a) with the regular classifier *gen* for 'rope', the interpretation is that only a single piece of rope is purchased. Similarly, in (7b) there could be a delivery of several fish, whereas in (8b) with the regular classifier *tiao* for 'fish', the interpretation is that only a single fish is delivered. Consequently the use of *ge* might seem to relate more to the event/predicate than to the nominal:

(7) a. wo qu mai ge sheng. (from Liu 1993)
     I   go buy GE rope
     'I'll go do a rope-buying.'
   b. wo qu song ge yu.
     I   go deliver GE fish
     'I'll go do a fish-delivering.'

(8) a. wo qu mai gen sheng.
     I   go buy CL rope
     'I'll go buy a rope.'
   b. wo qu song tiao yu.
     I   go deliver CL fish
     'I'll go deliver a fish.'

Examples in (9) exhibit the occurrence of a *locative* object introduced by *ge*:

(9) a. women lai tiao ge sheng. (see also Liu 1993)
     we   come jump GE rope
     'Let's do a rope-jumping.'
   b. women qu zou ge lu.
     we   go walk GE road
     'Let's go take a walk (do a walking on the road).'

Here (9) is in contrast with (7) and (8). In (7) and (8) it is possible to have either the specific classifiers for specific nouns *or* the 'event' classifier *ge*, but examples with locative objects such as those in (9) do *not* allow similar substitution of the specific classifiers for nouns, as shown in (10):

(10) a. *women lai tiao gen sheng.
      we   come jump CL rope
      '*Let's jump one rope.'
    b. *women qu zou tiao lu.
      we   go walk CL road
      '*Let's go walk on one road.'

From this it can be concluded that *ge* is *not* a simple replacement for more specific nominal classifiers and does not simply function to introduce a regular NP object. For example, in (9a) the sequence *tiao-sheng* 'jump-rope' *does*

16

allow *ge* to introduce *sheng* 'rope', but in (10a) it does not allow a regular classifier such as *gen* (which would be an appropriate classifier for *sheng* in other situations such as in 8a). There is consequently an important difference between *ge* and other classifiers whose function is to introduce and individuate simple NP objects.

Next, the post-verbal nominal following *ge* is often a numeral-measure phrase. This numeral-measure phrase can be an object of an activity verb as in (11) or a duration/frequency phrase as in (12).

(11) a. ta chi-le ge san wan fan.
    he eat-ASP GE three CL-bowl rice
    'He did an eating of three bowls of rice.'
  b. ta xiang shang-tai chang ge san duan qur.
    he want get-on-stage sing GE three CL-session song
    'He wants to get on the stage and do a singing of three operas.'

(12) a. women qu Bali wan-le ge liang tian.
    we go Paris play-ASP GE two day
    'We went to Paris and did a two-day playing (a two-day trip).'
  b. qing ba zhe-ben shu zixinde kan ge wu bian.
    please BA this-CL book carefully read GE five time
    'Please do a five-time reading of this book carefully.'
  c. yundongyuan dao caochang pao-le ge san quan.
    athletes go exercise-field run-ASP GE three lap
    'The athletes went to the track and did a three-lap running'

Comparing (11) and (12) with (13) and (14) it is found that when *ge* is used, the whole verb phrase is interpreted as 'one' single event or 'one group' of events. For example, in (11a), the inclusion of *ge* results in the interpretative effect that the eating of the three bowls of rice has to be understood to take place at one specific time, while in (13a), the three bowls of rice could be eaten at different meals.

(13) a. chi-le san wan fan.
    eat-ASP three bowl rice
    'ate three bowls of rice'
  b. chang san duan qur.
    sing three session song
    'sing three operas'

CHAPTER 2

(14) a. wan-le   liang tian
       play-ASP two days
       'played for two days'
   b. kan wu   bian
      read five time
      'read five times'
   c. pao-le   san   quan
      run-ASP three lap
      'ran three laps'

This single-event interpretation associated with the predicate can be highlighted by the interaction of quantified or plural NP subjects and *ge*-marked objects. Sentence (15) means Zhangsan ate three bowls of rice at one time and Lisi ate three bowls of rice at one time. Strictly speaking, although there may be two events involved, *ge* functions to set the boundary of the activity denoted by the *predicate*: for each person the three bowls of rice is necessarily consumed during one eating event.

(15) Zhangsan he Lisi ge   chi-le   ge san   wan fan.
     Zhangsan and Lisi each eat-ASP GE three bowl rice
     'Zhangsan and Lisi each at one time ate three bowls of rice.'

2.2.3 Ge *Introducing a Simple Resultative/Descriptive Adjective*

Ge can also be used to follow an activity verb and precede certain adjectives in an adverbial usage. As shown in (16), *ge* can be used to introduce a descriptive adjective, which otherwise cannot follow the verb. This intervention of *ge* again results in the interpretation that a single event (of 'fast-running') occurred:

(16) Pingchang   kan-bu-chu-lai, zuotian   de yundonghui ta dao
     in-daily-life can-not-see   yesterday DE sports-event he however
     pao-le   ge kuai.
     run-ASP GE fast
     'I can't see that in him in daily life, but he demonstrated a fast running in yesterday's sports meet.'

A more frequently seen case is when the following adjective is a resultative adjective. The interpretation here may be that the action depicted by the verb is carried out until the point is reached where the subject can be said to have the quality described by the adjective, as illustrated in (17) and (18): [1]

(17) a. ta xiang zai na-jia caniting chi ge bao.
       he want at that-CL restaurant eat GE stuffed
       'He wants to do a satisfying eating (keeping eating until stuffed) in that restaurant.'
    b. ta zai na-jia canting chi-le ge bao.
       he at that-CL restaurant eat-ASP GE stuffed
       'He did a satisfying eating (kept eating until stuffed) in that restaurant.'

(18) wo mama hui ba wo ma ge gou.
     I mother will BA me scold GE enough
     'My mother will do a satisfying scolding (keep cursing until enough) to me.'

(19) wo zuotian qu zhao ta, jieguo pu-le ge kong.
     I yesterday go look-for him, in-the-end catch-ASP GE empty
     'I went to visit him yesterday, but it was an empty house.'

(20a) and (20b) are further examples of adjectives combining with *ge* in similar fashion:

(20) a. sha-le ge ganjing
       kill-ASP GE clean
       'did a clean killing (killed everything)'
    b. shuo ge qingchu
       say GE clear
       'do a clear explanation'

In these cases, it might be suggested that *ge* intervenes in the middle of some kind of action-result *compound*. However, the examples in (21) indicate otherwise—without *ge* these sequences of verb-adjective would require some other elements such as a sentence-final *le* (as in 21b) or other continuing elements (as in 21c) to make the sentences acceptable. The contrast in (22) shows that when the action and the result are separated, and where there consequently cannot be any V-Adj compounding, *ge* shows that it is able to license the following adjective as a legitimate post-verbal element.

(21) a. *ta zai na-jia canting chi-bao.
        he at that-CL restaurant eat-full
     b. ta zai na-jia canting chi-bao le.
        he at that-CL restaurant eat-full LE
        'He is already full from eating at that restaurant.'
     c. ta zai na-jia canting chi-bao cai lai de.
        he at that-CL restaurant eat-full then come DE
        'He came here after he was full from eating at that restaurant.'

(22) a. *ta chi-le bao.
      he eat-ASP stuffed
   b. ta chi-le ge bao.
      he eat-ASP GE stuffed
      'He had a completely satisfying eating.'

An important point to note here is that an action-result string requires an aspect-marker *le* or some other elements for the predicate to obtain the perfective aspect, while *ge*-sentences do not. It can then be suggested that *ge* contributes significantly to the aspectual specification of the predicate and functions to provide an end point to the event, so changing an activity predicate into an accomplishment. This function of bringing out the end point of an activity also explains why *ge* makes an activity verb countable, shown previously in (3) and (4).

Anticipating somewhat, it can be suggested that a nominal object is necessary to make an atelic activity predicate into a telic bounded event, following ideas in Tenny (1987) and Borer (1994), and that *ge* functions to convert a non-nominal category into a nominal type which will result in such an interpretation (nominal elements 'measuring-out' an event and resulting in an event being bounded when the object is fully 'consumed'—see Tenny (1987)/Borer (1994). Basically then it might seem that the use of *ge* as a simple nominal classifier has become extended to a wider use and may now somehow be able to convert elements of *adjectival* type into *nominal* type elements.

A further peculiarity of the *ge*-construction is that when the adjective following *ge* can be made more complex by being combined with some kind of degree-type modifier, the expression with *ge* generally sounds better, as seen in (23) and (24). The modifier-head adjectives in these examples denote an extreme result or an extreme description.

(23) a. he-le   ge da-zui
        drink-ASP GE big-drunk
        'did a completely drunk drinking'
     b. ??he-le ge zui
        drink-ASP GE drunk
        'did a drunk drinking'

(24) a. zou-le   ge fei-kuai
        walk-ASP GE fly-fast
        'did a as-fast-as-flying walking'
     b. ?zou-le ge kuai
        walk-ASP GE fast
        'did a fast walk'

Concerning this effect of adding a modifier to an adjective in (23a) vs. (23b) and (24a) vs. (24b), it can be argued that if the object is modified and in a certain way made more specific/identifiable then this enables it to function as a delimiter more easily, either providing an end-point or otherwise measuring out the event to make it telic. If the end-point is some kind of extreme (a 'big drunk') then the telic reading is all the more easy to license.

2.2.4 Ge *Introducing an Idiom or Fixed Expression*

In section 3.3 it was shown that the element introduced by *ge* can be an adjective, and the suggestion was made that *ge* may be functioning to provide an essentially nominal complement to the verb which precedes it. Here it can be noted that the element which is introduced into the VP via *ge* can actually also be a *clause-like idiom*, expressing the extreme result of some action.[2] Again in such instances the preceding verb is an activity verb and the *ge*-XP contributes to convert the predicate into an accomplishment:

(25) a. pin ge ni-si-wo-huo
       fight GE you-die-I-live
       'make a terrible fight (aim to kill the other party)'
   b. nao-le   ge ji-quan-bu-ning
       fuss-ASP GE chicken-dog-not-peaceful
       'caused a big turmoil'
   c. wen ge shui-luo-shi-chu
       ask GE water-fall-rock-out
       'do a thorough interrogation until everything is clear'

2.2.5 Ge *with Perfective but not Imperfective Aspect*

There are also certain aspectual restrictions on *ge*-forms, and when the predicate has an overt aspect marker, as in (26) and (27), it is found that event classifier *ge* can co-occur with the *perfective* marker *le* (28), but not with the *imperfective* markers *zai-* (26) and *-zhe* (27). This may perhaps be because imperfective aspect markers function to focus on the internal stages of an event and event classifier *ge* objects are interpreted as constituting an unanalyzable single event with no visible internal stages, in this sense being more like instantaneous achievement-type predicates (see here Smith 1997 and chapter 6 for more discussion of the role of perfective/imperfective aspect). Such an unanalyzable single event property will also account for the fact that in *ge* objects which have numerals, such as (11/12/15) above, there can only be a single event interpretation and no possibility of a multiple event reading—the internal parts of a *ge* object are simply unavailable for individual interpretation/imperfective aspectual modification:

CHAPTER 2

(26) *wo zheng zai die ge tou-po-xie-liu.
    I right at fall GE head-break-blood-flow
  '*I am falling so hard that I'm getting a broken bleeding head.'

(27) *wo die-zhe ge tou-po-xie-liu.
    I fall-DUR GE head-break-blood-flow
  '*I am falling so hard that I am getting a broken bleeding head.'

(28) wo die-le ge tou-po-xie-liu.
    I fall-ASP GE head-break-blood-flow
  'I had a fall so bad that I got a broken bleeding head.'

2.2.6 *Apparent Constraints on Verb Selection*

While it was noted that the noun classifier *ge* can occur with a stative verb, an activity verb, or an achievement verb, most of the occurrences of the event classifier *ge* actually follow an *activity* or an *accomplishment* verb, and often it may *not* occur with a *stative* verb:

(29) *ta you ge san zhi bi.
    he have GE three CL pen
  'He has three pens.'

This constraint on verb selection can be shown to be aspectual in nature. If the *ge*-XP is able to express an end point and make the whole VP an identifiable event, even stative verbs are in fact permissible. For example, the stative verb 'love' in (31), with the help of *ge*-XP, similarly expresses an identifiable event: the subject wants to have 'one' exciting romance. Once again it seems therefore that the *ge*-XP functions to change an atelic predicate into a telic predicate.

(30) ta xiangyao ai ge si-qu-huo-lai.
    he want love GE die-go-live-come
  'He wants to experience an extreme romance.'

(31) ta ai-le ge si-qu-huo-lai.
    he love-ASP GE die-go-live-come
  'He experienced an extreme romance.'

In addition to activity verbs, certain achievement verbs can also occur with the event *ge*:

(32) a. ta xiang ba zhe-jian shi   wang ge ganganjingjing.
    he want BA this-CL matter forget GE   clean
    'He wants to forget this completely.'
  b. zhe-ci   wenyi, cun-li   de ren   si-le   ge jingguang.
    this-time plague village-in DE person die-ASP GE bright-clean
    'The people in the village died out because of the plague.'

As achievement verbs by definition inherently encode end points, it might perhaps be incorrect to suggest that the *ge*-XP functions to make the predicate telic by specifying the end point of the activity. The *ge*-XP in (32) might instead be said to *reinforce* the boundary of the event and make the event be perceived as a whole. However, without the *ge*-XP, the event boundary would in fact have to be expressed by some other means, for example by the use of a perfective aspect-marker as in (33a) and (33b):

(33) a. ta xiang ba zhe-jian shi   wang *(le).
    he want BA this-CL matter forget LE
    'He wants to forget this.'
  b. zhe-ci   wenyi, cun-li   de ren   *(dou) si-guang *(le).
    this-time plague village-in DE person all   die-clean LE
    'The people in the village all died because of the plague.'

Consequently it may in fact be the case that the *ge*-XP also in these cases does function to delimit the predicate and make it telic. Elsewhere in Chinese it is found that verbs which would be classed as telic in English and other languages need to be overtly specified as bounded by the addition of an aspect-marker or resultative complement. For example, (34) is possible in Chinese, though not in English. With English a predicate like 'kill' plus past tense implies that the event depicted by the predicate did have a successful completion, whereas in Chinese it is not necessarily true. It is suggested here that *ge*-XP functions as one of the means that make a predicate telic.

(34) zuotian   Zhangsan sha Lisi, keshi mei sha-si.
    yesterday Zhangsan kill Lisi, but   NEG kill-dead
    '!Yesterday Zhangsan killed Lisi, but Zhangsan didn't kill Lisi.'

2.3 Syntactic Properties

2.3.1 Event Ge *Introducing a Non-predicational Adjective*

Here I would like to note a further restriction on event *ge* which can be observed when *ge* combines with adjectives. Basically it is found that the adjective cannot be in 'predicational' form but rather must be 'bare'. When adjectives occur as predicates in declarative sentences in Chinese, they are invariably accompanied by a modifier such as *hen* 'very' or *tai* 'too' as in (35), whereas when they occur attributively they appear bare, as in (36):³

(35) a. ta hen piaoliang.
     ta very pretty
     'She is very pretty.'
   b. zhe-ge fangzi tai jiu.
     this-CL house too old
     'This house is too old.'

(36) xin shu
     new book
     'new books'⁴

Turning to *ge*-forms it is found that adjectives which occur following *ge cannot* be modified by *hen* 'very' or *tai* 'too', as shown in (37).⁵

(37) a. *shuo-le ge hen qingchu
       say-ASP GE very clear
   b. *chi-le ge tai bao
       eat-ASP GE too full

Secondly, there is a further restriction found in adjectival reduplication forms. Chinese allows for bi-syllabic adjectival reduplication in two basic forms commonly referred to as the AABB Form and the ABAB form. The AABB reduplication form is referred to as the 'vivid' adjectival form which expresses an extreme description, while an ABAB reduplication is said to be predicational reduplication and is shown to occur in standard predicate type positions in (38):

(38) a. mingtian women chuqu tongkuai-tongkuai.
       tomorrow we go out enjoy-enjoy
       'Let's go out and enjoy ourselves tomorrow.'
   b. jintian ni hua-yixia-zhuang, rang ziji piaoliang-piaoliang.
       today you put on makeup let self beautiful- beautiful
       'Why don't you put on makeup and make yourself look beautiful today.'

In the *ge*-construction it is found that adjectives may be reduplicated according to the AABB pattern but not the ABAB predicational pattern as shown in examples in (39) and (40):

(39) a. chi ge tong-tong-kuai-kuai
       eat GE enjoy-enjoy
       'do a completely satisfying eating'
    b. daban   ge piao-piao-liang-liang
       dress-up GE beautiful-beautiful
       'dressed up to be completely beautiful'

(40) a. *chi ge tongkuai-tongkuai
        eat GE enjoy-enjoy
        'ate until satisfied'
    b. *daban   ge piaoliang-piaoliang
        dress-up GE beautiful-beautiful
        'dressed up beautifully'

A third restriction on the combination of *ge* with adjectives is that the adjective following *ge* cannot be syntactically negated. As shown in (41a), *ge* cannot introduce an adjective which is syntactically negated by *bu* 'not'.[6]

(41) *shuo-le ge bu qingchu
      say-ASP GE not clearly
      'say (it) not clearly.'

However, if the negation is part of a fixed negative adjective, as in (42), it can legitimately follow *ge*. Being able to be syntactically negated is another characteristic of a syntactic predicate, so again there is evidence that a predicational adjective cannot follow *ge*.

(42) shuo-le ge bu-qing-bu-chu
     say-ASP GE not-clearly
     'make a vague statement'

Lastly, the adjective following *ge* can not be A-not-A questioned. As shown in (43), *ge*-sentences cannot be made into an A-not-A question by questioning the adjective.[7] This is another predicational characteristic that the adjective selected by *ge* is lacking.

(43) *ta shuo ge qing-bu-qing-chu?
      he say GE clear-not-clear
      'Did he make it clear?'

I would like to suggest that all of these restrictions are actually rather typical of *nominalization* forms in certain languages and may be explained if it is assumed that (a) *ge* is functioning as a nominalizer (a categorization in fact suggested in Lü 1984), and (b) *ge* selects for a complement which is syntactically 'less' than a full clausal predicate.

Specifically concerning point (b), it has been noted that in languages such as Korean there is variation in the type of predicate constituent selected by different nominalizers. Following initial work in Yoon (1990), Lapointe and Nielsen (1996) show that Korean 'Type II' and 'Type III' nominalizations have certain critically different clusters of properties. The nominalizer in the former selects for a full clausal complement which has an overt tense morpheme, a nominative subject and allows for sentential negation, sentential adverbs and clause-internal scrambling. The nominalizer in the latter however seems to select for a more restricted constituent which does not allow scrambling, negation, sentential adverbs, nominative subjects or tense/aux elements (subjects instead occur in genitive case). Lapointe and Nielsen show that such a contrastive patterning can be captured quite simply if it is assumed that the Type II nominalization involves selection by the nominalizer of a TP-level constituent, whereas in Type III nominalizations the nominalizer selects a VP-type level constituent.

Returning to Chinese, with *ge* one finds that although a predicate may be selected and even project its arguments (as in the idiom cases in 25), there are certain syntactic properties associated with full regular clauses which may not occur in the predicate sequence following *ge*, e.g., sentential negation and A-not-A question forms.[8] Such syntactic properties, and possibly also the type of reduplication found with predicational adjectives noted, may all be assumed to require a certain minimal amount of clausal structure in order to be licensed. For example, negation would occur located in the functional part of a clause and not low down attached to VP/AdjP, and A-not-A forms arguably require the presence of a Q-morpheme in I, hence the functional projection IP, etc. This absence of sentential negation, A-not-A questions and predicational adjectival reduplication can consequently be suggested to indicate that the functional structure necessary to support such properties is also absent, in a way which is rather similar to Korean Type III nominalizations. Similar to Korean Type III nominalizations, I would therefore now like to suggest that *ge* is in fact a nominalizer which takes as a potential complement simply a bare predicate (maybe an AdjP) without allowing any of the higher clausal functional projections which would be necessary to support negation, A-not-A and predicational reduplication, etc.[9]

2.3.2 *Event* Ge *Licensing an Extra Argument*

Thus far we have seen sequences of a verb followed immediately by *ge* and some other element. However, elsewhere it is also possible to find sequences of [verb + (in-)direct object + *ge*-object], i.e., the *ge*-XP can also follow an object of the verb.[10] These sentences are more acceptable to speakers from Mainland China; the examples in (44) are cited from novels written by writers from Mainland China, recorded in Fang Li 1993.

(44) a. ta da-le wo ge ban-si.
   he hit-ASP I GE half-dead
   'He hit me to the extent that I almost died.'
   (Wang Meng's <Qingchunmeng> [Youth dreams])
 b. da ni ge tou-po-xue-liu
   hit you GE head-break-blood-flow
   'hit you until you have a broken bleeding head'
   (Wang Shuo's <Wo Shi Ni Baba> [I am your father])
 c. bie yiwei nimen shi nusheng, fan-le gui zhaoyang da nimen
   don't assume you are girls, violate-ASP rule same hit you
   ge si-jiao-chao-tian.
   GE four-foot-face-sky
   'Don't just assume you are girls. I will still hit you to the extent that you all fall down on you back, if you break the rules.' (Wang Meng's <Qingchunmeng> [Youth dreams])
 d. er guniang cui-le baba yi ge man-lian-hua.
   second young lady spit-ASP father one GE full-face-messy
   'The second daughter spit at her father to the extent that his face got all messy.'
   (Lao She's <Liutunde> [Women from the Willow Village])

As is well-known, in Chinese it is generally not possible to have two discrete elements following the verb, unless one of these is a frequency complement as in (45):

(45) wo qu-guo Beijing hen-duo-ci.
   I go-EXP Beijing many times
   'I have been to Beijing many times.'

Normally if an element such as a descriptive or resultative complement occurs and the object of the verb is overt, the verb must be repeated to license the object:

(46) *Zhangsan da erzi de ban-si.
   Zhangsan hit son DE half-dead

(47) Zhangsan da erzi da de ban-si.
   Zhangsan hit son hit DE half-dead
   'Zhangsan beat his son until he was half-dead.'

However, it is found that a *ge*-XP *may* in fact co-occur with an overt object DP as in (48), in direct contrast to the non-*ge* resultative structure (46):

(48) Zhangsan da-le erzi ge bansi.
Zhangsan hit-ASP son GE half-dead
'Zhangsan hit his son to the extent that his son almost died.'

Such a structure with two elements following the verb in fact appears very similar to double object constructions (DOCs), roughly shown as (49).

(49) a. V + NP Object + *ge*-XP   *ge*-construction
b. V + Object 1 + Object 2   DOC

According to Li and Thompson (1981), an important characteristic of the double object construction in Chinese is that Object1 which directly follows the verb is always either an animate noun or an institution name, this being illustrated in (50).

(50) a. wo song-le ta yi-ben shu.
I give-ASP he one-CL book
'I gave him a book.'
b. tamen huan-le yinhang yi-bi daikuan.
They return-ASP bank one-CL loan
'They returned a loan to the bank.'
c. *ta song-le xinjia yixie jiaju.
he give-ASP new-house some furniture

Interestingly, *ge*-sentences seem to exhibit the same constraint on the object, as shown in (51), the (c) example is unacceptable because the direct object *yifu* is inanimate:[11]

(51) a. ta xiangyao xia wo ge hun-fei-po-san.
he want frighten I GE soul-fly-spirit-scatter
'frighten me until my soul and spirit leave my body'
b. naxie ren wei-le yiyuan yi ge
those people surround-ASP hospital one GE
shui-xie-bu-tong.
water-leak-not-through
'Those people surrounded the hospital to the extent that nothing can get through in the hospital.'
c. *ta xi-le yifu ge gan-gan-jing-jing.
he wash-ASP clothes GE clean

One might suggest that the occurrence of two overt DPs post-verbally in DOCs is permitted because the indirect object can be licensed via incorporation into the verb (cf. chapter 4 and Audrey Li 1990), leaving the direct object to receive the verb's structural accusative case. The same incorporation process might then be taken to be responsible for the well-formedness of sentences with a post-verbal direct object and a *ge*-DP.[12][13]

2.3.3 Ge *Licensing the Expletive 'It'*

Here we note a last interesting aspect of the *ge* paradigm: its occurrence with *ta* in object expletive contexts. Lin (1993) shows that expletive *ta* can often co-occur with object DPs and suggests that an expletive-associative chain is formed between *ta* and the real argument DP, the argument raising to replace *ta* in SpecAgrOP at LF. (52) illustrates this use of *ta* with an object associate:

(52) wo kan-le ta san-ben xiaoshuo.
     I read-ASP it three-CL   novel
     'I read three novels (at one time).'

Here it can be shown that *ge*-XPs may also often co-occur with the expletive *ta* 'it' (called by Lin 1993 as an expletive object). The element introduced by *ge* can be either an adjective or an indefinite nominal which is a measure phrase (or more marginally a bare noun), as shown in (53):

(53) a. chi ta ge tongkuai
       eat it GE satisfied
       'have a satisfying eating'
   b. pao ta ge san quan
       run it GE three CL-lap
       'do a three-lap running'
   c. ??tiao ta ge wu
       dance it GE dance
       'do an activity of dancing'

What is important to note is that *ta* in these object expletive structures always requires a *DP* associate. This therefore implies that *ge* is crucially functioning to provide a nominal DP expression in the event *ge* construction, sometimes converting non-nominal categories (such as adjectives) into DP elements. Secondly *ta* has been noted by Lin to tolerate only DP associates which are headed by *weak* determiners such as *ji*-CL ('several N') and *yi-xie* ('some NP'), but not *nei*-CL ('that NP') or *mei*-CL ('every NP'):

(54) wo yao kan ta ji-ben/yi-xie   lishi xiaoshuo.
     I want look it several-CL/some history novel
     'I want to read several/some history novels.'

(55) *wo yao kan ta nei-ben/mei-ben lishi xiaoshuo.
     I want look it that-CL/every-CL history novel
     'I want to read that/every history novel.'

This would seem to indicate that the *ge*-headed nominals must also be DPs with some weak determiner element in the D-head position.[14][15]

2.4 The Proposal—*Ge* as a Weak Unselective Determiner in D⁰

Having provided a characterization of a number of restrictions and patterns found with what has been referred to loosely as 'event *ge*', I would now like to argue that the evidence presented would all seem to indicate a single solution: the element *ge* is currently used not only as a regular numeral classifier, but also now as a *weak unselective determiner* with a non-specific indefinite specification. It will be pointed out that this element is similar in certain respects to the unselective determiners reported to exist in Salish languages by Davis and Matthewson 1997, and it also bears similarities with a certain use of Cantonese classifiers reported by Cheng and Sybesma (1999) and Audrey Li (1999a).

2.4.1 Ge *as a Nominalizer*

In order to reach the above conclusion, a brief review of the patterning observed in section 3 will be helpful. It was observed in Section 3 that the element *ge* may occur preceding nouns which are *already* quantified by numeral-classifier expressions, as for example in (56):

(56) he   ge san-ping jiu   (see also 11 and 12)
drink GE three-CL wine
'drink three bottles of beer at one time'

It was also significantly shown that *ge* may occur introducing not only elements which are clearly nominal (as in 56), but also other XP-types which may not be nominal at all, a common case being *adjectives* as in (57a), but also clause-like idiom expressions as in (57b) and sub-parts of V-V compounds as in (57c):

(57) a. chi ge bao   (see also 17)
eat GE full
'do a satisfying eating'
b. wen ge shui-luo-shi-chu (= 25c)
ask GE water-fall-rock-out
'do a thorough interrogation until everything is clear'
c. xue   ge xi (= 4)
study GE study
'do an activity of studying'

In this sense it seems that *ge* is rather unselective in terms of the syntactic category type it selects and introduces into the object position.[16]

A comparison was also made between *ge* and other regular classifier types and it was argued that *ge* is *not* simply replacing a more specialized regular classifier when it occurs in certain objects, as the attempt to replace *ge* with a regular classifier is often found to be unacceptable:

(58) tiao   ge/*gen   sheng   (see also the discussion in 7-10)
   jump GE/CL-strip rope
   'do a rope jumping/*jump one rope'

This would seem to indicate that *ge* is not simply occurring in the standard classifier position and that 'event *ge*' forms do not result from simple deletion of the numeral *yi* 'one'. Rather, *ge* would appear to have a rather different status from standard classifiers and arguably is occurring in a different syntactic position.

It was also shown that the *ge*-XP has an important *aspectual function*, often serving to provide either an end point for an activity predicate or an object which can be measured-out in the course of the event (and so also naturally bounding the predicate in this function too). Data reviewed indicated that *ge*-XPs could only occur with *perfective* and not *imperfective* aspect-markers (and marginally with stative predicates if an inchoative interpretation is forced, as in example 30), this being fully consistent with the assumption that *ge*-XPs function to convert a non-telic predicate into one which is aspectually bounded. Noting that work carried out by Tenny (1987) and Borer (1994) has argued that underlying nominal objects (or unaccusative subjects) may be necessary for the interpretation of a predicate as telic, it was suggested that *ge* might seem to be functioning as a *nominalizer* in part, converting certain non-nominal categories into object DPs which could then serve as the necessary input for the interpretation of a predicate as telic.

It was further noted that there are various restrictions on *ge*-XPs—it was shown that adjectives introduced by *ge* may not undergo predicate-type ABAB reduplication, that regular negation may not occur between *ge* and its complement, and that adjectives in *ge*-XPs may not undergo A-not-A question formation. It was suggested that restrictions of this type might be explained by likening such patterns to other similar restrictions found with *nominalization* phenomena in languages such as Korean. Nominalizers in Korean would seem to differ crucially with regard to the *size* of the syntactic constituent they may embed, Type II nominalizations embedding a full clausal constituent and allowing for all regular clausal elements and syntax to occur internal to the nominalization, while Type III nominalizations only embed VPs or smaller clausal/lexical projections and disallow elements and syntactic phenomena which are dependent on higher functional heads in the clause. Such differences have also been noted to occur in English (e.g., in Abney 1987), with the *-ing* nominalizer arguably being associated with either an IP-like constituent as in

(59), this licensing nominative case and accusative case, or selecting a VP-size complement and forcing genitive case and *of*-insertion for objects (due to the lack of T and AgrO heads) as in (60):

(59) [John reading his book] was encouraging.

(60) [John's reading of his book] was encouraging.[17]

Consequently there might seem to be good evidence for a nominalization hypothesis, the absence of ABAB reduplication, A-not-A question forms and regular negation being attributed to the possibility that *ge* as a nominalizer might be selecting a bare Adj(P) which would not be able to support such syntactic processes.

A final set of evidence relating to patterns found with object expletive *ta* was then argued to confirm this suggestion. Observing that object expletive *ta* always seems to require a weakly-quantified DP associate, a natural conclusion to make is that *ge*-XPs also have such a status, and that the element *ge* is critical in performing a nominalization category-conversion function.

Putting all this information together, it seems that *ge* can be convincingly argued to function as some kind of *nominalizer*. A natural question to ask now is what the descriptive term nominalizer actually corresponds to in formal syntactic terms, and what position in the Chinese DP/NP/ClP *ge* actually occurs in?

2.4.2 Ge *as a D^0*

Here I would like to suggest that the most natural interpretation of the evidence and patterning found may be to conclude that the element *ge* is actually a *determiner* in the D^0 position selecting for a variety of complement types and converting them into a 'nominal' output which can then function to provide an aspectual bounding for an activity predicate. The clues which lead to such a conclusion also come from various parts of the evidence presented. First the nominalization function of *ge* has been seen to be suggested by a number of phenomena. The patterns with object expletive *ta* then indicate that the overall category of the *ge*-XP can reasonably be argued to be that of DP, headed by some overt weak determiner (noting that object expletive *ta* will *not* combine with an NP which does not have any overt weak determiner, cf: **kan ta shu* 'read it book(s)'). This consequently might seem to indicate that *ge* itself must be interpreted as the weak determiner head of the DP.

As *ge* is elsewhere assumed to have the category of *classifier* however, one might perhaps question whether this suggested (re-)assessment of (event) *ge* as a determiner type is actually correct. Other evidence indicates that such a conclusion is in fact rather well-supported. First of all it was seen that (event) *ge* may often *not* be simply replaced by a more specialized classifier (example 58), which may be taken to indicate that *ge* is not just instantiating the regular classifier position but is inserted as some other syntactic category type. Secondly we saw that (event) *ge* may also *precede* a full numeral-classifier expression as in (56), which indicates rather clearly that *ge* cannot in fact be occurring in the regular classifier position but must in fact be located in some *higher functional head*.[18] A natural conclusion then is that this higher functional head is in fact D^0, and that the occurrence of *ge* in D^0 results in the nominalization of whatever complement it is that *ge* introduces. By drawing a parallelism between a V-O-*ge*-XP string and the double object construction, I have also shown how the event *ge* makes it possible for the *ge*-XP to act like an (extra) argument of the verb, which can furthermore be said to be a typical function of a determiner. Szabolcsi (1994) has proposed that the primary function of determiners and complementizers (which occur in similar structural positions in nominal and clausal constituents) is to act as "embedders" and enable a proposition or a DP to refer as an argument.

2.4.3 Further Evidence

Event *ge* is therefore now suggested to be a weak determiner instantiating D^0 and higher in the nominal functional structure than simple numeral-classifier sequences. There are two further consequences of such an analysis which can be argued to support it further. First of all if *ge* is in D^0 and not the regular Classifier position Cl^0, we can explain why *ge* may not be preceded by numerals such as and *san* 'three' and *si* 'four', etc.—numerals will occur lower in the functional structure and not raised in D^0 or SpecDP:

(61) a. wo xiang chi ge bao.
     I   want eat GE full
     'I want to keep eating until I am stuffed.'
   b. wo xiang chi yi ge bao.
     I   want eat one GE full
     'I want to keep eating until I am stuffed.'
   c. *wo xiang chi   san/si ge bao.
     I   want eat three/four GE full

Elsewhere (e.g., in Lü 1984) it has been suggested that event *ge* is actually the abbreviated form of *yi-ge* 'one-*ge*' and hence that *ge* should in fact be in the regular CL position, simply with a deleted number one. Here I would like to suggest that there may in fact be a deleted or covert *yi* occurring with *ge*, but that this element is not in fact the regular number one but rather an equivalent to the indefinite article *a/an* in English. While certain languages do have indefinite articles which are phonologically distinct from the number one (as e.g., English), there are many languages which make use of the number one also as an indefinite article (e.g., German *ein*, French *un*, etc.). Chinese can therefore be suggested to belong to this latter (far larger) group and allow for *yi* to be syntactically employed *either* as the number one *or* as an indefinite article.[19] The distributional facts reported here would also seem to support the treatment of *yi* as an indefinite article syntactically distinct from the number one *yi* too—only the article *yi* can occur (with *ge*) preceding a numeral-classifier-N sequence.[20]

(62) a. ta   e   jile,   henhende chi-le (yi) ge san-wan fan.
        he hungry extremely fiercely eat-ASP one GE three-CL rice
        'He was very hungry, so he fiercely ate three bowls of rice (all at once).'
    b. *ta   e   jile,   henhende chi-le si ge san-wan fan.
        he hungry extremely fiercely eat-ASP four GE three-CL rice

Such a syntactic difference between an indefinite article and a homophonous number one can be found elsewhere in Thai and supports the distinction suggested here. In standard Thai the number 'one' *nung* occurs preceding the classifier as in (63).[21] However, when the same element has the interpretation of an indefinite article 'a/an' significantly it occurs *after* the classifier, as in (64a). The post-classifier position is also the position occupied by definite articles, as in (64b), confirming that post-classifier *nung* is in fact an article rather than a numeral:

(63) a. phuu-ying nung-khon
        woman   one   CL
        'one woman'
    b. phuu-ying soong-khon
        woman   two   CL
        'two women'

(64) a. phuu-ying khon-nung
        woman   CL   a
        'a woman'
    b. phuu-ying khon-nii
        woman   CL   this
        'this woman'

The second set of evidence supporting treatment of *ge* as a weak determiner giving rise to an interpretation of the DP it heads as a non-specific indefinite comes from the unacceptability of *ge*-XPs in environments other than object position. The examples in (65) and (66) show that *ge*-XPs cannot occur in subject position and cannot be topicalized. This can be simply ascribed to the suggestion that *ge*, as a weak determiner with a non-specific indefinite interpretation, is barred from occurring in positions which only allow for either definite or specific indefinite DPs, hence neither subject nor topic position. Note that *bare* NPs/DPs *may* in fact occur in subject/topic position (with definite/generic interpretations); the fact that *ge*-XPs are fully unacceptable in subject/topic position can therefore only be related to the presence of *ge* and the proposal that *ge* as a weak determiner forces a particular non-specific indefinite interpretation.

(65) a. *ge wu   tiao-wan   le.
         GE dance dance-finish ASP
     b. *ge san quan pao-wan le.
         GE three lap run-finish ASP

(66) a. *ge wu, ta tiao le.
         GE dance he dance ASP
     b. *ge san quan, ta pao le.
         GE three lap he run ASP
     c. *ge bao, ta chi le.
         GE full he eat ASP
     d. *ge   ji-quan-bu-ning,   ta nao le.
         GE chicken-dog-not-peaceful he fuss ASP

Similar considerations account for the non-occurrence of *ge*-XPs in *ba*- and *bei*- constructions—in both such environments the *ba-/bei*-raised DP must be specific, but *ge*-XPs are necessarily non-specific.

(67) a. *ta ba ge wu   tiao le.
         he BA GE dance dance ASP
     b. *ta ba ge san quan pao le.
         he BA GE three lap run ASP
     c. *ta ba ge bao chi-le.
         he BA GE full eat-ASP
     d. *ta ba ge   ji-quan-bu-ning   nao le.
         he BA GE chicken-dog-not-peaceful fuss ASP

(68) a. *ge wu   bei ta tiao le.
         GE dance BEI he dance ASP
     b. *ge san quan bei ta pao le.
         GE three lap BEI he run ASP
     c. *ge bao bei ta chi le.
         GE full BEI he eat ASP
     d. *ge   ji-quan-bu-ning   bei ta nao le.
         GE chicken-dog-not-peaceful BEI he fuss ASP

Finally, the weak determiner analysis of *ge* can be suggested to account for the non-occurrence of *ge* with demonstratives as in (69):

CHAPTER 2

(69) *ta chi-le ge na san-wan fan. (cf. 11a)
    he eat-ASP GE that three-CL rice
    'He ate those three bowls of rice at one time.'

Examples such as (69) can be ruled out in either of two possible ways. Possibly it could be suggested that the demonstrative must be located in D^0 and therefore if *ge* is also an instantiation of D^0 they simply cannot occur. A second way to account for the unacceptability of (69) is to suggest that demonstratives are base-generated lower in the DP and not in D^0 (as per Simpson 2002), but that there must be necessary definiteness concord/agreement obtaining between a lower demonstrative/quantifier and any instantiation of D^0 and as *ge* is specified as being indefinite, this will conflict with the [+definite] specification of the demonstrative, so resulting in the unacceptability of (69).

Concluding this section, one might ask whether there is possibly any supporting precedent for the analysis of *ge* as an element of the type proposed. Essentially I have argued that *ge* is an *unselective determiner* which is able to embed a complement which may be of a variety of syntactic types, from clearly nominal types through to adjectives and apparent clausal idioms. Whereas determiners (and functional elements in general) cross-linguistically are commonly assumed to be lexically specified for a single complement type, the proposal that *ge* as a nominalizing determiner should tolerate a variety of complement types might seem to be somewhat unusual. However, looking further across languages one finds that a proposal of a highly similar type has in fact been made on the grounds of quite different evidence for a patterning found in the Salish languages of North America. Davis and Matthewson (1997) argue at length and present convincing evidence that there are determiners in Salish which are unselective in terms of their complement category, optionally selecting *either* for a nominal *or* a verbal complement, an NP or a VP: 'In Lilloet Salish the lexical projections of N and V are morphologically and syntactically distinct. However, this distinction is neutralized at the DP/IP level. In (70) [renumbered] the determiner *kwu* indiscriminately takes either an NP or an (infinitival small clause) VP as its complement:' (Davis and Matthewson 1997, handout p.3):

(70) wa   ka   ama-s-as   [kwu calis]/[kwu qwul-xal].
    PROG appear good-CAUS-3ERG [DET cherry]/[DET cook-INTR]
    'He likes cherries/likes to cook.'

Likewise the determiner [*ti..a*] introduces either an NP or a (finite small clause) VP:

(71) ama [ti citx sw   a] / [ti s   xiq   sw   a].
     good [DET house 2SG-POSS DET]/[DET FNT arrive 2SG-POSS DET]
     'Your house is good/Your arriving is good.'

The existence of unselective determiners of different types might then actually be a phenomenon which exists across a number of languages and would not be linguistically odd in any particular way.

Secondly, if one turns to another Chinese language, Cantonese, one can find further supporting evidence for the classifier-determiner connection. In Cantonese it has long been noted that bare classifiers occurring with nouns automatically give rise to readings of *definiteness* (see Cheng and Sybesma 1999 and Li 1999a).

(72) bo-sue hai bin do a?   Cantonese
     CL-book be where Q
     'Where is the book?'

(73) goh-ging-chaat waa ngoh jii   lak.   Cantonese
     CL-policeman   say I   know ASP
     'The policeman told me (that).'

Given that definiteness is standardly assumed to be a property of the D^0 position in DPs, if definiteness readings result from the use of a bare classifier in Cantonese, it may naturally be suggested that this is a function of the classifier occurring in D^0. Then a clear parallel is found with the *ge*-XP construction—in both instances there is the occurrence of a bare classifier in the D^0 position and a particular type of definite/indefinite interpretation results. The difference between Mandarin and Cantonese here being that indefiniteness is a lexically-associated property of Mandarin event *ge*, whereas all classifiers in Cantonese may potentially trigger definiteness readings when occurring in D^0. Cross-linguistically then it would seem that there is indeed support for the analysis proposed here, and that the functional element *ge* can be taken to occur high in the nominal functional structure as an unselective weak determiner, necessarily interpreted as being non-specific indefinite and functioning to provide a telic nominal bound to aspectually unbounded predicates.[22]

2.5 Grammaticalization, Reanalysis and *Ge*

In this last main section of the chapter, I would finally like to approach the question of how it is that *ge* might come to be an element in the D^0-position. I would like to suggest that a plausible explanation can be offered in terms of an approach to grammaticalization suggested in Simpson (1998b). Such an approach can be shown to not only allow for a hypothetical account of *ge*, but will also be further developed in chapter 6 to account for changes which have arguably occurred with verbal *le*.

CHAPTER 2

In Simpson (1998b) it is suggested that one possible way of understanding certain occurrences of grammaticalization is to see grammaticalization as frequently resulting from a combination of movement and reanalysis within the functional structure projected above a lexical element. It is proposed that various instances of 'category change' (i.e., reanalysis of an element of one category-type as instantiating a second category-type) may occur when a lexical element first raises up to some functional head dominating the lexical head and then later on becomes re-interpreted as actually being base-generated in the higher functional head position. For example, if a functional structure consisting of three functional heads F_1-F_3 is projected dominating a lexical head L as in (74), it is possible that F_1-F_3 may be filled by discrete overt functional elements which are actually base-generated in F_1-F_3, or it is possible that the lexical head L raises to these heads. In the latter case the lexical element may be taken to be base-generated with morphological features which are checked against the higher F-heads either overtly (as in N-to-D raising in DPs in Romance languages, see e.g., Longobardi 1994, Grosu 1988) or later on at LF.

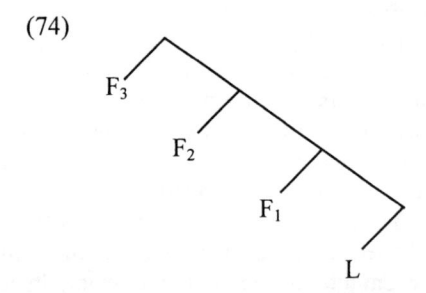

(74)

F_3
F_2
F_1
L

Considering still the second case where L raises up to one or more of the functional heads, supposing the morphological features corresponding to these heads are covert/phonologically zero, it is possible that the lexical element itself may become interpreted as actually instantiating the features of the higher functional head(s). If the lexical element also undergoes a loss of descriptive content ('bleaching') while simultaneously becoming more associated with the functional properties of the F-head/s it raises to, it is argued that the lexical element may then ultimately undergo categorial reanalysis and be re-interpreted as base-generated in the functional super-structure dominating L rather than originating in L. This will consequently result in a syntactic category change and grammaticalization of the lexical element L as a functional element of type F_1 (or $F_{2/3}$).

As a concrete illustration of this hypothetical process, Simpson discusses the creation of the French negative morpheme *pas*. Originally negation in French was expressed just by a pre-verbal negative element *ne*. Later on this changed somewhat and the pre-posing of certain verbal *objects* to a non-canonical object position preceding the verb came to signal emphatic negation.

Among these emphatic re-enforcers of negation was the element *pas* literally meaning 'a pace' or 'a step' and occurring naturally as the object of a variety of verbs of motion such as 'walk', 'run', etc. The effect of emphatic negation with *pas* was very similar to that in the English example (75):

(75) I didn't walk a STEP!

With other types of verbs different appropriate objects would be used, amongst which those in (76) below (see Gamillscheg 1957):

(76) *mie* 'crumb' — with verbs of eating
gote 'drop' — with verbs of drinking
point 'dot, point' — with verbs of writing

English again has certain similar uses, e.g.,

(77) I didn't drink/touch a DROP!

From a wide range of objects used as emphatic re-enforcers of negation in early French, by the sixteenth century only *pas* and the three elements in (76) actually remained, these elements having undergone sufficient generalization that they could be used with a wide variety of verbs. Later on still in modern French only *pas* and *point* are found, (without their original literal meaning) with *point* being more restricted in its use and only occurring to emphasize the contradiction of a previous statement (see here Hopper and Traugott 1993). Essentially then *pas* over time lost its original purely literal meaning of 'step' and has come to be used as a functional emphatic re-enforcer of negation with verbs which have no connection at all with walking or running or actions involving 'steps' as potentially genuine objects. In modern day French the original emphasis present with *pas* and other emphatic re-enforcers of negation has also significantly been lost and *pas* is now interpreted as signaling simple (non-emphatic) negation. Finally another highly important aspect of the process of historical change is that *pas* may now be used to express negation with transitive verbs which have overt objects. Whereas *pas* was originally understood to be the object of the verb, it has now been reanalyzed as a purely functional morpheme occurring in some other position. Because of this reanalysis, transitive verbs projecting other genuine object DPs may now co-occur negated with *pas* as in (78):[23]

(78) Je n'ai pas vu Jean.
I NEG-have PAS seen John
'I haven't seen John.' (Simpson 1998b)

In view of this collection of synchronic and diachronic properties, Simpson suggests that *pas* was originally base-generated as a simple object NP which

CHAPTER 2

optionally underwent raising to a pre-verbal emphatic-focus-type projection selected by the negation head *ne* when focus-features were added on to *pas*, as illustrated in (79):

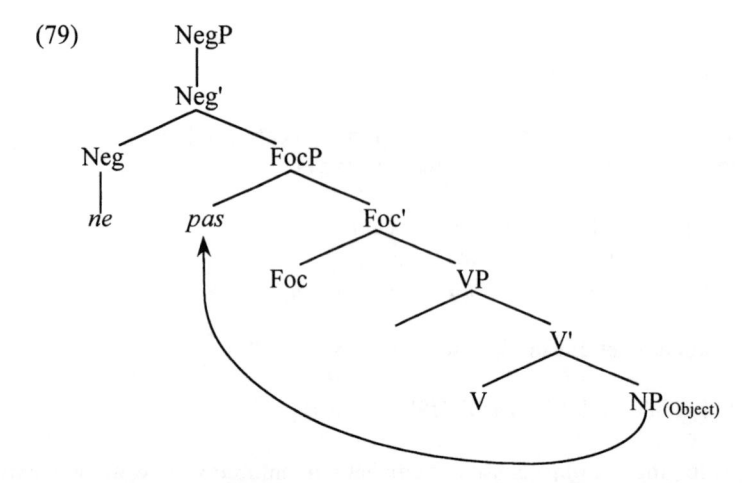

(79)
```
         NegP
          |
         Neg'
        /    \
      Neg    FocP
       |    /    \
       ne  pas   Foc'
               /    \
             Foc    VP
                    |
                    V'
                   /  \
                  V   NP(Object)
```

With the continued association of *pas* with focus and negation and the specialization of *pas* over other emphatic negative objects Simpson suggests that *pas* was mentally reanalyzed as occurring base-generated in the Spec of the focus-projection. Such reanalysis then allowed for the object position to be occupied by a genuine non-emphatic NP and gave rise to forms with overt objects in addition to *pas*, as seen in (78) and the tree in (80):

(80)
```
         NegP
          |
         Neg'
        /    \
      Neg    FocP
       |    /    \
       ne  NP    Foc'
           |    /    \
          pas  Foc    VP
                     /  \
                   NP    V'
                   |    /  \
                   je  V   NP(Object)
                   'I' |      |
                       vu    Jean
                      'seen' 'John'
```

40

The possibility of explaining the clustering of properties and developmental changes with *pas* in this way thus arguably supports the suggestion that grammaticalization may indeed consist in a sequence of movement and subsequent reanalysis in a functional projection targeted by a lexical element. Here *pas* is originally a lexical object which begins to undergo raising to the pre-verbal SpecFocP when it signals emphatic negation. Significantly later on after continued association of *pas* with negation and focus it is reanalyzed as being only a functional element and as therefore being base-generated in the functional projection itself. Such reanalysis frees up the object position in VP and a genuine thematic object can then be base-generated in this lexical position, leading to the co-occurrence of *pas* with overt lexical objects.

Simpson suggests that another instantiation of this 'upward' process of grammaticalization is the frequent change of lexical verbs into auxiliary-verb elements, a development in which a lexical V^0 first raises up to a higher Infl-type from V^0 and then is later simply base-generated in the higher functional head.[24] In support of the movement-based approach to grammaticalization, Simpson also notes that changes going in a 'downward' direction do not seem to take place. For example, whereas root modals which are canonically situated low down in the functional structure dominating VP commonly turn into structurally higher epistemic modals with sentential scope, the opposite type of change of epistemic modal into root modal is critically not found (see e.g., Bybee, Perkins and Pagliuca 1994). Significantly it would seem to be the case that change and reanalysis consistently occurs in an upward direction, mirroring the direction of syntactic movement.

Turning back to Chinese and *ge*, I would like to suggest that a rather simple natural hypothesis can now be made about *ge*'s occurrence in the D^0 position. It is fairly clear that *ge* must have originated as a classifier and would therefore have been originally base-generated in the classifier head position Cl^0. Synchronically it has been suggested that *ge* has however a rather different function and occurs as an unselective determiner in D^0 embedding a variety of complement types as a nominalizer, functionally allowing these elements to occur as the nominal objects of a verb. Historically I would like to suggest that the current status of *ge* is a direct result of *ge* undergoing a sequence of movement and reanalysis in the functional super-structure of the DP essentially very similar to that outlined for *pas* above. It can be suggested that *ge* was indeed originally base-generated in Cl^0 but then later underwent raising to the higher D^0 position and then ultimately became reanalyzed as an element of type D^0 directly base-generated in the D^0 head. Concerning the motivation for the hypothetical movement to D^0, here a useful clear parallel can be drawn with the development of English *a/an*. The English indefinite determiner *a/an* is well-documented as having developed historically from the numeral *one* (see e.g., Osawa 1998); if one assumes that numerals are base-generated in a distinct functional head Num^0 (as e.g., in Ritter 1991) and that indefinite determiners occur in D^0, then *a/an* can be taken to have developed from *one* via raising from Num⁰ to D⁰ and eventual full reanalysis in D⁰. It may be assumed that *a/an/one* underwent a change in its interpretation and functional role and that from a time when it was licensed as a numeral signaling the number one in contrast to other numbers it later came to be interpreted *primarily* as a simple indefinite element which 'embeds' an NP as its argument. As an indefinite counterpart to *the* it would therefore have raised to D⁰ and possibly then have undergone reanalysis as a D⁰ element. Now, Chinese *ge* is in ways quite similar to English *a/an*, functioning as an embedding element with a clear indefinite value like English *a/an*. Recall here also the fact noted earlier that when no numeral occurs with the simple classifier *ge* it has a natural default interpretation of 'one'; in such cases there is critically no feeling of contrast between the numerical value one and other possible numbers and *ge* is much more naturally translated as English *a/an*. Consequently it can be suggested that when *ge* was not accompanied by a numeral in the past, it came to be potentially licensed not just as a classifier associated with a covert numeral 'one' but also as an indefinite embedding element higher in D⁰. Essentially then in both English and Chinese an element such as *ge/a/an/one* would be base-generated and remain in CL⁰/Num⁰ if its role was primarily numerical and contrastive with other possible number values, but raise to D⁰ or be directly base-generated in D⁰ if its primary function were to serve as an indefinite embedding element. The hypothetical raising of *ge* to the D⁰ position can therefore be given a reasonable explanation which furthermore has cross-linguistic support.[25]

Diachronically, I would therefore like to suggest the following sequence of developments:

(81) a. Stage 1: *ge* was base-generated and remained in CL⁰ as a classifier.
b. Stage 2: *ge* was base-generated in CL⁰ and also raised to the D⁰ position
c. Stage 3: *ge* was fully reanalyzed as a D⁰ and consequently base-generated directly in the D⁰ position

Supposing one were to assume a simple DP structure with D⁰ selecting for a NumP which in turn selects a CLP headed by a classifier, structures in (82-84) would represent the hypothetical sequence of change:[26]

(82) Stage 1

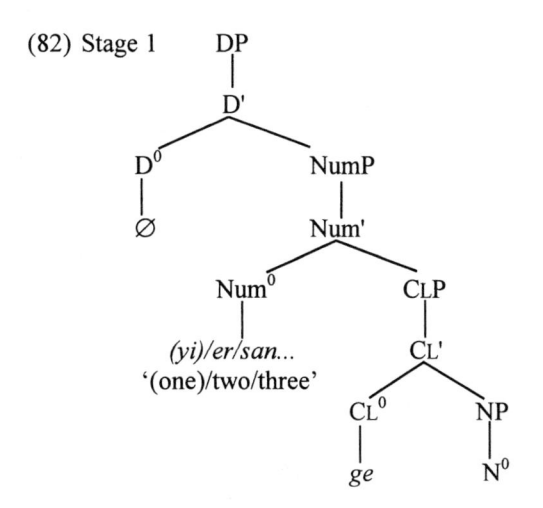

```
          DP
          |
          D'
         / \
        D⁰  NumP
        |    |
        ∅   Num'
           /    \
         Num⁰   CLP
          |      |
     (yi)/er/san... CL'
     '(one)/two/three' /  \
                    CL⁰   NP
                     |    |
                    ge   N⁰
```

(83) Stage 2

```
          DP
          |
          D'
         / \
        D⁰  NumP
        |    |
        ∅   Num'
           /    \
         Num⁰   CLP
          |      |
       (yi 'one') CL'
                  /  \
                CL⁰   NP
                 |     |
                ge    N⁰
```

43

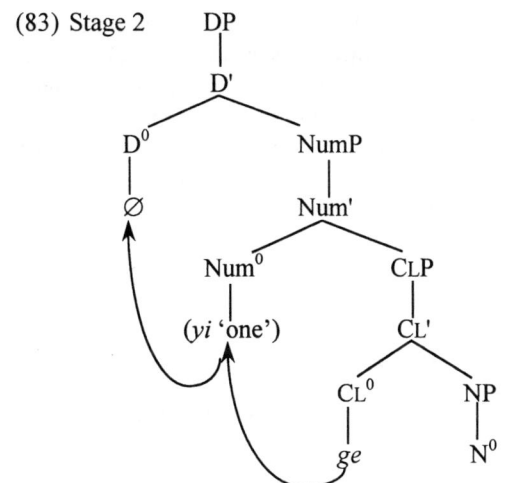

(84) Stage 3

```
        DP
        |
        D'
       / \
      D⁰   NumP
      |     |
      ge   Num'
          /    \
        Num⁰    CLP
                |
                CL'
               /   \
             CL⁰    NP
                    |
                    N⁰
```

In (83) where no numeral (other than 'one') occurs in Num⁰ ge raises here and is essentially interpreted as 'one', and then moves higher to D⁰ where it is licensed as an embedding indefinite determiner-type element.[27] In stage 3, ge is reanalyzed as being base-generated in D⁰ and functions just as an embedding indefinite determiner. Significantly at this point when *ge* is not interpreted as having undergone raising from CL⁰ and Num⁰ it then becomes possible for these positions to become filled with other overt elements and sequences such as (85) are fully possible:

(85) ta   he-le   ge san-ping jiu.
     he drink-ASP GE three-CL wine
     'He did a drinking of three bottles of wine.'

The sequence in (82-84) then really has a close resemblance to the changes found with the French negation element *pas*. Like *pas*, after *ge* has raised from its base-generated position to a higher functional projection and eventually undergone reanalysis and full grammaticalization as instantiating only the higher functional position, its original base-generated site then once more becomes available for the lexical insertion of other elements. Somewhat different to the development with *pas* though, because *ge* has become an *unselective* determiner, once stage 3 is reached *ge*'s complement is actually not forced to be a NumP but as noted in earlier sections can also be a variety of other syntactic types.

Ultimately then it has been possible to arrive at a plausible and reasoned explanation of how *ge* has grammaticalized and developed from a classifier into a functional element of some higher type within the DP, thereby adding further good support and justification for its synchronic treatment as an element of type D⁰ as proposed here.

2.6 Concluding Remarks

In this chapter I have shown that the general classifier *ge* can be employed to count out an event. Semantically this 'event' *ge* functions to make an atelic predicate telic by bringing out (or reinforcing) the end point of the event depicted by the predicate. Syntactically event *ge* has been suggested to be a weak *determiner* in the D position selecting for a variety of complement types and converting them into a 'nominal' output which can then function to provide an aspectual bounding for an activity predicate. As a D^0, *ge* is essentially equivalent to a non-specific indefinite article, this property also accounting for the fact that the DP headed by *ge* can only occur in object position in Chinese. Finally, I attempted to show how *ge* may have diachronically undergone change from being an instantiation of CL^0 to become a D^0, basically following a hypothetical path of change upwards in the DP equivalent to the development of the English indefinite article 'a/an' from the numeral 'one'.

Notes

[1] Here the *ge* construction exhibits interesting differences from resultative constructions in English where a resultative secondary predicate may only refer to an *object* (or to the subject of an *unaccusative* verb, i.e., an underlying object) but not to regular transitive/unergative subjects:

   (i)   *John swam tired.

   (ii) John ran his horse tired.

   (iii) John arrived tired.

   (iv) John laughed *(himself) hoarse.

[2] These sequences are 'clause-like' in the sense that a full (and overt) argument structure is present.

[3] Note that the use of *hen* does not *necessarily* result in an interpretation of 'very' but appears to be necessary to fulfill some rather unclear structural requirement that the pre-adjectival position be filled by some overt element in clauses.

[4] If *hen* 'very' is added to the adjective, the element *de* must also occur, indicating that this is a relative clause structure and a predication, e.g.:

   (i)   hen xin *(de) shu
       very new DE book
       'books that are very new'

[5] Compare (37) to the sentences with the resultative *de* in (i):

(i) a. shuo de hen qingchu
       say DE very clear
       'said it very clearly.'
    b. chi de tai bao
       eat DE too full
       'ate too full'

Resultative *de* selects for a complement which may be instantiated by a predicational adjective here, this contrasting with *ge* which cannot introduce predicational form adjectives.

[6] Compare the sentence in (41) with the resultative *de*.

(i) ta shuo de bu qingchu.
    he say DE NEG clearly
    'He said it unclearly (He did not say it clearly).'

[7] Compare *ge* in (43) to the resultative *de*:

(i) ta shuo de qing-bu-qingchu?
    he say DE clear-NEG-clear
    'Did he make it clear?'

[8] Note that the negative element *bu* in (42) occurs in a frozen expression and therefore is not part of the process of a syntactic negation, while (41) is a case of syntactic negation. I assume that syntactic negation in examples such as (41) involves a clausal structure. According to Cinque (1999), clausal negation can occur in different positions cross-linguistically. It is therefore not unreasonable to find two or more clausal negative elements co-occurring in one sentence:

(i) ta mei-you bu xiang qu. (p.c., Audrey Li)
    he NEG-have NEG want go
    'He didn't not want to go.'

The argument here is that the XP following *ge* can not be a clausal structure. Different negative items can occur as long as it does not involve a process of syntactic negation (and hence a clausal structure). For example, the negative item *mei* can also occur in the frozen expression following *ge* in (ii):

(ii) ta shuo-le ge mei-wan-mei-liao.
     he speak-LE GE not-end-not-finish
     'He made an endless talk.'

[9] Given the well-formedness of (42) one might have to assume that some instances of negation may in fact be combined with other elements *in the lexicon*. This is a position which has actually frequently been adopted in the past, for example by certain authors working on negative auxiliary elements such as English 'can't', 'won't', etc. (in Zwicky 1977), or Cantonese *mo* = *mei* + *yau* in (Matthews and Yip 1994).

[10] Objects occurring between the verb and *ge* are however rather uncommon, it being usually preferred to position them pre-verbally licensed by *ba* as in (i):

(i) wo ba ta da-le ge ban-si.
I BA he hit-ASP GE half-dead
'I hit him half-dead.'

[11] An explanation of the animacy patterns in DOCs put forward in Kayne (1994) suggests that the fact that the indirect object in DOCs must always be +animate (or an institution) is because the indirect object comes to be in *possession* of the direct object in DOCs. The evidence from the *ge*-construction here might seem to indicate that such a generalization may not be entirely correct—basically a parallel [+animate] constraint characterizes both DOCs and the *ge*-construction, but there is no possession relation arising in the latter syntactic forms. However, note that in 'di-transitive' *ge* constructions such as (51) the result depicted by the *ge*-XP always predicates of the NP following the verb rather than the subject of the sentence. In order to explain this, one might assume that the post-verbal NP and the *ge*-XP form a single small clause-type constituent with the *ge*-XP naturally predicating of the post-verbal NP as the small clause subject. Such an analysis would then actually come to resemble the small clause-type analysis of indirect object and direct object proposed by Kayne.

[12] A second possible explanation might be that the *ge*-XP is always a non-specific indefinite and hence can be licensed via some kind of inherent partitive case.

[13] Elsewhere however the parallelism in behavior between DOCs and di-transitive *ge*-forms diverges somewhat. Specifically the object directly following the verb exhibits differences in the two constructions in its ability to undergo *movement*. Whereas the object following the verb can be topicalized in both constructions and also *ba*-raised or *bei*-raised in *ge*-sentences, object 1 in the double object construction cannot occur raised with either *ba* or *bei*:

(i) a. nei-ge ren, wo da-le ge ban-si.
that-CL person I hit-ASP GE half-dead
'That person, I hit him until he almost died.'
b. ?nei-ge ren, wo song-le yi-ben shu.
that-CL person I send-ASP one-CL book
'That person, I gave a book.'

(ii) a. wo ba nei-ge ren da-le ge ban-si.
I BA that-CL person hit-ASP GE half-dead
'I hit that person until he almost died.'
b. *wo ba nei-ge ren song-le yi-ben shu.
I BA that-CL person send-ASP one-CL book
'I gave that person a book.'

(iii) a. nei-ge ren bei wo da-le ge ban-si.
that-CL person BEI I hit-ASP GE half-dead
'That person was hit by me and he almost died because of it.'
b. * nei-ge ren bei wo song-le yi-ben shu.
that-CL person BEI I send-ASP one-CL book
'That person was given a book by me.'

Both *ba*-constructions and *bei*-constructions involve affectedness of the theme or the patient. In the double object construction, what is affected is the direct object (i.e., the book in the examples), not the indirect object. I assume that it is the affectedness

CHAPTER 2

effect which in fact prevents the indirect object of a di-transitive verb from being *ba*- or *bei*-preposed. In the di-transitive *ge*-construction by way of contrast, the NP following the verb is affected and so can be *ba-/bei*-preposed. Consequently the syntactic parallelism between DOCs and di-transitive *ge*-forms still holds.

[14] Lin (1993) and Borer (1994) essentially both assume that the DP-object-associate raises to SpecAgrO/AspP at LF. For Borer this has the effect of inducing a telic reading, activating the Asp-head which is associated with telicity.

[15] Note that when *ge* is not present, only the (b) example in (53) survives, as shown in (i).

(i) a. *chi ta tongkuai
eat it satisfied
'ate until fully satisfied'
b. pao ta san quan
run it three CL-lap
'do a three rounds of running'
c. *tiao ta wu
dance it dance
'do a dancing'

This is because the expletive *ta* requires a weakly-quantified DP associate, as noted. Where *ge* is present, this provides the necessary type of DP object associate for *ta*, but when it is removed only (b) remains a weakly-quantified DP; (a) and (c) can be suggested to unacceptable because *tongkuai* and *wu* are interpreted as verbal/non-nominal and hence of the wrong categorial type to constitute associates for *ta*.

[16] The *output* of applying *ge* to any of its possible complement XP types is however assumed to be consistent, and *ge* as a nominalizer applied to any of these XP will result in a constituent YP [$_{YP}$ ge XP] which is outwardly specified as being a nominal-type projection.

[17] Note also that negation can occur in the (59)-type form and not in (60), supporting the suggestion that (59) contains an IP clausal projection whereas (60) is a simple nominalized VP:

(i) a. [John not reading his book] upset us.
b. *[John's not reading of his book] upset us.

[18] It might perhaps be suggested that *ge* in these cases corresponds to something like a 'group classifier' and therefore does still occur in a higher classifier position. However, event *ge* can also embed adjectives with no group meaning. If one intends to aim for a uniform analysis of event *ge* it would therefore seem that *ge* is best analyzed as something other than a straightforward classifier in Cl^0.

[19] Concretely I would actually like to assume that *yi-ge* is a single grammaticized X^0 head and does not consist in two discrete parts/heads (noting that neither *yi* nor *ge* can be substituted for by any other numbers or classifiers when this unit occurs in the D^0 position preceding other numerals and classifiers or adjectives, etc). It is *yi-ge* therefore which is the D^0 indefinite determiner equivalent to English 'a/an'. I furthermore suggest that simple bare *ge* is fully equivalent to *yi-ge* and results from simple reduction of *yi-ge* to *ge*.

[20] Note that although *(yi)-ge* as an indefinite determiner can freely precede other numerals and classifiers as in (62) and other examples in the chapter, it cannot occur before the numeral one and a classifier:

(i) *wo chi-le (yi)-ge yi wan fan.
    I eat-ASP one-GE one CL-bowl rice

A restriction on the legitimate use of the indefinite determiner *(yi-)ge* seems to be that if the complement introduced by *(yi-)ge* is already nominal, it necessarily has to be a plural-collective XP. This may well be a primarily pragmatic restriction on the use of the determiner *(yi-)ge*. *(Yi-)ge* is commonly used to introduce a complement which is unusual or sometimes excessive in some way as e.g., in (62a). Singular NP complements (such as for example *yi wan fan*) however normally do not represent unusual/excessive amounts and so the use of the *(yi-)ge* determiner is pragmatically unjustified. If a situation can however be created in which the consumption of a single unit of the N may in fact be interpreted as being excessive/unusual, the use of *(yi-)ge* actually is permittable with a following *yi* + CL:

(ii) ta pingchang bu he   jiu.   jintian tai gaoxing le.
     he regularly NEG drink alcohol tomorrow too happy LE
     jingran   zai wu-fenzhong nei he-le   ge yi da   ping jiu.
     surprisingly at five-minute within drink-LE GE one big CL-bottle wine
     'He does not drink regularly. He was too happy today. Surprisingly he drank a big bottle of wine in 5 minutes.'

[21] See Simpson (2001) for a full discussion of the Thai patterns.

[22] Earlier I noted that there is a special restriction that indefinite determiner *ge* seems to occur only as part of an aspectually-bounded predicate: *ge*-XP either follows an activity verb and provides the predicate with an end point or follows an achievement verb to reinforce the end point (the restriction addressed in examples 29-31). If one follows Borer (1994) and assumes that the object DPs which provide measures for telic predicates are licensed in the Spec of an AspP dominating VP, it can now be suggested that the event *ge* is an instantiation of D^0 which will formally only be licensed when such an AspP is projected in the structure. Consequently, where stative predicates occur no such AspP will be projected and the indefinite determiner *ge* will not be licensed as an instantiation of D^0:

(i) *ta you ge san-ge haizi.
    he have GE three-CL child

(ii) *ta xihuan ge san-ge nüren.
     he like   GE three-CL women

[23] It can also be noted that in colloquial French the original negative marker *ne* is fast disappearing so that *pas* is taking over as the sole marker of negation.

[24] Such a change and re-analyis is indeed assumed to have occurred in the 'creation' of the modal verb series in English (Lightfoot 1979).

[25] See here Szabolcsi (1994) and chapter 3 on the suggestion that elements in D^0 may be licensed in virtue of being embedding elements similar to complementizers in the clausal domain. See also Longobardi (1994) and Vergnaud and Zubizarreta (1992) on the idea that the D^0 position sometimes must be filled, even if this is with an expletive

CHAPTER 2

determiner element which has no obvious definiteness value. Here I do not attempt to approach the question of whether the D^0-position in Chinese might always need to be filled, and if so how this is achieved. For interesting relevant discussion here see Audrey Li (1998).

[26] There are many suggestions as to how D^0, Num^0 and Cl^0 might be structurally related. I have adopted the structures in (82)-(84) for ease of explanation, but other structures might also be accommodated with the basic proposals put forward here. See Audrey Li (1999a) for further analysis of the internal structure of Chinese DPs.

[27] Earlier it was noted that *ge* alternates with *yi-ge* as an indefinite determiner in D^0 and that *ge* and *yi-ge* are essentially equivalent (see footnote 19). There are two possible ways in which *ge* could have come to combine with *yi* in D^0. One possibility is that *yi* was located in Num^0 in Stage 2 and allowed for *ge* first to raise up to it and then *yi* and *ge* together raised higher to D^0 as *yi-ge*. A second possibility is that *yi* was actually located in D^0 as an indefinite determiner in Stage 2 and *ge* raised up to adjoin to it in D^0. Although one cannot be sure which of these possibilities might be correct, there is interesting evidence in favor of the second hypothesis. In classical Chinese it can be argued that *yi* occurred as an indefinite determiner in NPI examples such as (i) below:

(i) bu jian yi ren
NEG see one person
'did not see anyone'

If such examples do indicate that *yi* could function as an indefinite determiner before *yi-ge* sequences occurred in D^0, then possibly *ge* did raise up to *yi* in D^0 rather than to *yi* Num^0.

3

RELATIVE CLAUSE *DE*
DIRECTIONALITY, CLAUSAL RAISING AND SENTENCE-FINAL PARTICLES

3.0 Introduction

This chapter examines the structure of relative clauses in Chinese and aims to develop and defend an analysis of relativization which will be made critical use of in the examination of *shi-de* cleft structures in Chinese in chapter 4. Section 1 of the chapter considers certain very general properties of relative clauses cross-linguistically and how these have been modeled in Chinese by standard Government and Binding/GB style analyses. Section two then goes on to examine the problem of directionality and headedness with regard to relative clause structures in Chinese, highlighting the fact that Chinese is an exceptional language which combines prenominal relative clauses with a basic V-O word order. Concerning the 'relativizing' element *de*, it is argued that GB analyses of *de* as a complementizer are at odds with the general directionality of Category-selection in Chinese and that there is evidence that elements in C in Chinese do indeed select for rightward complements. In section 3.3 I then attempt to show how adopting a Kaynean approach to relativization may resolve these problems, following in part a discussion of relative clauses in Simpson (2002). This Kaynean analysis is subsequently compared with an alternative approach to prenominal relative clauses suggested in Murasugi (1998) for Japanese. I argue that the Kaynean account is preferable for Chinese for three essential reasons. First it allows for a more uniform account of other noun-complement clause structures which make use of the element *de*. Secondly it is able to resolve the headedness/directionality issue (which is not a problem of relative clauses in Japanese). Thirdly some of the critical features of relativization in Japanese which lead Murasugi to propose a fully base-generated analysis of Japanese relative clauses are absent from relative clauses in Chinese. In section 3.4 I discuss the relevance of tone sandhi phenomena in Taiwanese for the account of relativization developed, indicating how it can be shown to provide interesting support for an analysis in which there are leftward clausal movement as part of the construction of relative clauses. Section 3.5 is an extension of the Taiwanese tone sandhi patterns discussed in section 3.4. The grammaticalization process of Taiwanese sentence-final "particle" *-kong* adds further support for the leftward clausal movement proposed for relative clauses. Section 3.6 is a brief conclusion.

3.1 Relative Clauses in Government and Binding Theory

Relative clauses are standardly taken to be descriptions which semantically represent properties or sets, e.g., the relative clause: 'who helped John on June 12th 1998' linguistically represents the set of all (human) entities which have the property that they helped an individual named John on a certain day. Such elements are optionally combined with nouns which also represent sets (e.g., the bare noun 'policeman' being a property which characterizes all those human individuals with a particular profession) and in doing so simply function to pick out the intersection of the sets represented by both noun and relative clause. Such a subset may then be combined with a determiner or other quantifier to yield a nominal phrase with particular reference, as in: 'the policeman who helped John.'

This assumption that relative clauses first combine with nominals and then with a quantifier/determiner naturally leads to the view that relative clause structures have the form in (1) below.[1] Due to their optionality, relative clauses are syntactically taken to be adjuncts and so adjoin to NP before application of any element in D:

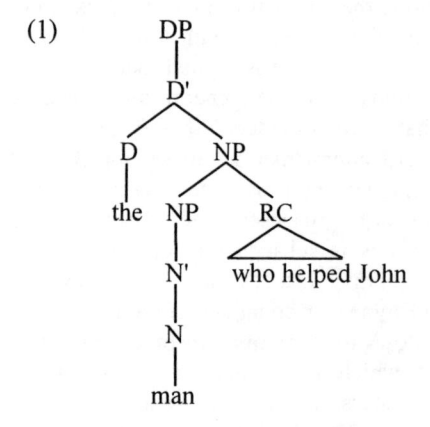

(1)
```
           DP
           |
           D'
          / \
         D   NP
         |  /  \
        the NP   RC
            |   /\
            N' who helped John
            |
            N
            |
           man
```

From a syntactic point of view, within Government and Binding Theory it has been widely argued that relative clauses themselves are CPs, commonly with an operator element of some type raised to the Specifier of C from a position within the IP complement of C. While this may often be an overt relative pronoun in many languages (e.g., in English), in the absence of such an overt element Subjacency tests still provide good evidence for assuming the existence of null operators undergoing the same type of movement. A simple 'that'-relative in English may therefore be represented as in (2):

(2)
```
        DP
        |
        D'
       / \
      D   NP
      |   / \
     the NP  CP
         |  / \
         N' Oᵢ  C'
         |    / \
         N   C   IP
         |   |   △
        man that John saw tᵢ
```

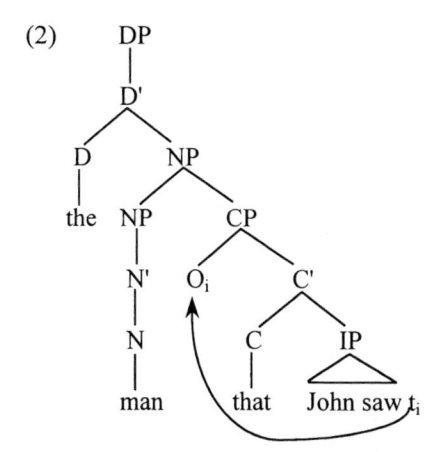

Turning to Chinese, relative clauses are found to precede the nominal element with which they are combined, the 'linking' element *de* occurs between the relative clause and the nominal and no relative pronoun is present. Quantifiers and demonstratives are optional:

(3) [wo zuotian mai] de shu
    I yesterday buy DE book
    'the book(s) I bought yesterday'

The purpose of this chapter is to arrive at an analysis of how the various parts of relative clause structures in Chinese are syntactically related, i.e., how the noun head, the relative clause and the functional element *de* are formally combined with one another.

If such structures do indeed have a similar underlying syntax to relative clauses in English and other languages (as e.g., represented in example 1), a first question which arises is whether there is any evidence of a null operator and null operator movement in Chinese. Although an answer to this question is not immediately obvious, Chiu (1993), (1995) presents interesting arguments that one can in fact conclude that at least a subset of relative clauses in Chinese must be formed by some kind of movement strategy and suggests a structure for Chinese relative clauses which in many ways is very close to that in (1), this also being largely endorsed by further argumentation in Ning (1993).

3.1.1 Chiu (1993/1995) and SuoP; Ning (1993)

Chiu (1993/1995) discusses in particular the significance of the occurrence of the element *suo* in relative clauses such as (4):

CHAPTER 3

(4) [Lisi suo mai ___] de shu
     Lisi SUO buy   DE book
     'the books that Lisi bought.'

Chiu points out that there are various restrictions on the occurrence of *suo* (which is also always purely optional). First of all, *suo* may only occur if the relativized noun-head corresponds to a gap which is in *object* position:

(5) *[___ suo mai shu] de ren
          SUO buy book DE person

Secondly, *suo* appears only if there is a genuine gap in the relative clause, and may not occur if a resumptive pronoun is present (Chiu notes that resumptive pronouns in object position are not liked by all speakers, but for those speakers who do tolerate them as objects, *suo* is not at all possible):

(6) [Lisi (*suo) renshi ta$_i$] de [nei-ge ren]$_i$
     Lisi SUO   know   him DE that-CL person
     'the person that Lisi knows'

Chiu then notes certain critical interactions of *suo* with locality phenomena. When *suo* is present it is not possible for the gap corresponding to the head noun to occur either inside a Complex NP, a Sentential Subject or a *wh*-island containing a *wh*-adjunct:

(7) *[[Lisi suo kan ___] zui heshi]   de shu
       Lisi SUO read   most appropriate DE book
     intended: 'the book that it is most appropriate for Lisi to read'

(8) *[[___$_i$ suo zu ___$_k$] de ren$_i$ hen duo] de nei-dong fangzi$_k$
              SUO rent   DE person very many DE that-CL house
     intended: 'the house that the people who rented (it) are many'

(9) *[Lisi xiang-zhidao [Akiu weishenme suo mai-le ___] de nei-ben shu
      Lisi wonder   Akiu why   SUO buy-ASP   DE that-CL book
     intended: 'the book that Lisi wonders why Akiu bought'

From this Chiu makes the natural conclusion that relativization does indeed involve movement of an empty operator in Chinese. The effects of this movement may at times be obscured because Chinese might also seem to allow for a resumptive *pro* element to occur in islands to overcome Subjacency violations (and the equivalents on (7)-(9) are indeed acceptable if *suo* does not occur). However, when *suo* appears, the relativization strategy does indeed show itself to be fully island-sensitive. Chiu gives arguments that *suo* may in fact only occur in structures where movement has taken place and instantiates an Accusative Case Projection (labeled SuoP) whose overt appearance is only

54

triggered when an object has been raised through it to some higher position. In this sense *suo* is highly similar to the occurrence of object agreement in French which also only appears overtly when there has been some movement of the object (relativization, *wh*-movement, passivization or cliticization, as discussed in Kayne 1975). Such an analysis is nicely supported by the fact that *suo* may *not* occur in the presence of an overt resumptive pronoun where movement has not taken place—example (6). Consequently it may be assumed that relativization in Chinese does indeed involve movement of some element, and Chiu suggests that this element is an empty operator moving to SpecCP, just as in English that-relatives.[2]

In a second treatment of relativization in Chinese, Ning (1993) argues for similar conclusions to those in Chiu (1993/1995), but from a rather different set of observations. Ning again points out the fact that some cases of relativization in Chinese might seem able to violate Subjacency/the CED, licitly linking a head-noun to a position within Sentential Subjects, Adjunct Islands, and CNPs. For example, (11) is an example of an apparent subjacency violation involving relativization from within the sentential subject in (10). Ning argues that (11) is acceptable only because the gap in (11) can be identified as a (resumptive) *pro*; therefore there is no movement involved and no subjacency violation occurs.

(10) [na-ge xuesheng kai zhe-zhong che] shuoming ta baba youqian.
that-CL student drive this-CL car show his father rich
'That that student drives this kind of car shows that his father is rich.'

(11) [[*t* kai zhe-zhong che] shuoming ta baba youqian] de na-ge xuesheng
drive this-CL car show his father rich DE that-CL student
'*the student who that (he) drives this type of car shows that his father is rich'

Ning then shows that certain gaps may however not be identified as (resumptive) *pro* elements as this would violate Huang's (1982) Generalized Control Rule (GCR) on the identification and control of *pro*. This type of gap may *not* in fact be located inside any island configuration, as for example in (12). The conclusion Ning draws is that gaps of relativization not licensed as *pro* by the GCR must indeed result from movement and therefore that at least a substantial sub-section of relative clauses in Chinese are formed by movement.

(12) *[[na-ge xuesheng kai *t*] shuoming ta baba youqian] de na-bu che
that-CL student drive show his father rich DE that-CL car
'*the car which that the student drives (it) shows that his father is rich'

Ning (1993) also considers the phenomenon of so-called 'gapless' relative clauses in Chinese discussed in Tsai (1992) and elsewhere. Ning argues contra

Tsai that Chinese does not in fact have relative clauses which do not contain a gap (either a gap of movement or a trace resulting from operator-movement), and provides arguments that all relative clauses in Chinese do contain some operator-variable chain. Ning suggests that structures such as (13)-(16) below result from the movement of a null wh-operator which may correspond to one of four universally available values—*place, time, manner* and *reason*:

(13) [ta xiu che]-de cheku
 he repair car-DE garage
 'the garage where he fixed the car'

(14) [ta xiu che]-de wanshang
 he repair car-DE evening
 'the evening when he fixed the car'

(15) [ta xiu che]-de fangfa
 he repair car-DE method
 'the method how he fixed the car'

(16) [ta xiu che]-de yuanyin
 he repair car-DE reason
 'the reason why he fixed the car'

Ning goes on to show that relations between a head-noun and a clause which do not fall within any of these four basic types may not license a relative clause structure, for example, neither *comitative* nor *source* interpretations of the head-noun are possible in (17) or (18):

(17) *[ta tiaowu]-de guniang
 he dance-DE girl
 intended: 'the girl he danced with'

(18) *[ta lai]-de na-ge xiaozhen
 he come-DE that-CL town
 intended: 'the town he came from'

There are therefore good reasons for believing that relative clauses in Chinese are licensed by the coindexation of the head-noun with some position in the relative clause, such dependencies arising either via movement or otherwise via the linking of a base-generated *pro*, and that Chinese relative clauses are not in fact simply licensed by any 'Aboutness Relation' (as e.g., in Kuno 1973).

3.1.2 DE *as a Complementizer*

The next question which needs to be answered is: what might be the status of the element *de* in relative clause structures? It can be noted that *de* is certainly obligatory in relative clauses and in this sense might seem to be similar to the occurrence of the element 'that' in English relative clauses where the subject position is relativized and no relative pronoun occurs:

(19) [wo zuotian mai] *(de) shu hen gui.
     I yesterday buy   DE book very expensive
     'the book I bought yesterday is very expensive'

(20) the man *(that) __ helped me

In Chiu's (1993/1995) and Ning's (1993) accounts, the relative clause in Chinese is analyzed as a CP with a null operator (often) moving to the Spec position of CP, in which *de* occurs as a relativizer in the C position, just as 'that' does in English. Such a proposal means that C must naturally be assumed to select its IP-clausal complement to the left, an assumption which has been justified in the literature on the basis of the occurrence of question particles in clause-final position—if one takes such particles to instantiate a Q-morpheme located in C, then C must be clause-final and IP to its left in Chinese:

(21) [[ni qu-guo Beijing] ma] ?
     you go-ASP Beijing Q
     'Have you ever been to Beijing?'

Putting all the components of relative clause forms together and making the assumption that Specifiers uniformly branch leftwards in Chinese, one arrives at the structure in (22) representing (3), which is the analysis put forward in Ning (1993) and in somewhat more articulated form also in Chiu (Chiu has NomP in her structure in place of the IP here):[3]

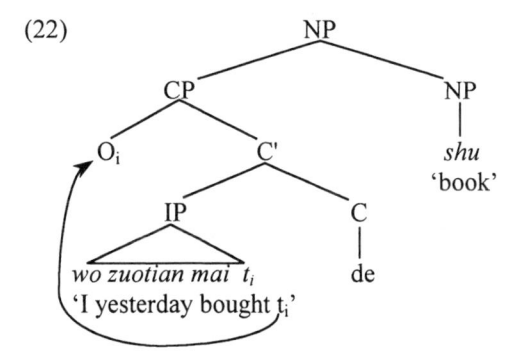

(22)
```
              NP
            /    \
          CP      NP
         /  \      |
        O_i   C'   shu
             /  \  'book'
           IP    C
          /|\    |
  wo zuotian mai t_i  de
  'I yesterday bought t_i'
```

Such a structure is very much a direct equivalent of the standard GB-type analysis of English relative clauses in (2) and has by and large been the regular approach taken to relative clause formation in Chinese for a number of years.[4]

In what follows, however, I would like to argue that there are reasons to prefer another type of analysis for relative clause structures in Chinese, one which is based on more recent general proposals concerning phrasal projection made in Kayne (1994). I will attempt to show both that there is empirical evidence in favor of a Kayne-based approach and that such an approach should also be favored for reasons of theoretical simplicity.

3.2 Directionality and C-selection—a Theoretical Problem for Standard Analyses

In this section I would like to suggest that a reason to be somewhat 'suspicious' of and disprefer a structure such as (22) is that the analysis of *de* as a C selecting an IP complement *to its left* might seem to go against the general directionality of selection in Chinese. Although there has been considerable debate about the head-parameter setting in Chinese and some linguists (notably Li and Thompson 1974) have argued that Chinese displays the beginnings of an O-V order (in *ba*-construction sentences), the present general consensus of typologists, historical linguists and generativists would appear to be that Chinese neither was a head-final language in the past nor does it show real signs of changing from a basic head-initial ordering at present (see e.g., Mulder and Sybesma 1992, Sun 1996, Peyraube 1996).[5] Both in the lexical domain and in the functional domain one finds that X^0 heads select their complements in a rightward direction, so for example verbs and prepositions consistently take their objects to the right as in (23) and (24), and auxiliaries which can be taken to occur in I similarly have rightward VP complements, as seen in (25):

(23) [$_{VP}$ [$_V$ mai [$_{NP}$ yi-suo-fangzi]]]
        buy   one-CL-house
   'buy a house'

(24) [$_{PP}$ [$_P$ zai [$_{NP}$ wo-jia]]]
        at   my home
   'at my house'

(25) [$_{IP}$ ta [$_I$ hui [$_{VP}$ qu Beijing]]].
        he will   go Beijing
   'He will go to Beijing.'

If one attempts to suggest that the relative clause element *de* is occurring in a C position to the right of its complement IP, the directionality of this selection relation would seem to be opposite from what is otherwise attested in Chinese.

One piece of evidence given in support of the assumption that C is final in Chinese was however the occurrence of question particles such as *ma/a* in clause-final position, as in (26). It has been suggested that such particles occur in C and that C hence follows IP to its right. Here I would like to argue that this argumentation is not particularly strong for a number of reasons, and that it is more likely that C is initial in Chinese selecting its complement IP in a canonical rightward direction.

(26) ni qu ma/a?
you go Q
'Are you going?'

The first argument against an analysis of question particles such as *ma* occurring in C is that similar elements occur in many other languages which are clearly head-initial and which have complementizers occurring to the left of their complement IPs. Two such languages which can be mentioned here are English and Thai (p.c., Andrew Simpson), both very regular SVO head-initial languages. In both English and Thai it is found that question particles occur sentence-finally as illustrated in (27)-(30):

(27) You're going home, eh?

(28) She left already, right?

(29) wan-nii khun ca hen khaw mai? (Thai)
today you will see him Q
'Will you see him today?'

(30) khaw ca maa meuarai le? (Thai)
he will come when Q
'When is he going to come?'

The occurrence of these question particles in sentence-final position would seem to be very similar to that in Chinese, yet in English and Thai it is not possible to argue that the particles occur in C as C is IP-initial in both languages with clear complementizers occurring in positions preceding IP:

(31) John said that [$_{IP}$ Mary left].

(32) Daeng book waa [$_{IP}$ Dam mai maa]. (Thai)
Daeng say C   Dam not come
'Daeng said that Dam didn't come.'

It therefore seems that one needs to recognize that sentence-final question particles may regularly occur in surface positions which do not correspond to regular complementizer positions and that the position of *ma* in Chinese does not necessarily indicate the locus of C in Chinese.

A second reason to reject the idea that *ma* is located in C comes from the observation that *ma* (and other questions particles such as *a*) show an important difference from question particles such as *ka* in Japanese which might be more reasonably located in C.[6] Whereas *ka* productively occurs in all kinds of embedded interrogative clauses such as (33), Chinese *ma/a* in (34), just like English 'right/eh' in (35) and Thai particles *mai/le* in (36), are restricted to occurring only in root/main clauses. If *ma/a* are taken to be simple instantiations of C, there is no obvious reason why they should not also occur in embedded questions, as embedded clauses obviously do also contain a complementizer/C position. The root/main clause restriction on *ma/a* then suggests that *ma/a* is perhaps not in C (but perhaps in a higher matrix head) and therefore that the position of *ma/a* is not a good indication that C is final in Chinese:

(33) watashi-wa [dare-ga kuru ka] shirimasen. (Japanese)
I-TOP   who-NOM come Q   not-know
'I don't know who is coming.'

(34) *ta xiang-zhidao [ni qu ma/a].
he wonder   you go Q
intended: 'He wonders whether you are going.'

(35) *John wonders [you're going right/eh].

(36) a. *Daeng yaak ruu (waa) [Dam chalaat mai]   (Thai)
Daeng want know C   Dam clever   Q
intended: 'Daeng wonders if/whether Dam is clever.'
b. *Daeng thaam waa [khrai maa le]
Daeng ask   C   who come Q
intended: 'Daeng asked who came.'

Original suggestions that *ma/a* might be in C were made because Chinese seems to lack any obvious equivalent to the Indo-European general-purpose embedding complementizers (such as English 'that') which might disambiguate where C is located. However, it is not in fact true that Chinese lacks any likely candidate for C. Elements such as 'if' and 'whether' and their counterparts in other languages are commonly taken to be complementizers located in C, and equivalent elements do exist in Chinese, e.g., *ruguo/yaoshi* 'if', etc. Significantly, such elements are found to occur clause-*initially* and so would seem to indicate that C in Chinese does indeed select its complement IP in a regular rightward direction:

(37) [$_{CP}$ ruguo/yaoshi [$_{IP}$ ni bu xihuan nei-ge ren]], ni...
       if   you NEG like that-CL person you
   'If you don't like that person, you...'

Finally, Hwang (1998) notes that the verb to 'say' in Mandarin, Taiwanese and Cantonese is currently following a typical pattern of grammaticalization and becoming reanalyzed as a regular complementizer in certain environments, e.g., following cognitive verbs such as 'think' or informative verbs such as 'tell.' In such instances it is found that the newly grammaticalized complementizers linearly *precede* their sentential complements, strongly suggesting that the position of C in Chinese is in fact IP-initial rather than IP-final.[7] (38) contains examples of Mandarin *shuo* 'say' as a complementizer; the same verb in Taiwanese and Cantonese behaves the same.

(38) a. ta xiang shuo ta bu lai le.
       he think C he NEG come ASP
       'He thinks that he is no longer coming.'
    b. ta gaosu wo shuo ta bu lai le.
       he tell me C he NEG come ASP
       'He told me that he is no longer coming.'

As a result of the above argumentation, the analysis of relative clause *de* as occurring in a C position with a *leftward* complement seems rather unlikely. All the evidence available suggests that C in Chinese selects for a rightward IP complement, in line with the general direction of selection in the language. Therefore it might seem that a different account of the positioning (and possibly syntactic category type) of *de* is called for, which may well have further consequences for the general analysis of internal structure of relative clauses in Chinese. This I now turn to in section 3.3.[8]

3.3 Kayne (1994) and a Uniform Theory of Relativization

Kayne (1994) develops a theory of phrase structure projection, the Linear Correspondence Axiom/LCA, which attempts to encode the idea that there can be no ambiguity in the way that terminal/head elements are linearly sequenced. One consequence of the LCA is that rightward adjunction structures may no longer be posited in any syntactic structures. Standard GB-style relative clause analyses in which CPs are taken to be right-adjoined to NPs as in English (1) repeated below therefore have to be reanalyzed by Kayne:

(1)
```
         DP
         |
         D'
        / \
       D   NP
       |  /  \
      the NP  RC
          |   /\
          N' who helped John
          |
          N
          |
         man
```

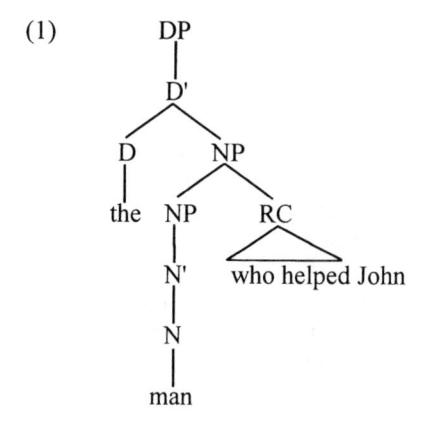

Kayne's solution to the problem created for relative clauses created by the LCA involves two key components. First of all it is suggested that D selects directly for a CP complement. Secondly it is suggested that the relative clause noun-head actually undergoes movement to its surface position from some position within the IP unit. The latter suggestion is in part justified by the observation that it allows for idiom chunks to be base-generated together and then split by the process of relativization, and is a return to a style of analysis originally put forward for similar reasons by Vergnaud (1985). In forms such as (39) below, an analysis in which the NP 'headway' is base-generated as the object of the verb 'make' and then raised leftwards is fully consistent with the general assumption that complex idioms must be stored in the lexicon as a single unit and introduced into syntactic structure together. Alternative null operator-type analyses of similar examples have been criticized as failing to capture the well-formedness of such idiomatic cases; it is argued that a word such as 'headway' is listed in the lexicon *only* as part of the idiom 'make headway' and not as an independent noun which could be taken and directly inserted as the head-noun of a relative-clause structure:

(39) the [headway]$_i$ that we made t$_i$ on the project

A simple *that*-relative according to Kayne is formed via movement of the NP to the SpecCP position as diagrammed in (40):

(40)
```
        DP
        │
        D'
       ╱ ╲
      D   CP
      │  ╱ ╲
     the NP  C'
         │  ╱ ╲
      [book]ᵢ C  IP
              │  ╱╲
           (that) I bought tᵢ
```

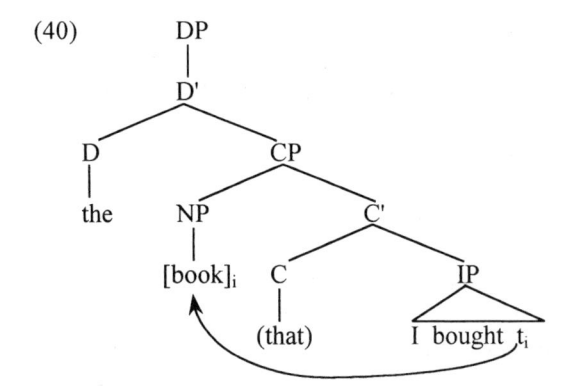

The same essential head-initial structure is then also suggested to underlie prenominal relative clauses in other languages, with the addition of a single extra movement raising the IP constituent to the Specifier of D as in (41), using English words for ease of exposition:

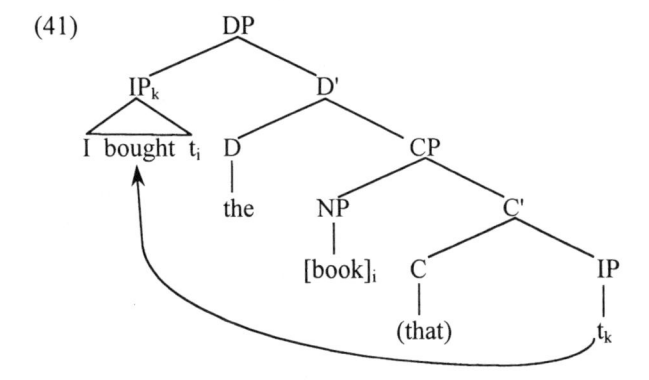

(41)
```
             DP
            ╱  ╲
          IPₖ    D'
         ╱╲    ╱  ╲
  I bought tᵢ D    CP
              │   ╱ ╲
             the NP   C'
                 │   ╱ ╲
              [book]ᵢ C  IP
                     │   │
                  (that) tₖ
```

If one were to allow movement to be able to affect C' as a constituent (although generally it is argued that X'-level constituents are invisible for the purposes of movement), then one might also expect languages to show the surface order indicated in (42), and this might in fact seem to be what is found in Amharic (p.c., R. Hayward, again using English words for ease of exposition):

(42) [[that [I bought tᵢ]]ₖ [D the [CP bookᵢ [tₖ]]]]

Such an analysis essentially allows Kayne to suggest that there is a fully universal structure underlying relative clause forms in all languages, the surface differences attested being simply due to whether (and how much of) the relative clause is moved to SpecDP overtly.

Now, concentrating on the possible positions that *complementizers* can occur in languages with prenominal relative clauses, it can be seen that they

63

may be found either finally after the head-noun as in (41) after IP-movement, or initially as in (42), and so schematically as in (43):

(43) (C) IP D NP (C)

(44) (that) [I bought] the [book] (that)

If one now takes the *pre-nominal* relative clauses found in Chinese, e.g., (45), and compares them with the template in (43), paying particular attention to the linear positioning of the element *de* and the possible positions of complementizers according to Kayne, an interesting discovery is made. It is found that the position which *de* occurs in does *not* correspond to any potential complementizer position. Such a conclusion is highly interesting because it is exactly what has been argued for in section 3.2. There it was suggested that it would be quite unnatural to analyze *de* as a complementizer in C and that some other analysis seemed to be required.

(45) [$_{IP}$ wo zuotian mai] de [$_{NP}$ shu]
 I yesterday buy DE book
 'the book I bought yesterday'

In fact, as pointed out in Simpson (2002), it seems that the only likely category that *de* could conceivably correspond to in such structures is actually D, which is initially somewhat surprising as *de* would not seem to exhibit the standard patterning of determiner elements, neither having any obvious inherent definiteness value nor co-occurring with NPs outside of relative clause and possessor modification environments. However, rather than immediately reject the possibility that *de* may be taken to be a determiner in D, one might instead reconsider what is understood by such a term and re-examine how the notion of definiteness may be represented in a DP. This is indeed the path taken in Simpson (2002) and shortly I consider a number of the points raised in that work. Before doing so, it may be helpful to indicate how relative clauses might look in a Kaynean-style approach under the assumption that *de* is in fact located in D. Structures in (46) and (47) represent the sequence of movements necessary to convert a fully head-initial structure into the surface string attested in (45). The first step in (46) is the raising of the NP which first proposed in Vergnaud (1985) and later suggested in Kayne (1994) to take place in relativization in all languages. (47) follows this with further raising of the IP, as occurs (by hypothesis) in Amharic but not English:

(46) [tree diagram]
```
           DP
           |
           D'
          / \
         D   CP
         |   /\
      de [shu]i C'
        'booki'/\
              C  IP
                 /\
            wo zuotian mai ti
            'I yesterday bought ti'
```

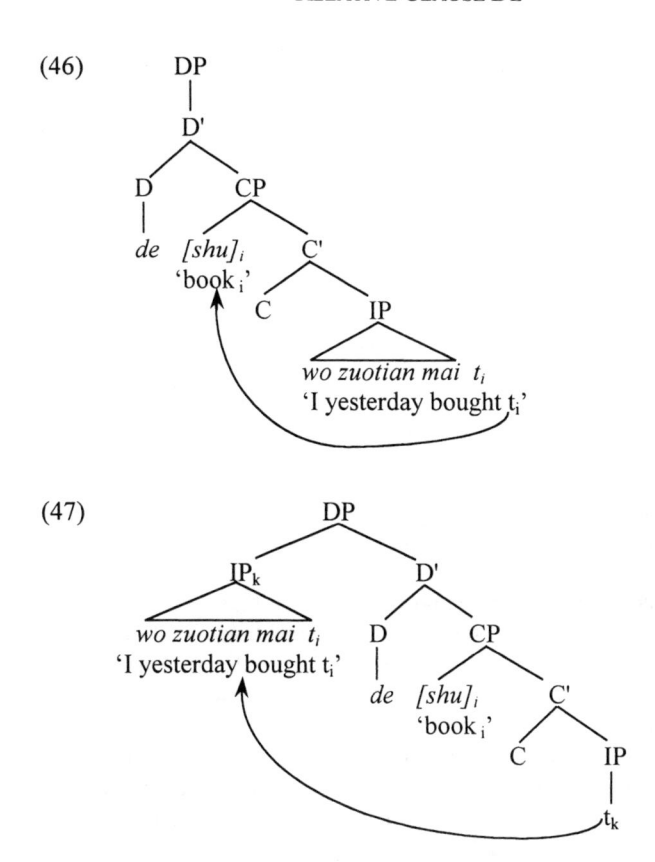

(47) [tree diagram]
```
               DP
              /  \
            IPk   D'
           /\    / \
   wo zuotian mai ti  D   CP
   'I yesterday bought ti' |  /\
                       de [shu]i C'
                        'booki' /\
                               C  IP
                                  |
                                  tk
```

3.3.1 Determiners, Demonstratives and Definiteness Agreement

Referring to work carried out by Greenberg (1978) on African languages, Hopper and Traugott (1993) and Abraham (1997) among others, Simpson (1998a, 1998b, 2002) notes that it is a fairly common process for functional elements such as determiners to pass through a number of stages of grammaticalization. Generally it is documented that determiners are initially derived from *demonstratives* after a loss of the deictic force present in such elements. For example, the French determiners *le/la* have been grammaticalized from the Latin demonstratives *ille/illa*, German *der* from *dieser* and English 'the' from the 'this/that' demonstrative series. Greenberg (1978) writes that after further time determiners may then also go into a process of further decay, ultimately losing their definiteness specification with the end result that they either disappear from a language or else remain on with some additional function. As determiners undergo bleaching of their definiteness specification, it is common that languages develop some compensatory mechanism to encode the definiteness of a DP. Certain languages may make

65

use of word order possibilities, while others may employ means such as aspectual marking on the verb to distinguish definite from indefinite DPs (e.g., Abraham 1997 on the development of determiners in German and the use of aspectual systems in Slavic languages). A third common way to compensate for the loss of definiteness specification in determiners is for a language to develop a new series of demonstrative elements in adjective-like positions within the DP. Such demonstratives are then frequently found to co-occur with determiners in a single DP representing a classic example of the typological notion of 'layering'.

Simpson suggests that this is indeed the case of Chinese *de*. *De* is argued to be a determiner which no longer has any intrinsic or overt definiteness value and which consequently may often occur 'doubled' by a demonstrative (or other quantifier) specifying the definiteness of a DP:

(48) [wo zuotian mai] de nei-ben shu
I yesterday buy DE that-CL book
'that book which I bought yesterday'

In more theoretical terms, Simpson suggests that the overt locus of definiteness in a DP need not always be the D position. Following original ideas in Vergnaud and Zubizarreta (1992), developed also in Szabolsci (1994) and Longobardi (1994), it is noted that many languages would seem to have an EPP-like condition on the D position that it be overtly filled by some element prior to Spell-Out. The element filling the D position need not necessarily have any definiteness specification and could be an 'expletive' determiner with no definiteness value; the EPP-like condition on D is then similar to the clausal EPP which requires that SpecTP be filled, even if only with a semantically empty expletive element.

In languages such as English, if a demonstrative is generated in the DP, this necessarily occurs in D. However, in other languages it seems possible to find either a demonstrative in the initial D-position *or* a determiner in D with a demonstrative occurring lower down in the DP. Such a pattern is found in Spanish, Irish, Greek and a number of other languages. Example (49) illustrates this alternation with data from Spanish taken from Giusti (1997):

(49) a. la reaccion alemana esa a las criticas
the reaction German that to the criticisms
'that/the German reaction to the criticisms'
b. esa reaccion alemana a las criticas
that reaction German to the criticisms
'that/the German reaction to the criticisms'

Data such as (49a/b) allow one to draw a number of conclusions. First it is argued in Grosu (1988), Szabolsci (1994), Giusti (1997) and various other works that demonstratives are not in fact base-generated in D but actually in lower DP-internal adjective-like positions. In many languages they are suggested to undergo raising to an initial position and so appear as if they had been directly inserted into D. Other languages however show that their demonstratives will only raise to the initial position *if* no determiner has been inserted there. In Spanish for example, if no determiner is present in the initial position in (49a) the demonstrative is forced to raise to the initial position as in (49b) and it may not remain lower down:

(50) *reaccion alemana <u>esa</u> a las criticas
 reaction German that to the criticisms

This has led to the view mentioned above that determiners are often 'place-holders' or expletives, and that the definiteness specification of a DP may be primarily encoded by other elements such as demonstratives. Simpson (2002) points out however that it is not sufficient for just any type of D-compatible element to occur in D in the presence of a lower demonstrative, and that generally only the definite determiner is possible, as in the contrast seen in (51):

(51) el/*un hombre este
 the/a man this

This is attributed to the existence of a requirement of 'definiteness agreement' or 'definiteness concord' between the D-position and lower elements such as demonstratives or other quantifiers.

Consequently it is argued that it is in fact rather natural to find that determiners co-occur with demonstratives within a single DP. Historically this is suggested to be due to a process in which determiners originally grammaticalized from demonstratives may gradually be bleached of an original definiteness value and then tolerate doubling by a secondary set of demonstrative elements which are the primary encoders of definiteness in the DP.[9] In languages such as Spanish, Greek and Romanian, the plain determiners may still maintain a definiteness value, though frequently also functioning as expletive place-holders. Chinese, by way of contrast Simpson suggests, is a language in which a determiner element occurs in D which has lost all trace of any definiteness specification, with the result that definiteness concord between the D-position and a lower demonstrative is only covertly encoded.

Such a mode of explanation allows one to make certain sense of the idea that *de* may be an instantiation of D without necessarily having any obvious definiteness value. It therefore provides a way of reconciling the distribution of elements within the relative clause in Chinese with the structure predicted by a Kaynean approach. Returning to the forms suggested by Kayne for typical prenominal relatives (as in 46 and 47), one now might ask what motivation could be given for the suggested IP- raising operation shown in (47), repeated immediately below:

(47)

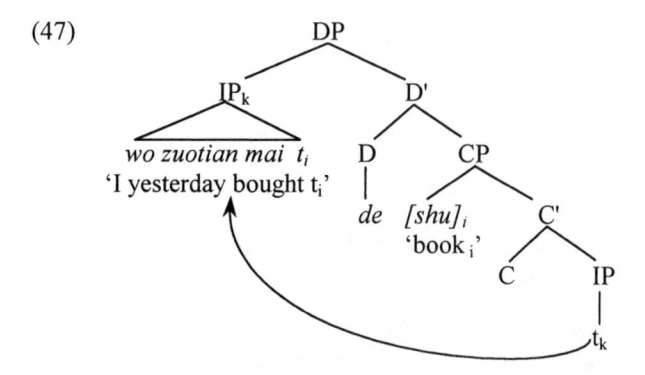

```
              DP
            /    \
          IP_k    D'
         /   \   / \
    wo zuotian mai t_i  D    CP
    'I yesterday bought t_i'  |   / \
                          de [shu]_i  C'
                          'book_i'  / \
                                   C   IP
                                       |
                                       t_k
```

Pointing out that Chinese is possibly the only language known to exhibit the combination of *pre-nominal* relative clauses and a basic head-initial/V-O order (as in Dryer 1992), Simpson suggests that any explanation of the IP-raising should be somewhat exceptional in nature and therefore necessarily related to a particular lexical item rather than being a general syntactic property (such as a parameter setting). Simpson proposes that the exceptionality present in Chinese relative clauses relates directly to the element *de* and suggests that *de* is an enclitic determiner similar in nature to the enclitic definite determiners found in Romanian, Mokilese and Buginese, attracting an element (in Chinese the IP) to its Specifier position for phonological support. Such a proposal takes its lead from Grosu's (1988) analysis of the definite determiner in Romanian. Grosu convincingly shows that the definite determiner is an enclitic which attracts an element to the DP-initial position preceding the determiner, so that the determiner can phonologically attach to this element. The element attracted may be a noun or an adjective if present, as in (52) and (53). Cases such as (52) and (53) with the definite determiner contrast strongly with the use of the indefinite article in (54) which is not an enclitic and does not result in the attraction of either adjectives or nouns:

(52) potret_i-ul   t_i unei   fete
      portrait-the   a-GEN girl
      'the portrait of a girl'

(53) frumos_i-ul   t_i baiat
      nice-the   boy
      'the nice boy'

(54) un portret   al   fete
      a   portrait of-the girl
      'a portrait of the girl'

So for Chinese the suggestion in Simpson (1998a, 2002) which I would also now like to assume, is that *de* is an enclitic determiner very similar to *ul* in Romanian, and that *de* attracts the IP-clause to SpecDP to attach to it, thus giving rise to the surface distortion and the typologically very unusual prenominal ordering.[10]

As additional support for the *de*-as-determiner analysis, Simpson notes that there are a number of languages which visibly make use of determiners in the formation of their relative clauses, among them Lhakota, Diegueno, Tzeltal and Hebrew, a cross-linguistic patterning which indicates that it is indeed (relatively) common to find determiners in such positions.

Finally I would like to point out that there is potentially strong historical support for the contention that *de* is indeed a determiner element in the D position. Earlier it was observed that determiners frequently develop from demonstratives when the latter lose their strong deictic force. Given such a process, it is now significant to note that there is in fact a direct connection between modern Mandarin *de* and an earlier demonstrative element. Commonly it is assumed that the modern Mandarin morpheme *de* developed from an earlier element *zhi*, which in classical Chinese had a distribution largely parallel to contemporary *de* (see for example Pulleyblank 1995). Importantly in addition to contexts such as relative clauses in which modern Mandarin *de* occurs, classical Chinese *zhi* was also used as a clear demonstrative (example cited from Pulleyblank 1995):[11]

(55) zhi er chong you he zhi
these two worm again what know
'And what do these two worms know?' (*Zhuangzi* 1.10)

If modern Mandarin *de* has indeed developed from classical Chinese *zhi*, and if classical Chinese *zhi* was a demonstrative, a highly natural analysis of modern Mandarin *de* is that it is a determiner descended from this earlier demonstrative via the common process of "definiteness bleaching."

The end result of this is that an analysis based on a Kaynean model coupled with an account of *de* as a bleached enclitic determiner might indeed seem able to accommodate the typological oddity of relative clauses in Chinese in a principled and satisfactory way which is also successful in avoiding the directionality problem faced by earlier GB-style approaches.

3.3.2 *Further Evidence for the NP-raising Analysis: (1) Language Acquisition: Chiu (1998); (2) Connectivity and Idiom-chunks*

In addition to providing an analysis of Chinese relative clauses which is in accord with the general direction of selection dominant in Chinese, there is also interesting language acquisition evidence discussed in Chiu (1998) which supports Vergnaud's (1985) idea (adopted by Kayne 1994) that it is the N-head which undergoes raising rather than an empty operator. Chiu observes that children produce not only relative clauses with regular resumptive pronouns but also relatives with full NPs in place of an extraction-gap (Resumptive NP Relative Clauses/RNP RCs), as in (56):

(56) luotuo chi <u>caomei</u>   de <u>caomei</u>
camel eat strawberry DE strawberry
'the strawberry which the camel ate'

Following Guasti and Shlonsky (1992) in essence, Chiu suggests that the use of an empty 'linking' operator in relativization is a complex strategy which only becomes available to children at a later stage of development. Chiu suggests that children therefore initially form relative clauses via simple movement of an NP from a base-generated position within the relative clause (via SpecCP) to a surface position right-adjoined to the relative clause. RNP-RCS such as (56) occur when children optionally spell-out both the lower extraction-site copy of the NP as well as the head of the chain, instead of just the latter:

> Because linking operators are maturationally unavailable for children before the age of 6 (cf. Guasti and Shlonsky 1992), children begin forming relatives by directly moving the head noun from within the CP to its surface position, leaving an exact copy at the extraction-site. (Chiu 1998, p.18)

In addition to forms such as (56) and 'regular' relative clause structures such as (57) in which only the head of the chain is phonetically spelled-out, children also produce sequences such as (58). Chiu suggests that forms of this 'head-internal' type are the result of spelling-out just the lower copy of the relativization chain:

(57) luotuo chi __ de <u>caomei</u>
camel eat   DE strawberry
'the strawberry which the camel ate'

(58) ganggang nei-ge <u>daxiang</u> tiao de
just-now that-CL elephant jump DE
'the elephant which just jumped'

Consequently such patterns would indeed seem to provide further support for an N(P)-raising account of relativization and are rather difficult to account for in analyses in which the head-noun is simply base-generated in its surface position following *de*. If the head-noun were to be base-generated following *de* and commonly associated with a gap position via an operator-trace/*pro* linking, one would expect for the argument position in the relative clause to be occupied by either just a trace, a phonologically null *pro*, or possibly an overt resumptive pronoun, but certainly not a copy of the head-noun as in (56). The only explanation for the occurrence an overt copy of the head-noun inside the relative clause would seem to be that this is left by movement of the head-noun itself, not any operator.[12][13]

In addition to the above language acquisition evidence for an NP-raising analysis of Chinese relative clauses, there is further evidence from connectivity and idiom-chunks in favor of such an account. Connectivity effects occur in English relative clauses such as (59):

(59) the picture of himself that John likes the best

(59) contains an anaphor 'himself' which must be bound in order to comply with Principle A of the Binding Theory. This requires that the anaphor must at some point be c-commanded by its antecedent 'John' and as the NP 'John' is located *inside* the relative clause, this would appear to mean that the NP [picture of himself] must in fact have been base-generated within the relative clause as the object of 'like' (in which position it will be c-commanded by 'John') and then raised to its surface position. The existence of connectivity effects such as this has been taken to be a strong argument in favor of a Kayne-style account of relativization, and was originally discussed in earlier accounts such as Vergnaud (1985). Connectivity has been shown to be dependent upon *movement*, so that where a movement analysis is blocked, as in the Left Dislocation structure (61) compared to the Topicalization example (60), the connectivity effect disappears:

(60) [That picture of himself]$_i$, John liked t$_i$

(61) *[That picture of himself], John liked it.

Turning now to consider Chinese relative clauses, one finds that connectivity effects are also present in such structures as for example in (62):

(62) Zhangsan$_i$ bu xihuan [na-jia chubanshe chuban de] youguan ziji$_i$ de
Zhangsan NEG like that-CL publisher publish DE regarding self DE
shu.
book
'Zhangsan does not like the books about himself that are published by that publisher.'

Such patterns are clearly unexpected in an analysis in which the only element which moves is an empty operator as in (22), as then the anaphor will at no point in the syntactic be c-commanded by its antecedent. In an NP-movement analysis, however, the anaphor *ziji* will straightforwardly be c-commanded by its antecedent prior to movement of the NP *youguan ziji de shu* 'books about himself' to Spec of CP.

A similar point can be made with respect to the possibility of idiom-chunks in relative clause structures. Vergnaud (1985) notes that parts of an idiom may occur modifying the head noun of a relative clause as already noted in examples such as (39) repeated below:

(39) the [headway]$_i$ that we made t$_i$ on the project

Given that the element 'headway' is part of an idiom 'make headway', it has to be assumed that it is base-generated together with the verb 'make' inside the relative clause and then raised to its surface position. Again, such patterns clearly favor an NP-raising analysis over a null-operator approach which has no obvious way to account for the existence of such forms. Related patterns occur in Chinese relative clause structures as illustrated in (63):

(63) [[ta kai t$_i$ de] dao$_i$] dou hen chenggong.   (from Audrey Li 1999b)
he open   DE knife all very successful
'The operations that he performed were all successful.'

In (63), *dao* 'knife' is part of an idiom *kai-dao* literally 'open-knife' meaning 'perform an operation'. It would seem that one should therefore assume that it is base-generated together with the verb *kai* 'open' inside the relative clause and subsequently raised to the head noun position. In an empty operator analysis such as (22), one would not expect for such idiom chunks to be able to occur as head nouns in relative clauses, as in such a structure the head noun cannot be lexically inserted together with material internal to the relative clause.

Before concluding that the analysis put forward here is necessarily to be preferred to previous accounts, I will finally consider an account of relativization in Japanese which rejects a straight Kaynean approach to pre-nominal relative clauses and attempt to assess whether such an account might also be appropriate for Chinese. Arguing that the analysis developed here is actually to be preferred, in section 3.3.4 and 3.3.5 I then show how the wider patterning of complex NPs in Chinese adds further support to the Kayne-based analysis.

3.3.3 Relativization in Japanese, Murasugi (1991/1998)

Murasugi (1998) takes the original account of Japanese relative clauses which she developed in Murasugi (1991) and examines whether it might be compatible with Kayne's theory of Antisymmetry. Her conclusions, following work in Kuno (1973) and Hoji (1985), are that there are various critical aspects of relativization in Japanese which seem to distinguish Japanese from English-type languages and render a direct translation of Kayne's proposals inappropriate for Japanese.

The first important point that Murasugi makes with regard to relative clauses in Japanese is that they do not seem to need to contain any gap corresponding to the head-noun. Similar remarks appear in a number of works on Japanese relative clauses with this property being first commented on by Kuno (1973). (64) and (65) are typical examples of what are frequently referred to as 'gapless' relatives, where it seems highly difficult to re-site the head-noun in any position within the relative clause without adding in a lot of additional material (which could not be simply deleted in the process of relativization):

(64) [John-ga hako-o nutta] omochabako
John-NOM box-ACC painted toy-box
'the toy box that John created by painting a box'

(65) [atama-ga yoku naru] hon
head-NOM well become book
'the book (by reading) which one's head becomes better'

Murasugi takes the existence of gapless relatives to be evidence against a straightforward Kaynean analysis of relative clauses in Japanese. An important aspect of Kayne's account is that the head-noun is base-generated within the IP in the relative clause and moved to its surface position; if there arguably is no position within the IP from which it could have originated in gapless relatives, then at least a subset of relative clauses in Japanese must be constructed without any movement.

The second point raised by Murasugi, here following Hoji (1985) is that Japanese might not seem to show the important connectivity effects which have been argued to occur in English relative clauses such as (59) in section 3.3.2. Hoji (1985) notes that the occurrence of an anaphor such as *jibun* modifying the relative clause head-noun in (66) seems to cause the relative clause structure to be unacceptable:

(66) *[John$_i$-ga __ taipu-shita] [jibun$_i$-no-ronbun]
John-NOM type-did self-GEN-paper
lit: 'self$_i$'s paper that John$_i$ typed'

This may then be taken as evidence that the head-noun present in relative clauses in Japanese does *not* in fact originate within the IP in relative clause structures in Japanese, and that Japanese relative clauses do not involve any Kayne-style movement.[14]

A third related point brought up by Murasugi concerns relative clauses in Japanese and locality. Kuno (1973), Kameshima (1989) and others have noted that the process of relativization in Japanese might not seem subject to Subjacency or the CED. Kuno gives examples of the dependency between the head-noun and a gap position licitly crossing Complex NPs, Sentential Subjects, and Adjunct Clauses:

(67) [[__ kawaigatte-ita] inu-ga shinde shimatta] kodomo
          was-fond-of dog-NOM dying ended-up child
     'the child who the dog (he) was fond of died'

(68) [watakushi-ga __ au koto/no]-ga muzukashii hito
     I-NOM   meet thing-NOM be-difficult person
     'the person who [that I see (him)] is difficult'

(69) [__ shinda no de] minna-ga kanashinda   hito
         died because all-NOM was-distressed person
     'the person who everyone was upset because (he) died'

Murasugi suggests that this is a further reason to believe that there is no movement involved in relative clause formation in Japanese and that a Kayne-style approach to relative clauses is therefore not suitable for Japanese.

Murasugi proposes instead that any apparent gap in a relative clause is actually a base-generated *pro* controlled by the head-noun which is also base-generated in its surface position and not moved from any other position. Referring back to a set of arguments in her 1991 thesis, Murasugi argues that relative clauses in Japanese should actually be taken to be IPs rather than CPs and then suggests the possible structure in (70), noting that this is similar in certain ways to the structure she proposed in her thesis, given in (71):

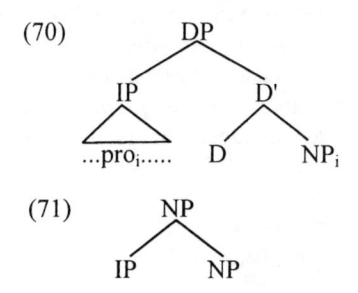

(70)   DP
              /   \
            IP   D'
           /\   / \
       ...pro$_i$..... D   NP$_i$

(71)   NP
            / \
           IP   NP

(70) is a potential reflection of the various conclusions/points argued for by Murasugi. If Japanese does not show connectivity effects and if there are fully gapless relatives in Japanese, then one need not assume that the head-noun is base-generated within the IP and it may be directly inserted in its surface position. If the lack of Subjacency/CED effects indicate that there is no movement of *any* kind, including any null operator movement, then there need not be any CP layer of structure present to host an operator in a raised SpecCP position, and the relative clause itself can be argued to be an IP-level constituent. Finally, if the head-noun is not raised to its surface position from within the IP, there is no need to assume that the IP must have been base-generated in a position to the right and lower than the head-noun as in Kayne. Consequently it is possible to suggest that the IP is actually base-generated in its surface position in Spec of DP, this essentially being an updated rather more

articulated version of the 1991 base-generation analysis represented in (71). It may be noted that a somewhat similar approach is suggested for Korean relative clauses in Young-Kook Kim (1997), with the relative clause being base-generated in a left-branch preceding the head-noun and no movement of the head-noun being involved.

So, if there are reasons for believing that (70) may be a plausible analysis for pre-nominal relative clauses in Japanese, the question arises as to whether a fully base-generated structure such as (70) should not also be appropriate for pre-nominal relatives in Chinese rather than the Kaynean analysis proposed. I would like to argue that (70) is not suitable for Chinese on the basis of two rather general sets of arguments.

First of all, the structure in (70) arises as a possible analysis of relative clauses in Japanese as a direct result of the conclusion that there would not appear to be any movement involved in the formation of relative clauses in Japanese. This allows one to suggest that the head-noun is base-generated in its surface position rather than moved there and that the relative clause itself is simply an IP with no internal movement to any Spec of CP. In Chinese however it has been argued (in section 3.1.1) that there are in fact good reasons for assuming some kind of movement in relativization (either of an empty operator or the head-noun). In a number of very clear cases, Chiu's data relating to the patterning with *suo* and Ning's arguments concerning the Generalized Control Rule convincingly show that relativization in Chinese crucially is island-sensitive when one controls for and blocks the possible use of a resumptive *pro* strategy.[15]

Consequently there must be more to the structure of relative clauses in Chinese than indicated in (70). Either one may assume that the head-noun undergoes movement in Chinese, as in the Vergnaud-Kaynean analysis proposed earlier, or one could suggest that there is some kind of empty operator movement. Both such accounts would seem to require (70) to be non-trivially modified. If the first option is taken, then the relative clause must originate to the right of the head noun in a position from which the head-noun may undergo *raising* (i.e., one cannot assume that the head-noun is lowered from an IP base-generated in Spec of DP as in 70). (70) will have to be modified into (72):

(72)

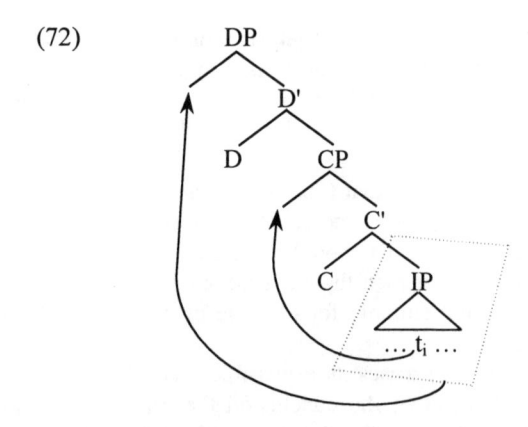

If the second possibility is taken, it might also seem to lead to an analysis in which the relative clause is base-generated lower than the head-noun and to its right in the structure. When there is null-operator movement rather than movement of the head-noun, the null operator must be assumed to move to a SpecCP operator position (hence the clause must be a CP rather than an IP). As it is a reasonable assumption that operators whose reference is controlled within a sentence should be c-commanded by the element controlling this reference (as e.g., in *easy-to-please* constructions, topicalization, standard relative clause structures, etc.), this would seem to require that the relative clause CP should be base-generated in a position c-commanded by the head-noun, hence to its right in a modified form of (70), such as (73).[16][17] Either way, the fact that Chinese relative clauses seem to give clear evidence of movement has for effect that a base-generated structure similar to (70) can arguably not be taken to be appropriate for Chinese.

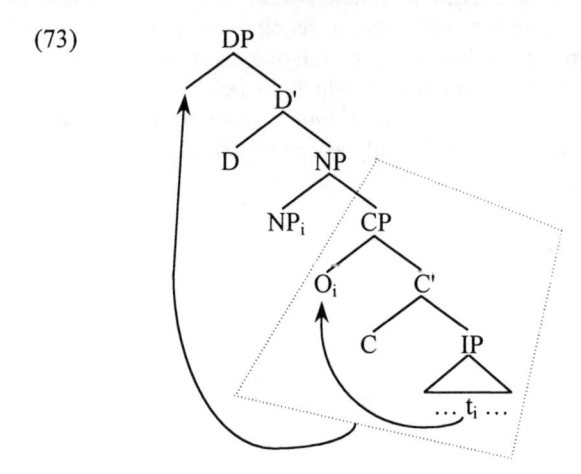

(73)

In fact, as noted earlier, it is not only the Subjacency/CED facts which appear to distinguish Chinese from Japanese, Murasugi's first argument for a non-movement analysis of relative clauses in Japanese, namely the occurrence of gapless relatives such as (64) and (65), would also seem to be inapplicable for Chinese. Examples such as (64) and (65) when translated into Chinese are quite unacceptable, suggesting that Chinese does not tolerate *truly* gapless relative clauses, as indeed argued by Ning. Furthermore, as noted earlier in example (62), Chinese also displays connectivity effects which Murasugi takes to be absent from Japanese.[18] Murasugi assumes that such patterns are indicative of movement; their presence in Chinese but apparent absence from Japanese would further seem to argue against adopting Murasugi's account of relativization in Japanese for Chinese:[19, 20]

The second broad piece of argumentation against a structure such as (70) and for the Kayne-based approach outlined earlier relates to the syntax of noun-complement clause structures in Chinese. Essentially it will be argued that noun-complement clause forms have an underlying syntax which is very similar to that of relative clauses, and that as the structure in (70) can be shown to be inappropriate for noun-complement clause units, it may by extension also be taken to be inappropriate for relative clauses. The line of argumentation will take its lead from significant work on the syntax of process nominals presented in Fu (1994) as well as an extension of this in Simpson (2002). After briefly describing the basic intuitions of these two works, I will then indicate how they can be shown to favor the Kayne-based account of relativization rather than any fully base-generated structure such as that in (70).

3.3.4 *Process Nominals and the Structure of Noun-Complement Clause CNPs*

Noun-complement clause structures in Chinese appear very similar to relative clauses. The clausal unit precedes the selecting noun and *de* is found to occur in between these two elements:

(74) [Deng Xiao-Ping shishi] de xiaoxi
Deng Xiao-Ping died DE news
'the news that Deng Xiao-Ping died'

Such structures again raise the problem of the direction of selection. Elsewhere in Chinese there is consistent, good evidence that both lexical and functional heads select their complements to the right, i.e., Chinese is a descriptively head-initial language. Here however in the NP/DP the surface patterns seem to show the opposite, i.e., the complement of N seems to be selected to its left. Certain linguists (e.g., Lin 1994 and Tang 1990) have suggested that the bracketed string preceding *de* in sequences such as (74) is not in fact a complement, despite its connection to the head noun in terms of meaning. In the spirit of Grimshaw (1990) it is suggested that such elements may actually be syntactic adjuncts and so the directionality issue is not a problem after all. However, in a detailed study of the syntactic properties and structure of process and result nominals in Chinese, Fu (1994) provides convincing evidence that the elements occurring with the former type of derived nominal are indeed syntactic complements. He shows that when a process reading of these derived nominals is forced by means of duration phrases and the process verb *jinxing* 'to last', the object of the noun head is indeed forced to appear, this being a good indication of its argumenthood:

(75) ta ??(dui zaiqing) de baodao jinxing-le san-ge xiaoshi.
he towards disaster DE report last-ASP three-CL hour
'His reporting of the disaster lasted three hours.' (Fu 1994)

Fu also shows that with a process reading, only a single *de* may occur and this has to be placed after all of the arguments associated with the noun. Specifically, the subject argument may not be marked by *de* although one does find multiple instances of *de* elsewhere with clearer cases of adjuncts:

(76) [Zhangsan (*de) dui zhei-ge anjian de diaocha] jinxing-le
Zhangsan DE towards this-CL case DE investigation last-ASP
liang-ge xiaoshi.
two-CL hour
'Zhangsan's investigation of this case lasted two hours.'

Fu takes this as evidence for a process of nominalization in which the head noun (*baodao* in (75), *diaocha* in (76), etc.) is inserted as a verb in a regular verbal/clausal constituent (the bracketed string in the examples above), projecting its argument structure in a regular way inside this VP/clause, and then raises rightward over *de* to an empty nominal head position, so being converted into a nominal category. Simpson (2002) points out that such an account still leaves the directionality problem unaddressed and proposes a modification of Fu's analysis, suggesting that the verb raises leftwards to an N which selects for the clause in a rightward direction. This first movement is then followed by raising of the clausal remnant to the SpecDP position, with *de* assumed to be in D. The derivation of a string such as (77) will then be as in (78) and (79):

(77) [tamen dui zhei-ge wenti] de taolun
they towards this-CL problem DE discussion
'their discussion of this problem'

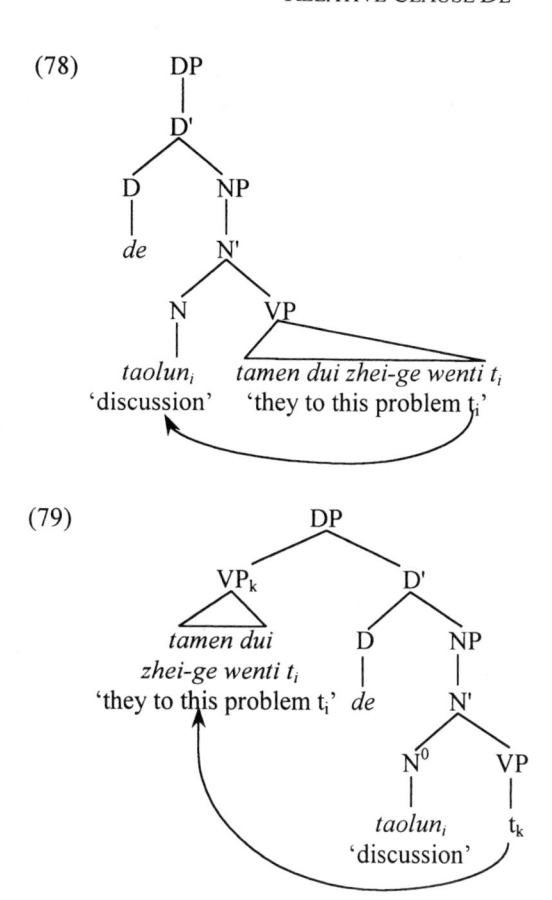

(78) [tree diagram]

DP
│
D'
├── D: de
└── NP
    └── N'
        ├── N: taolun$_i$ 'discussion'
        └── VP: tamen dui zhei-ge wenti t$_i$ 'they to this problem t$_i$'

(79) [tree diagram]

DP
├── VP$_k$: tamen dui zhei-ge wenti t$_i$ 'they to this problem t$_i$'
└── D'
    ├── D: de
    └── NP
        └── N'
            ├── N^0: taolun$_i$ 'discussion'
            └── VP: t$_k$

Interestingly this analysis actually results in a form closely resembling the potential surface structure for Japanese relative clauses proposed by Murasugi in (70), i.e., there is a clausal element in the SpecDP position and the noun-head is selected in a rightward direction by D (which has an overt instantiation in Chinese). However, there is an extremely important difference between (79) and the form in (70). In (79) the clause is raised to its surface position from a position in which it is: (a) base-generated in a regular structural complement relation with the selecting N, and (b) this selection relation follows the canonical direction of selection as observed in Chinese. If the VP in (79) and other similar cases is indeed a complement of N, it should not be possible to *base-generate* it in a SpecDP position, as there is no structural relation of complementation between the N head and the SpecDP position (in fact there is no standardly definable structural relation between these two positions at all). Consequently a fully base-generated structure such as (70) would seem to be quite inappropriate for noun-complement clauses in Chinese, and a plausible analysis which accommodates the problem of the unexpected exceptional directionality found in such strings is that the complement clause is in fact raised to its surface position. Now, if there is indeed such a productive process of clausal raising to the Specifier of DP headed by the enclitic determiner *de* (and this raising is triggered by the particular properties of *de*), this would seem to provide natural support for the analysis of relative clauses outlined earlier. In other words, if the base-generated structure (70) cannot be applied to noun-complement clause strings and a clausal raising analysis appears independently necessary to account for such structures in a theoretically undisruptive way, this same essential analysis should be available for relative clauses as well (the particular lexical properties of *de* remaining constant). Coupled with the suggestion that an operator present in the relative clause should be c-commanded by the noun/NP which controls it, this would seem to clearly favor the derivation and representations given earlier over the possible alternative analysis in (70).[21]

3.3.5 *Other Noun-Complement Clause CNPs*

Before closing this section, I would finally like to suggest that structures similar to those in (78/79) but without any V-to-N-raising may be appropriate for certain other CNP types in Chinese, CNPs such as those in (80)-(83) below:

(80) [ta xue Zhongwen] de yuanyin
he study Chinese DE reason
'the reason he studies Chinese'

(81) [ta jiejue wenti] de fangfa
he solve problem DE method
'the way he solved the problem'

(82) [ta changchang lai Zhongguo] de shihou
he often come China DE time
'the time he often came to China

(83) [wo kanjian ta liang ci] de difang
I see he two time DE place
'the place I saw him twice'

Ning (1993) assumes that such structures are actually relative clauses and suggests that because there is no obvious gap corresponding to the head nouns, relative clauses of this type must be formed by the movement of an empty operator (see section 3.1.1 above). If an empty operator analysis is indeed taken to be necessary for (80)-(83), such examples might be argued to constitute evidence against the general suggestion of the chapter that relative clauses are formed via raising of the NP-'head' in Chinese rather than resulting from empty operator movement. If one is forced to concede that an empty operator strategy might occur in this particular subset of cases, it might be objected that such a strategy might possibly also underlie all other cases of relativization (though the connectivity arguments in (62) and acquisition patterns in 3.3.2 would still remain difficult to explain for any hypothetical operator account). In defense of the proposed raising analysis of relative clauses in Chinese, the following points and suggestions can however be made. First of all it can be noted that even if one were forced to concede an empty operator analysis for examples such as (80)-(83), this would actually NOT force the conclusion that ALL relative clauses should necessarily be formed via such empty operator movement and that other cases of relative clauses might not be formed by NP-raising as suggested. It is certainly possible that languages might in fact have more than a unique strategy for relativization. In English, for example, it is commonly assumed that relative clauses may either be created by movement or alternatively be fully base-generated when a resumptive pronoun occurs, and in Hindi Dayal (1995, 1996) suggests that three significantly different strategies of relativization are actually available. Supposing that (80)-(83) were to be formed via empty operator movement, the evidence considered here in the chapter could still be taken to support a second NP-raising analysis of other more regular relative clause structures. Secondly, there is actually a rather simple and natural way to avoid Ning's conclusion that (80)-(83) are formed via empty operator movement. Rather than automatically assuming with Ning (1993) that such structures are necessarily relative clauses, one can instead assume that they are simple noun-complement clause CNPs similar to 'the claim [$_{CP}$ that...]' CNPs in English and many other languages where a head noun selects a complement clause specifying its content, as in (84)-(86):

(84) the claim [$_{CP}$ that John was a liar]

(85) the news [$_{CP}$ that there was an earthquake]

(86) the rumor [$_{CP}$ that she was engaged]

In this second widely available type of CNP it is regularly assumed that the head noun directly selects a complement CP and there is no relativization of an empty operator. Such a noun-complement clause strategy can also be argued to be responsible for direct English equivalents to the Chinese cases in (80)-(83) such as (87)-(90) below:

(87) the reason [$_{CP}$ he studies Chinese]

(88) the way [$_{CP}$ he solved the problem]

(89) the time [$_{CP}$ he came to China]

(90) the place [$_{CP}$ he studies Chinese]

Note furthermore that although English allows *wh*-elements to be used as relative pronouns, such CNP forms frequently resist the occurrence of any attempted *wh* relative pronoun indicating that it must be possible for such forms to be created by the noun-complement clause non-relativization strategy:[22]

(91) *the way how he solved the problem

(92) */??the second when you come here

In Chinese, as in English, it can therefore be suggested that the clauses which occur with head nouns such as *yuanyin* 'reason' and *fangfa* 'way', etc. can be considered to be complement clauses specifying the content of the selecting nouns in the same way that CPs occurring with head nouns such as 'news/rumor/claim' specify their content. Cases such as (80)-(83) can therefore be analyzed in a way similar to their English counterparts and in a way which is also similar to the Chinese structures (78/79), as in (93/94) below, with *yuanyin/fangfa* selecting a rightward complement clause which then undergoes raising to SpecDP to support the enclitic *de*:

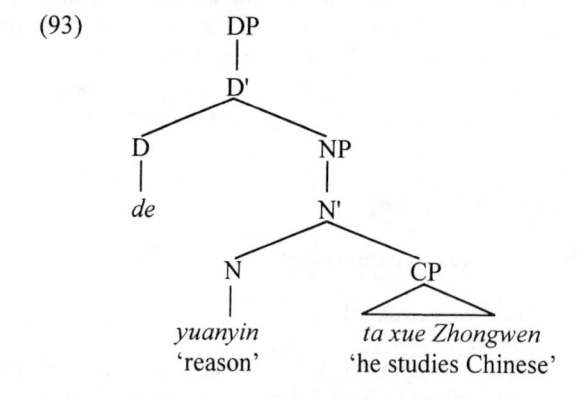

(93)

```
            DP
            |
            D'
           / \
          D   NP
          |   |
          de  N'
             / \
            N   CP
            |   |
         yuanyin  ta xue Zhongwen
         'reason' 'he studies Chinese'
```

(94)

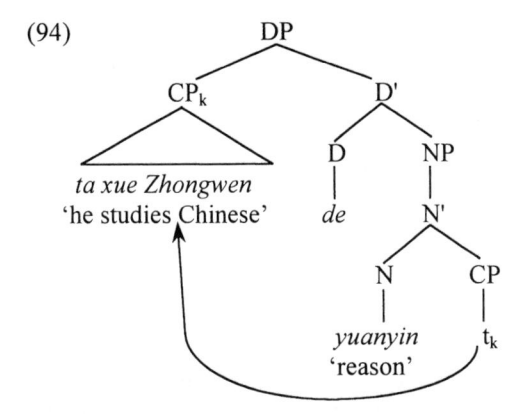

```
                    DP
                   /  \
                CPₖ    D'
               /  \   /  \
              /    \ D    NP
         ta xue Zhongwen |    |
        'he studies Chinese' de   N'
                              /  \
                             N    CP
                             |    |
                          yuanyin tₖ
                          'reason'
```

Cross-linguistically this type of CNP strategy is subject to certain lexical variation and not all (types of) head-noun syntactically license a complement clause in such a way. For example, in English 'way' licenses a complement CP as in (88), but the semantically similar 'manner' does not, as shown in (95). Note that if (88) were to be formed by a process of relativization with some kind of empty operator rather than being a complement clause structure, it is quite unexpected that such an operator-relative clause possibility should not be available when the head-noun is instead 'manner.' Processes of relativization should be fully blind to the lexical properties of the head noun and it should be possible to relativize any head noun if an appropriate operator is available. The fact that (95) is not acceptable therefore clearly suggests (88) is not formed by relativization. In a similar way, whereas English 'rumor' and 'news' license complement clauses specifying their content (examples 85/86), the nouns 'sound' and 'smell' by way of contrast do not, as seen in (96/97). This contrasts with languages such as Japanese and Mandarin where equivalents to 'sound' and 'smell' do indeed license complement clauses specifying their content:

(95) *the manner [CP that John walked]

(96) *the sound [CP that Bill hit the drum]

(97) *the smell [CP that Mary cooked the garlic]

(98) [Taroo-ga   kitaa-o   hiku] oto   (Japanese)
     Taroo-NOM guitar-ACC play sound
     lit: *'the sound that Taroo played the guitar'

(99) [Zhangsan da gu] de shengyin   (Mandarin)
     Zhangsan hit drum DE sound
     lit: *'the sound that Zhangsan hit the drum'

CHAPTER 3

It can therefore be suggested that Chinese is to some extent more permissive than English, and that Chinese allows such noun-complement clause structures with a whole range of noun types, potentially specifying the content/identity of nouns in terms of reason, manner, time, place and also other sensory properties.[23]

3.4 Taiwanese Tone Sandhi and the Clausal Raising Hypothesis

In this last section I would like to present a further set of evidence in favor of the basic account of relative clauses suggested here, based on the phenomenon of tone sandhi in Taiwanese. I will argue that a certain tone sandhi patterning occurring in relative clause structures in the Taiwanese dialect of Chinese can be given neat explanation if one indeed assumes the approach to relativization proposed here. I will also argue that this patterning remains puzzling and unaccounted for in a GB/Murasugi-type base-generation analysis. In order to make such arguments, it will first be necessary to provide a very brief background sketch of basic tone sandhi phenomena in Taiwanese and then turn to relative clauses in particular.

3.4.1 Tone Sandhi Patterns in Taiwanese

Taiwanese is a variety of Chinese with eight tones:[24] The 1st: high-level 5-5, the 2nd: high-falling 5-1, the 3rd: low-falling 2-1, the 4th: low-entering tone (a syllable with a final stop), the 5th: contour-tone 2-1-4, the 6th: high-falling 5-1 (the same as tone 2), the 7th: mid-level 3-3, the 8th: high-entering. In addition to these eight tones there are also syllables which do not carry any tone, this sometimes being referred to as 'neutral tone' (NT). In the phenomenon of *tone sandhi*, the lexically listed tone of a syllable is generally able to undergo modification according to fully regular rules when preceding some other tone-bearing syllable in the same tone sandhi domain. For example, if a syllable with tone 1 precedes another tone-carrying syllable, the tone 1 changes into a tone 7, as illustrated in (100):

(100) **khi3** pak8kiang1 → **khi2** pak8kiang1
     go   Beijing
     'go to Beijing'

Table (101) below shows how the full range of these modifications are made. Note that the changes in tone are not triggered or conditioned by the particular type of tone that the following syllable carries, hence a syllable with tone 1 will change its tone to tone 7 no matter whether the following syllable has tone 1, 2 or 3, etc.; the essential requirement for tone sandhi to apply is that the following syllable have some type of lexical tone rather than just 'neutral tone.'

(101) a. $1^{st} \rightarrow 7^{th}$
b. $2^{nd} \rightarrow 1^{st}$
c. $3^{rd} \rightarrow 2^{nd}$
d. $4^{th} \rightarrow 8^{th}$ when the syllable ends in p/t/k;
$\rightarrow 2^{nd}$ when the syllable ends in a glottal stop
e. $5^{th} \rightarrow 7^{th}$ (southern Taiwan);
$\rightarrow 3^{rd}$ (northern Taiwan)
f. $6^{th} \rightarrow 1^{st}$
g. $7^{th} \rightarrow 3^{rd}$
h. $8^{th} \rightarrow 4^{th}$ when the syllable ends in p/t/k;
$\rightarrow 3^{rd}$ when the syllable ends in a glottal stop

As mentioned just above, tone sandhi may not occur in a syllable if it precedes a syllable which has only neutral tone/no tone. Consequently *zau* in example (102) may not change its tone-2 when occurring before the toneless element *a* in (102):

(102) **zau2** a-NT → **zau2** a-NT
run already
'already left'

Similarly, a syllable may not undergo tone sandhi if it occurs sentence-finally. This is due to the fact that tone sandhi is restricted to apply within certain specific domains. In (103) below, the citation tone-2 of sentence-final *ho* may not be converted into tone-1 even though followed by a syllable (Ahui) which does carry tone because this latter syllable occurs in a separate sentence. Note that from this point on, for simplicity of representation, I will indicate tone sandhi by means of a simple bolded dot following the relevant syllable. Thus if a syllable is followed by a bolded dot, this indicates that it undergoes tone sandhi, and if a dot is absent, no tone sandhi is possible. In (103) sentence-final *ho* is therefore not followed by a dot as no tone sandhi can occur in sentence-final position:

(103) A•sin chin• **ho**.   A•hui ma• chin• ho.
Asin very good   Ahui also very good
'Asin is fine, and Ahui is also well.'

Sentence-internally there would also seem to be other tone sandhi/TS domains relevant for the operation of tonal change, and broadly-speaking every syllable in such a domain will change its tone unless it is the last tone-bearing syllable. Significantly, tone sandhi in Taiwanese appears to relate to and reveal the underlying syntactic structure in a way which is not found in tone sandhi phenomena in Mandarin, Shanghainese and certain other varieties of Chinese. For present purposes it is important to point out the following three significant generalizations:

(104) **Generalization A: a head and its complement occur in the same TS domain**
The presence of an overt complement consistently triggers tone sandhi on the selecting head, indicating that a head and its complement are in a single TS domain:

(105) a. V-NP_{object}
be• [lng•-pun• chhe]
buy   two-CL book
'buy two books'
   b. P-NP
tui• [goan• lau•pe]
to   my   father
'to my father'
   c. Aux/I-VP
e•   lai
will come
'will come'
   d. Comp-IP
na•**si•** [A•sin m• lai]…
if   Asin NEG come
'If Asin is not coming…'

(106) **Generalization B: a head and its Specifier do not occur in the same TS domain**
It is found that a head does not trigger tone sandhi on the final syllable of its Specifier. Consequently the Specifier of a head constitutes an independent TS domain. In (107) below, the final syllable of the subject does not change its tone, despite being followed by the tone-bearing head *u* 'have':

(107) [A•sin] u• lng• chhing• kho.
Asin have two thousand dollar
'Asin has two thousand dollars.'

In addition to (107) above with the final syllable of a subject in SpecIP failing to undergo tone sandhi, further examples of Specifiers being isolated TS domains are given in (108) and (109) below, where the DP *tai-oan-oe* 'Taiwanese' occurs as either a moved or base-generated topic relating to the object position. In such a Specifier position, its final syllable *oe* does not undergo any tone sandhi:

(108) A•sin [tai•oan•**oe**] be• hiao• kong.
Asin Taiwanese NEG know speak
'Asin, Taiwanese, can't speak (Taiwanese, Asin can't speak).'

(109) [tai•oan•**oe**] A•sin be• hiao• kong.
Taiwanese Asin NEG know speak
'Taiwanese, Asin can't speak.'

(110) **Generalization C: adjuncts are self-contained TS domains**
The final syllable of an adjunct does not undergo tone sandhi even when followed by other tone-bearing syllables. This is illustrated below with the case of a CP adjunct. No tonal change in its final syllable is possible:[25]

(111) [na•si• A•sin m• **khi**], A•hui ma• be• khi
if Asin NEG go Ahui also NEG go
'If Asin is not going, Ahui also won't go.'

3.4.2 Tone Sandhi in Taiwanese Relative Clauses

Turning back to relative clauses now, there are certain critical aspects of their tone sandhi patterning in Taiwanese which argue against a standard GB-type account of their structure. A simple relative clause in Taiwanese and the structure that such a form would be naturally assigned under Ning's (1993) and Chiu's (1995) analysis of Chinese relative clauses is illustrated in (112) and (113). In (113) the functional element *e* (=Mandarin *de*) is analyzed as a relativizing complementizer in C similar to English 'that' (following the Ning/Chiu assumption that Mandarin *de* is a C), and the CP relative clause is taken to be left-adjoined to the final NP (again as in the Ning 1993/Chiu 1995 analysis of Mandarin Chinese):

(112) [$_{IP}$ A•sin **be**] **e**• [$_{NP}$ **chhe**]
Asin buy REL book
'the book Asin bought'

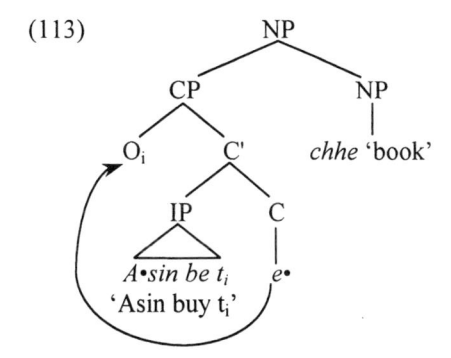

(113)

```
            NP
           /  \
         CP    NP
        /  \    |
      O_i   C'  chhe 'book'
           /  \
         IP    C
         /\    |
   A•sin be t_i  e•
   'Asin buy t_i'
```

Considering forms such as (112), three fully general and important tone sandhi facts can be noted:

(114) a. The (final syllable of the) head-noun does not undergo tone sandhi.
   b. The functional element *e* does undergo tone sandhi.
   c. The final element in the IP preceding *e* does not undergo tone sandhi.

Taking these properties one by one and reflecting on how they might be accounted for in a structure such as (113), it is found that the first property (114a) (that the final syllable of the head-noun does not undergo tone sandhi) is not difficult for a GB-style analysis to explain. Above in (103) and (106) it has been noted that the final syllable of a sentence and the final syllable of a Specifier do not undergo tone sandhi. If relative clause forms such as (112) then occur either sentence-finally as objects or as subjects in a specifier position it is expected that the final syllable in the structure will not undergo tone change.

Property (114b) however is very difficult for a GB-style account to explain. If one assumes an analysis such as (113), in which *e* heads a CP left-adjoined to the NP/head-noun, it is unexpected that the functional element *e* would change its tone. Note here that the Taiwanese element *e*, unlike Mandarin *de*, does indeed carry a tone; its lexically-listed citation tone is tone 5, and this undergoes tone sandhi modification when preceding a (tone-bearing) head-noun to tone 7. In (111) it has been noted that CP adjuncts constitute their own isolated tone sandhi domains and tone sandhi does *not* take place between the final syllable in a CP adjunct and the element it is adjoined to. Consequently, if the relative clause is assumed to be a CP adjunct as in (113) it should *not* be possible for the head-noun to trigger tone sandhi leftwards onto the last syllable of the CP adjunct *e*, yet *e* clearly does change its tone.

Property (114c) is also quite unexpected in an analysis such as (113). If the IP-clause is taken to be a leftward *complement* to the functional *head e* in C, then this IP and *e* in C should constitute a single tone sandhi domain. In (104) it was noted that the presence of an overt complement consistently triggers tone sandhi on the selecting head, and in (105d) it was seen that a C head and its IP complement constitutes a tone sandhi domain and therefore every syllable but the last syllable in the domain should change its tone. This being so, and given that Taiwanese *e* is a genuinely tone-bearing syllable, it is expected that the C-element in (113) should be able to trigger tone sandhi onto the last syllable of the preceding IP-complement—the verb 'buy', but this is *not* possible.[26]

There are consequently good reasons to doubt the correctness of the GB-type analysis of Chinese relative clauses as illustrated in (113). The Kaynean-type analysis of relativization in Chinese argued for earlier by way of contrast is indeed able to explain all of the tone sandhi patterns observed without any of the difficulties found in the more traditional analysis in (113). (115) and (116) are representations of the hypothetical derivation of Taiwanese (112) in a Kaynean analysis:

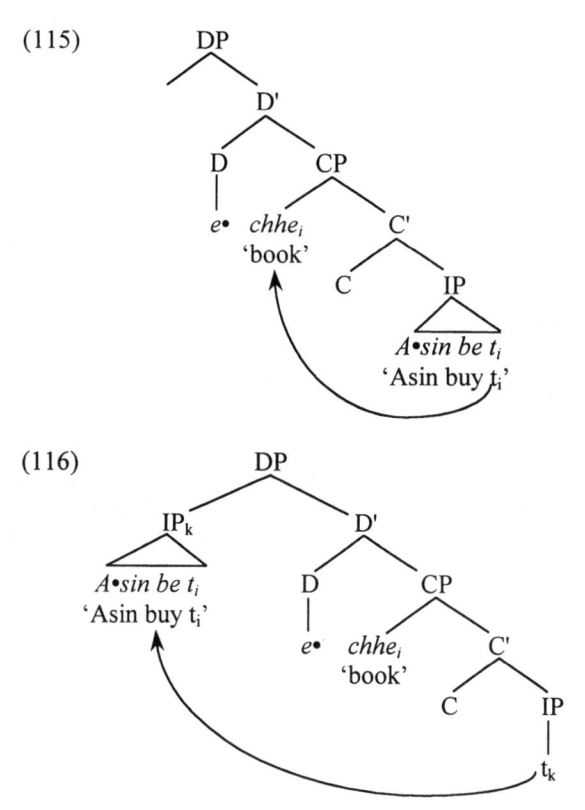

(115)

```
        DP
        /\
          D'
          /\
         D   CP
         |   /\
        e• chhe_i  C'
          'book'  /\
                 C   IP
                    /\
                   A•sin be t_i
                   'Asin buy t_i'
```

(116)

```
              DP
              /\
           IP_k   D'
           /\    /\
      A•sin be t_i  D   CP
      'Asin buy t_i' |   /\
                    e• chhe_i  C'
                      'book'  /\
                             C   IP
                                 |
                                 t_k
```

First of all, property (114a) that the NP *chhe* 'book' does not show any tone change can be simply assumed to be due to one of two facts. First it occurs in a Specifier position, SpecCP, and the final syllables of elements in Specifier positions do not undergo any tone sandhi, as per (106). The second fact is that the NP 'book' is linearly final in the whole DP which itself may occur as an object sentence-finally or as a subject in a Specifier position, and neither of those positions allow it's final syllable to undergo tone change.

Secondly and more significantly, (115) and (116) are able to account for property (114b), the fact that the functional element *e* undergoes tone sandhi. In the GB analysis this is a problem because *e* occurs in a CP *adjunct* and so should not be visible outside this domain for any tone sandhi operations. In the structure in (115/116) however, no adjunct relation is present, and *e* is instead a D selecting a rightward complement. As a head and its complement occur in a single tone sandhi domain and complements consistently cause tone changes in their selecting heads, it is actually very natural that the element following *e* in its complement CP does trigger tone sandhi on *e*.[27]

The third property (114c) is also importantly explained, namely that the final element in the IP of the relative clause (the verb *be* 'buy') does not undergo tone sandhi. In the GB analysis this is unexpected because this element is assumed to be in the unmoved complement IP of the C head instantiated by *e* and so the C should trigger tone sandhi on the preceding element *be* 'buy.' In (115/116) however, the IP is analyzed as being base-generated as the rightward complement of a phonetically null C and then raised to its surface position in SpecDP, where *e* actually instantiates D. Occurring in a Spec position, it is fully expected that the IP will constitute an isolated tone sandhi domain and that the final syllable in such a constituent (i.e., the verb *be* 'buy') should *not* undergo any tonal change.

Consequently then, it would seem that there is good evidence from tone sandhi supporting a Kaynean analysis of relative clauses in Chinese of the type outlined in the chapter here. Whereas a more traditional GB approach assuming *de/e* to be an instantiation of a C selecting a leftward complement IP is arguably unable to account for the patterns of tonal change revealed in Taiwanese, a uniformly right-branching analysis of relative clauses with *de/e* taken to be in D provides a principled and natural account which accords with other general patterns of tone sandhi phenomena productively observed in the language. To the extent that such evidence therefore further bears out the Kaynean analysis already justified on other grounds, it might seem that such an analysis is indeed well able to capture the diverse range of properties associated with relative clauses in Chinese.[28]

3.5 Extensions: Grammaticalized Complementizers in Taiwanese

Before concluding this chapter centered mainly on the syntax of relative clauses in Chinese, I would like to suggest that ideas on the interaction of tone sandhi and syntax presented above in section 3.4 can also account for a second interesting phenomenon in Taiwanese—the grammaticalization of a verb of saying *'kong2'* as a complementizer in an unexpected sentence-final position. This section will also attempt to show how sentence-final particles in head-initial languages may quite generally come into being as the result of processes of grammaticalization, and addresses directly the important issue of directionality and surface linear ordering in CP-type constituents in Chinese. Finally, the section will also argue that the paradigms investigated provide evidence for Chomsky's (1998) idea of Cyclic Spell-Out.[29]

Earlier in section 3.2 it was noted that cross-linguistically it is fairly common for certain very general verbs of communication (typically equivalents to English 'say') to undergo grammaticalization as complementizers when they occur after other more specific verbs of communication or cognitive state such as 'yell', 'answer', 'inform', 'think' or 'believe.' Frequently this occurs when a language has serial verb constructions which allow for a sequence of two verbs of communication (one more specific the second less specific) to become reanalyzed as a sequence of verb + complementizer, schematically as in (117):

(117)   Verb1 Verb2   →   Verb(1) Complementizer
        shout say   shout   that

What is of particular interest and relevance here is the position of the verb 'to say' when it becomes grammaticalized as a complementizer. The cross-linguistically common pattern is for the grammaticalized complementizer to occur in the same position that the earlier fully verbal form occurred in. In the many head-initial SVO languages of West Africa and S.-E. Asia which show this type of grammaticalization this means that the new complementizer will occur *preceding* its clausal complement. In Thai for example, the morpheme *waa* is currently both a verb meaning 'to say' as seen in (118) and also grammaticalized as a complementizer preceding its IP complement as in (119). The fact that *waa* may co-occur with verbs of cognition such as *khit* 'think' in (119) no longer with its literal meaning 'to say' is evidence that *waa* has indeed grammaticalized as a complementizer in such positions and is no longer just a verb-in-series. Such an assumption is further supported by the observation that *waa* may now also occur after *nouns* as in (120), which shows that *waa* is no longer a verb 'say':

(118) kae waa arai?
      you say what
      'What did you say?'

(119) khaw book/khit waa Daeng suay.
      he   say/think that Daeng be-pretty
      'He says/thinks that Daeng is pretty.'

(120) kham-phaasii waa "tham bun dai bun"
      proverb   that do   good get good
      'the proverb (that says) if you do good, you will receive goodness'

In West African Ewe (Heine and Reh 1984: p.252) it is found that the verb *be* 'say' grammaticalized as a complementizer no longer occurs with the tense-aspect markings or pronoun prefixes which would otherwise be normal for real verbs in serial verb constructions, again indicating rather clearly that a category change from verb to complementizer has taken place. Similarly in Twi (Lord 1993: p.176) the verb *se* 'say' occurring as a complementizer also now no longer takes verbal affixes such as negation concord which would otherwise occur with verbs-in-series, confirming as with Ewe and Thai that a category change from verb to complementizer has taken place.

In Mandarin Chinese and Cantonese, Hwang (1998) argues that the same type of grammaticalization is taking place, and as Mandarin (121) shows, the verb *shuo* 'to say' occurs following a verb of cognition. As in Thai (119), this element in (121) no longer has its original verbal meaning of 'saying' but instead appears to be functioning as a general embedding complementizer element:

(121) Zhangsan xiang shuo Lisi bu lai le. (Mandarin)
Zhangsan think that Lisi NEG come ASP
'Zhangsan thinks Lisi is no longer coming.'

Examples such as (121) are important, as they show that where a complementizer/C is developing in Chinese, it occurs in a pre-IP position and hence conforms with the otherwise head-initial pattern in Chinese preceding its complement. As noted briefly in section 3.2, where other suggestions have been made that CP is a head-final projection in Chinese, this has been based on the occurrence of sentence-final question particles and the assumption that Chinese has no other regular instantiations of C equivalent to English 'that.' Here however one finds that a fairly simple equivalent to English 'that' is indeed beginning to occur and significantly it identifies CP as being head-initial and quite regular in its directionality.

A similar pattern also occurs in Taiwanese, and one finds that the verb *kong* occurs following other verbs of communication and verbs of cognition as in (122):

(122) A•hui siong•sin• kong• A•sin m• lai.
Ahui believe KONG Asin NEG come
'Ahui believes that Asin is not coming.'

Again, as with Thai *waa* and Mandarin *shuo*, the fact that *kong* occurs without its normal verbal meaning of 'saying' with verbs of cognition strongly suggests that it has grammaticalized away from its original verbal source. This is confirmed by the fact that the verb preceding *kong* can take an (experiential) aspectual suffix, while *kong* in such a position cannot occur with any aspectual suffixes. This suggests that *kong* in these instances has indeed undergone a category change from verb to some other non-verbal category and now occurs as a complementizer:[30]

(123) a. goa bo• sioN•-koe kong• A•sin m• lai.
I haven't think-ASP KONG Asin NEG come
'I haven't thought that Asin was not coming.'
b. *goa bo• sioN• kong•-<u>koe</u> A•sin m• lai.
I haven't think KONG-ASP Asin NEG come

This position preceding the embedded IP in (122) is precisely where one would expect to find *kong* occurring as a grammaticalized complementizer, and *kong* as a new C here seems to be fully parallel to Mandarin *shuo*, Thai *waa* and equivalents in other SVO serializing languages. However, in addition to forms such as (122), another arguably more interesting pattern is found with *kong*, as briefly noted in the introduction. For no immediately clear reason, the same element *kong* also seems to occur as a complementizer in clause-*final* position, hence *following* its clausal complement, as in (124) and (125) repeated below:

(124) A•hui liau•chun• A•sin si• tai•pak• lang kong•.
    Ahui thought   Asin is Taipei person KONG
    'Ahui thought that Asin is from Taipei.'

(125) A•hui siong•sin• A•sin m• lai kong•.
    Ahui believe   Asin NEG come KONG
    'Ahui believes that Asin is not coming.'

As Taiwanese like other varieties of Chinese elsewhere shows evidence of being head-initial (see here the examples in 105), and *kong* otherwise does occur as a genuine grammaticalized complementizer in clause-initial pre-IP position (as in 122), this apparent clause-final V-to-C grammaticalization of *kong* is rather strange and seems to go against the general headedness specification of the language. It clearly also does not correspond to any serial verb position from which *kong* could have naturally grammaticalized as a complementizer.

In order to explain the puzzle of clause/sentence-final *kong*, I will shortly suggest that the canonical position of the grammaticalized comeplementizer *kong* is indeed *preceding* its IP complement as in (122) and show that there is certain rather clear evidence from tone sandhi patterns indicating that the unexpected exceptional order in (124) and (125) is one which is actually *derived*, via a process of IP-raising to SpecCP.

3.5.1 Tone Sandhi Patterns with Kong

Considering the ordering of C and IP found in (122), one finds quite regular expected patterns of tone sandhi. The C grammaticalized verb *kong* undergoes tone sandhi in its position preceding the IP complement, this caused by a regular head-complement relation, and the final element in the embedded IP *lai* does not undergo tone sandhi. This is fully anticipated as sentence-final elements do not undergo tone sandhi (as seen above in (103) and other examples).

Turning to (124) and (125), with the unusual ordering of IP-C in the embedded clause, one now finds two quite unanticipated tone sandhi patterns. The first of these is that the IP-final element *lang* in (124) and *lai* in (125) do *not* undergo tone sandhi. If one assumes that the IP is the leftward complement of *kong* in a final C position, this should mean that the IP and the C are in the same tone sandhi domain and it is expected that the head-complement relation should result in tone sandhi occurring between the C and the element left-adjacent to it in this tone sandhi domain, i.e., the final syllable in the IP, yet this doesn't happen.

The second extraordinary tone sandhi patterning in forms such as (124) and (125) is that the *sentence-final* element *kong* does in fact undergo a tone change. This is very much unexpected as no other elements in sentence-final position are known to undergo tone sandhi, the sentence being a self-contained tone sandhi domain as noted earlier when discussing example (103). Furthermore, the grammaticalization of *kong* might be expected to result in it either maintaining its citation tone2 or simply reverting to a neutral tone/absence of tone as is commonly found in other cases of grammaticalization (e.g., Mandarin, *de, le* and *zhe*, and various functional elements in Taiwanese). However, instead of this, *kong* undergoes a fully regular tone sandhi in sentence-final position. Examples such as (124) and (125) need also not be followed by any other sentence for tone sandhi to occur on *kong* and so it would appear that there is nothing following *kong* which could trigger its tonal change.

Both such patterns can now be argued to have a rather simple explanation. Critically, both of the odd patterns observed in (124) and (125) are exactly parallel to those occurring in "regular" examples such as (122) and (126) below where the complementizer *kong* occurs preceding its complement IP:

(126) A•hui liau•chun• kong• A•sin si• tai•pak• lang.
      Ahui thought KONG Asin is Taipei person
      'Ahui thought that Asin is from Taipei.'

In (122) and (126), as just noted, the final syllable in the lower IPs, *lai* and *lang* respectively, do not undergo tone sandhi (as expected), and *kong* preceding its IP complement does undergo tone sandhi (again as expected). Comparing (122)/(126) and (124)/(125) it can therefore be seen that precisely the same tone sandhi patterns occur both when *kong* precedes its complement IP in a regular head-initial C position and when *kong* occurs finally in a rather unusual position:

(127) a. *kong* – IP: expected order, expected tone changes
       (i) final syllable in IP does not undergo tone sandhi
       (ii) *kong* does undergo tone sandhi
   b. IP – *kong*. unexpected order, unexpected tone changes
       (i) final syllable in IP does not undergo tone sandhi
       (ii) *kong* does undergo tone sandhi

The simple conclusion from such a comparison is that *kong* in its unusual sentence-final position is behaving for tone sandhi purposes exactly as if it occurred in a regular pre-IP position. Syntactically in order to capture this striking parallelism it can now be suggested that IP-*kong* forms such as (124)/(125) are actually the result of an IP-raising operation applying to underlying fully regular *kong*-IP forms *before* they are converted into IP-*kong* sequences. Such a pair of assumptions allows for a very straightforward explanation of the otherwise unanticipated tone sandhi facts, as follows. Prior to IP raising, the final element *lang/lai* in the embedded IP in (124/125) will occur in sentence-final position and *kong* will occur as a regular C preceding an IP-complement. If the tone sandhi rules are applied at this derivational point, the result will be (a) that the final syllable in the IP *lang/lai* does not undergo any tone sandhi, being in sentence-final position, and (b) that *kong* does undergo tone sandhi, being in a head-position preceding its IP complement.

Observe how the assumption of IP-raising will explain both the unusual tone sandhi patterns in *kong*-final sentences and the odd sentence-final position occupied by *kong*, (bearing in mind that *kong* occurs as a regular CP-initial complementizer in embedded clauses such as 122/126). It might now naturally be assumed that the hypothesized IP-raising operation applies in the embedded clause in (124)/(125) converting a string such as (122) into (125), as schematized in (128):

(122) A•hui siong•sin• kong• A•sin m• lai.
    Ahui   believe   KONG   Asin NEG come
    'Ahui believes that Asin is not coming.'

(125) A•hui siong•sin• [$_{CP}$ [$_{IP2}$ A•sin m• lai]$_i$ kong• t$_i$]

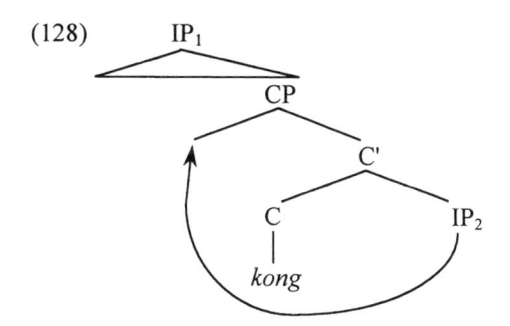

(128)   IP$_1$
           CP
             C'
           C   IP$_2$
           |
          kong

However, there is actually good reason to believe that this is not exactly how IP$_2$ and *kong* become re-positioned relative to each other. Although *kong* might seem to bear all the hallmarks of an embedded complementizer grammaticalized from a general verb of communication as in many other languages, further data reveals that *kong* in fact syntactically embeds not just a lower clause but *the entire matrix sentence* in which it occurs sentence-finally.

The evidence that this is so comes in two forms. First of all, in sentences such as (124) and (125) it is possible to have not only a *kong* in sentence-final position, but also a second *kong* in a regular grammaticalized embedded Comp position preceding the embedded IP, as in (129) and (130):

CHAPTER 3

(129) A•hui liau•chun <u>kong</u>• A•sin si• tai•pak• lang   <u>kong</u>•.
Ahui   thought   KONG   Asin is   Taipei   person KONG
'Ahui thought that Asin is from Taipei.'

(130) A•hui siong•sin• <u>kong</u>• A•sin m•   lai   <u>kong</u>•.
Ahui   believe   KONG   Asin NEG come KONG
'Ahui believes that Asin is not coming.'

This indicates that the sentence-final *kong* does not originate in an embedded C position, as this position can clearly be filled by a second distinct *kong*. Consequently, the natural assumption to make is that sentence-final *kong* is actually in the matrix C in (124), (125), (129) and (130) and that the entire IP$_1$ (i.e., the whole sentence consisting of both clauses IP$_1$ and IP$_2$) is raised to the Specifier projected by this matrix C. Clear confirmation that this is true comes from the fact that it is possible to have a sentence-final *kong* in *single-clause* sentences, as in (131)-(133). This indicates that *kong* here can only possibly be occurring in a matrix Comp as there obviously is no embedded C in such clausal structures:

(131) A•sin m•   lai   kong•.
Asin NEG come KONG
'Asin is not coming.'

(132) goa chahng   bo• khi• tai•pak• kong•.
I   yesterday NEG go   Taipei   KONG
'Yesterday I didn't go to Taipei.'

(133) goan• lau•pe si• tai•pak• lang   kong•.
my   father is Taipei person KONG
'My father is from Taipei.'

Furthermore, if one compares (125) which has a single sentence-final *kong* with (122) where *kong* occurs preceding the embedded IP, one finds that the interpretation of the two structures is not fully equivalent. Use of *kong* in (122) essentially adds nothing extra to the meaning of the sentence, much in the way that the optional addition of the English complementizer 'that' adds no extra semantic content when it precedes an embedded clause. Use of sentence-final *kong* however does add clear extra meaning to the sentences it accompanies, and encodes speaker-related emphatic assertion of the sentence which in English can often be naturally glossed with the expression 'I'm telling you X!' (where X = the content of the sentence). This emphatic assertion resulting from the use of S-final *kong* in (134) below implies the interpretation that: "Asin has written in his letter saying he is coming, so why do you, the person listening to me (the speaker), think that he will not come?".

RELATIVE CLAUSE *DE*

(134) A•sin e• phoe sia• kong• bin•a•chai beh• lai kong•.
Asin GEN letter write KONG• tomorrow want come KONG
'Asin's letter wrote that he will come tomorrow.'

As a result of the above observations, it can be suggested that *kong* is indeed a grammaticized C element, but one which critically occurs in matrix clause positions. Quite possibly this restriction results from *kong* being licensed by a speaker-centred propositional attitude (the special emphasis of *kong*) which can only be encoded in matrix clauses where the speaker is the clear source of the information.[31] Assuming *kong* then to be in the matrix C, the surface forms found in (125) and (131) can actually be argued to have the underlying derivation and structure indicated in (135) and (136):[32]

(135)

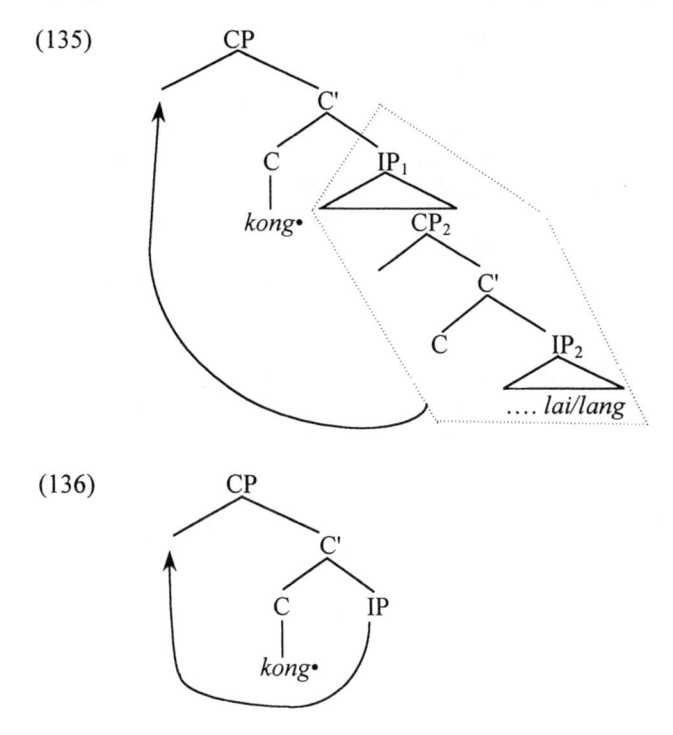

(136)

(135) and (136) will then allow for the basic explanation of the tone sandhi patterns already given. Considering (135) which represents the examples considered in (124) and (125), what needed to be accounted for in (124)/(125) were the two significant facts that (a) the final syllable in IP$_2$ *lang/lai* does not undergo any tone sandhi, and (b) that sentence-final *kong* does undergo tone sandhi. If one assumes that (135) is the underlying structure for (124)/(125) and that the tone sandhi rules apply to (135) before the movement of IP$_1$ (and IP$_2$, etc.) to SpecCP$_1$, these two patterns are simply explained. The final

97

CHAPTER 3

element *lang/lai* of IP₂ will be in sentence-final position when tone changes are applied, and so no tonal change will occur in *lang/lai* as there is no tone-bearing syllable following it at this point. As for *kong* in C of the matrix CP₁, it will be followed by its complement IP₁ at the point of tone sandhi application and so this will naturally cause tone change on *kong*. The conclusion that *kong* is in the matrix C thus essentially alters nothing in the basic account of the unusual tone sandhi patterns in *kong*-final sentences, and the suggestion that there is IP-raising in such forms is seen to account both for the odd tone sandhi with *kong* and its non-canonical sentence-final position.[33]

3.5.2 Grammaticalization of Kong and Motivations for IP-movement

I now turn to consider the obvious question of why IP-raising takes place in *kong* sentences, and also examine a little further how *kong* has undergone grammaticalization in structural terms. Importantly, because IP-final *kong* has grammaticalized into the *matrix* clause C, the process of its grammaticalization must actually have been somewhat different from the grammaticalization of other verbs of saying as *embedded* clause complementizers noted in section 3.1.1. In the latter cases, the source of the new sequence of verb and complementizer is a serial verb construction consisting of two verbs, as diagrammed in (31). With IP-final *kong* however, the most likely explanation of its grammaticalization as a *matrix* clause C is that this has occurred when earlier two clause structures containing *kong* as the higher clause predicate have over time been reanalyzed as single clause structures, as outlined in (137). In such a sequence of development, *kong* reanalyzed as a C will come to occur as the C of the single matrix clause which remains after the collapse of bi-clausal forms into new mono-clausal structures:

(137) a. Stage 1: bi-clause structure, *kong* a real verb meaning 'to say' with an NP subject and a clausal complement:
[NP$_{subject}$ *kong* [$_{IP}$ .....]]
b. Stage 2: the 2-clause structure reanalyzes as a single clause; *kong* deverbalizes and loses its NP subject, *kong* grammaticalizes as a new matrix clause C
[$_{CP}$ [$_C$ *kong* [$_{IP}$ ......]]]
c. Stage 3: the IP complement of *kong* raises to SpecCP (motivation for IP-raising discussed below)·
[$_{CP}$ [$_{IP}$ .....]$_i$ [$_C$ *kong* t$_i$]]

Noting also that it is specifically an emphatic assertion of the first-person speaker which is communicated by the use of *kong*, such a first-person restriction can be suggested to have resulted from *kong* in the original two-clause structure having commonly had a first person subject when used as an emphatic assertive form. As part of the grammaticalization process I suggest that the first person subject specification associated with *kong* emphatic forms may have subsequently become reanalyzed and absorbed directly into the element *kong* as an inherent restriction on its use. Such a process of reanalysis has indeed been attested elsewhere in similar cases with the grammaticalization of quotative complementizers and the creation of evidential morphemes. Harris and Campbell (1995, p.169), for example, note that the Georgian quotative complementizer *metki* can only be used to quote the words of the speaker and point out that *metki* grammaticalized from an original sequence *me vtkvi* which literally meant 'I said (it).'[34] Similarly, in many American Indian languages evidential suffixes on verbs have grammaticalized from verbs of seeing and hearing following the collapse of two-clause structures into mono-clausal forms in the same way hypothesized for *kong*. Examining Maricopa, Gordon (1986) notes that the addition of the suffixes -*'yuu* and -*'a* to verbs results in the interpretation that the speaker respectively saw or heard the action described:

(138) lima-'yuu
 dance-EV
 'He danced (I know because I saw it).'

(139) ashvar-'a
 sing-EV
 'He sang (I know because I heard it).'

The restriction that it is the speaker who has the visual or aural evidence for the truth of the proposition simply results from the fact that these suffixes are derived from the first person singular verbal forms of the verbs *yuu-k* 'to see' and *av-k* 'to hear' (the prefix element ['] being a first person singular marker). As the morphemes *'yuu* and *'a* are synchronically no longer verbs but clause-final particles, it can be assumed that the first person subject specification has become reanalyzed as an inherent property of these X^0 heads, restricting their use and resulting in the interpretation that it is specifically the speaker who has the visual/aural evidence for the proposition. In Taiwanese, IP-*kong* forms are here suggested to have developed from two-clause structures in a similar way, with *kong* as the higher clause verb undergoing deverbalization and incorporating a first-person speaker-related interpretation from its former syntactic subject.[35]

Assuming this much, I can now outline two possible explanations for the IP-raising which has accompanied grammaticalization of *kong* as a C element, one phonological, the other syntactic. The first phonological possibility is that as *kong* has grammaticalized into a particle-like element, like other particles it has become increasingly more clitic-like and dependent and in need of some kind of phonological support.[36] Normally in Chinese such support should critically come from an element to the particle's *left*, as stress in most varieties of Chinese including Taiwanese is phrase-initial and commonly leads to encliticization rather than the occurrence of proclitics. One potential explanation of IP-raising with *kong* is therefore to suggest that the tendency for functional clitic-like elements to attach to their left may directly trigger movement of the IP complement of *kong* to a position to its left in order to provide *kong* as an enclitic with phonological support.[37]

A second possible syntactic explanation of the IP re-positioning is to suggest that this movement occurs as the result of the particular informational structure of *kong* sentences. Recall that in section 3.1.2 it was noted that S-final *kong* adds to the proposition expressed in its IP complement an assertive interpretation equivalent to English: 'I'm telling you IP!' or 'Why do/would you doubt IP?' When S-final *kong* is used, it importantly seems to imply that the hearer may already entertain the proposition expressed in the IP, but perhaps be somewhat doubtful of it for no good reason in the speaker's opinion. Use of *kong* by the speaker then expresses the speaker's strong endorsement of the truth of the proposition, in a way similar to the use of 'I'm telling you!' in English as in (140):

(140) He's gone, I'm telling you!

In S-final *kong* sentences then, the proposition encoded in the IP is a possibility which may be entertained as true by both speaker and hearer but with different degrees of certainty. In this sense the IP therefore represents old, topic-like information largely presupposed by the participants in the conversation, and the clear focus of attention and force of *kong* sentences lies in the *assertion* of the proposition by the speaker via the explicit use of *kong*. Because of this topic-like property of the IP and the strong focus on the asserting act with *kong*, an alternative to the encliticization account of IP-raising is therefore to suggest that movement of the IP takes place in order to topicalize the IP, placing the IP in sentence-initial topic position and leaving *kong* in prominent sentence-final position where it is naturally interpreted as being in focus. In such a syntactic analysis, the IP-raising in *kong* sentences would essentially be an operation of defocusing, or 'p-movement' in Zubizarreta's (1998) terms, carried out in order that a secondary element (*kong*) is cast into focus in a prominent position (sentence-finally here).

Both of the above two possible explanations of IP-raising in *kong* sentences, I believe, may in fact be plausible as quite general causes of S-final particle creation in SVO languages. If bi-clausal structures may perhaps more regularly collapse into mono-clausal forms with higher clause predicates grammaticalizing into particles in the way outlined, I suggest that either encliticization or topic-focus reasons might then in many cases possibly lead to the displacement of IP-like clausal constituents in a leftward direction resulting in the creation of S-final particles. Both phonology and information structure may therefore possibly be genuine forces underlying the frequent occurrence of particles in S-final position in different instances. Considering the particular case of *kong* however, it would seem that an explanation in terms of defocusing is most likely to be the real motivation for the IP-movement, accounting as it does for the particular topic-focus interpretation of *kong*-final forms, and encliticization/phonology taken as a potential trigger for the movement would seem to miss this link with the meaning of *kong* sentences. I therefore now assume that in the case of *kong*, IP-raising does indeed take place for defocusing reasons and turn to see how such a conclusion interacts with a consideration of the *derivational timing* of IP-movement.

3.5.3 Evidence for PF Movement?

An important part of the IP-raising account of the tone sandhi patterns in *kong*-final sentences has been the suggestion that tone changes are made at a particular point in the derivation of such sentences when the IP-complement of *kong* in C is still *in situ* and has not yet been raised to SpecCP. Only if the tone sandhi rules are applied at this point can the unusual patterns be given a principled explanation in line with other tone sandhi patterning in Taiwanese.[38] Concerning the essential nature of tone sandhi, given that tone sandhi rules alter the phonetic interpretation of an element and so apply to specifically phonetic features, it is most natural to assume that such rules are indeed *phonological rules* and consequently apply in the PF component after Spell-Out. This being so, it can be shown that one seems to be led to the further conclusion that the hypothesized IP-raising operation itself significantly has to occur in the PF component too.

The critical sequence in the derivation of *kong*-final sentences is that underlying forms such as (136) repeated below are created in the syntactic component and then *prior to IP-raising* presented for tone sandhi alternation. Assuming that tone sandhi is a phonological process, under standard assumptions it should only take place after a syntactic sequence has entered the PF component. Now, because the IP-raising operation has to take place *after* the tone sandhi rules have applied, it seems that one therefore should conclude that the IP-raising also occurs in the PF component and hence is importantly an instance of movement in PF rather than syntactic movement.

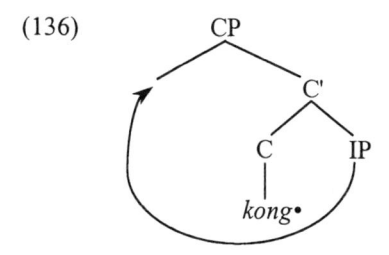

(136)

```
         CP
        /  \
           C'
          /  \
         C    IP
         |
        kong•
```

Under such assumptions, the derivation of a *kong*-final sentence such as (46) can be schematized as in (141):

101

(141) [$_{CP}$ [$_C$ kong [$_{IP}$ Asin m lai]
　　　　　↓
　　　Spell-Out
　　　　　↓
　　　PF—tone sandhi rules apply (changing the tone on *kong* and maintaining the citation on *lai*)
　　　[$_{CP}$ [$_C$ kong• [$_{IP}$ Asin m• lai]]]
　　　　　↓
　　　IP-raising
　　　[$_{CP}$ [$_{IP}$ Asin m• lai]$_i$ [$_C$ kong•] t$_i$]]

At first sight, the tone sandhi patterns of *kong*-final sentences might therefore seem to offer good support for the general possibility that not all movement operations are necessarily syntactic and that certain occurrences of raising potentially take place in the PF component too. However, further reflection reveals that a serious problem is also introduced by the conclusion that IP-raising occurs after the application of tone sandhi and hence apparently in PF. Elsewhere in the past where claims have been made that movement occurs in PF, such suggestions have importantly been made when the visible repositioning of certain constituents appears to have no impact on *interpretation*. In such cases it is suggested that if the relevant movement is assumed to take place only in PF after the derivation has left the syntactic component, its effects will not be present in the structure presented for interpretation at LF, and the fact that the movement is semantically vacuous can be simply explained. Operations of PF movement are therefore clearly expected not to have an impact on the meaning of a sentence and not to be associated with any particular interpretation. Considering the IP-raising in *kong*-final sentences, such movement does however appear to be associated with a particular interpretation, and structures in which an IP is raised before *kong* are regularly interpreted as topic-focus forms with the IP instantiating old information and *kong* encoding a highlighted assertive focus, similar to other structures generated by operations of defocusing p-movement. Such a connection between IP-movement and the creation of a particular interpretation therefore suggests that IP-raising should be assumed to take place not in PF but actually during the course of the syntactic derivation in order to be present in the input to LF. The patterns with *kong* consequently lead to an apparent contradiction. On the one hand there is evidence that IP-raising follows the application of phonological rules and so should be taken to be PF movement, yet on the other hand there are interpretative effects indicating that the movement should in fact be assumed to occur in the syntax. As there is no obvious way of resolving such a paradox in a traditional T-model of grammar, the patterns with *kong* may therefore seem to suggest that there is actually a rather different interaction between syntax and phonology than assumed such a model, and that a solution to the *kong* dilemma may perhaps lie in (somehow) allowing phonology greater access to mid-derivational syntactic structures.

Discarding the possibility of a PF movement analysis of the *kong* patterns, I will now show how the conflicting properties of *kong* sentences can in fact be naturally reconciled with Chomsky's (1998) idea of cyclic Spell-Out and that the *kong* paradigm consequently provides good support for such an approach to the phonology-syntax connection.

3.5.4 An Alternative—Cyclic Spell-Out

In contrast to earlier GB and Minimalist models, Chomsky (1998) suggests that there is in fact no single point of Spell-Out where the phonetic features of a sentence are fed off to PF and phonology, but that sub-parts of a derivation may be given phonetic interpretation during the course of a single derivation and before a structure is finally completed. A single syntactic derivation is therefore taken to be potentially spelt-out in a number of successive cycles which Chomsky tentatively identifies as CPs and *v*Ps, the "phase" constituents. Once such a phase constituent has been syntactically created, the suggestion is that it may possibly also be spelt-out phonetically before being merged into a higher syntactic unit.

The tone sandhi patterns investigated here can be argued to provide good evidence in support of such a cyclic Spell-Out approach and also allow for a better understanding of certain aspects of the process of cyclic Spell-Out.[39] The critical patterning in *kong*-final sentences in need of some account is the fact that the IP-movement seems to have to take place *after* the application of a phonological process, the tone changes. This led us above to the initial hypothesis that IP-raising perhaps takes place at PF, but such a possibility was then rejected on the grounds that the movement seems to be associated with interpretative effects. If a model incorporating cyclic Spell-Out is however adopted and it is assumed that sub-parts of syntactic structure may be given phonetic interpretation mid-way in the course of a derivation, a rather simple second explanation for the sequencing of tone sandhi and IP-raising automatically becomes available which does not require the assumption of movement at PF. Significantly the element *kong* is taken to occur grammaticalized in C and hence instantiates the head of a phase-type constituent, CP. It can therefore be suggested that after construction of the phase CP with *kong* in C merged with its complement IP to the right (i.e., [$_{CP}$ kong [$_{IP}$...]]), this sequence is given phonetic interpretation and spelt-out in PF. Entering PF the tone sandhi rules will apply to the sequence and cause a tone sandhi alteration in *kong* but not in the final element in the IP, resulting in the surface attested tone sandhi patterns. Following this, the syntactic derivation will then continue, with the IP undergoing raising to a Specifier position to the left of *kong*. On completion of the full syntactic derivation, the sequence will then be spelt-out and will surface with the linear sequence [[$_{IP}$...] kong]. In such a cyclic Spell-Out approach the IP-raising therefore occurs as a fully regular *syntactic* movement, and movement at PF importantly need not be

103

assumed. The apparent paradox that IP-movement must take place in the syntactic component yet after the application of certain phonological rules can consequently be captured rather simply with the idea of cyclic Spell-Out, and to the extent that *only* such an approach seems able to capture the patterning found with *kong*, the *kong* paradigm then clearly offers good support for such a view of syntax and phonology.

The Taiwanese tone sandhi patterns also allow for certain further conclusions about the actual process of cyclic Spell-Out and a finer understanding of the nature of phase constituents. A first point concerns the input forms to cyclic Spell-Out. Quite generally, Chomsky (1998) suggests that there is a distinction between Specifiers that are semantically selected by a head and "extra" Specifiers which it is argued are licensed with the categories C, T and *v* in addition to any selected external argument (EA). Non-selected Specifiers of this second type are taken to host the subject (SpecTP), raised *wh*-phrases (SpecCP), and shifted objects (Spec*v*P). Projections of the "core functional categories" C, T and *v* are accordingly schematized as in (142), with H being the head, YP its complement, EA a semantically selected Specifier, and XP the extra non-selected Specifier:

(142) [XP [(EA) H YP]]

The outer Specifier XP is furthermore suggested to be a position which is critically visible to syntactic heads which occur higher than a CP or *v*P phase, allowing for an element in XP to raise to satisfy EPP requirements of a higher head. Elements inside the inner pair of square brackets in (142) are taken to be largely invisible to higher positions due to the opacity of phases ("phase impenetrability"). The outer Specifier is therefore a position which is in a sense importantly not inside the phase proper and not part of the phase's core. Turning back to Taiwanese and *kong*-sentences now, it has been suggested that the IP complement of *kong* raises to a Specifier associated with *kong* after the sequence *kong*-IP has been spelt-out. Such a Specifier (SpecCP) is not semantically selected and is therefore of the extra "outer" type just described (XP in 142). It can therefore now be argued that the input to cyclic Spell-Out may quite possibly be the inner core of phases consisting of the head of a phase, its complement YP and any external argument Specifier (EA), but not necessarily a phase's outer phase-peripheral Specifier XP. Such a Spec position is perhaps created only after the inner core of a phase has been sent to Spell-Out. In *kong* sentences then, the inner core of the phase headed by C (*kong*) is constructed resulting in the linear sequence [kong IP/TP] and then this is spelt-out phonologically, critically also undergoing tone sandhi alteration at this point. Following Spell-Out of the inner core of the phase, an outer Specifier position is created and the IP (TP) complement of *kong* is moved to this position. Finally the full and final syntactic structure is presented to the phonological component again and the linear order [IP/TP kong] is pronounced.[40] This sequencing is now diagrammed in (143) below (using example (46) again):

(143) **Syntactic creation of the inner core of phase headed by C *kong*:**

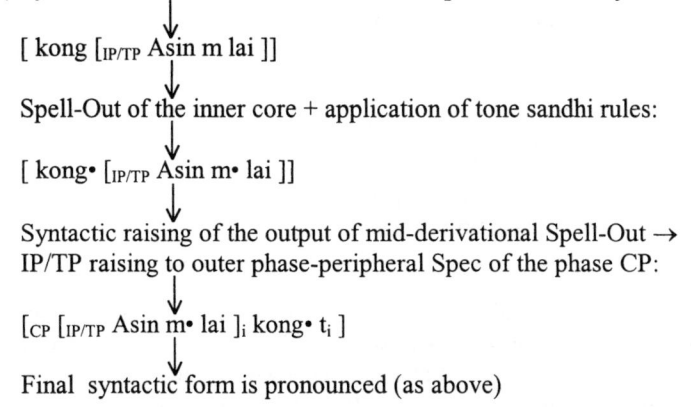

↓

[kong [IP/TP Asin m lai]]

↓

Spell-Out of the inner core + application of tone sandhi rules:

↓

[kong• [IP/TP Asin m• lai]]

↓

Syntactic raising of the output of mid-derivational Spell-Out →
IP/TP raising to outer phase-peripheral Spec of the phase CP:

↓

[CP [IP/TP Asin m• lai]$_i$ kong• t$_i$]

↓

Final syntactic form is pronounced (as above)

Such conclusions about the input forms to cyclic Spell-Out are further strengthened and confirmed by an independent pattern found in English, the interaction of *wh*-movement and sentential stress discussed in Bresnan (1971), which largely anticipates the idea of cyclic Spell-Out. Bresnan convincingly shows that *wh*-phrases which appear raised in surface forms in fact behave as if they were *in situ* for purposes of sentential stress assignment. Bresnan notes that whereas sentential stress is normally placed on the final element in a sentence, in *wh*-questions and relative clauses it is placed on a raised *wh*-phrase, as in (144), with 'what books' receiving the sentential (non-contrastive) stress:

(144) John asked what BOOKS Helen had written.

Bresnan argues that in order to explain the stress on the *wh*-phrase and the lack of stress on the sentence-final verb, sentential stress must be assigned when the *wh*-element is *in situ* in sentence-final object position prior to raising to SpecCP. As sentential stress is a phonological rule and this must apply before syntactic raising of the *wh*-phrase to SpecCP, Bresnan concludes that phonological rules apply to each transformational cycle in syntax before further syntactic operations occur in higher cycles, and that phonology will therefore be interwoven with syntax in a single derivation (i.e., there is cyclic phonological Spell-Out). Here I would like to point out two significant points relating to the *wh* data Bresnan presents. First of all, if sentential stress as a phonological rule is naturally applied to a CP constituent, then importantly it applies to the CP *before* the SpecCP position is created by raising of the *wh*-phrase (i.e., sentential stress applies to the object *wh*-phrase in its *in situ* position before any raising). This therefore seems to result in the same

105

conclusion arrived at on the basis of Taiwanese IP-raising that the mid-derivational input to Spell-Out and phonology is indeed the inner core of a CP phase without its external outer Specifier position.[41]

A second important point results from a comparison of Bresnan's patterns with object topicalization in Taiwanese, a construction whose tone sandhi patterns independently require some re-consideration here. As mentioned in footnote 38, and seen in example (109) repeated here below, tone sandhi is not triggered in the verb which precedes the object in the underlying form of an object topicalization sentence (i.e., *kong* in 109):

(109) [tai•oan•**oe**] A•sin be• hiao• kong.
Taiwanese Asin NEG know speak
'Taiwanese, Asin can't speak.'

If it is assumed that objects are necessarily topicalized to the same SpecCP position that IP-raising targets in *kong*-final sentences, this lack of tone sandhi in the verb would be rather surprising. One would expect that the object would first trigger tone sandhi on the preceding verb during cyclic Spell-Out of the CP phase and then undergo raising to the phase's outer Spec. Because tone sandhi does not however occur in the sentence-final verb it can be suggested that this may then indicate that object topicalization actually does *not* target SpecCP but some other lower adjoined/Focus-phrase position located in the inner core of the CP phase, and that this will explain the lack of tone sandhi in the verb. Any topicalization/focus-raising to a position lower than C/SpecCP will critically take place *before* the CP phase is spelt-out and objects raised and phonetically interpreted in such a higher position will consequently not be able to cause tone sandhi in the lower selecting verb. Good empirical support can also importantly be given for such an explanation of the lack of verbal tone sandhi with object topicalization. If it is assumed that IP-*initial kong* is grammaticalized as an embedding C in subordinate clauses as argued in section 3.1.1, this allows one to test whether object topicalization occurs to a SpecCP position preceding *kong* in C or to an adjoined/Focus position following C. As seen in the contrast in (145) and (146) below, object topicalization can legitimately occur only to a position below *kong* in C and consequently inside the CP's inner core:

(145) A•sin sioN• **kong•** [hit• pun• chheh]$_i$ A•hui m• be t$_i$.
Asin think C that CL book Ahui NEG buy
'Asin thinks that Ahui doesn't want to buy that book.'

(146) *A•sin sioN• [hit• pun• chheh]$_i$ **kong•** A•hui m• be t$_i$.
Asin think that CL book C Ahui NEG buy

The lack of parallelism between IP-raising and object topicalization with regard to tone sandhi on the sentence-final element therefore has a reasonable and simple explanation. It also has an interesting consequence when explored a little further in comparison with English *wh*-movement and sentential stress patterns.

Note that Bresnan's *wh*-sentential stress patterns could in fact be given a slightly different explanation from the one offered immediately above. Supposing that the input to cyclic Spell-Out could possibly be phases of either CP or *v*P type, it could be suggested that sentential stress is actually assigned to an object *wh*-phrase when *v*P rather than CP is inputted to cyclic Spell-Out, the object *wh*-phrase occurring unraised in *v*P-final position at such a point and hence in the necessary position to be assigned the relevant stress.[42] The patterns found with Taiwanese object topicalization now importantly seem to exclude this as a possibility and suggest the conclusion that *only* CP phases can occur as the input to cyclic Spell-Out. The reason for this is that if *v*P phases could occur as the input to cyclic Spell-Out, one would expect (incorrectly) that Taiwanese topicalized objects would indeed be able to trigger tone sandhi on their selecting verbs, as at the hypothetical point of *v*P cyclic Spell-Out, such objects would occur *in situ* following the verb in VP.[43] The fact that tone sandhi does not however occur in the verb in such cases therefore clearly suggests the broad conclusion that phonology has access to mid-derivational syntactic forms only at the clausal level after CPs have been constructed, and does not apply directly to smaller syntactic cycles such as *v*P phases.

The Taiwanese *kong* paradigm thus generally both adds interesting positive empirical support for the idea of cyclic Spell-Out itself and also allows one to understand more precisely what may be involved in such a process, indicating that the input to cyclic Spell-Out is a clausal CP constituent prior to the creation of its external Specifier position.[44]

3.6 Concluding Remarks

This chapter set out to provide an account of the basic architectural properties of relative clauses in Chinese and focused primarily on how the noun-head, the 'linking' element *de* and the relative clause syntactically combine together. Rejecting analyses in which the relative clause is taken to be an exceptional leftward complement to *de* for the reason that the directionality of selection should (ideally) not be subject to different parameter settings within a single language, a variety of evidence was presented in favor of adopting an analysis of relativization in Chinese along lines outlined in Kayne (1994), Vergnaud (1985) and Simpson (2002). It was suggested that the apparent exceptionality of relative clauses in Chinese (i.e., the fact that they are prenominal when no other V-O languages seem to have prenominal relative clauses) should be related to exceptional properties of the lexical item *de* and that following Simpson (2002) in essence, *de* should be analyzed as an enclitic determiner grammaticalized from an earlier demonstrative, synchronically triggering leftward IP-raising for phonological support. I then went on to show how such an approach is preferable to base-generated accounts of superficially similar relative clause structures in Japanese and pointed out a variety of differences in the patterning of relative clauses in the two language types which suggest that a fully unitary analysis is not in fact appropriate. Finally I presented a set of evidence relating to tone sandhi phenomena in Taiwanese which added further empirical support to the IP-raising view of relativization. I also developed the idea that such IP-clausal movement may be further widespread in Chinese in sentences in which a new sentence-final particle has grammaticalized from a verb of saying, collapsing earlier bi-clausal forms into new mono-clausal structures.

Notes

[1] With *non*-restrictive relative clauses such as (i) below it is commonly assumed that the head-noun first combines with the determiner/demonstrative to form a DP and this DP is then joined with the relative clause. This encodes the intuition that in non-restrictive relative clause structures the reference of the DP is established independently of the relative clause, and the relative clause simply adds in a further property attributed to the DP (see Safir 1986 for further discussion of the interpretation of non-restrictive relative clauses). Syntactically then, the relative clause is adjoined to a full DP rather than an NP:

(i) [$_{DP}$ [$_{DP}$ that man] [$_{RC}$ who you met last night]]

[2] Note that if an object is relativized but *suo* does not occur, it need not necessarily be concluded that there has been no movement. In French the triggering of overt object agreement is purely optional even when there has been movement of the object. One can therefore suggest that Chinese may be similar to French and *suo* is optional when movement of an object takes place.

[3] See also Audrey Li (1999b) for similar assumptions about the structure of relative clauses in Chinese.

[4] Strictly speaking Ning (1993) is written from an early Minimalist rather than a GB perspective. By including it here I simply mean to contrast it with a Kaynean-style analysis.

[5] Though see Audrey Li (1990) and Travis (1984) for interesting discussion of alternate views.

[6] It is actually quite possible that *ka* is not in C in Japanese either, as *ka* may co-occur with the quotational complementizer to as in (i):

(i) Mary-wa [John-ga itsu   kuru ka]-to kikimashita. (p.c., Yuka Kumagai)
     Mary-TOP John-NOM when come Q C   asked
     'Mary asked when John was coming.'

Possibly the standard complementizer domain is split into a number of heads with quotational and interrogative complementizers occurring in discrete heads in certain languages. Generally when languages allow for multiple instantiations of C in this way however, such functional heads all occur together on one particular side of the clause and hence show a single directionality relation in their c-selection, i.e., all would seem to be heads selecting their complements in the same direction, and one does not seem to find languages in which a quotative complementizer occurs on one side of a clause and an interrogative complementizer on the other. Dutch below is another example of a language with an overtly split-C system:

    (ii)   Ik weet niet of dat hij komt.
           I know NEG Q C he come
           'I don't know whether he is coming.'

[7] The verb 'say' can also follow a subordinator, which itself can be considered as a C. For example, in (i), the Mandarin verb 'say' is grammaticalized as a complementizer which follows another complementizer 'if.' This can be said to be an example of multiple instantiations of C, which is discussed in footnote 5. All instantiations of C occur together on one side of the clause and hence show a single directionality relation in their selection.

    (i)   ruguo shuo ni bu xiang qu, women jiu bie qu le.
          if say you NEG want go we then don't go ASP
          'If (that) you don't want to go, then let's not go.'

[8] There remains the question of where sentence-final question particles such as *ma/a* actually occur. If there is independent evidence from the positioning of elements such as *ruguo/yaoshi* that C is initial in Chinese, and abstracting away from the problem noted that *ma/a* are restricted to matrix clauses, one possibility might be that the rightward IP complement to a sentence-initial C occupied by *ma/a* is raised (leftwards) to SpecCP in question forms giving rise to the *ma/a*-final surface word-order observed, as schematized in (i):

    (i)   [$_{CP}$ [ni qu Beijing]$_i$ [$_C$ ma t$_i$]]
          you go Beijing   Q
          'Are you going to Beijing?'

An analysis along these lines has been suggested by Dominique Sportiche (1996 class lectures) for French and English intonation questions and accounts for certain facts concerning the licensing of NPIs. For example, in English it is possible to form yes/no questions both by means of subject-auxiliary inversion (SAI), and with a particular type of sentence-final intonation (a rising pattern):

    (ii) Did you see John? → subject-auxiliary inversion (SAI)

    (iii) You saw John?   → rising intonation only

However, whereas SAI questions license NPIs, intonation-questions do not:

    (iv) Did you see <u>anyone</u>?

    (v) *You saw <u>anyone</u>?

Sportiche makes the standard assumption that an NPI is licensed if the Q-morpheme in C is able to c-command the NPI, and this occurs unproblematically in SAI questions such as (iv). Sportiche suggests that a possible explanation why NPI licensing fails in intonation questions is that the entire IP actually undergoes raising to SpecCP, so destroying the c-command relation between the Q-morpheme in C and the NPI in SpecCP.

CHAPTER 3

In section 5 of this chapter I return to the general issue of sentence-final particles and suggest that there is actually good evidence for an IP-raising analysis with the Taiwanese S-final particle *kong*, and therefore that such an analysis might indeed be appropriate for other similar particles in Chinese too. In section 5 it is suggested that generally the surface position of phonetically reduced particle-like elements is not necessarily a reliable indication of any underlying head-complement order and the fact that such elements are phonologically dependent and enclitic may result in significant surface distortions of underlying linear order.

Note though that Chinese S-final Q-particles do in fact license NPIs, which might seem to be puzzling given that the hypothetical IP-raising in (v) does not. A possible explanation here might relate to the derivational point at which IP-raising occurs. Supposing IP-raising in Chinese questions were to occur at PF, it might be expected that such raising would *not* affect any licensing of NPIs in the IP. Possibly the IP-raising assumed by Sportiche in English and French may take place not in PF but during the syntactic derivation and for this reason block the licensing of NPIs in these languages.

[9] For discussion of how demonstratives develop into determiners, see for example Vincent (1997). Vincent notes that demonstratives may also develop into pronouns. Latin *ille* for example, developed in two ways in modern French; the second syllable *le* of *ille* became the modern French masculine singular definite determiner, and the first syllable *il* became a masculine singular subject pronoun.

[10] Following Simpson (1998a), it can be suggested that *de* is a D which only selects CP complements, and therefore cannot occur simply with an NP as in *de NP/*NP de. In the case of possessive forms such as *Zhangsan de* 'Zhangsan's', Simpson suggests such sequences are not simply NP + *de*, but arise from relativization and the raising to Spec DP of an IP containing a null predicate of possession.

[11] Pulleyblank notes that *zhi* could also occur as a pronoun in object positions. As the occurrence of *zhi* in (55) is clearly in subject position, Pulleyblank takes *zhi* to be a demonstrative here, not a pronoun.

[12] Possibly one might attempt to suggest that forms such as (56) relate to English non-movement structures such as (i) below:

(i) the strawberries such that the camel ate the strawberries

However, such an approach could not be extended to cover cases such as (58) where there is only an NP inside the relative clause—critically there must be an external head for 'such that' clauses to be possible. The example in (ii) is an attempted 'such that'-relative clause without an external head, and is quite unacceptable, even if one adds a pronominal element such as 'those':

(ii) ??those such that the camel ate the strawberries

To the extent that a 'such that'-relative approach to (56) cannot extend to cover related cases such as (58), a unified Kaynean/Vergnaud-type treatment of all (56-58) suggesting movement of the head-noun (and some optional deletion) is clearly to be preferred.

[13] Note that Chiu is of the opinion that the N(P)-raising strategy suggested to occur in children's language is actually later replaced by empty operator movement in adult

Chinese. Presumably Chiu assumes this because forms such as (56) and (58) are not found in adult speech. However, one might alternatively suggest that it is the Spell-Out option which changes in adult speech rather than the fundamental relativization process, i.e., adults would continue to form relative clauses via direct raising of the N(P) as children do, but then only Spell-Out the head of the chain. Indeed in languages such as Korean forms both equivalent to head-external structures such as (57) and head-internal relatives such as (58) continue to be produced in adult speech, though William O'Grady interestingly reports (p.c. via Ruth Kempson) that there is a marked change in preference—whereas children seem to produce more head-internal relative clauses such as (58), at around the age of six they start to switch much more regularly to using head-external forms such as (57). The fact that both types of structure continue to exist in adult Korean (and Japanese) might seem to indicate that they result from stylistic (Spell-out) options associated with a single basic relativization strategy rather than being due to two fundamentally quite different strategies associated with different stages of cognitive development.

Kayne (1994) also suggests that one might expect for both head-internal and head-external relatives to occur in a single language where the relative clause linearly precedes the head-noun because (in his analysis) there will be no c-command relation between the head-internal position and the external head, and hence either of these (or in theory both) could be spelled-out, the choice being assumed to be largely stylistic (see Kayne 1994 for details).

Finally it should be noted that (contra proposals made here) Chiu assumes throughout a basic structure in which the CP relative clause is a left-adjoined to the head-noun/NP and the IP is a leftward complement to *de* in C, i.e., the same structure as in Chiu (1993/1995) and Ning (1993)—tree (22). The issues of directionality and selection and the categorial status of *de* discussed here are therefore left unaddressed (not being the focus of Chiu's paper).

[14] Here however there *may* also be additional non-structural aspects of the data which contribute to the unacceptability of examples such as (66). Certain other structurally similar examples with *jibun* modifying the relative clause head-noun are felt to be far more acceptable, e.g.:

(i) [John$_i$-ga __ suki-na] [jibun$_i$-no-shashin]
John-NOM   likes   self-GEN-picture
'the pictures of himself which John likes'

[15] Possibly Japanese might also show itself to be island sensitive if one could establish a similar sort of test and control. That is, maybe the apparent island violations noted in Kuno (1973) are cases where a resumptive *pro* is made use of and that there otherwise is indeed some kind of movement similar to Chinese. Possibly if the head-noun were to be a quantificational equivalent to 'no-one' or 'more than two people' one might find the re-appearance of Subjacency effects (a resumptive *pro* not being available in such necessarily restrictive relative environments).

[16] If the head-noun is only co-referenced with a *pro* as in Murasugi's analysis of Japanese, there is no parallel necessity for a c-command relation between the head-noun and the *pro*, pronouns in general not needing to be c-commanded by their antecedents.

CHAPTER 3

[17] The surface order of the pre-nominal relative clause results from the CP undergoing raising to precede the head noun. At LF the raised CP will then either reconstruct to the position where the operator in SpecCP is c-commanded by the head-noun, or one might assume that a copy is left in the position from which the CP moves, this satisfying the c-command requirement.

[18] Such connectivity also indicates that standard GB analyses, in which an operator movement is proposed (Chiu 1993/1995 and Ning 1993 discussed above, for example), are less appropriate than the analyses with the head-noun movement.

[19] Another interesting difference between relative clauses in Chinese and Japanese which may be noted here concerns the positions of demonstratives and restrictive/non-restrictive interpretations. In both languages (and also Korean, which patterns like Japanese and different to Chinese, see Young-Kook Kim 1997) it is possible to position demonstratives either before the pre-nominal relative clause or between the relative clause and the head-noun. However, this seems to result in opposite interpretations in Chinese and Japanese. In Chinese if the demonstrative occurs between the relative clause and the head-noun, a regular restrictive interpretation is possible, but such a positioning automatically triggers a *non*-restrictive interpretation in Japanese. When the demonstrative occurs preceding the relative clause, this may give rise to a *non*-restrictive interpretation in Chinese (Huang 1982), whereas it normally results in a restrictive interpretation in Japanese (and Korean):

   (i) [wo zuotian mai]-de *zhei-ben* shu
       I yesterday buy DE this-CL book
       'the book that I bought yesterday'

   (ii) [watashi-ga kinoo katta] *kono* hon
       I-NOM yesterday bought this book
       'this book, which I bought yesterday'

   (iii) *zhei-ben* [wo zuotian mai]-de shu
       this-CL I yesterday buy DE book
       'this book, which I bought yesterday'

   (iv) *kono* [watashi-ga kinoo katta] hon
       this I-NOM yesterday bought book
       'the book that I bought yesterday'

I do not propose to attempt an explanation of this difference here, but just note it as another example of how apparently similar surface structures in Chinese and Japanese actually seem to have quite different properties on closer examination.

[20] Having argued that there is good evidence in favor of a Kaynean-type movement account of relativization in Chinese, I have suggested that structures such as (46/47) represent the derivation of regular relative clauses in Chinese. For those cases in which it appears that a resumptive *pro* can be base-generated in relative clauses in Chinese (and Subjacency violated), I assume that this results from a modification of the basic movement structure in (46/47) below simply with the head noun/NP being base-generated in Spec of CP and a resumptive *pro* occurring in some position in IP. This follows the approach commonly adopted towards relative clauses with resumptive pronouns in other languages that these are simply due to base-generation

of the resumptive pronoun and the relative-operator in the same relative clause positions that would otherwise be linked via movement. Such an approach seems more natural than to posit quite different structures for resumptive pronoun cases—if a relative clause movement-type structure such (46/47) is anyway necessary and available for minor modification via base-generation of a resumptive pronoun, this would seem to be simpler than to assume some different structural form.

[21] A general question concerning the account of clausal raising outlined here is why *de* as an enclitic needs to attract a clausal constituent rather than, say, the highest XP within that clause. Although I have no great insight to offer here, it can be noted that clitics cross-linguistically do show considerable variation in the hosts which they target. In some languages clitics may attach themselves to a wide variety of hosts, whereas in other languages clitics may only tolerate a single type of host (as e.g., the pronominal clitics in French/Italian, which only attach to verbal elements, discussed in Spencer 1991). Here it can be said that *de* is also rather selective as a clitic and will only attach to verbal projections. In order to implement such an idea technically within a Minimalist approach, one can suggest that the D position is generated with a strong *v*-feature which triggers raising of some verbal constituent to its Specifier. In the case of possessive structures such as *Zhangsan de shu* 'Zhangsan's book' which might seem to be a counter-example here, one might assume Simpson's (1998b) analysis in which possessor structures result from relativization and an empty predicate of possession, as noted earlier in footnote 10. If this is so, then possessor forms will actually have the structure: [$_{DP}$ [$_{IP}$ Zhangsan __ t$_i$]$_m$ de [$_{CP}$ [shu]$_i$ t$_m$]] and *de* will still be attracting an IP category.

[22] Sometimes for certain speakers a *wh* relative pronoun does seem possible, as in (i-ii):

(i) % the reason why Mary likes John

(ii) % the time when he met Mary

Informants indicate that such forms often seem to be dispreferred in speech, that not all speakers accept them, and that in many cases overt *wh* elements are completely rejected by all speakers (such as for example 91). I would here like to speculate that all CNPs of the type seen in (84)-(92) are formed as noun-complement clause structures parallel to [the claim [$_{CP}$ that...]]-forms. When *wh* elements do occur for certain speakers, they are actually occurring base-generated in C as selected *wh*-variants to the default C *that*, similar to the fact that C elements are in other instances also arguably selected by embedding heads, as in (iii) and (v).

(iii) John wonders [if/whether Mary will come].

(iv) Bill denied [that he is in love with Mary].

(v) Sue asked [for Bill to leave].

Consequently such structures in (i) and (ii) will again not be instances of relativization.

[23] Note that there is also another quite simple analysis of structures such as (82) and (83) in which they can in fact be assumed to be relative clauses resulting from a Kaynean process of NP-raising. Kuno (1973) argues on the basis of a variety of data that relative clauses are commonly formed from *topic structures* and that it is the topic of a sentence which is relativized as the head-noun/NP of a relative clause. If this is so,

because the head nouns/NPs in structures such as (82) and (83) can occur as topics preceding the bracketed IP as in (i) and (ii) below, it can be suggested that such NPs are relativized to their surface position from an underlying topic position and that such structures are therefore not 'gapless' relative clauses:

(i) nei-ge shihou, wo changchang lai Zhonguo.
 that-CL time I often come China
 'At that time I often came to China.'

(ii) nei-ge difang, wo kan-guo ta liang ci.
 that-CL place I see-ASP him two time
 'In that place I saw him twice.'

An analysis along these lines would consequently seem to allow one to maintain that Kaynean-type NP-raising does occur also in cases where there is perhaps no obvious gap in the relative clause—the extraction gap of the NP would actually be in the topic position.

Note that in such an approach, examples such as (80) and (81) would however still have to be analyzed as being N+ CP complement structures, as the nouns *yuanyin* 'reason' and *fangfa* 'way/method' cannot occur as topics connected to the relative clause IP as in (iii) and (iv):

(iii) *nei-ge yuanyin, ta qunian xue Zhongwen.
 that-CL reason he last-year study Chinese

(iv) *nei-ge fangfa, ta jiejue wenti.
 that-CL method he solve problem

[24] Two of the 'eight' traditionally recognized tones, tone2 and tone6 are actually identical in phonological terms—both are high-falling 5-1.

[25] Note that a quite different approach to the description of tone sandhi generalizations is offered in R. Cheng (1968, 1973). Rather than stating (Taiwanese-type) Min dialect tone sandhi as a set of phonological rules which applies to major syntactic units as input (i.e., specifiers, heads, complements and adjuncts), Cheng suggests that such tone sandhi is instead sensitive to the particular *categorial type/label* of a syntactic constituent, and that tone sandhi is a process which is blocked and fails to apply if a syllable occurs specifically at the end of an NP, a VP, IP, sentential AdvP or CP. Such a categorial-based approach is however criticized in Chen (1985). Chen vigorously points out that truly productive phonological processes such as tone sandhi are nowhere else found to be directly sensitive to and restricted by particular categorial labels and phonological rules instead seem to be blind to categorial distinctions (for example, one never finds cases of other phonological processes such as vowel harmony, palatalization, spirantization, etc. being restricted by categorial type and therefore only occurring in AdjPs or PPs, or NPs and AdjPs, etc., although such processes may be subject to other more general boundary conditions). Chen argues that it would be consequently implausible to assume the exceptional existence of rules which do refer to a subset of such labels just in the case of Min tone sandhi. In contrast to the lack of such category-specific phonological rules however, Chen notes that cross-linguistically there are many phonological processes which are sensitive to *more general* syntactic divisions in sentential structure, indicating that phonology (potentially) does recognize distinctions between arguments and adjuncts

and other major syntactic relations, and that such more general distinctions are more likely to be relevant for Min tone sandhi. I agree with Chen's argumentation that phonological rules should be assumed to be unable to refer specific category labels and would also like to thank Monik Charette, Moira Yip and Jean-Roger Vergnaud for useful discussion and confirmation of this point. The chapter consequently continues to assume that Taiwanese tone sandhi is indeed a function of more general syntactic structure and the generalizations suggested in the text and is not a result of categorial labels. For further discussion of how Min tone sandhi patterns are sensitive to argument/adjunct type syntactic relations, see Chen (1990) and also Chen (2000).

[26] One might perhaps wonder whether an alternative account of the patterning might be possible, relating it to the paradigm of *wh*-trace interference in *wanna*-contraction where the occurrence of an A'-trace between two elements blocks the phonological process of contraction from occurring (i.e., **Who do you wanna win?* is unacceptable as the A'-trace of 'who' occurs between 'want' and 'to'). Movement of an empty operator to Spec of CP might leave behind a trace of A'-movement which would linearly intervene between the element targeted for tone sandhi application *be* 'buy' and the following tone-bearing element potentially able to license tone sandhi (*e*). This A'-trace intervention could then possibly be held responsible for the impossibility of tone sandhi in the verb *be*. However, tonal change on the final element in the IP is equally impossible when a subject is relativized from within the IP and no trace intervenes between the final IP element and the C *e*, as in (i).

(i) [O$_i$ t$_i$ be• chhe] e• lang
    buy book REL person
    'the person who bought books'

It would therefore seem that it is not the occurrence of an A'-trace before *e* in (112/113) which blocks it from licensing tone sandhi (one can also note that A'-traces in fact do *not* seem to block contraction processes in any clearly uniform way—Sag and Fodor (1995) observe that the *wh*-trace resulting from extraction out of *tensed* subject positions does not block auxiliary contraction: *Who do you think'll/'s come?*).

[27] Note that if there is no overt NP following *e*, then *e* does not undergo tone sandhi, as shown in (i):

(i) [$_{IP}$ A•sin **be**] **e** [$_{NP}$ __]
    Asin buy E
    'the one(s) Asin bought'

This confirms that the tone sandhi rules significantly apply *after* the IP has undergone raising to SpecDP, as otherwise the presence of the IP following *e* might be expected to trigger tone sandhi on *e*. The IP-raising therefore can be assumed to take place in the syntax and not be movement at PF (i.e., after the application of tone sandhi)—see sections 3.5.3 and 3.5.4 for further discussion of the "derivational timing" issues relevant here.

[28] It could perhaps be argued that the tone sandhi patterns here might also be explained if a slightly adapted version of the Murasugi-type structure in (70) is adopted with the relative clause base-generated in SpecDP. In such a structure no tone sandhi would be expected on the final element in the IP preceding *e* as this would be occurring in a Specifier (SpecDP) and *e* itself would be expected to undergo tone sandhi as it would

115

CHAPTER 3

be a D head preceding an overt NP complement. However, earlier arguments given against such an analysis are still valid here. Because there is evidence of movement in Chinese relative clauses, it must be assumed that a CP is projected with some element raising to SpecCP; if this is assumed to be an empty operator rather than the head-noun, such an operator will need to be c-commanded by the head-noun and so the CP should be base-generated to the right of the NP in structure (70). Consequently it should *not* be possible to base-generate the CP relative clause in SpecDP and, as before, a Murasugi-type structure has to be rejected (for Chinese).

[29] Note that the work in this section results from a fruitful collaboration with Andrew Simpson in 1999-2000, and appears in a different form as Simpson and Wu (2002a).

[30] Note that Mandarin (i) below is perfectly acceptable with aspectual *guo* attached to *ting-shuo* 'hear-say.' This indicates that Mandarin *shuo* in the sequence *ting-shuo* is still verbal:

(i) wo mei ting-shuo-guo ta bu lai.
 I NEG hear-say-ASP he NEG come
 'I didn't hear that he was not coming.'

Elsewhere however, Mandarin *shuo* occurs as a grammaticalized complimentizer similar to Taiwanese *kong*, and if it occurs following a verb of cognition, such as *xiang* 'think', *shuo* 'say' may not be accompanied by *guo*, as seen in (ii) below:

(ii) wo xiang-shuo(*-guo) ta bu lai.
 I think-say -ASP he NEG come
 'I thought that he was not coming.'

[31] Note that this is similar to the observation that various propositional attitude adverbs in English and other languages cannot occur easily in embedded contexts:

(i) John said that (??frankly) Mary was crazy.

Embedding the adverb under a higher clause subject seems to block the speaker's control of the propositional attitude expressed by the adverb, a licensing requirement which appears to be necessary for the use of certain adverbs.

[32] The analysis of IP-raising suggested here would be further supported if it could be shown that extraction of an element from the IP could not licitly occur, as extraction from within a leftward Spec position (as opposed to from within a complement position) might be expected to violate Subjacency. Unfortunately because IP-final *kong* is a root/matrix clause C, such tests cannot be constructed, as there is no higher position in the clause that an element could be legitimately extracted to. Note however that it might be suggested that the unacceptability of *wh* elements in *kong* sentences could be due to Subjacency applying to LF extraction in some way:

(i) *Asin be sia-mih kong?
 Asin buy what KONG
 'What did Asin buy?'

I would like to suggest though that the *wh* elements actually cannot co-occur with IP-final *kong* because *kong* instantiates a declarative and hence non-interrogative value of C, *kong* functioning to emphatically assert the IP. If the C is non-interrogative it will simply not be able to license *wh* elements (and the unacceptability of cases such as (i) will therefore not be due to any LF Subjacency violation).

In this regard note furthermore that yes/no question particles can also not co-occur with *kong*:

(ii) *Asin u   lai bo kong?
     Asin AUX come Q KONG
     'Did Asin come?'

Such complementary distribution of *kong* and question particles can be taken as indication that *kong* and interrogative X⁰ elements occur as alternative competing instantiations of the same basic C head position with *kong* and question particles encoding opposite semantic values—declarative assertion vs. interrogative +Q.

[33] Concerning the question of whether other older S-final particles in Taiwanese also result from IP-raising, when one examines these (e.g., aspectual *a* (Mandarin *le*)), one finds that they are now phonetically reduced to the extent that they no longer carry any positive tone which could undergo tone sandhi. Such a lack of possible tone sandhi does not indicate that IP-raising does not occur with these particles, and only has for effect that any (hypothetical) raising can no longer be made visible by possible tone sandhi. Essentially then it is necessary to catch a particle at a particular point in its development in order to be fully confident about its underlying syntax, Taiwanese *kong* being especially clear and revealing here in still having both an obviously recognizable source as the verb 'to say' and the positive tone which allows it to undergo tone sandhi.

[34] *Me* is the pronoun 'I' and *v-tkv-i* is the first person singular subject (*v-*) aorist indicative (*-i*) of the verb 'say.' Note that in the case of Taiwanese, as Taiwanese subjects can be phonetically null (i.e., *pro*), there is no necessary phonetically overt reflex/trace of the incorporation of the first person specification into the reanalyzed *kong* (unlike in Georgian).

[35] Speculating a little on why bi-clausal structure might collapse into simplified monoclausal forms in this way, it can be suggested that this perhaps takes place when there is no longer any pressure to see the content of the higher clause predicate as instantiating a highlighted discrete event.

[36] See Bybee, Perkins and Pagliuca (1994, p.107) for discussion of the fact that grammaticalization frequently leads to phonetic reduction, causing phonological dependency and cliticization.

[37] See here Grosu (1988) and Giusti (1997) and section 3.3.1 for clear evidence that dependent enclitic definite determiners in Romanian attract elements to D/SpecDP in order to support them phonologically and hence that this kind of attraction for phonological support is indeed attested elsewhere.

[38] The *kong* paradigm therefore seems to provide a clear argument in favor of a *derivational* model of grammar, and would not seem to be easily accounted for in any fully representational approach. In a non-derivational approach, *kong* sentences would have the (single) representation in (i) with the IP in its surface position relating to a trace/copy following *kong*:

(i)   [[IP]$_i$ *kong* t$_i$]

CHAPTER 3

The problem here is that the element following *kong* in (i) is phonetically null and therefore should not be able to trigger tone sandhi in *kong*. Elsewhere it is clearly only phonetically overt elements (which furthermore must have non-neutral tone) that can trigger tone sandhi on a preceding element (hence, for example, an object *pro* does not cause tone sandhi on a verb). Note that it is also not possible to allow for copies of movement (as opposed to base-generated empty categories) to exceptionally cause tone sandhi as the copies left by other types of movement such as object topicalization do not cause tone sandhi on the elements which precede them. There would therefore seem to be no obvious way to account for the tone sandhi patterns with *kong* without assuming a derivational approach where the overt IP triggers tone sandhi on *kong before* raising to its left.

[39] Thanks go to both Joseph Aoun and David Pesetsky for pointing out how the tone sandhi patterns might be considered evidence for cyclic Spell-Out.

[40] It can be assumed that such an end-of-derivation re-presentation of the completed syntactic form to the phonology will not result in any second application of tone sandhi rules and that tone sandhi alterations occur only once to any phase.

[41] As with Taiwanese IP-raising, there are also clear interpretational effects associated with English *wh*-movement indicating that it clearly cannot be analyzed as PF movement and that a cyclic Spell-Out approach is therefore necessary instead.

[42] Note that Chomsky (1998) suggests that prior to *wh*-movement to SpecCP, *wh*-phrases may have to raise to Spec*v*P. However, if such an outer Spec is not created until after the *v*P phase has been interpreted by cyclic Spell-Out as argued above with CP, then a *wh*-object will indeed still be *in situ* at the point that cyclic Spell-Out may hypothetically apply to a *v*P.

[43] Again, as noted in footnote 19, raising of an object to Spec*v*P and higher positions should only come after the *v*P is spelt-out.

[44] If one assumes a more articulated structure in the left periphery/C-domain, perhaps as in Rizzi (1997), it might be possible to suggest that IP-raising in Taiwanese takes place to a Specifier position which is higher than the Specifier of the projection headed by *kong*. If this were to be so, one needs to ask to what extent the conclusions reached here might possibly be different. I believe that that the main conclusions would essentially not be much changed, and largely just be re-presented with a somewhat different labelling. The basic thrust of the argumentation has been to suggest that the input to cyclic Spell-Out is a clausal constituent which is actually (just) less than a full CP—a CP lacking an outer Specifier in the terms used here. If one now concludes that *kong* is perhaps the head of a Mood/QP which encodes the assertive-declarative/interrogative force of the clause (*kong* occurring in complementary distribution with other Q-morphemes and not allowing for the licensing of *wh*-elements, see footnote 38, and if its IP complement perhaps raises to a higher TopP/CP, then the generalization in essence remains as before but just makes use of different terms: the input to cyclic Spell-Out is a clausal constituent which is somewhat less than a full clause, being a Mood/QP and not a full TopP/CP.

I believe however that there is actually a good reason for wishing to maintain the original generalization in the text. What needs to be captured is the observations in (i) and (ii) below:

118

(i) The XP input to cyclic Spell-Out in Taiwanese is optionally headed by an X^0 (*kong*) which encodes declarative force in alternation with interrogative Q-morphemes (and hence occurs in C/Q/Mood).

(ii) The XP input to cyclic Spell-Out in English *cannot* be the *full* XP headed by the X^0 (C/Q/Mood) which encodes interrogative force, as this input is formed and spelt-out before *wh*-phrases undergo raising to Spec of the XP.

If it is reasonable to assume that cross-linguistically there is a uniform input to cyclic Spell-Out, the two generalizations above indicate that this input form must be (at least) an XP headed by a declarative/interrogative head (due to the Taiwanese evidence with *kong*), but that it cannot be a full XP of this type (due to Bresnan's English *wh* patterns). An obvious way of capturing these two generalizations is therefore to maintain the suggestions in the text that the input to cyclic Spell-Out is indeed a CP (or perhaps a Mood/QP) which has not yet projected its external Specifier position.

4

DE IN FOCUS SENTENCES
FROM D TO T*

4.0 Introduction

This chapter sets out to investigate the syntactic and categorial status of the element *de* found in clause-final position in Mandarin Chinese cleft-type sentences such as (1), and also attempts to account for the alternation found where the object optionally appears positioned after *de* as in (2):

(1) wo shi zuotian mai piao de.
     I BE yesterday buy ticket DE
     'It was yesterday that I bought the ticket.'

(2) wo shi zuotian mai de piao.
     I BE yesterday buy DE ticket
     'It was yesterday that I bought the ticket.'

Structures such as (1) have been the subject of a number of pieces of research in recent years, e.g., Chiu (1993), Huang (1982), D. Shi (1994) among many others. There and elsewhere it is noted that *shi-de* sentences consistently give rise to interpretations similar to English clefts, with the focused element commonly following the copula *shi* and frequently being an adverb or PP referring to the time or place where some event has occurred, as for example in (3):[1]

(3) ta shi zai Zhongguo xue Yingwen de.
     he BE in China study English DE
     'It was in China that he studied English.'

Most research on the *shi-de* construction has centered itself on the focus properties of such sentences and has attempted to offer accounts of how the focus interpretation may be syntactically encoded. In general this has led to a concentration on the function of *shi* and various suggestions that LF movement of the focus may be involved.[2] Comparatively little attention has however been given to the role and status of the element *de* in the construction, possibly due to the fact that *de* may sometimes seem to be optional in its occurrence, and to date there has not been any serious discussion of the alternation illustrated in (1) and (2). Such apparently optional occurrence of the object either before or after *de* is puzzling as there is no obvious interpretative difference triggering the alternation and purely optional, unmotivated movement should not occur under current Minimalist assumptions. This chapter suggests that a study of the role played by *de* and the alternation found in examples such as (1) and (2) leads to a better understanding of the *shi-de* construction and the interesting conclusion that *de* is currently undergoing a significant reanalysis. It is argued that *de* is changing category from an original source as a D^0 element to become a new past tense instantiation of T^0, and that the reason for such a shift is in large part the increase of a past time conversational implicature strongly present in *shi-de* forms. Syntactically, such D-to-T conversion is suggested to be an example of 'lateral grammaticalization', a process in which a functional head from one type of syntactic domain may under appropriate circumstances undergo re-interpretation as an equivalent functional head in a second domain, D and T here both being elements which (potentially) assign deictic reference to their complements and therefore having largely corresponding functions in the nominal and clausal domains. The chapter also presents a variety of evidence suggesting that *de* is actually still ambiguous at present and in different instances may potentially instantiate either tense or a D^0 head, this having direct effects on a number of syntactic phenomena. Speakers are therefore argued to significantly maintain a dual analysis of *de* in the current period of change, with different underlying structures being possible depending on the temporal interpretation of *de* in *shi-de* sentences.

The organization of the chapter is briefly as follows. Section 1 focuses on the alternations in (1) and (2) and argues that the only plausible explanation of the full patterning observed is that *de* is undergoing movement to the verb. Considering further the interpretation of *shi-de* forms and the interaction of this with object positioning, it is proposed that *de* is being reanalyzed as a past tense element, raising as a clitic to the verb from a T^0 position. Section 2 then considers S-final non-past occurrences of *de* and suggests that these however occur in CNP structures, showing how such a second dual analysis of *de* can account for a number of otherwise conflicting patterns in *shi-de* forms. Section 3 then goes on to present a formal syntactic account of the hypothesized reanalysis of *shi-de* structures and provides further justification for the route of grammaticalization suggested as well as an examination of the structural position of *shi* in past tense *shi-de* sentences. Section 4 considers the D/T relations from a general cross-linguistic perspective and the idea of cross-domain grammaticalization suggested by D-to-T reanalysis. Finally the chapter is closed with an examination of how focus is formally encoded in *shi-de* sentences.

CHAPTER 4

4.1 Object-*De* Repositioning in the *Shi-de* Construction

The important alternation illustrated in (1) and (2) above can be schematically represented in simplified form as (4a) and (4b) below, which highlights the part of the structure in need of some explanation, i.e., how the object and the element *de* come to be repositioned with respect to each other:

(4) a. V – Ob – *de*
    b. V – *de* – Ob

Concerning the relation of these two orders to each other, given that the order in (a) is found in all Chinese dialects, while that in (b) is more restricted in its occurrence, a first fairly natural assumption that can be made is that the ordering in (b) should somehow be derived from the more basic order (a). It can also be noted that the order in (a) diachronically precedes that in (b), again suggesting that the (b) order has been derived from the (a) order. Assuming this much, there seem to be three possible ways of analyzing the optional positioning of the object relative to *de*, as now examined.

A first fairly obvious possible way of relating (b) to (a) is to suggest that (b)-type surface forms might result from underlying (a) forms via simple rightwards movement of the object over *de* to clause-final position, as schematized in (5):

(5) V t_i *de* Ob_i

Such a possibility is however unlikely to be right, for a number of reasons. Rightward object extraposition of this kind is cross-linguistically observed to occur predominantly when an object is either heavy or focused, as e.g., in heavy NP shift in English or finite clausal extraposition in Hindi and German:

(6) John gave t_i to Mary [everything he possessed]$_i$/*it$_i$.

(7) Er hat t_i gesagt, [dass er heute kommen würde]$_i$. (German)
    he has said that he today come would
    'He said that he would come today.'

In *shi-de* constructions when the object occurs following *de*, it is however neither necessarily heavy nor focused and in fact the opposite is actually true. In examples such as (2) the post-*de* object *cannot* indeed be focused as the focus is here automatically interpreted as being the adverbial element directly following *shi*. Furthermore a post-*de* object will by preference actually be light rather than heavy for reasons to do with the representation of old information. Specifically, as the focus in examples such (1-3) is taken to be the adverbial/PP element directly following *shi*, any object present either preceding or following *de* will be part of the presupposition and so necessarily old information; as such, it will normally be represented by a simple bare (hence light) NP rather than a longer descriptive form of the type which might naturally occur when an NP is introduced for the first time as new information (as for example is often the case in English heavy NP shift). Informants furthermore indicate that when the object is a clausal complement and necessarily somewhat heavy, they in fact strongly prefer for it to be placed before *de* as in (8) rather than 'extraposed' as in (9):[3]

(8) ta shi zuotian shuo [ta bu xihuan Mali] de.
he BE yesterday say he NEG like Mali DE
'It was yesterday that he said that he didn't like Mary.'

(9) ?(?)ta shi zuotian shuo de [ta bu xihuan Mali].
he BE yesterday say DE he NEG like Mali
'It was yesterday that he said that he didn't like Mary.'

It therefore seems rather unlikely that (b)-type forms result from any rightwards movement of the object from its post-verbal base position in (a). This being so, a second possibility to account for the order in (4b) may be to posit that it is actually the verb which is undergoing movement in (4b), raising leftwards to adjoin to the element *de* which would then be base-generated in some kind of higher functional head as indicated in (10). Such an approach would also have to assume that there is movement in (4a) of the whole VP containing the verb and its object as in (11):

(10) V_i-*de* t_i Ob (=4b)

(11) VP_i-*de* t_i (=4a)

Such a possibility is however also unlikely to be correct. If *de* is base-generated in a clausal functional head position, it should clearly occur located above VP-adverbs, yet such elements occur preceding *de* (as in 2) and cannot occur following *de* as shown in (12). This is clearly unexpected if *de* were indeed to be located in a position in the functional structure dominating the VP.

(12) ta shi qunian xue de (*zai xuexiao) Yingwen.
he BE last year study DE in school English
'It was last year that he studied English.'

If it is therefore concluded that neither movement of the object nor movement of the verb is likely to be responsible for the (b)-type orders, a third logical possibility is that it is actually *de* itself which is the element changing its position, moving leftwards from a base-generated clause-final position as in (13):

(13) V de_i Ob t_i

Given the additional observation that *de* prosodically attaches to the right-hand side of the verb in examples such as (2) in the way of an enclitic element (i.e., it is not possible for there to be any intonational pause between the verb and *de*), such movement could perhaps be suggested to be an instance of clitic-movement/cliticization, movement driven by the needs of an element to attach to a particular type of host for phonological support. Furthermore, just as clitics may over time often show a change in the host they target for attachment, here it could be suggested that the alternation in (4a) and (4b) results from *de* as an enclitic simply switching to attach to a different, more restricted phonological target. In the more widespread/earlier pattern in (4a) it could be assumed that *de* in clause-final position unselectively cliticizes to whatever element is present clause-finally (i.e., the verb or a DP object), whereas in (4b) it could be suggested that *de* is now showing signs of coming to be more selective and deliberately targeting the verb as its host, hence moving over any clause-final object in order to encliticize to the verb. This kind of behavior and a gradual narrowing of the target for attachment is noted to be quite typical of the development of clitics (see e.g., Spencer 1991), such elements often becoming more selective in what they attach to over time and ultimately developing into affixes morphologically attached to just a single type of host.

This enclitic hypothesis of the alternation in (4a/b) which suggests that *de* in pattern (4b) moves to specifically target the verb as a phonological host can now importantly be shown to be supported in a strong way by the behavior of *de* in double object constructions (DOCs). In DOCs, in addition to the fully S-final positioning of *de*, it can be noted that the order in (14/15) is significantly also possible with *de* preceding *both* the direct object *and* the indirect object:

(14) NP shi Adv/PP V *de* IO DO

(15) wo shi zuotian   gei de tamen san-ben shu.
     I BE yesterday give DE they three-CL book
     'It was yesterday that I gave them three books.'

Such patterns indicate fairly clearly that sequences where *de* precedes the direct object as in (4b) (i.e., V *de* Ob) cannot in fact be assumed to result from simple movement of the object over *de* as here *two* elements are found following *de*, both the direct object and the indirect object. As it is unlikely that there is an operation moving both direct and indirect objects rightwards here (and no motivation for any such movement as noted earlier), it would seem that cases such (15) instead provide strong support for the view that it is instead the element *de* which is undergoes movement leftwards from a clause-final base position in (4b)-type forms and that this movement of *de* also specifically targets the verb, in DOCs potentially raising to the verb over both the direct and the indirect objects. Given as noted that *de* does also exhibit clear enclitic properties in its leftward prosodic attachment to the verb, the most reasonable explanation of the alternation in (4a/b) can now indeed be concluded to be the encliticization hypothesis, that *de* moves to cliticize to the verb in *shi-de* sentences of type (4b) and this is therefore why it ends up linearly preceding the object.

Such a hypothetical process of cliticization to the verb of a clause-final element can also be noted to have a well-documented precedent in Chinese adding further potential plausibility to a clitic analysis of pattern (4b). Many researchers (e.g., Cao 1987, Li and Shi 1997, Z. Shi 1989, G. Wu 1999 among others) have noted that historically the perfective aspect suffix verbal *le* developed from a clause-final full verb *liao* 'to finish.' Originally *liao* occurred following the object of the descriptive verb as schematized in (16a). Later on however it underwent reduction and attached itself arguably as a clitic (and later still as a suffix) to the right of the verb and so now occurs between the verb and its object as in (16b). Such a path of development is clearly similar to what is argued to be taking place with S-final *de*—from an original clause-final position, *de* becomes attracted to the verb and in cliticizing to the verb moves over the intervening direct object as in (17):

(16) a. V Ob liao   later →
     b. V-le$_i$ Ob t$_i$

(17) a. V Ob de   now (optionally) →
     b. V-de$_i$ Ob t$_i$

If it is indeed correct that *de* is specifically targeting the verb when it undergoes displacement in examples such as (2) and (15), one now needs to ask why this should be happening and what kind of verb-related clitic *de* could plausibly be. As noted above, when clitics come to target a single host-type rather than just a position and any category filling that position, they are characteristically close to the point at which they may develop further and be reanalyzed as morphological affixes. If this consequently suggests that *de* may be en route to becoming a new verbal suffix, one needs to consider what type of verbal inflection *de* might actually be turning into. In the case of *liao/le* becoming a verbal suffix, it is widely assumed that *le* now instantiates the verbal category of perfective aspect, a category which cross-linguistically often occurs affixally attached to the verb. The element *de,* I would now like to argue, also instantiates a syntactic category which commonly occurs in affix form on verbs in a wide range of languages. Specifically, I would like to suggest that various properties of *shi-de* sentences all point towards the single conclusion that *de* is currently in the process of becoming a past tense morpheme, and that as such it is undergoing repositioning and developing into a suffix on the verb in a way which is cross-linguistically very common with tense morphemes.

A first important point leading towards such a conclusion is that quite generally in *shi-de* sentences one tends to find a very strong preference to interpret the event described by the predicate as having taken place in the past, even in the absence of any past time adverbials. For example, (18) below *only* seems to allow for a past time interpretation:

(18) wo shi zuo huo-che qu Beijing de.
       I BE sit train go Beijing DE
       'It was by train that I went to Beijing.'

Secondly one finds that *de* is in fact also often *necessary* for a past time interpretation. In (19) below, if *de* is present, only a past time interpretation is possible, and if *de* is not included a past time interpretation is actually not available:

(19) wo shi gen Zhangsan qu Beijing (de).
       I BE with Zhangsan go Beijing (DE)
       with *de*: 'It was with Zhangsan that I went to Beijing.'
       without *de*: 'It IS (indeed) with Zhangsan that I'm going to Beijing.'

This indicates that although the occurrence of *de* might seem to be 'optional', in fact if a past time interpretation is necessary, then *de* is actually obligatory with *shi*, as further illustrated in (20) where the presence of a past time adverbial necessitates a past time reading and this in turn forces the occurrence of *de* in the structure:

(20) ta shi zuotian qu Beijing *(de).
       he BE yesterday go Beijing DE
       'It was yesterday that he went to Beijing.'

There is consequently a clear strong connection between the presence of *de* and past time/tense interpretations. Despite this strong connection however, *shi-de* sentences with *de* can in fact have non-past interpretations if this is forced by the use of non-past/future adverbials together with the occurrence of future/modal elements such as *hui* 'will' or *yao* 'will.' Note that the latter modal elements are indeed necessary for the non-past reading and it seems that a non-past adverbial on its own is not enough to license a non-past interpretation:

(21) ta shi mingtian *(cai hui) qu Beijing de.
       he BE tomorrow only-then-will go Beijing DE
       'It is (only) tomorrow that he will go to Beijing.'

It can therefore be concluded that the connection of *de* to past time interpretations instantiates a heavy *preference*, and that not all occurrences of *de* necessarily have to be interpreted as past time events. In pragmatic terms, the default tendency for past time interpretation with *de* has the status of a generalized conversational implicature—a preference which is clearly strong, but which can still be over-ridden with the deliberate use of certain elements/strategies, such as the occurrence of non-past adverbials and modals as in (21).

A highly significant new piece of evidence bearing directly on the status of *de* when it occurs in pattern (4b) can now be added to the general patterning observed here. Interestingly it is found that when *de* precedes the object and is by hypothesis raised and attached to the verb as an enclitic en route to becoming a verbal suffix, it is no longer possible to use modals and adverbs to over-ride the past time implicature of such constructions any more, and *only* a past time interpretation is possible in such a configuration:

(22) *ta shi mingtian cai hui qu de Beijing.
he BE tomorrow only-then-will go DE Beijing

Examples such as (22) which instantiate the structure in (4b) here show an important contrast with those in (18)-(21) which represent (4a). The latter cases showed that while a past time interpretation is strongly associated with the use of *de*, it still effectively constitutes a preference which can nevertheless be over-ridden with appropriate means. When however *de* shows signs of really becoming a verbal element and is suggested to undergo reanalysis as an instantiation of (past) tense, moving to cliticize to the verb, at this point it seems that the past time conversational implicature (i.e., the 'preference' for past time interpretation) has actually become strengthened to the extent that it is now part of the genuine meaning of (verbal enclitic) *de* and can therefore no longer be over-ridden (i.e., *de* in such a position can *only* mean past). The suggested analysis of *de* in the pre-object pattern of (4b) as a new past tense morpheme therefore seems to be strongly supported. It can also be noted that the occurrence of syntactic change as the result of the strengthening of the preference for a particular interpretation is a path of development which has been argued to be a common pattern of reanalysis. Hopper and Traugott (1993) in particular suggest that the strengthening of a conversational implicature to the point where it becomes standardized and triggers a formal reanalysis is a mode of syntactic and semantic change which underlies much diachronic change.[4] In the case of *de*, the preference for a past time interpretation can be taken to have finally strengthened to the extent that it has eventually allowed for a reanalysis of *de* as a genuine instantiation of the category of past tense, such a reanalysis now indeed being manifested in its movement to the verb.

The development of *de* as a verbal clitic encoding past time/tense can also be suggested to have been functionally assisted by the natural structuring of information in *shi-de* forms. As noted earlier, the *shi-de* construction commonly encodes a clear focus set off against a strongly presupposed background which often consists of the verb and its object as in examples (1-3) and (18-20). As the object is then frequently part of the presupposition and hence old information, there will be a natural tendency for representing it by means of a pronominal element rather than a repetition of a full descriptive NP form. As Chinese furthermore allows for null pronominal objects (*pro* or topic-operator-bound trace as in Huang 1984), *shi-de* sentences then frequently occur without any overt object, and also often without any overt *shi*, as in (23), such forms being preferred to fully-specified examples like (24) which are grammatical but generally felt to be rather awkward/over-specified:

(23) (wo) jintian mai de.
 (I) today buy DE
 'I bought it *today*.'

(24) wo shi jintian mai nei-ben shu de.
 I BE today buy that-CL book DE
 'I bought that book *today*.'

A presupposed/old object may alternatively also occur placed in topic position:

(25) nei-ben shu wo jintian mai de.
 that-CL book I today buy DE
 'That book I bought *today*.'

The clear result in commonly-heard forms such as (23) and (25) is therefore that the verb and *de* are importantly heard adjacent to each other unseparated by other overt material. Such common verb-*de* adjacency with *de* prosodically attaching to the verb can be argued to be a clear functional factor favoring the development of *de* as a specifically verbal clitic and therefore leading to and licensing its attachment to the verb even in the presence of an overt post-verbal object. As a clitic optionally attaching to the verb and being strongly associated with a past time interpretation, the possibility of *de* becoming reanalyzed as a past tense morpheme therefore seems to be both natural and perhaps even anticipated as a further stage in its development.

In sum then, there are a variety of good reasons for assuming that the element *de* in *shi-de* structures of type (4b) has indeed come to be a new instantiation of (past) tense in Mandarin Chinese. Before we go on to see how this is formally produced in the syntax in section 3, I will first turn to consider what the source of *de* is in *shi-de* forms and also rather importantly what the identity of *de* may be when it occurs in full sentence-final position in the post-object pattern (4a).

4.2 Post-object *De*

Let us now reconsider what kinds of interpretations arise with *de* in the different *shi-de* patterns (4a) and (4b). If *de* occurs in the pre-object position as in (4b), it has been noted that *de* has a necessary/strict interpretation as past time/tense. If *de* however occurs in pattern (4a) following the object of the verb in clause-final position, there is a preference for past time interpretations of the event described by the predicate, but non-past interpretations are also possible if certain modals and adverbials are used. When *de* is present with such non-past interpretations, it is obvious now that it cannot be instantiating the category of past tense. Assuming the analysis of *de* as a past tense morpheme in pattern (4b) to be correct for the various reasons given, this therefore leads to the conclusion that *de* is in fact potentially ambiguous in its categorial status in *shi-de* sentences and in addition to instantiating past tense in certain instances, it must also be able to occur as some other non-tense category in pattern (4a), relating to an underlying syntactic structure which may possibly be quite different from that in past tense occurrences of *de*.

If we consider now what category and status *de* might have in these other non-past cases, it can be noted that linguists describing the *shi-de* construction in previous work (e.g., Chao 1968, Paris 1979, Li and Thompson 1981) have frequently identified *de* as the same element *de* which occurs in relative clauses and possessor structures introducing a modification on a following nominal as for example in (26) and (27):

(26) [wo zuotian mai] de shu
 I yesterday buy DE book
 'the book I bought yesterday'

(27) Zhangsan de shu
 Zhangsan DE book
 'Zhangsan's book'

This is indeed a reasonable assumption and cross-dialectical evidence within Chinese clearly favors identifying the element *de* in *shi-de* forms with 'nominal modifying' *de*. In Mandarin Chinese, there are in fact a number of elements having the same pronunciation *de*—cleft sentence *de*, relative clause *de*, possessor/genitive *de*, potential *de*, descriptive-clause *de*, and resultative-clause *de*. These elements have a variety of different syntactic properties and do not all derive from the same source, there being essentially two clear groups of *de*'s. Etymologically, the cleft-sentence *de*, relative clause *de*, adjectival *de*, and possessor *de* are all written in the same character, while the potential *de*, descriptive-clause *de*, and resultative-clause *de* are written differently, suggesting that *de* in *shi-de* forms really does relate to nominal modifying *de* in terms of its origin. The latter group of elements is illustrated in (28):

(28) a. kan-de-jian
      look-DE-see
      'is able to see'
   b. ta zou de hen kuai.
      he walk DE very fast
      'He walked very fast.'
   c. ta qi ma qi de hen lei.
      he ride horse ride DE very tired
      'He rode a horse until he was very tired.'

A survey of non-Mandarin Chinese dialects/languages also significantly reveals that the morphemes all pronounced *de* in (26), (27), *shi-de* sentences such as (1) and the group of elements in (28) in Mandarin are consistently split up and grouped in a particular way. In Cantonese, Taiwanese and Shanghainese, the morphemes corresponding to *de* in *shi-de* sentences, possessor structures and relative clauses all have a single pronunciation, whereas those corresponding to *de* in (28) have different pronunciations, as illustrated below in Cantonese (29), Shanghainese (30) and Taiwanese (31):

(29) Cantonese:
   a. kui hai tingyat maai sue ge.
      he BE yesterday buy book GE
      'It was yesterday that he bought a book.'
   b. kui mai ge sue
      he buy GE book
      'the book that he bought'
   c. kui ge sue
      he GE book
      'his book'

(30) Cantonese:
   a. maai-dak-hei
      buy-DAK-lift
      'be able to buy'
   b. kui ja che ja dak ho faai.
      he drive car drive DAK very fast
      'He drove very fast.'
   c. kui duk sue duk do/dak ho gwooi.
      he read book read until/ DAK very tired
      'He studied until he was very tired.'

130

DE IN FOCUS SENTENCES

(31) Shanghainese:
    a. i si zonie qi Zeben <u>ge</u>.
       he BE yesterday go Japan GE
       'It was yesterday that he went to Japan.'
    b. i ma <u>ge</u> su
       he buy GE book
       'the book that he bought'
    c. i <u>ge</u> su
       he GE book
       'his book'

(32) Shanghainese:
    a. koe-<u>de</u>-ji
       look-DE-see
       'is able to see'
    b. i zou <u>de/le</u> lao kua.
       he walk DE/LE very fast
       'He walked very fast.'
    c. i dzi mo qi <u>de/le</u> lao chili.
       he ride horse ride DE/LE very tired
       'He rode a horse until he was very tired.'

(33) Taiwanese:
    a. i1 si7 cha1-hng1 khi3 jit8-pun2 <u>e5</u>.
       he BE yesterday go Japan E
       'It was yesterday that he went to Japan.'
    b. i1 be2 <u>e5</u> chhe3
       he buy E book
       'the book that he bought'
    c. goa2 <u>e5</u> chhe3
       I E book
       'my book'

(34) Taiwanese:
    a. chau2 <u>e7</u> kin2
       run can fast
       'be able to buy'
    b. i1 khui1 chhia1 khui1 <u>kah4</u> chin1 kin2.
       he drive car drive KAH very fast
       'He drove very fast.'
    c. i1 thak8 chhe3 thak8 <u>kah4</u> chin1 thiam2.
       he read book read until very tired
       'He studied until he was very tired.'

Through all of Cantonese, Shanghainese and Taiwanese, the morpheme occurring in the cleft-focus equivalent to Mandarin *shi-de* therefore has the same pronunciation as the element used in relative clauses, adjectival structures and possessor structures, and is different from the morpheme occurring in potential verb constructions, the descriptive verb construction and resultative clauses. It can therefore be concluded with reasonable certainty that clause-final cleft *de* is indeed in its origin nominal modifying *de*.

Returning to consider the underlying structure of *shi-de* forms now, if the *de* in such constructions has indeed developed from nominal modifier *de*, given that this latter element regularly precedes a nominal/N one might expect that there would be some kind of (phonetically null) nominal projected in *shi-de* forms too. Here it can be noted that in relative clause and possessor structures in Chinese it is not uncommon for the head noun following *de* to be omitted if it is anaphoric and/or can be recovered from the discourse context, as in (35), indicating that phonetically null/'deleted' head nouns are most certainly possible with *de*:

(35) na shi wo zuotian mai de (dongxi).
 that BE I yesterday buy DE (thing)
 'That's what/the thing/the one I bought yesterday.'

Shi-de sentences are however unlikely to be simple covert relative clause structures with a deleted/empty head noun, as the interpretation of overtly-headed relative clauses following the copula *shi* is rather different from *shi-de* forms and such sequences lack the cleft-like focus interpretation present in *shi-de* sentences. A second more likely possibility can be suggested to be that *shi-de* forms are instead more closely related to Complex NP/CNP structures of the 'the fact/news that IP' type where the same *de* occurs linking a *complement* clause to a following nominal, as for example in (36):

(36) [$_{IP}$ ta bu hui lai] de xiaoxi
 he NEG will come DE news
 'the news that he will not come'

In an earlier examination of *shi-de* sentences, Kitagawa and Ross (1982) indeed propose an analysis along such lines and suggest that there is a phonetically null head-noun following *de* with an interpretation something like '(the) situation.' Such a proposal is inspired by the observation frequently made in the literature (e.g., in Chao 1968, de Francis 1963) that *shi-de* sentences always seem strongly linked to the direct discourse setting and function to clarify information relating to some aspect of the discourse situation which is obvious to both speaker and hearer (for example, explain when or where some obvious, presupposed event has taken place). Kitagawa and Ross suggest that Chinese *shi-de* sentences (and equivalents in Japanese) therefore have interpretations something like the second gloss given for (1) repeated below:

(1) wo shi zuotian mai piao de.
    I BE yesterday buy ticket DE
    'It was yesterday that I bought the ticket.' OR:
    'As for me, the <u>situation</u> is that I bought the ticket YESTERDAY.'

Quite generally, given that nominal-modifying *de* is indeed the most natural default source to presume for *de* in the *shi-de* construction, it is not unnatural to suppose that speakers do in fact also assume the presence of some kind of semantically very light N following *de* in the way that Kitagawa and Ross essentially suggest. Here it can also be noted that in an equivalent cleft-like construction in Burmese, a 'dummy' head-noun *haa* is actually physically present in the structure. This element elsewhere occurs as the nominal complement of the demonstrative *dii* 'this' meaning 'this one', and is either pronounced as *haa* or collapsed with *dii* as the form *daa*, as shown in (37):

(37) a. *dii haa* 'this (one)'
     b. *daa* 'this (one)'

In clefts, *haa* regularly collapses with the non-irrealis morpheme *teh* to result in *taa*:

(38) dii-nee weh <u>taa</u> paa.
     today buy TAA POL
     'It was today that I bought it.'

There is consequently also comparative empirical support for the possibility that Chinese *shi-de* clefts may contain a kind of light N as suggested.

A possible alternative account of the source of *de* in *shi-de* forms which still recognizes the obvious connection to nominal modifying *de* but avoids the assumption of any empty N-head following *de* might instead be to follow Paris (1979), and Li and Thompson (1981) rather than Kitagawa and Ross, and suggest that nominal modifying *de* in both CNPs and in *shi-de* forms is essentially just a (clausal) nominalizer. In *shi-de* sentences it could then be assumed that *de* simply functions to nominalize the clausal constituent preceding *de*, and unlike the case of relative clauses and other CNPs such a clausal nominalization might possibly not be syntactically combined with any following (null) head noun.

Either of the above plausible assumptions about the original source of *de* in *shi-de* forms can now be noted to have interesting consequences. First of all, it is possible to observe parallels between *shi-de* forms and the behavior and interpretations of certain other clear *nominal/nominalization* forms elsewhere, suggesting that the *shi-de* construction may well be rooted in an original nominal(ization) form and that this may then have possibly influenced the way that *shi-de* structures have come to be interpreted. Secondly, a nominalization/CNP analysis of current non-past *shi-de* forms allows for a principled account of various restrictions on the occurrence of *wh*-adjuncts and adverbial modification found to pattern differently in *shi-de* forms in past and non-past interpretations, and leads to conclusions about differences in the structures which may underlie *shi-de* sentences.

Considering the particular interpretation associated with the use of *de*, *de* is essentially argued to be pragmatically appropriate when it marks a structure in which a focused constituent (following *shi*) is set off against a strongly *presupposed* background event. In this sense, the use of *de* can be suggested to provide a 'guarantee' of the occurrence of the background event, clearly signaling that the relevant event either has already taken place in the past or will certainly occur at some point in the future. This function of marking the background event as fully presupposed can now be argued to be largely responsible for the preference for a past time interpretation commonly noted with *de*. Clearly it is possible to have the greatest confidence and be able to guarantee that an event will occur *at some point* if it is in fact known that the event has indeed *already* occurred, and one can be confident about the future occurrence of any event with much less certainty. *De* is therefore naturally found marking and guaranteeing the occurrence of past time events much more frequently than non-past events. As has been noted in section 1 though, the past time interpretation of the predicate when *de* follows the object (i.e., pattern 4a) still remains a *preference* which can indeed be over-ridden with appropriate means (non-past time adverbials and modals). From a comparative point of view, it can now be noted that the important strongly presuppositional property associated with *shi-de* sentences is also found in certain nominalization forms in English, which seem to heavily imply or guarantee the occurrence of a particular event. Furthermore, as with *shi-de* forms this 'guarantee' most frequently gives rise to a past time interpretation. For example, in (39) the events represented by the nominalizations are *most naturally* understood to have taken place in the past:

(39) The panel will discuss [the destruction of the village]/[the killing of the hostages].

However, exactly as with *shi-de* forms, the past time interpretation would only seem to be a default interpretation, and may be over-ridden with the use of adjectives such as 'planned' and 'scheduled' which function to guarantee the occurrence of the event in the future:

(40) The panel will discuss tomorrow's ??(planned) killing of the hostages.

(41) They're talking about tomorrow's ?(scheduled) destruction of the bridge.

Given the clear similarities between the interpretational preferences in *shi-de* sentences and the English nominalizations in (40-41) (and their over-ridability), and given the likelihood that *shi-de* forms have as their source a nominalization/nominal construction, it is tempting to see the common past time interpretation with *shi-de* sentences as being potentially related to the existence of an original nominal(ization) syntax, and possible that such a source structure may have to a certain extent been responsible for the past time conversational implicature arising in *shi-de* sentences.[5]

A nominalization/CNP source of *shi-de* forms can now also be suggested to account for certain restrictions on the distribution and interpretation of adverbs and *wh*-adjuncts in *shi-de* sentences. Broadly one finds two types of restrictions. First of all, *wh*-adjuncts such as *weishenme* 'why' and *zenme* 'how' cannot occur following *shi* when there is an intended future interpretation of the predicate, as in (42) and (43):

(42) ?*ni shi weishenme cai hui qu Beijing de.
 you BE why only-then will go Beijing DE

(43) *ni shi zenme cai hui qu Beijing de.
 you BE how only-then will go Beijing DE

Secondly, adverbs cannot occur preceding *shi* and modify the predicate following *shi* when there is a non-past interpretation of the predicate in *shi-de* forms, as seen in (44) and (45) below (compared with 21 above):

(44) *wo meitian dou shi hui qu Beijing de.
 I every-day all BE will go Beijing DE

(45) *mingtian ta shi (cai) hui qu Beijing de.
 tomorrow he BE (only-then) will go Beijing DE

Such restrictions can be straightforwardly explained if it is assumed that non-past *shi-de* forms have as their underlying syntactic form an original CNP or nominalization structure. Concerning the latter adverb cases (44) and (45), elsewhere it has often been observed that adverbs which occur external to DPs cannot quantify into DPs or modify events depicted internal to a DP. As a result of this opacity of DPs, in (46) below it is not possible to understand 'yesterday' as referring to the time when Bill betrayed Sue, only to the time of John's discussion:

(46) Yesterday John discussed [Bill's betrayal of Sue]

Consequently, if the sequence following *shi* in non-past *shi-de* sentences is indeed a DP/nominal structure of some kind it is indeed anticipated that adverbs external to this sequence (i.e., preceding *shi*) should not be able to quantify in to the predicate inside the DP. As for the unacceptability of *wh*-

adjuncts such as *zenme* and *weishenme* following *shi* in future-type interpretations of the predicate, this is again expected if the sequence following *shi* in such interpretations is a CNP. Elsewhere CNPs in Chinese do not allow such *wh*-adjuncts to occur inside them, as shown in (47/48):

(47) *ta shi [[DP weishenme lai] de ren]?
     he BE   why   come DE person

(48) *[DP ta weishenme/zenme piping Meiguo]-de xiaoxi] bu zhengque?
          he why/how   criticize USA   DE news NEG accurate

Such patterns can now be shown to significantly contrast with the occurrence of adverbs and *wh*-adjuncts in *shi-de* forms in pattern (4b) where *de* encliticizes to the verb and precedes the object, and the predicate accordingly has a past time interpretation. Here it is found that adverbs can in fact occur preceding *shi* and still quantify over the predicate following *shi*, as in (49), and that *wh*-adjuncts such as *weishenme* and *zenme* can occur either following *shi* or preceding *shi* and in both cases refer to/question the event in the predicate following *shi* as in (50):

(49) zuotian ta shi gen Zhangsan lai   mai de piao.
     yesterday he BE with Zhangsan come buy DE ticket
     'It was with Zhangsan that he bought the ticket yesterday.'

(50) ni   qunian shi weishenme/zenme qu de Beijing?
     you last-year BE why/how   go DE Beijing
     'How/why was it that you went to Beijing last year?'

If the analysis of verbal clitic *de* in pattern (4b) put forward here is correct, such contrasts have a simple explanation. If *de* in pattern (4b) is an instantiation of past tense and categorially different from non-past *de* in pattern (4a), the presence of *de* in examples such as (49) and (50) can be suggested to signal the occurrence of a simple TP rather than a nominal CNP island constituent. As TPs are not islands for *wh*-adjuncts nor opaque constituents for external adverbial modification, it is quite expected that both *wh*-adjuncts and pre-*shi* adverbs should indeed be able to occur in cases such as (49) and (50). The contrasts between (44-45, 47-48) and (49-50) therefore seem to add good support first of all for the general hypothesis that *de* may correspond to two distinct syntactic types in its past and non-past interpretations, and secondly for the possibility that significantly different syntactic structures may correspond to these different instantiations of *de*, in the case of non-past *de* this being an opaque nominal constituent which is an island for *wh*-adjuncts (a CNP or perhaps a clausal nominalization), and in the case of past tense *de* this being instead some kind of non-opaque, non-island constituent marked by *de*, quite plausibly a simple TP.

The above conclusions now also raise a further important question about the syntactic status of *de* in the S-final [V Obj *de*] pattern (4a) when *de* has a past time interpretation. Specifically, one would like to know whether *de* in such cases gives rise to a past time interpretation simply as the result of a pragmatic conversational implicature, or whether *de* may be formally reanalyzed as a (past) tense morpheme also in these cases as with pattern (4b). Now having considered the patterns with adverbs and *wh*-adjuncts we have a potential structural diagnostic for resolving this issue. If past time interpretations of *de* in pattern (4a) allow for the occurrence of *wh*-adjuncts following *shi* and adverbs preceding *shi*, then it can be concluded that *de* in such cases is not associated with the projection of any opaque, island-like nominal projection, but instead relates to a different TP structure headed by *de* as an instantiation of past tense. If on the other hand past time interpretations of *de* in pattern (4a) pattern like future-time interpretations and disallow the occurrence of external adverbs and internal *wh*-adjuncts, then one can conclude that past time *de* in pattern (4a) is indeed associated with the same CNP-type underlying structure and is only interpreted as past by conversational implicature. What one finds, as shown below in (51) and (52), is that *wh*-adjuncts and adverbs in past time interpretations of *de* in pattern (4a) significantly show none of the unacceptability of the same elements occurring with non-past *de* in pattern (4b):

(51) zuotian wo shi zai xuexiao kanjian ta de.
yesterday I BE in school see he DE
'It was in the school that I saw him yesterday.'

(52) ni shi weishenme/zenme lai xuexiao de?
you BE why/how come school DE
'Why/how is it that you came to school?'

This clearly suggests the interesting conclusion that *de* has allowed for a formal reanalysis as a past tense element projecting a TP not only in pattern (4b) but also in full S-final position (i.e., pattern 4a). How this may be possible and what kinds of formal syntactic structures underlie *shi-de* forms in patterns (4a) and (4b) will now be shortly examined in section 3 below.

Summarizing the conclusions made so far, in section 1 I presented evidence and argumentation that *de* in sequences of [V *de* Obj] instantiates past tense. I then noted that as *de* in [V Obj *de*] sequences can have a non-past interpretation, this indicates that *de* in such occurrences must be a different syntactic element from past tense *de* and therefore that speakers must be assumed to currently maintain a dual analysis of *de* in *shi-de* forms. Considering what this latter non-past *de* might be, it was noted that its most likely source is the 'nominal modifying' *de* found in CNP (and possessor) type structures. I then saw how the assumption that non-past *de* might still relate to a nominalization/CNP structure may account for contrasts in the acceptability of certain *wh*-adjuncts and adverbs in past and non-past interpretations of *de*. Finally it has been argued that the lack of restrictions on adverbs/*wh*-adjuncts with past time interpretations of *de* in the S-final pattern (4a) suggests that *de* is also instantiating past tense here and that a non-island TP is projected in the structure rather than an opaque nominal category. In section 4 now I will consider a little more closely what kind of underlying syntactic structures are projected in the different *shi-de* forms and how an original nominal structure may have come to be reanalyzed as a projection of past tense.

4.3 The Syntax of Reanalysis in *Shi-de* Sentences

In attempting to compare the structures underlying past and non-past *shi-de* forms and how the latter may have undergone reanalysis as a new past tense structure, I will first outline what I assume to be the underlying syntax of non-past *shi-de* forms. Taking *de* in non-past *shi-de* forms to be the nominal modifier *de* of regular CNPs, I assume as noted in section 2 that non-past *shi-de* forms contain a CNP structure headed by a light N element.[6] Concerning the analysis of CNPs in Chinese, chapter 3 has defended a Kayne-style (1994) analysis of relative clauses and other noun-complement clause CNPs in Chinese with the following properties:

(53) a. *De* is a an element of type D in all CNP type structures.
b. *De* selects a *rightward* clausal complement, in line with the dominant head-initial direction of complement selection in Chinese.
c. In relative clauses the relativized noun/NP raises to SpecCP and then the IP remnant raises higher to SpecDP.
d. The motivation underlying this IP movement is that *de* as an enclitic determiner triggers movement of the IP element to its SpecDP position for phonological support.

The derivation of a relative clause structure such as (54) was then argued to be as indicated in (55):

(54) [wo zuotian mai] de shu
I yesterday buy DE book
'the book I bought yesterday'

(55) a.

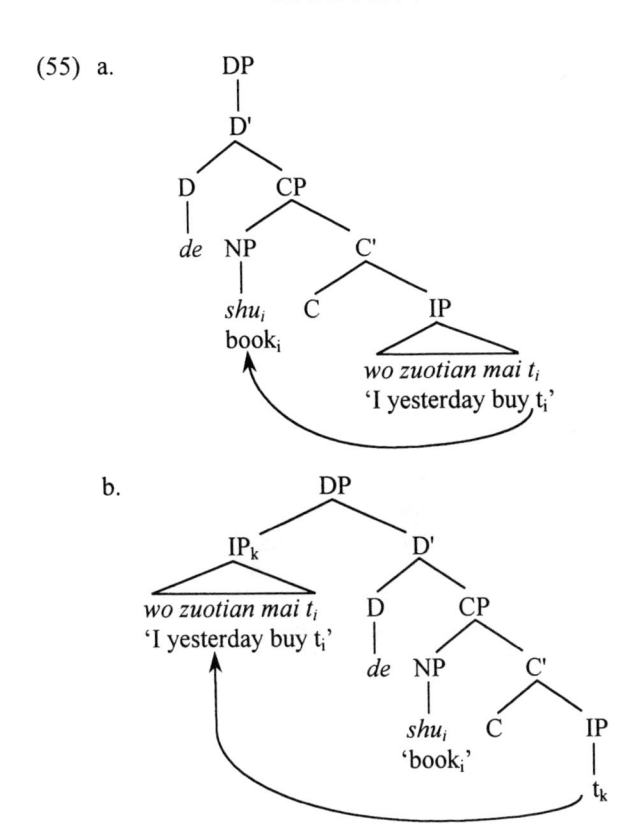

[Tree diagram: DP → D' → D (de) + CP; NP (shu_i 'book_i') raised to Spec; CP contains C' → C + IP (wo zuotian mai t_i 'I yesterday buy t_i')]

b.

[Tree diagram: DP → IP_k (wo zuotian mai t_i 'I yesterday buy t_i') + D'; D' → D (de) + CP; CP contains NP (shu_i 'book_i') and C' → C + IP (t_k)]

In the similar treatment of noun-complement clause CNPs, *de* in D was suggested to select a rightward NP (rather than CP) complement, with the N head of this NP in turn selecting a rightward IP/AspP complement as in (56), representing example (36) repeated below. The element *de* was furthermore taken to have the same enclitic requirements as in relative clauses, triggering raising of the IP/AspP clausal constituent to SpecDP as in relative clauses:

(36) [IP ta bu hui lai] de xiaoxi
     he NEG will come DE news
     'the news that he will not come'

CHAPTER 4

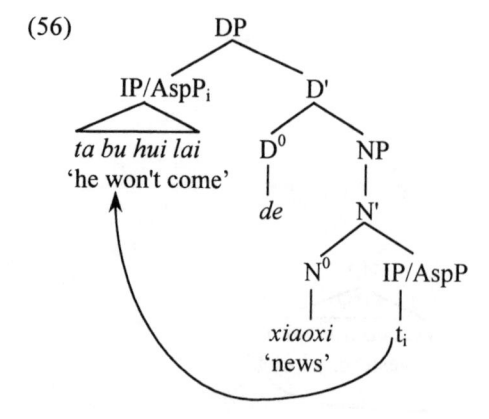

(56)

```
         DP
        /  \
   IP/AspPᵢ  D'
   /|\      / \
  ta bu hui lai  D⁰  NP
  'he won't come'  |   |
                   de  N'
                       / \
                      N⁰  IP/AspP
                      |    |
                    xiaoxi  tᵢ
                    'news'
```

Turning now to *shi-de* forms, under the assumption that such structures in non-past interpretations contain a noun-complement clause CNP headed by a phonetically null light N as suggested, the underlying structure and derivation of examples such as (21) can be suggested to be as in (57):

(21) ta shi mingtian *(cai hui) qu Beijing de.
 he BE tomorrow only-then-will go Beijing DE
 'It is (only) tomorrow that he will go to Beijing.'

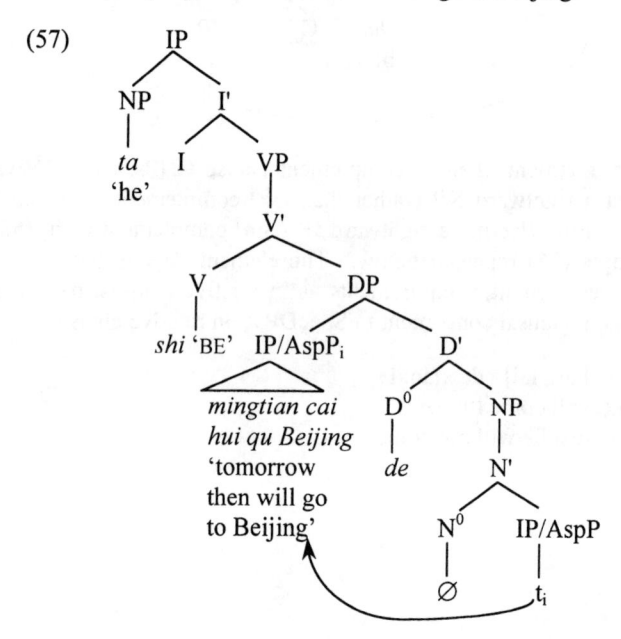

(57)

```
            IP
           /  \
          NP   I'
          |   / \
          ta  I  VP
         'he'    |
                 V'
                / \
               V   DP
               |   / \
           shi 'BE' IP/AspPᵢ  D'
                  /|\        / \
             mingtian cai   D⁰  NP
             hui qu Beijing  |   |
             'tomorrow       de  N'
             then will go        / \
             to Beijing'        N⁰  IP/AspP
                                |    |
                                ∅    tᵢ
```

Taking (57) to be the representation of *non-past shi-de* forms, we are now in a position to see how such structures may be reanalyzed into rather different

140

syntactic forms when *de* comes to instantiate past tense, as well as how further aspects of the syntax of past tense *de* may be accounted for.

The central contention of the analysis argued for in sections 1-2 above is that nominal modifying *de* undergoes reanalysis as a new instantiation of past tense. In categorial terms it can therefore now be suggested that an original D head of the CNP taken to occur in the source construction becomes reanalyzed as an element of type T. Such a reanalysis of the head of the construction will then automatically result in the original DP complement of *shi* in non-past *shi-de* forms being reinterpreted as a new TP complement to *shi*. Concerning the rest of the CNP structure in (57), a further change which can be suggested to follow from the reanalysis of D as T is that the light N head present in (57) is pruned and lost from the underlying structure so that T comes to directly select for a clausal rather than a nominal complement, as indeed elsewhere with T elements.[7] Such simplification and pruning of the NP projection can be suggested to be possible for two reasons. First, it may be possible because the N head is a semantically light expletive-type N (similar, for example, to Japanese *koto* 'thing') assumed to simply fill the regular N-position of the source CNP construction, and it is therefore not an element which is really required for any interpretative purposes (and is hence rather easily 'eliminable'). Secondly, the hypothesized N may be essentially ignored and eliminated during the reanalysis of the DP as a TP, as the N is phonetically covert and there is consequently no overt phonetic material which might have to be reanalyzed as some other category.[8] Such a hypothetical reanalysis of the structure will then result in new TP forms such as (58) occurring as complements to *shi* in place of DPs, with the clausal complement of T^0 (arguably an AspP, potentially containing the perfective aspect marker *le*) undergoing raising from its base position to SpecTP, essentially as in the original DP structure. Note that here I concentrate on and present the lower *de*-related part of the full *shi-de* structure and later return to consider the upper half of the structure:

(1) wo shi [$_{TP}$ zuotian mai piao de].
     I BE   yesterday buy ticket DE
     'It was yesterday that I bought the ticket.'

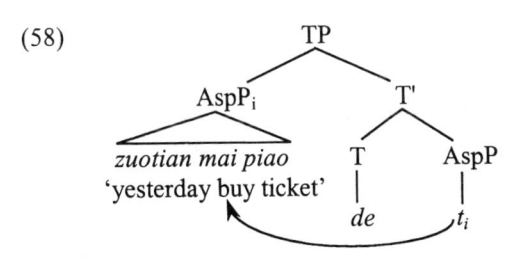

(58)
```
                    TP
                   /  \
               AspPᵢ   T'
              /    \   / \
      zuotian mai piao  T   AspP
      'yesterday buy ticket' |    |
                            de   tᵢ
```

CHAPTER 4

(58) above represents pattern (4a) when *de* has a past time interpretation. In section 2 I argued that *de* encodes past tense not only in pattern (4b) but also when it appears following the object as in (1). *De* in (1) and other similar examples can therefore be taken to be occurring base-generated in the new T^0 position as indicated in (58). Concerning pattern (4b), where *de* attaches directly to the verb and precedes the object, here I suggest as before that this is the result of a cliticization operation in which *de* moves to target the verb, and that prior to cliticization and movement, *de* in such cases is base-generated in the same basic T^0 position as in pattern (4a) and tree (58). The critical *optionality* between pattern (4a) and pattern (4b) therefore does not relate to any difference in the underlying structure projected, but is taken to relate to *de* targeting different hosts for cliticization: in the case of (4a), *de* simply cliticizes to the right edge of the AspP in SpecTP; in (4b) however, *de* alternatively targets the verb as a more specific phonological host and so moves leftwards from its base position to do this. Such an approach to the optionality in the positioning of *de* which essentially ascribes this to the availability of different possible targets for cliticization can be suggested to be potentially more appropriate as an analysis of *de*-positioning in *shi-de* forms than other pure-syntax-based possibilities. Given that the optional repositioning of *de* in pattern (4b) appears to result in no real perceptible differences in interpretation (with *de* encoding past tense in both patterns 4a and 4b), it might seem difficult to account for such an alternation in *purely* syntactic terms, as random, optional syntactic movement having no effects on interpretation is assumed to be unavailable in current Minimalist approaches to syntax. Processes of cliticization driven by primarily phonological considerations are however often observed to display optionality of exactly this kind. As one example of this, Spencer (1991, p.372-373) notes that auxiliary clitics in Polish optionally move and attach to a wide variety of phonological hosts: pronouns, complementizers, adverbs, NPs and numerals (these not necessarily occurring in any fixed clausal P2 position either), and hence that there is a considerable degree of optionality in the placement of aux clitics in this language. Elsewhere studies of the development of clitics have shown that clitics may over time gradually become more selective and switch from targeting general syntactic positions or constituents as hosts to targeting certain more specific syntactic categories, and that during the period of change apparently optional attachment to either original or new host category is possible. In the case of past tense *de*, it can therefore be suggested that *de* is currently in just such a transitional stage, tolerating attachment both to an original general syntactic host (AspP) as well as also showing signs of becoming more selective and optionally targeting the specific syntactic category of the verb for phonological support.[9, 10]

A movement-cliticization account of *de* in pattern (4b) can also be argued to be preferred to an alternative affixation analysis which might suggest that *de* is now simply base-generated on the verb as a suffix in examples such as (2). Essentially there are two types of argument against the latter possibility. The first is that it is clear that past tense *de* in pattern (4a) cannot be a verbal suffix as it encliticizes to whichever direct or indirect object DP occurs finally in the AspP preceding it. As it is implausible to imagine that the same past tense morpheme *de* has two lexical entries, one as a suffix and the other as a clitic, it would seem that a natural uniform analysis of past tense *de* needs to recognize it as a special clitic which (optionally) moves to the verb from a T^0 position. A second argument in favor of such a treatment comes from a further consideration of the double object construction (DOC). Earlier it was noted that in addition to a possible S-final position, past tense *de* can also occur attached to the verb in DOCs, hence both a *de*-final [V IO DO-*de*] sequence and a *de*-raised [V-*de*$_i$ IO DO t$_i$] form occur as noted in example (15):

(15) wo shi zuotian   gei de tamen san-ben shu.   [V-*de* IO DO]
 I   BE yesterday give DE they three-CL book
 'It was yesterday that I gave them three books.'

Here it can now be noted that in addition to the patterning illustrated in (15), many speakers also allow for *de* to occur intervening between the indirect object and the direct object as in (52):

(59) wo shi zuotian   gei tamen de san-ben shu.   [V IO-*de* DO]
 I   BE yesterday give they DE three-CL book
 'It was yesterday that I gave them three books.'

This might initially seem to go against the verbal-encliticization analysis argued for in section 1, as here *de* seems to be attaching to the indirect object pronoun not the verb. However, in addition to the clear fact that the order in (15) with *de* enclitic on the verb does show *de* to be targeting a verbal host, it can be suggested that the order in (59) results from syntactic incorporation of the indirect object pronoun into the verb prior to *de* attachment. Following Baker and Hale (1990) and Bresnan and Mchombo (1987) who argue for the general possibility of pronominal incorporation phenomena, it can be suggested that indirect object incorporation in cases such as (59) creates a complex verbal element to which *de* may subsequently attach as a verbal clitic. As indirect object incorporation may be reasonably assumed to be a syntactic operation, this indicates that *de* encliticization/attachment should also be assumed to occur during the syntactic derivation rather than be the product of lexical suffixation, and only such a movement-encliticization analysis of *de* seems able to account for the patterns noted here that *de* can occur both finally, between the indirect object and direct object, and also attached directly to the verb.[11] Here it can also be noted that such patterns distinguish *de* from verbal *le* which can only attach directly to the verb and is unacceptable if positioned after an indirect object as indicated in (60):

143

CHAPTER 4

(60) a. wo gei-le tamen san-ben shu.
   I give-ASP they three-CL book
   'I gave them three books.'
   b. *wo gei tamen-le san-ben shu.
   I give they-ASP three-CL book

The contrast between (55b) and (54) can be simply accounted for if it is assumed as suggested above that *de* is a clitic moving in the syntax to attach to the verb together with any incorporated indirect object, and that verbal *le* is (as commonly assumed) a suffix directly attached to the verb prior to insertion in the syntax and therefore prior to any possible indirect object incorporation to the verb.

The cliticization-movement analysis of *de*'s attachment in *shi-de* sentences can also be suggested to allow for a possible account of the otherwise unexplained observation that when perfective aspect verbal *le* occurs in *shi-de* forms only pattern (4a) and not pattern (4b) is possible, as shown in (61):

(61) a. wo shi zuotian mai-le piao de.
   I BE yesterday buy-ASP ticket DE
   'It was yesterday that I bought the book.'
   b. *wo shi zuotian mai-le-de piao.
   I BE yesterday buy-ASP-DE ticket

Here it can be suggested that the encliticization of *de* and its attachment for phonological support may be subject to a restriction that *de* can only target and attach itself to a host which is phonologically 'strong' in the sense of being a syllable which bears a tone and is not destressed. Verbal *le* is always destressed and has lost any original tone it may have had and can therefore be suggested not to be strong enough to constitute a suitable target for *de*'s cliticization, blocking pattern (4b) and *de*'s movement to the verb.[12] Instead, as pattern (4a) is available as an option, *de* in such cases will simply cliticize to the right edge of the AspP (which does contain a strong syllable). Such an account of (60a) and (61b) in terms of the suitability of the potential phonological host for encliticization can also be argued to be supported by further patterns with *de*. First of all it can be noted that the unacceptability of (61b) is actually not specifically due to the fact that it instantiates pattern (4b) with movement of *de* over the object; if there is no overt object present at all as in (62), it is similarly unacceptable for *de* to attach to a verbal base suffixed with *le*:

(62) wo shi zuotian mai(*le) de.
   I BE yesterday buy (ASP) DE
   'It was yesterday that I bought (it)'

As (62) could in theory be an instantiation of either pattern (4b) or (4a) (i.e., in syntactic terms *de* in (62) could either be moving to the verb or it could be attaching to the right edge of AspP), this indicates that it is the creation of a sequence of [*V-*le-de*] *in any way* in *shi-de* forms which is unacceptable and that it is not pattern (4b) which is specifically blocked by the occurrence of *le* on the verb. Clearly something in the surface string [*V-*le-de*] (rather than its derivation) must therefore be responsible for the unacceptability of such forms, and here this is suggested to be the weakness of the suffixed base that *de* as a clitic is attempting to attach to. Secondly, it can be observed that when *de* is attached to a base suffixed with the experiential marker *guo* as in example (63), *guo* in such cases is regularly pronounced with its optional tone 4 rather than being destressed into neutral tone as is common elsewhere, supporting the assumption that *de* needs to cliticize to a phonologically stronger syllable:

(63) (?)naxie difang wo shi qunian gang qu-guo-de. jinnian bu qu le.
those place I BE last year just go-EXP-DE this year NEG go ASP
'It was only last year that I visited those places. I don't want to go again this year.'

Such patterns then seem to suggest that *de* can only attach to host element which is phonologically unreduced. Given that clitics are commonly defined as being elements which are syntactically independent but in need of phonological support, and that clitics also frequently undergo movement to find an appropriate phonological host, the restrictions observed in (61-63) then add additional plausible support for the general encliticization analysis of *de*'s attachment and repositioning.[13]

Two further syntactic arguments can now also be added on here as general support for the structure in (58) and the assumption that there is movement of the AspP constituent from complement-of-T position to SpecTP. The first of these requires a reconsideration of how it is that *wh*-adjuncts can legitimately occur in past tense examples such as (47) and (48). In section 2 it was noted that if non-past occurrences of *de* in *shi-de* relate to an underlying CNP structure but past time interpretations project instead a TP, then various contrasts in acceptability between past and non-past *shi-de* structures with *wh*-adjuncts and pre-*shi* adverbs could be reasonably explained, CNPs but not TPs being syntactic islands for the licensing and interpretation of such elements. If however it is now assumed that the AspP constituent in *shi-de* forms occurs in a *specifier* position as in (58), such a structure might in fact be expected to constitute an island for the licensing of *wh*-adjuncts as configurationally it closely resembles a sentential subject structure and such constituents have indeed long been observed to be islands for *wh*-adjuncts (see e.g., Huang 1982). Here it can be suggested that in order to allow for the legitimate occurrence of *wh*-adjuncts in past tense *shi-de* constructions it has to be assumed that at some derivational point the AspP containing such elements must also occur in some other non-specifier position which does not constitute an island for *wh*-adjunct licensing. The suggestion that the AspP originates as a rightward complement to T^0 prior to raising to SpecTP combined with the copy-theory of movement (Chomsky 1995a) or simple reconstruction now offers the possibility of explaining the relevant lack of island effects with *wh*-adjuncts here.[14] If it is assumed that the licensing of *wh*-elements in Chinese occurs at the level of LF in some way (either via movement or *in situ* binding), it can be suggested that either the AspP clause reconstructs to its base complement position and any *wh*-adjunct present inside is licensed in this reconstructed non-island constituent, or that *wh*-adjuncts are licensed as part of the copy left in the complement-of-T^0 position by movement of the AspP. Consequently it can be argued that it is indeed necessary to assume that the AspP originates in complement position before being raised to the surface SpecTP position, and it cannot be suggested that the AspP is perhaps reanalyzed as being somehow directly base-generated in the leftward SpecTP position.

An argument can also be made that the AspP does indeed *raise* from its underlying complement position to a higher specifier position. An alternative to such an assumption might possibly to suggest that the AspP is instead *base-generated* as a *leftward complement* to T^0 and does not occur in a specifier position at any point in the derivation. Against such an analysis, which would clearly be a head-final structure out of alignment with the dominant head-initial direction of selection in Chinese, it can be suggested that the AspP arguably needs to occur in a higher specifier position in order for raising and cliticization of *de* to the verb to be possible. Elsewhere cliticization has been regularly found to be movement upwards rather than downwards in a tree; if the optional cliticization of *de* to the verb is also naturally assumed to follow this strong cross-linguistic generalization, it would seem that the AspP containing the verb targeted by *de* cannot be in simple complement position as this would clearly involve *de* undergoing a *lowering* operation to its target. Rather, it would seem that such a constituent should instead be assumed to be located in a higher position in the tree in order for raising of *de* to occur, such as indeed the specifier position suggested. The derivation suggested in (58) with the AspP constituent originating as the rightward complement of T^0 and then raising higher to the leftward SpecTP position is then generally supported by a range of phenomena.[15]

Finally in this section, having motivated and defended the structure and derivation in (58), I will turn to consider how this partial structure combines with the element *shi* to result in full *shi-de* focus forms and what the status of *shi* may be in these larger reanalyzed structures. I will also attempt to offer an answer to a general question raised by the claim of D-to-T reanalysis with *de*, which is: why is it that *de* as a new instantiation of past tense does not in fact occur with every verb having a past time interpretation?

Approaching these issues, I would like to suggest that recent ideas on the syntax and structure of tense proposed in Stowell (1996) allow for a modeling of *shi-de* sentences which accurately reflects both the syntactic properties and the interpretation of *shi-de* forms, and it can be argued that past tense *shi-de* sentences are in fact largely similar to English complex perfect tense forms.

An important piece of information concerning the status of *shi* in *shi-de* sentences comes from the way that A-not-A questions are composed. As illustrated in (64), significantly it is the element *shi* which is doubled in such question forms:

(64) ni shi-bu-shi zuotian lai de?
you SHI-NEG-SHI yesterday come DE
'Is it yesterday that you arrived?'

This patterning is potentially important and revealing, as elsewhere it is generally found that the element which is repeated in A-not-A forms is a verb/auxiliary which is interpreted as being finite (i.e., the doubled element is the highest verb/auxiliary in a finite clause). Examples such as (64) therefore seem to suggest that *shi* is both verbal and also finite not only in non-past *shi-de* forms where its complement is assumed to be a DP, but also still in past-time interpretations where it has been argued that *de* heads a TP constituent.[16] This hypothetical co-occurrence of two finite specifications in *shi-de* structures (with both *shi* and *de*) is clearly in need of some explanation and possibly might seem to challenge the past tense analysis of *de*, suggesting that *shi* rather than *de* should be considered to be the head of TP in *shi-de* sentences. Here I believe that a comparison of *shi-de* structures with English *have -en* perfect tense forms such as (65) and in particular Stowell's (1996) analysis of the perfect tense now offers a simple and natural solution to this apparent problem:

(65) a. John has eaten all the doughnuts.
b. Mary has bought War and Peace.

Set within a broad new theory of the syntactic structure of tense, Stowell (1996) suggests that the English perfect tense form made up of the verb 'have' together with a second inflected verb is in fact a complex tense construction which critically comprises *two* finite tense forms, rather than a single tense+participial form. Stowell argues that the interpretation of (present) perfect forms such as (65) is that a past event described by the *en*-inflected lexical verb is related to a present speech time encoded in the auxiliary *have*, and that syntactically *both* lexical verb and auxiliary project discrete instantiations of tense in the complex structure, present (or sometimes past in past perfect forms) with the auxiliary and past with the lexical verb. The result of the presence of the two tense forms is that the event described by the lexical verb is interpreted as having taken place prior to the speech time (hence in the past) and to have relevance to the (present) speech time.

Turning back to Chinese *shi-de* sentences, such an analysis of the perfect tense can be suggested to be exactly what is necessary to capture the apparent properties and interpretation of *shi-de* forms. Having seen that both *shi* and *de* individually show signs of being +finite and consequently associated with discrete tense positions, it can now be pointed out that *shi-de* sentences significantly also have interpretations similar to English perfect forms in depicting past time events which are stressed as having clear relevance to/in the present/speech time. Such aspects of the *shi-de* construction can be simply captured if it is assumed, following Stowell's analysis of the English perfect, that both *shi* and *de* in fact project tense positions and TP constituents and that the past tense encoded in *de* is embedded under a present tense specification with *shi* as in (66) below:[17]

(66)

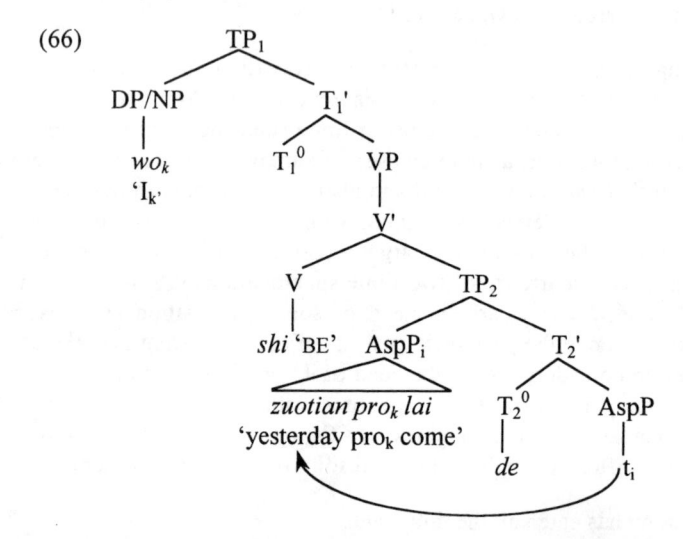

```
                    TP₁
                   /    \
              DP/NP      T₁'
                |       /    \
              wo_k    T₁⁰     VP
              'I_k'            |
                               V'
                              /  \
                             V    TP₂
                             |   /    \
                        shi 'BE' AspP_i    T₂'
                                /    \   /    \
                        zuotian pro_k lai  T₂⁰   AspP
                        'yesterday pro_k come'  |     |
                                                de    t_i
```

Such a structure not only licenses the A-not-A patterning found, *shi* being associated with the structurally higher +finite T⁰ and therefore naturally being the element repeated in A-not-A forms, the embedding of past-time TP₂ under present-time TP₁ can also be argued to naturally encode the interpretation of strong present relevance of a past event. (66) furthermore provides an explicit answer to the initial question of how *shi* and the *de*-headed TP combine together—*shi* as a higher verbal/auxiliary element in such structures selects for the TP headed by *de*.

Considering the question of why *de* as a new instantiation of past tense is not found to occur with every verb having a past time interpretation, the analysis in (66) can be suggested to offer the relevant answer here and a TP headed by *de* will essentially only appear if it is indeed selected by the element *shi* (or a phonetically null equivalent, as *shi* need not always be overt in *shi-de* structures). In this sense the occurrence of *de* in T⁰ will be very similar to that of the English past tense form *-en* in perfect constructions such as (65), *-en* only surfacing as an instantiation of past when selected by the auxiliary verb 'have.' Concerning the element *shi* itself, given its regular association with the creation of a cleft-like focus interpretation, *shi* will in turn only be selected from the lexicon when a focus interpretation is indeed required, and in this sense will be similar to the common (optional) use of the English auxiliary verb 'do' to cause readings of emphatic focus in examples such as (67):

(67) a. I do like this cake
b. Jane does know how write a good letter.

The distribution, syntax and interpretation of *de* as a past tense morpheme can consequently be given a principled account in line with recent assumptions about the structure of complex tense forms and the properties of similar elements in other languages. Having also discussed how other aspects of the syntax of past tense *shi-de* forms can be explained under the assumption of D-to-T reanalysis and the conversion of a CNP-type structure into a simple TP constituent, I now close the chapter with a brief summary and consideration of D-to-T reanalysis as a general hypothetical phenomenon, and (in an appendix to the chapter) with a discussion of how focus may be formally encoded in the *shi-de* construction.

4.4 Summary: D-to-T and Paths of Grammaticalization

This chapter set out to establish the categorial status and syntax of clause-final *de* in the Chinese *shi-de* construction. Section 1 began by arguing that the optional repositioning of *de* adjacent to the verb together with the necessary past time interpretation of the verb in such configurations strongly suggests that *de* instantiates the category of past tense when cliticized to the verb. As non-past interpretations of *shi-de* forms are however possible with *de* in post-object position, section 2 concluded that *de* must also be able to instantiate a category distinct from tense and that speakers consequently allow for a dual analysis of the element *de*. Taking this non-past *de* to be nominal-modifying *de*, section 2 then suggested that non-past *shi-de* sentences may be assumed to contain a CNP type structure with a phonetically empty head, and that such a hypothetical structure would allow for a natural account of restrictions on *wh*-adjunct and adverbial occurrence in non-past interpretations. The lack of similar restrictions with post-object past time interpretations of *de* then resulted in the conclusion that *de* in such instances has also undergone reanalysis as the past tense head of a TP and that the optionality in placement of past tense *de* is essentially due to cliticization of *de* targeting two potentially different hosts V and AspP, clitics elsewhere frequently showing such optionality in their attachment. Section 3 finally motivated the formal syntax assumed to underlie the reanalysis of *de* in T, and argued that this is reanalysis of an original D element, resulting in the creation of a complex new tense form similar to the English perfect. In this last (main) section of the chapter, I would like to now briefly reflect on certain general aspects of the hypothesized D-to-T reanalysis and on implications of the analysis for the theory of grammaticalization.

A first issue which arises from the suggestion that there is D-to-T reanalysis in the *shi-de* construction is whether it is in fact *generally* plausible and likely that an element of type D actually would undergo reanalysis as an element of type T, or whether such a category change is fully unexpected and therefore rather suspicious despite the empirical evidence supporting the assumption of a D-to-T reanalysis. Here I believe it can in fact be positively concluded that a D-to-T category switch is in fact a rather natural change because the functional roles performed by D and T elements in their respective nominal and clausal domains can be argued to be fundamentally very similar, both being deictic elements providing reference to their respective complement constituents. In D-to-T reanalysis it can therefore be suggested that the definite reference-fixing property of a D element may simply come to be reinterpreted in the locus of temporal reference and definiteness in the clause, the T-position, and that such a categorial reanalysis is therefore not an unnatural change, a functional element effectively just re-applying its underlying deictic/referential function in/to a new (clausal) type of domain. Reconsidering the particular case of *de* in the *shi-de* construction, it was earlier noted that use of this element consistently results in an interpretation in which the past or future occurrence of some background event is heavily presupposed and therefore constitutes knowledge which the speaker assumes is shared by the hearer. In this sense the use of *de* consequently signals and marks the background event encoded in the predicate as being *definite* (i.e., identified, unique, shared knowledge) and so functions in a way which is similar to other D/determiner elements. In the D-to-T reanalysis argued for in *shi-de* forms, it can therefore be suggested that this definite reference-marking function present with *de* is simply reinterpreted in the clausal domain as applying in a purely temporal manner and *de* indeed not unnaturally comes to be understood as marking past tense, deictically fixing the reference of its clause as being identified at some point prior to the present/speech time.

Assuming that D-to-T reanalysis is then in principle not an implausible type of categorial switch, this raises the natural question of whether it is a reanalysis which might in fact have occurred in other instances besides *de*. Here there are indeed two other cases which can be mentioned which I believe may also qualify as occurrences of D-to-T conversion, adding further potential support for such a possibility in general. The first of these relates to a language known as Panare (Venezuela) studied in Gildea (1993), where it is found that demonstrative pronouns occur as linking elements between subject DPs and predicate nominals. Gildea points out that the proximal/distal deictic orientation of such linking demonstratives may often be different from and apparently in conflict with that of other demonstrative elements present in predicate nominal constructions. Gildea argues that in such cases there actually is no conflict in spatial deixis and suggests that the linking 'demonstratives' have now in fact been reanalyzed as copulas, with their original proximal and distal deixis value now giving rise to interpretations of future time and past time reference rather than any spatial deixis. If Gildea is correct here, and demonstratives are assumed to be elements of type D^0, the Panare predicate nominal construction can then similarly be argued to be an instance of D-to-T reanalysis. Another possible case of D-to-T conversion may actually have occurred in English in the apparent reanalysis of the demonstrative element 'that' as a clausal complementizer. In Pesetsky and Torrego (2001) a wide range of syntactic arguments and evidence have recently been presented for the assumption that the English complementizer 'that' is in fact synchronically first base-generated in T^0 and then subsequently raised up to C^0. If Pesetsky and Torrego are indeed right and 'that' is an instantiation of T^0 as well as C^0, given that such an element is known to have developed from a demonstrative/D^0 this offers once again the clear possibility of a further case of D-to-T reanalysis.

The conclusion that D-to-T conversion is a reanalysis which has occurred in Chinese and possibly also elsewhere can now be noted to have consequences for the general theories of categorial reanalysis and the mechanisms which underlie and permit grammaticalization phenomena. In Simpson (1998a, 1998b), Simpson and Wu (2001, 2002a), Roberts and Roussou (1999) and chapters 2 and 6 of the present book, it is argued at some length that grammaticalization is a process of reanalysis resulting from *movement* within a syntactic tree. In all these works it is suggested that if a lexical element α regularly undergoes movement from an original position X to a higher position Y in the functional structure projected over X, then over time the element α may eventually come to be reanalyzed as a simple instantiation of Y rather than X. When such grammaticalization and reinterpretation of the lexical element α occurs, α is subsequently base-generated directly in the higher functional head (or alternatively specifier) position Y as indicated in (68), and the lower position X is instantiated by a new lexical element (β in 68b):

(68) a.

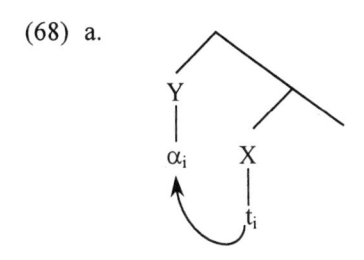

CHAPTER 4

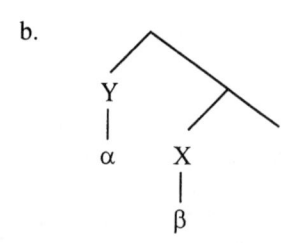

b.

```
        Y
        |
        α    X
             |
             β
```

    This general process of movement-dependent reanalysis and grammaticalization also occurs when α is in fact already a functional (rather than a lexical) element, the result in such cases being that α becomes re-grammaticalized as a higher head/X^{MAX} occurring in the functional structure (see chapters 2 and 6 of this volume). With the creation of new tense/auxiliary morphemes, the natural expectation is that such elements will also follow this common path of grammaticalization and arise from the reanalysis of lower light verbal elements raised into the functional structure dominating VP. While such reanalysis does seem to regularly occur as expected (as, for example, in the common development of future tense verbs from original lexical verbs of desire such as English *will*), the patterns found with *de* and the creation of a new past tense morpheme from a functional element originating in the nominal domain now significantly seem to offer good evidence for the general availability of a second quite different path of grammaticalization. This additional route of categorial reanalysis does not result from any movement and reanalysis within a single lexical-functional domain, but instead critically involves the reanalysis of a functional category from one lexical-functional domain as a functional head in a discrete second type of domain, a kind of 'lateral' cross-domain reanalysis/grammaticalization. Although such reanalysis may (perhaps) be more restricted in its occurrence than the alternative movement-assisted grammaticalization, it can nevertheless now be argued to constitute a genuine possibility when assisted and permitted by properties of the embedding syntactic structure, as indeed seen with *de*, where a null-headed CNP/clausal nominalization (by hypothesis) allows for reinterpretation as a simple clause headed by *de* in T^0. The *shi-de* paradigm and the reanalysis of *de* consequently allow for potentially important insights into general mechanisms of grammaticalization.

    Finally, D-to-T conversion also allows us to speculate on possible constraints on the general process of cross-domain reanalysis. In recent years, researchers such as Abney (1987), Szabolcsi (1994) and many others have suggested that there is a significant similarity and parallelism in the internal structure of DPs and clauses with various functional elements in the nominal domain corresponding to similar elements in the clausal domain. If there is indeed such a correspondence relation between functional heads in DPs and clauses, the occurrence of D-to-T conversion may suggest that a natural restriction on lateral grammaticalization linking elements in different domains may perhaps be that this is an operation only possible between nominal and clausal functional heads which indeed stand in a formal equivalence relation. Precisely how the various functional heads in nominal and clausal domains do in fact parallel and relate to each other is clearly a matter for much further investigation, however the obvious similarity of D and T elements in their reference-providing functions suggests that these two elements at least should be considered to be functional equivalents and that it is this parallelism in role and correspondence relation which has licensed conversion from one domain to the other.[18]

4.5 Appendix: on the Focus Interpretation of *Shi-de* Forms

The central interest of this chapter has been on the hypothetical grammaticalization of *de* as a new tense marker in *shi-de* forms and how this has had interesting observable effects on the syntactic structure of such constructions. The chapter has therefore concentrated primarily on aspects of the past/non-past tense interpretation in *shi-de* forms rather than on the focus interpretation which is more frequently the center of discussion in analyzes of the *shi-de* construction. For completeness and before closing the chapter I would however briefly like to consider how the focus interpretation may perhaps be syntactically encoded in *shi-de* forms, and note that there are two fairly obvious possibilities here—either LF movement or (LF) binding.

In both Chiu (1993) and D. Shi (1994) it is suggested that the element *shi* instantiates the X^0 head of a focus projection which Chiu refers to as ShiP. If one assumes that the selection of *shi* either results in the projection of a FocusP over VP or that the VP headed by *shi* is itself interpreted as a focus-licensing projection, the question then arises as to how an element in focus syntactically relates to this projection and how the focused interpretation of an element such as *zuotian* 'yesterday' in (69) below is licensed in the structure:

(69) wo shi zuotian mai piao de.
     I   BE yesterday buy ticket DE
     'It was yesterday that I bought the ticket.'

Frequently it has been observed that it would seem to be the element which is right-adjacent to *shi* which is the focus in *shi-de* forms, and hence that *gen Zhangsan* in (70) cannot encode the sole focus, rather this must be *zuotian*:

(70) wo shi zuotian gen Zhangsan mai piao de.
     I   BE yesterday with Zhangsan buy ticket DE
     'It was yesterday that I bought the ticket with Zhangsan.'

Possibly one might imagine that this necessary interpretation of the right-adjacent element as the focus results from some kind of overt movement of the element to a position related to the focus head *shi*. However, there is fairly

153

simple evidence that this is not so and that the focused element is not related to *shi* via overt movement. In (71) and (72) for example, it is not possible to overtly move the object of the verb either to a position following *shi* nor to a position preceding it in order to contrastively focus it (note that (72) is grammatical, but the object is not contrastively focused, rather it is *zuotian* which is contrastively focused):

(71) *wo shi nei-zhang piao zuotian mai de.
     I BE that-CL ticket yesterday buy DE

(72) wo nei-zhang piao shi zuotian mai de.
     I that-CL ticket BE yesterday buy DE
     'It was yesterday that I bought the ticket.'

If overt movement therefore does not relate a focused XP to *shi* and FocusP, there are two other plausible ways in which the focus relation might be established and licensed. One possibility is that an element in focus might raise to SpecFocusP at LF in order for this focus relation to be licensed, as essentially suggested in Chiu (1993) and D. Shi (1994). A second possibility is that *shi* or the head of FocusP might alternatively *bind* a focused element in its *in situ* position at LF and license its focus in this way. Both potential approaches would be fully compatible with the structures argued for in this chapter, with *shi* selecting a rightward DP/TP in (57) and (66).

What both types of account do need to explain in some kind of way is the observation that there appears to be a Spell-Out adjacency requirement holding between *shi* and the focused XP in *shi-de* sentences (as noted above in 70). This might seem to be somewhat surprising given that the licensing of the focus relation between *shi* and the XP is arguably only established at LF either via LF movement or binding.[19] However, there are in fact ways of understanding the apparent Spell-Out adjacency requirement in both LF movement and LF binding approaches which avoid the conclusion that it is linear adjacency of *shi* and the focused XP which is really required at Spell-Out. In order to show this as clearly as possible, I will first provide a clarification of the fuller restrictions on what may be interpreted as a legitimate focus in *shi-de* forms.

With regard to the licensing of focus in *shi-de* sentences, the following observations need to be explained in any account. First of all, if two adjuncts occur following *shi* as in (70), it is only the structurally higher adjunct adjacent to *shi* which can be licensed as the sole contrastive focus in the sentence, as already noted above. Secondly, it appears that only an XP/X^{MAX} constituent can be focused by *shi* and not a head X^0-level element such as a verb/V^0. Consequently in (73) it is not possible to contrastively focus just a verb (either *lai* 'come' (73iii) or *kan* 'see' (73iv)). In (73) either the embedded VP$_2$ [*kan Zhangsan*] 'see Zhangsan' (73i) or the DP object 'Zhangsan' (73ii) can constitute the focus in the sentence:

(73) wo shi [[$_{VP1}$ lai [$_{VP2}$ kan [$_{DP}$ Zhangsan]]] de].
       I   SHI   come   see   Zhangsan   DE
       (i) 'Its to see Zhangsan that I've come (here).'
       (ii) 'Its Zhangsan that I've come to see.'
       (iii) NOT: 'Its to SEE Zhangsan that I've come (not to BEAT him).'
       (iv) NOT: 'I CAME to see Zhangsan (I didn't GO to see him).'

The above patterning can essentially be captured if the constraints in (74) and (75) below are assumed as relevant for the determination of focus-licensing in *shi-de* forms:

(74) The licensing of focus in *shi-de* sentences
      The focus in a *shi-de* sentence is the structurally highest overt X^{MAX} YP c-commanded by *shi*/Focus^0, or the structurally highest and overt X^{MAX} ZP contained within YP.

(75) Maximality restriction on the focus in the *shi-de* construction
      It is not possible for the focus to be the entire overt sequence following *shi*.

If we consider (70), the adjunct *zuotian* adjoined to IP will be structurally higher than *gen Zhangsan* (which is perhaps adjoined to VP) and so will be selected as the natural focus, c-commanded by *shi*/the Focus head. In the absence of any time, place or manner adjuncts as in (73), there will be two potential choices for the focus. The sequence [*lai kan Zhangsan*] is the structurally highest overt constituent c-commanded by *shi* but this sequence cannot be the focus due to the pragmatic maximality restriction in (75), which essentially seems to require that at least *some* of the material following *shi* be old, presuppposed information not in the focus. The structurally highest overt X^{MAX} c-commanded by *shi* which is not the maximal overt string following *shi* is the embedded VP$_2$ [*kan Zhangsan*]. This VP is therefore a legitimate candidate for the focus of the sentence (a YP in 74 which does not violate 75). (74) also allows for the structurally-highest and overt X^{MAX} ZP contained within such a YP to be a potential focus, and so the object DP *Zhangsan* is also a legitimate focus in (73).

It can therefore be seen that the apparent linear adjacency restriction found in cases such as (70) is in fact just a part of a wider configurational restriction on the availability of a constituent as a possible focus in *shi-de* forms. Furthermore, there are elements such as DP objects *not* linearly adjacent to *shi* which the configurational restrictions in (74) and (75) allow to legitimately function as foci in *shi-de*.

Finally it can be suggested that the structural/hierarchical constraint in (74) together with the more pragmatic maximality condition in (75) may potentially be understood as being restrictions on either movement or perhaps binding relations relating the focused XP to *shi*/FocusP. If an XP is licensed as the

CHAPTER 4

focus of a *shi-de* sentence as the result of LF movement, it can be suggested that (74) and (75) essentially determine what is structurally visible to *shi*/Focus^0 and so constrain what is potentially available as a target for attraction by the focus head to SpecFocusP. Alternatively, however, if focus is licensed in *shi-de* forms by a non-movement LF binding relation, it can be argued that (74) and (75) similarly restrict which elements are visible to *shi*/Focus^0 for binding and licensing as an associated focus. Licensing via binding in such a way could then be naturally understood as being similar to the non-movement licensing of *wh* elements *in situ* by a c-commanding +Q C^0 as originally proposed in C. L. Baker (1970) and more recently in Tsai (1994).

Notes

[*] It should be noted that this chapter is largely the result of joint work carried during 1999-2000 with Andrew Simpson and published independently as Simpson and Wu (2002b).

[1] Various other options are also attested, though not so frequently, e.g., focusing of a whole IP including its subject when *shi* precedes the subject, focusing of the entire VP, and focusing of the object (see the above-cited references and section 5 of the present chapter for further details).

[2] As for example in Chiu (1993) with LF movement of the focused XP to Spec-ShiP, Huang (1982) with *shi* as an adverb undergoing LF raising together with the focus, and D. Shi (1994) for a similar LF-related idea.

[3] Note that the contrast between (8) and (9) again indicates that the neutral underlying base form should be (4a) rather than (4b).

[4] A simple example of this given in Hopper and Traugott concerns the development of the English connective 'since' which originally encoded only a temporal relation between two clauses as in (i):

(i) Since I started playing the lottery, I have won four times.

Later on a *causal* relation between the two clauses became a common conversational implicature:

(ii) Since Yeltsin came to power, there has been nothing but economic trouble.

Currently 'since' may sometimes also be used with only a causal meaning simply because of the long-term strengthening of this implicature, as seen in (iii):

(iii) Since you know about economics, can you give me a hand?

A similar story underlies German *weil* 'because', which developed from a relative to the English noun 'a while' (German: *eine Weile*); however, unlike 'since', *weil* may now no longer be used with a temporal meaning and can only encode causality (see again Hopper and Traugott 1993).

[5] Although the precise connection between nominalization and presupposition certainly requires more formal understanding, one can note that it is nevertheless a phenomenon which surfaces in a wide range of languages in different ways. For example, in Thai, Japanese and various other languages one finds that predicates which embed *factive* complements (whose content is hence definite and presupposed) may syntactically nominalize such clausal complements (in Thai with the nominalizer *thii*, in Japanese with *no*), whereas non-factive clausal complements are embedded as simple (non-nominalized) clauses.

[6] Or alternatively a headless clausal nominalization; here in the text I will generally pursue the former CNP possibility, and note that assuming the latter headless nominalization analysis may perhaps not lead to any very different results.

[7] The alternative is to assume that there is no N-head present and there is just a simple clausal nominalization preceding *de* in *shi-de* forms as noted earlier. However, the assumption that there is a CNP analysis with a phonetically null N-head has the advantage that it allows for an account of the unacceptability of *wh*-adjuncts in non-past interpretations of *shi-de* forms as discussed in section 2, CNPs being clear islands for *wh*-adjuncts elsewhere. As it is not clear that clausal nominalizations would necessarily instantiate islands for the interpretation/licensing of such elements, this would seem to favor the CNP analysis over a bare clausal nominalization approach.

[8] Here it can be noted that where a similar light N does have phonetic content in Burmese, and a similar kind of reanalysis appears to be occurring, the light N undergoes 'fusion' with the T element, collapsing as a single morphological form. As pointed out in examples (37) and (38), in cleft forms similar to Chinese *shi-de* sentences the light N *haa* 'one/thing' collapses with the preceding T morpheme *teh* to result in *taa*. Significantly, when this happens, the result cannot be optionally separated out into *teh* and *haa* (**teh haa*) and only the fused form *taa* occurs. This is unlike the behavior of *haa* elsewhere with D^0 demonstrative elements where the fusion of the D^0 *dii* and *haa* is quite optional and allows for either of the forms in (37) repeated here as (i):

(i) a. *dii haa* 'this (one)'
 b. *daa* 'this (one)'

If a nominal-based cleft construction is indeed undergoing reanalysis in Burmese in a way similar to Chinese, it can be argued that part of this reanalysis is the elimination of the light N via a process of incorporation of the N into the (new) T^0 element. Chinese, which does not have the problem of the need to re-interpret any phonetic material associated with a light N can perhaps just eliminate such an element without any prior syntactic N-to-D incorporation being necessary.

A similar kind of fusion may however elsewhere have occurred in classical Chinese resulting in modern Chinese *-zhe* '(the) one who does the V' as in *jizhe* 'reporter (one who reports/records).' One can speculate that here some nominal element incorporated into the classical Chinese D^0 *zhi* (modern Chinese *de*) changing the vowel quality of *zhi* and resulting in a new complex fused/collapsed element.

[9] This of course indicates the conclusion that Chinese is a language which has 'special' clitics, i.e., clitics which undergo movement and repositioning. Such a suggestion has in fact been previously made in Tang (1990) about the element *de* in descriptive and

CHAPTER 4

resultative constructions, which Huang (1988) notes occur in early Chinese in forms parallel to (i) and (ii). Tang (1990:250) suggests that these are formed via movement of the clitic *de* over the objects *shu* and *du* to the verb:

(i) du [-de shu duo]
 read DE book many
 'to read a lot'

(ii) zhong [-de du shen]
 get DE poison deep
 'to be seriously poisoned'

A similar implication that *de* in modern-day resultative constructions may be attached to the verb via cliticization from a non-adjacent position in a lower clause is present in work by Yafei Li (1998), who convincingly shows that the post-*de* 'subject' *Lisi* in *de*-resultatives embedded by transitive verbs such as in (iii) is actually the object of the higher clause. If it is then assumed that *de* originates as the complementizer of the lower clause, it has to be concluded that it reaches its surface position via cliticization movement over the object of *kua* to the verb *kua* itself:

(iii) Zhangsan kua-de Lisi dou bu xiang gan huor.
 Zhangsan praised-DE Lisi all NEG want do work
 'Zhangsan praised Lisi to the extent that she didn't want to do any work.'

[10] Note that the cliticization of past tense *de* to the verb resulting from a base structure such as (53) will involve cliticization of *de* from the head T^0 to an element (the verb) inside SpecTP. Cliticization of this type to a position contained within a higher constituent has been observed to occur in a number of instances elsewhere, for example Serbo-Croat where pronominal and auxiliary clitics attach to an element inside the constituent in SpecTP as in (i). Here the clitics *mi* and *je* occur encliticized to the demonstrative heading the DP in SpecTP:

(i) [DP Taj-mi -je pesnik] napisao knjigu.
 that me AUX poet wrote book
 'That poet wrote me a book.' (Spencer 1991)

It can also be noted that there is further clear optionality of attachment here and the same clitics may be attached to the right-edge of the DP instead of inside the DP:

(ii) [DP Taj pesnik] -mi -je napisao knjigu
 that poet me AUX wrote book
 'That poet wrote me a book.'

[11] In order to account for the possibility that *de* may occur either directly attached to the verb or to the V+IO complex, one can assume that indirect object incorporation is not always forced to occur. Note also that there are additional restrictions on the acceptability of DOCs combined with *de* which relate to complex constraints on the relative definiteness values of direct and indirect object. These I do not attempt to investigate here for simple reasons of space.

[12] The fact that *le* and *de* share the same shwa vowel sound may perhaps be another factor contributing to the unacceptability of V-le-de sequences, given that languages frequently disprefer the adjacent positioning of distinct morphemes which are either

158

identical in sound or have a high degree of similarity (see, for example, Boskovic 1999).

[13] Example (63) is not fully acceptable however, due to the fact that the same sentence without *guo* actually sounds better. Quite possibly some aspect of the meaning of experiential *guo* is not fully compatible with the meaning of *de*. However, there is indeed a contrast between (62) and (63). I am suggesting that an unreduced syllable is a better candidate for the clitic *de* to attach to. (63) is a better sentence because *guo* allows for an unreduced tone (tone 4), whereas (62) is completely unacceptable because *le* is always reduced.

The patterns noted here might also seem to distinguish the *clitic* status of *de* from the suffix status of other elements such as verbal *le*. In contrast to *de*, verbal *le* can in fact easily be attached to a weak destressed syllable, and in (i) the experiential marker *guo* can be quite naturally pronounced in neutral tone reduced form when followed by *le*:

(i) wo qunian yi-nian   jiu qu-guo-le henduo difang.
    I last year one year then go-EXP-ASP many   place
    'Within last year alone I had been to many places.'

This difference between *le* and *de* may reasonably follow if *le* and *de* are indeed attached at different derivational points as indeed suggested by the patterning noted with DOCs in (59) and (60) above. If *le* is attached in the lexicon as a suffix and *de* is attached in the syntax as a clitic, they might well be subject to somewhat different restrictions. Clitics in particular seem to need phonological support from a stronger element present in the structure and so might consequently be more likely than suffixes to require this host to be regularly stressed/not destressed.

[14] For arguments that clausal-type constituents obligatorily reconstruct see Heycock (1995) and also Huang (1993).

[15] The conclusion that the AspP has to occur in both positions combined with the observation that *de* can cliticize to either AspP or V^0 has an additional consequence which needs to be pointed out here. Previously, in the CNP structure (52), it was suggested that movement of the AspP is triggered by *de*'s need to encliticize to an element in its Spec position. If past tense *de* can now undergo cliticization to the V^0 as well as the AspP, it is difficult to maintain that movement of the AspP prior to cliticization of the *de* to the verb is itself for cliticization purposes. Here I suggest that movement of the AspP has simply been 'inherited' by the new TP structure as a part of the general process of reanalysis and is now a 'fossilized' automatic movement no longer driven by cliticization requirements but instead formally legitimized by the occurrence of strong *v*-features on T attracting the AspP constituent to SpecTP. For further discussion of how grammars may allow the introduction of categorial features on heads as a means to legitimize movements whose initial motivation has undergone change, see Simpson (2001).

[16] See also Huang (1990) for claims that *shi* is an auxiliary verb in *shi-de* sentences.

[17] Note that TP here actually is a simplification of the tense structure proposed in Stowell's works, but sufficient to represent the basic intuition here.

[18] For further evidence of the close relation of D and T elements see Lecarme (1996) where it is suggested that demonstratives in Somali give rise to temporal interpretations and may even be coming to encode tense *within* DPs.

[19] Given that the focus relation is one of *interpretation*, it might be difficult to suggest that it is established via binding at any point prior to LF such as Spell-Out/PF.

5

RESULTATIVE CONSTRUCTIONS
DIRECTIONALITY AND REANALYSIS

5.0 Introduction

Chapter four discussed in detail the ongoing syntactic change taking place in *shi-de* structures when a sentence-final *de* re-positions itself between the verb and its object. In the course of the chapter it was mentioned that such re-positioning of an element from a sentence-final position to one right-adjacent to the verb in fact has a clear historical precedent in Mandarin Chinese and that the element *le/liao* is known to have undergone a similar change in position. This surface parallelism in the re-positioning of *de* and *le* discussed in chapter four is schematized below in (1):

(1) a. V Object de → V-de Object
    b. V Object liao → V-liao/le Object

The present chapter focuses on a third potential instantiation of the same patterning diachronically found in the creation of resultative constructions such as Modern Chinese (2) and (3) below:

(2) ta xi-ganjing yifu le.
    he wash clean clothes LE
    'He washed the clothes clean.'

(3) wo kan-wan shu le.
    I look-finish book LE
    'I have finished reading the book.'

Forms such as (2) and (3) in which two verbal elements occurring adjacent to each other produce a resultative meaning historically derive from sequences in which the second verbal element actually followed the object of the first verb.[1] The development of the modern resultative construction therefore seems to parallel the patterns noted in (1a) and (1b) with a sentence-final element re-positioning itself over the object of the main descriptive verb to be right-adjacent to this verb, as indicated in (4):

161

CHAPTER 5

(4) V_1 Object V_2 → $V_1 - V_2$ Object

Chapter five attempts to see how a better understanding of the change in pattern (1a) as established in chapter four may now offer useful insights into the earlier change which took place in pattern (4) with resultative constructions, continuing this general theme in chapter six with a detailed re-examination of the similar diachronic re-positioning of *le/liao* in (1b).

In both chapter five and chapter six I set out to answer the following important questions:

(5)   a. What was the reason for the re-positioning of the sentence-final element into a new position right-adjacent to the main lexical verb?
      b. What is the current syntactic status of such constructions?

Broadly this chapter will argue that the second verb V_2 in resultative constructions has the status of an aspectual suffix combined with the main verb V_1 in the lexicon and licensed/checked by discrete aspectual projections which dominate the VP, contra recent syntactic accounts of resultative V-V sequences in Zou (1993) and Sybesma (1999). In sections 5.2 and 5.3, which concentrate on resultative forms, it is suggested that the movement/re-positioning of V_2 to its present position right-adjacent to V_1 occurred as part of a reanalysis process in which V_2 became reanalyzed as instantiating an aspectual head. Specifically it is proposed that the following steps took place in the reanalysis process. First of all, assuming that V_2 may have originally been licensed in some kind of predication relation with the object of V_1, it is suggested that a significant increase in focus on the telic aspectual contribution of V_2 in the construction subsequently led to the reanalysis of V_2 as *primarily* an aspect marker (with certain additional inherent lexical content). Secondly, as a direct result of this re-orientation of the primary contribution of V_2 from being one of direct predication of a lexical property onto the object of V_1 to being one of aspectual modification of the predicate, syntactically V_2 came to be reanalyzed as predicating of the V_1 and its object together. Formally this resulted in V_1 and its object being reanalyzed as a VP occurring in the Spec of an aspectual projection headed by V_2. Thirdly, V_2 as Asp^0 underwent re-positioning and apparent movement to V_1 in a way highly similar to the movement of *de* to the verb after *de* reanalyzed as T. However, whereas movement of *de* to the verb occurring (in the VP) in SpecTP is resulting in a new *tense* suffix on the verb, in the case of resultative V_2 re-positioning this has created new aspectual suffixes. The chapter then argues that this V_2-re-positioning was actually not triggered by any phonological reasons or clitic properties of the V_2 but significantly occurred in order to re-align the relevant AspP in accord with the canonical direction of selection in Mandarin and harmonize the location of the AspP with the head-initial parameter setting in Chinese.

Quite generally the chapter shows how current changes in *shi-de* forms and the conclusions reached in chapter four allow for critical insights into the restructuring process when sentence-final elements undergo re-positioning over objects and attach to verbs, using this to arrive at a new account of Chinese resultative constructions. The chapter also shows how the development of a general process of suffixation in head-initial languages has a natural explanation in terms of headedness and directionality. This offers a formal interpretation of typological claims that in every language there is internal pressure for a single direction of selection and that any examples of non-canonical directionality in selection relations will undergo 'correction' over time on account of such pressure. Finally, the chapter adds certain speculations on how alternations in resultative constructions in English and various other languages might be re-considered in the light of the suggested analysis of Chinese.

The structure of this chapter is as follows. In section 5.1.1, I introduce the phenomena of resultative verb constructions (henceforth RVCs) in full, and then follow this in 5.1.2-5.1.4 with a critical overview of certain recent lexical and syntactic approaches to RVCs, notably those in Yafei Li (1990), Zou (1994) and Sybesma (1999). In 5.1.5, I raises a number of objections to the syntactic accounts in Zou and Sybesma. In 5.2 and 5.3 I then gradually develop an alternative and fully general analysis of the synchronic and diachronic syntax of RVCs which argues for an aspectual suffix status of V_2 elements and invokes the notion of directionality in functional selection as an explanation for the re-positioning of the V_2 element. In 5.4 I give a brief look at the consequences of the analysis for certain other structures, and close the chapter in 5.5 with a speculation on how the analysis suggested for Chinese resultatives can offer insights into English verb-particle constructions.

5.1 Previous Analyses

5.1.1 *Resultative Verb Constructions: an Introduction*

In Li and Thompson (1981), Yafei Li (1990) and many other works, V-V sequences such as (2) and (3) above are actually referred to as resultative verb *compounds,* which necessarily infers that they result from a *lexical* concatenation process. Here I employ instead the more neutral term resultative verb construction/RVC to refer to such strings, in order to avoid any premature classification of their origin as either lexical or syntactic. This term RVC does however refer to the same set of V-V sequences in all major accounts.

In Li and Thompson (1981) RVCs are basically defined as consisting of a sequence of two adjacent verbal elements in which the second element 'signals some *result* of the action or process conveyed by the first element.' (p.54). RVCs are then broadly divided into three basic sub-types which can be referred to as *literal RVCs, directional RVCs* and *phase RVCs*. Literal RVCs are those RVCs which do not fall into the latter two RVC categories and are illustrated in examples (6-9) below:

Literal RVCs
(6) ta   zuotian   cai   xi-ganjing yifu.
    she yesterday then wash-clean clothes
    'She just washed the clothes clean yesterday.'

(7) Zhangsan yijing   pao-lei-le.
    Zhangsan already run-tired-LE
    'Zhangsan has already got tired from running.'

(8) Baoyu xia-shu-le   qi.²
    Baoyu play-lose-LE chess
    'Baoyu play chess and lost.'   (Yafei Li 1990)

(9) Lisi da-si-le Baoyu.
    Lisi hit-dead-LE Baoyu
    'Lisi beat Baoyu until Baoyu died.'

Directional RVCs are those RVC sequences which involve a V_2 which signals some clear directionality to the action denoted by V_1. As noted in Li and Thompson, there may even be more than one directional verb following the V_1 action verb, as seen in (12) and (13):

Directional RVCs
(10) ta song-lai   yi-ge xiangzi.
     he send-come one-CL case
     'He sent over a case.'

(11) wo   fang-xia   wo-de-shubao le.
     I   put-descend my-satchel   LE
     'I put down my satchel.'

(12) ta   tiao-guo   he le.
     he jump-cross river LE
     'He jumped across the river.'

(13) tamen pao-chulai le.
     they   run-out   LE
     'They came running out.'

Finally, 'phase' RVCs are classed by Li and Thompson as sequences 'in which the second verb expresses something more like the *type* of action described by the first or the degree to which it is carried out rather than its result' (p.65). Typically phase RVCs encode simply the completion of an event/action rather than providing additional lexical description of the result state that an object might be in after application to it of the first verb. Hence in the literal RVCs (6) and (9) the V_2 explicitly classifies the object as being respectively 'clean' and 'dead' as a result of the action of the V_1, whereas in phase RVCs such as (14-17) below the V_2 indicates primarily just completion of the action and no finer description of the end-state of the object is included:

Phase RVCs
(14) ta nian-wan shu le.
  he study-end book LE
  'He finished studying.'

(15) Zhangsan xie-hao-le xin le.
  Zhangsan write-good- LE letter LE
  'Zhangsan finished writing the letter.'

(16) ta mai-dao nei-ben shu le.
  he buy-arrive that-CL book LE
  'He managed to buy that book.'

(17) ta mei jie-zhu nei-ge qiu.
  he NEG receive-live/fix that-CL ball
  'He did not catch that ball.'

Precisely how all such sequences should be syntactically analyzed poses many challenging and interesting questions and has consequently been the subject of a large number of theoretical works in recent years. In what follows I now present an overview of two contrastive views of RVCs which can be taken to broadly represent two fundamentally different approaches commonly adopted in the literature—the 'lexical' approach and the 'syntactic' approach.

5.1.2 *The Lexical Approach—Yafei Li (1990)*

In a careful and interesting piece of work, Yafei Li (1990) provides a lexical compounding analysis of RVCs which largely succeeds in accounting for constraints on the productivity of V-V sequences. Prior to Li's work, no serious formal attempt had been made to model the creation of RVCs in a way which also reflected the many restrictions on their interpretation, and in this regard Yafei Li (1990) constitutes a significant step forward in the analysis of RVCs.

Yafei Li begins by considering examples such as (18) which have been noted to have two possible interpretations as indicated:

CHAPTER 5

(18) Baoyu qi-lei-le nei-pi ma.
Baoyu ride-tired-LE that-CL horse
(a) 'Baoyu rode the horse and as a result Baoyu got tired.'
(b) 'Baoyu rode the horse and as a result the horse got tired.'

Li points out that if the two verbs are compounded together in the lexicon as traditionally believed, then technically the combination of *qi* 'ride' and *lei* 'tired' might be expected to result in a compound verb with a total of three theta-roles—two theta roles from the transitive verb *qi* and one from the intransitive stative verb *lei*. As there are only two argument NPs present in (18) and hence the compound RVC projects only two theta roles, it is clear that any lexical compounding account of RVCs needs to explain precisely how the theta-grids of two verbs are combined into a single argument structure. In particular a lexical account needs to explain: (a) how the number of theta roles in the theta grid of a new compound verb may often be less than a simple total of the theta roles associated with each verb, and (b) what constraints there might be on the combination of the theta grids of both verbs when compounded. These two explanations together should then account for why it is that only a specific sub-set of the imaginable interpretations in compounding is available.

To capture a wide range of restrictions on the interpretation of RVCs, Li proposes a mechanism of 'theta-identification' in which a theta role from one verb may be identified with a theta role in the second verb's argument structure and consequently assigned to a single argument of the newly compounded V-V form. For example, if V_1 *qi* 'ride' in (18) has an external and an internal theta role labeled $[_{V1}1]$ and $[_{V1} 2]$ and V_2 *lei* 'be tired' just has a single theta role $[_{V2} 1]$, then either $[_{V1}1]$ and $[_{V2} 1]$ can be identified and assigned to the same DP resulting in interpretation (a), or $[_{V1} 2]$ and $[_{V2} 1]$ can be identified and assigned to the same DP to give interpretation (b):

(19) a. V1   V2
        qi 'ride' *lei* 'be tired'
        $[_{V1}1]$ = $[_{V2} 1]$
        $[_{V1}2]$
        → X rides and X gets tired: 'the rider became tired'
    b. V1   V2
        qi 'ride' *lei* 'be tired'
        $[_{V1}1]$
        $[_{V1}2]$ = $[_{V2} 1]$
        → X rides Y and Y gets tired: 'the horse was ridden and got tired'

When two transitive verbs are combined, and if one restricts one's attention to instances where there are two overt DP arguments licensed by Case in a sentence, it is noted that there are four ways in which the theta grids might potentially be integrated together via theta identification. However, only one of these four potential combinations actually is instantiated in natural language, the one depicted in (20) and illustrated with example (21):

(20) V1V2
    [V1-1] = [V2-1]
    [V1-2] = [V2-2]

(21) Jiaoda de zhuren da-ying-le zhe yi zhang.
    Jiaoda DE master hit-win-LE this one battle
    'Jiaoda's master fought and won that battle.'

In order to account for the non-occurrence of other potential combinations (and also to explain complex restrictions on further combinations of transitive and intransitive V_1-V_2 pairs), Li proposes a number of constraints on the combinatorial/identification process. These include assuming that V1 is the head of the compound in Chinese, that external theta roles have a greater prominence than internal theta roles and that there is also a critical 'prominence-sensitive' *ordering* in the way that theta identification is carried out. Without going into the full details of the proposals here, it can be said that generally what emerges is in fact a highly successful lexical account of restrictions on the combination process, and one which offers a formally tight implementation of the view that V_1-V_2 RVC formation is indeed an instance of compounding in the lexicon. It should also be noted that Li rejects the possibility that RVCs might be created in the syntax and opts for a lexical-compounding approach for a rather simple but important reason. Li suggests that if both V_1 and V_2 were to project discrete VPs in the syntax and be combined by head-movement from V_2^0 to V_1^0 then one would have to assume that V_1 *selects* for the VP headed by V_2 as a complement.[3] However, as there would not seem to be any obvious selection relation holding between V_1 and a complement VP headed by V_2 in V_1-V_2 pairings (Li maintains), such a syntactic analysis is argued to be unrealistic and unavailable.

5.1.3 The Syntactic Approach—Zou (1994)

A recent example of a syntactic approach which reacts to the lexical proposals in Yafei Li (1990) is found in Zou (1994). Zou argues that Li is incorrect when he dismisses the possibility of a selection relation existing between V_1 and a separate VP headed by V_2. Noting the observation made commonly in the literature that V_2 consistently encodes a result which is directly caused by the activity of V_1, Zou suggests that there is indeed a semantic relation between V_1 and V_2, and that V_1 "implicates" V_2 in V_1-V_2 pairs. Zou then proposes that this semantic implication relation between the two verbs may be captured by suggesting that V_1 selects for a second VP depicting the outcome of V_1 and that this latter VP is indeed headed by V_2. In Zou's words:

"The event conveyed by the first verb "implicates" the event conveyed by the second VP. Following Chomsky (1985) and Hale and Keyser (1993), this implication relation is then "canonically structurally realized" as a complementation relation between the first verb and the second VP, as the syntactic embedding corresponds to a semantic composite in which the event denoted by the second VP is a proper part of the event denoted by the first verb." (p.279)

An RVC such as (22) with the (b) reading will then have a structure approximately as in (23), the V_2 *lei* 'be-tired' raising overtly to V_1 *zhui* 'chase':

(22) Baoyu hui zhui-lei Lisi.
Baoyu will chase-tired Lisi
(a) 'Baoyu will chase Lisi and Baoyu will get tired as a result of it.'
(b) 'Baoyu will chase Lisi until Lisi gets tired.'

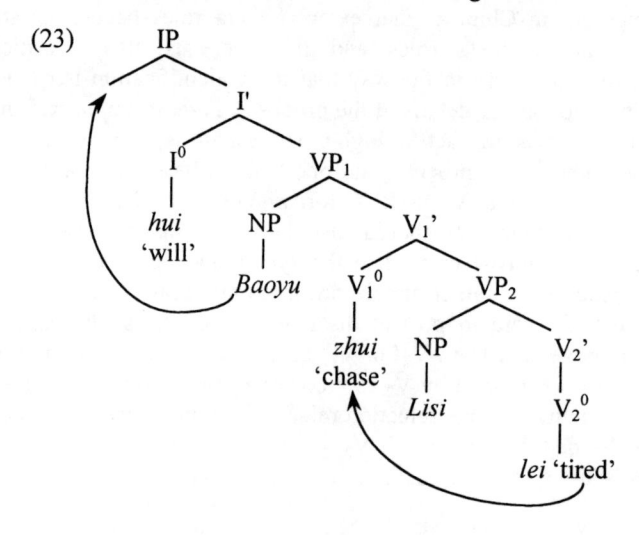

(23)

In fact, because (22) is ambiguous, there will be other syntactic structures which will correspond to the other interpretations. For example, the (a) interpretation that Baoyu chased Lisi and Baoyu got tired is suggested to result from the structure in (24).

(24)

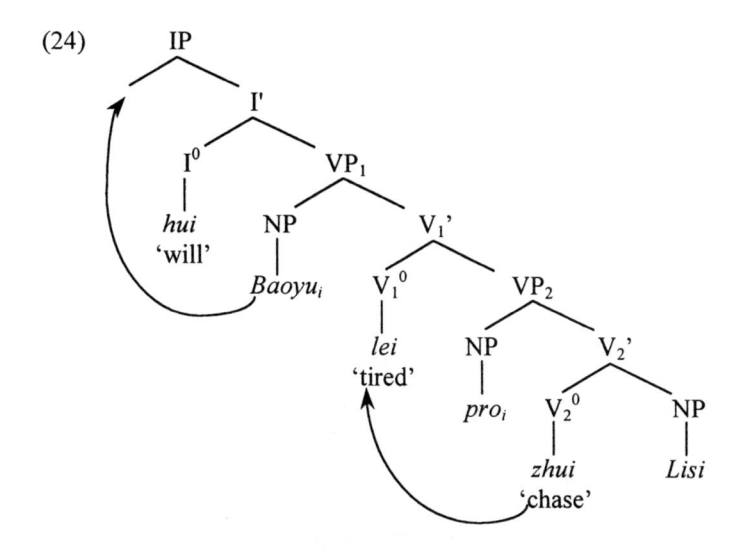

```
                IP
               /  \
              /    I'
             /    /  \
            / I⁰     VP₁
            | |      /  \
            | hui   NP   V₁'
            | 'will' |   /  \
            |     Baoyuᵢ V₁⁰  VP₂
            |          |    /  \
            |          lei NP   V₂'
            |         'tired' |  /  \
            |              proᵢ V₂⁰  NP
            |                   |    |
            |                  zhui  Lisi
            |                 'chase'
```

Note that the underlying linear order of *zhui* 'chase' and *lei* 'be-tired' in (24) is in fact actually the reverse from the order in (23). Zou assumes that the surface linear order of the V_1 and the V_2 will in all cases be determined by the following independent linearization principle which applies after V_2 has raised up to V_1:

> The verbal morpheme denoting an activity linearly precedes the verbal morpheme denoting the result of such an activity, no matter what their prior order is. (p.280)

In both (23) and (24) the relations between the predicates and their arguments is syntactically clear and all theta roles are assigned in standard ways. Where the subject *Baoyu* is interpreted as receiving a theta role from both V_1 and V_2 this results from the additional presence in the structure of a *pro* controlled by the subject of VP_1. As VP_2 is taken to be selected by V_1, the raising of V_2 to V_1 is also syntactically legitimate. Zou therefore suggests that a syntactic account of RVCs is consequently not only possible once one recognizes the existence of a selection relation between V_1 and $V(P)_2$, but also desirable for the reason that it is well able to represent the thematic relations in V_1-V_2 forms in a highly transparent way. Finally Zou adds that a syntactic account is superior to a lexical approach because it can be easily adapted to model certain other 'causative' RVCs which may be problematic for Li's lexical account. In examples such as (25), the surface subject *zhei-ping-jiu* 'this bottle of wine' has no direct thematic relation with either of the verbal predicates present *zui* 'get/be drunk' and *dao* 'fall-over'; consequently it is not obvious how it might be licensed to appear in Li's approach:

(25) zhei-ping jiu zui-dao-le Lisi.
this-bottle wine drunk-fall-LE Lisi
'Due to this bottle of wine, Lisi got drunk and fell over.'

Zou suggests that in (25) there is an additional third VP dominating the regular RVC V_1-V_2 shell and that *zhei-ping-jiu* 'this bottle of wine' is base-generated as a causative argument in the specifier of this VP. The syntactic account proposed by Zou therefore allows for relatively easy extension to cover such cases.

5.1.4 Sybesma (1999), Hoekstra (1992)

A second more recent syntactic treatment of RVCs which explores a VP-shell type approach in much greater depth is Sybesma (1999). This interesting work draws its original inspiration in large part from ideas on resultative constructions set out in an imaginative paper by Hoekstra (1992). In the latter paper, Hoekstra isolates a number of canonical properties of resultatives cross-linguistically and uses them to build a novel account of resultatives. Specifically it is noted that resultatives consistently seem to exhibit the following classic properties:

(26) a. The main predicate is a dynamic activity verb:
   John washed the clothes clean.
   b. A secondary element (an adjective, particle or PP) predicates a property of the object of the main verb, but never predicates on the subject:
   John$_k$ washed [$_{NP}$ the clothes]$_i$ clean$_{i/*k}$.
   Mary$_k$ looked [$_{NP}$ the words]$_i$ up$_{i/*k}$.
   Sue$_k$ sang [$_{NP}$ Mary]$_i$ to sleep$_{i/*k}$.
   c. The result state predicated of the object of the main verb serves to make the main activity verb aspectually bounded and telic
   d. Frequently an *intransitive* activity verb may be followed by an 'object NP' and a predicate:
   John laughed himself weak.
   Bill ran his sneakers threadbare.

Putting this information together, Hoekstra suggests that both transitive and intransitive dynamic activity verbs may select for a *small clause* representing a (result) state predicated of an NP which is the subject of that small clause. Aspectually the small clause functions to provide an endpoint to the activity depicted by the main verb and convert it into a telic predicate, and critically it is this aspectual role which licenses the selection relation between the main verb and the small clause as its complement.

Subsequently considering Chinese RVCs, Sybesma (1999) then focuses in on the well-documented property of such constructions that inclusion of the V_2

element results in the V_1 becoming telic, and proceeds to build the Hoekstra approach to resultatives into a well-developed account of Chinese RVCs. For V_1-V_2 sequences such as (27) below, Sybesma suggests that the V_2 occurs base-generated in a small clause selected by V_1 and that V_2 predicates directly onto the NP subject of the small clause from this position.[4] At some point prior to Spell-Out the V_2 will then raise up to right-adjoin to V_1, as depicted in (28) (where only the VP structure is shown, and the subject of V_1 is not included).

(27) xi-ganjing yifu
    wash-clean clothes

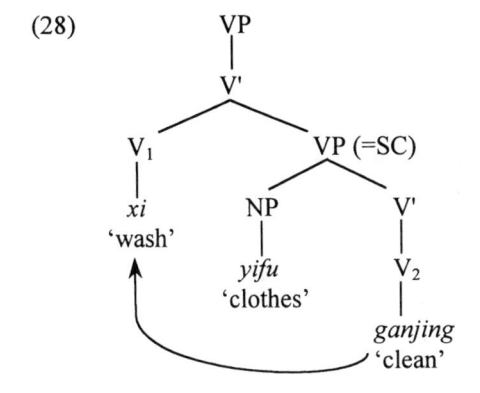

(28)
```
              VP
              |
              V'
             / \
           V₁   VP (=SC)
           |   / \
           xi NP  V'
         'wash' |  |
              yifu V₂
            'clothes' |
                   ganjing
                   'clean'
```

In support of the small clause analysis Sybesma observes that historically there were indeed linear sequences of [V_1 NP V_2] which parallel the posited underlying structure in (28) and that such [V_1 NP V_2] sequences at a later stage became [V_1 V_2 NP] sequences. The small clause analysis then suggests that synchronic [V_1 V_2 NP] forms still actively derive from a base order which was that of earlier resultatives.

Sybesma also points to the existence of a similar resultative construction built with the resultative morpheme *de* (meaning 'to the extent of') where the V_2 is again lower than the NP following V_1, as in (29):

(29) ta xi-de   yifu   hen ganjing.
    he wash-DE clothes very clean
    'He washed the clothes clean.'

Sybesma suggests that the NP *yifu* 'clothes' can be suggested to be in a predication relation with V_2 *ganjing* 'be-clean' here, and that V_1-V_2 resultatives and [V_1-de NP V_2] resultatives are similar in many ways. The occurrence of forms such as (29) with the linear sequence of [V_1 NP V_2] might then again be seen as suggestive of a V_2-raising analysis of V_1-V_2 sequences, with (29) being something like the base underlying order which results in V_1-V_2 surface forms.[5]

Chapter 5

As in Hoekstra's analysis of resultatives above, Sybesma suggests that the small clause structure in (28) encodes a result state predicated of an NP and that this result state critically functions to make the V_1 predicate aspectually telic. Such an aspectual relation is also taken to license the selection of the small clause by V_1. Note also that an important bi-product of the Hoekstra/Sybesma small clause approach is that there is no direct selection relation between V_1 and the NP which might standardly be considered to be its object. For example, in the English resultative: *John washed [sc the clothes clean]*, it is the small clause AdjP which is the complement selected by the V_1 *washed* and there is no thematic selection relation between V_1 *washed* and the NP *clothes*. This NP is licensed solely by its predication relation with the small clause predicate *clean*. The same is true in Chinese (28) and there is no thematic relation between V_1 *xi* 'wash' and the NP *yifu* 'clothes' which is base-generated inside the VP-small clause as subject to the predicate *ganjing* 'clean.' Commenting on the relation between V_1 and the NP, and following an idea in Kayne (1985), Sybesma suggests that there is only a pragmatic linking between V_1 and the NP, and that the interpretation of a structure such as (28) is essentially as in (30):

(30) interpretation of (28): wash [clothes (are/become) clean]
 + There is a washing event.
 + The state of the clothes being clean aspectually closes the washing event.
 → Pragmatic implicature: if the clothes are clean and they are part of a washing event, then they can be assumed to have been washed.
 → Pragmatically the NP is inferred to be the object of V_1.

Considering the interaction of verbal *le* and V_1-V_2 sequences, Sybesma makes the interesting and novel suggestion that verbal *le* is actually also a resultative predicate and therefore occurs as the head of a small clause. The subject of its small clause in the case of a V_1-V_2-le sequence will in fact also be a small clause and the proposed underlying (VP) structure and derivation of (31) is shown in (32):

(31) xi-ganjing-le yifu
 wash-clean-LE clothes
 'washed the clothes clean.'

(32)

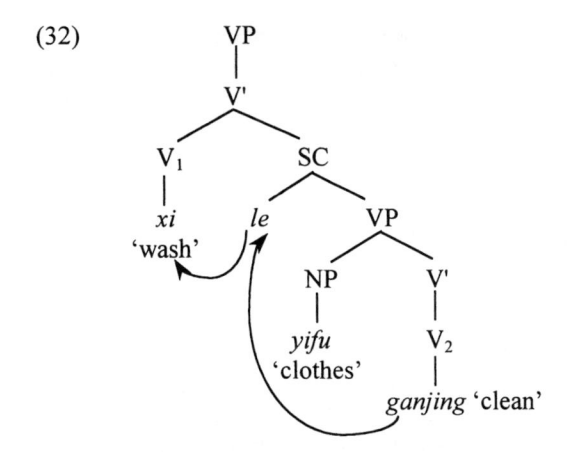

```
           VP
           |
           V'
          / \
        V₁   SC
        |   / \
       xi  le  VP
     'wash'   / \
             NP  V'
             |   |
            yifu V₂
         'clothes' |
                ganjing 'clean'
```

The V₂ *ganjing* 'be-clean' will raise to *le* forming *ganjing-le* and then this unit will move higher to V₁ and result in the surface sequence: *xi-ganjing-le yifu*.

Sybesma's account highlights interesting parallels between the posited underlying structure for RVCs and earlier diachronic sequences and current [V₁-de NP V₂] resultatives. Together with Zou's analysis, it furthermore demonstrates that a genuine syntactic alternative to Yafei Li's lexical account can indeed be carefully formulated. Finally, Li's principal objection to a syntactic approach that V₁ cannot be taken to select for a second VP headed by V₂ is intelligently responded to: such a selection relation arguably may be motivated on aspectual grounds, VP₂/SC serving to provide a telic bound to the action depicted by V₁.

5.1.5 *Objections to the Syntactic Approach*

In spite of the attractions mentioned above, I would however like to argue that there are a number of reasons why such a syntactic account is not fully satisfactory and that one might therefore pursue an alternative solution.

First of all neither Zou nor Sybesma actually provide any real explanation of the movement of V₂ to V₁, so it is not clear why it takes place and why one doesn't instead find sequences with the earlier historical order: [V₁ NP V₂]. Zou states that: "the verb-raising from V₂ to V₁ is motivated by the V-V compound formation (p.282)." However, compounding is obviously a *lexical* operation and so critically may *not* be invoked in a syntactic analysis. Whereas V₁-V₂ adjacency is a natural consequence of a lexical compounding approach, it really remains significantly unaccounted for in a syntactic treatment of the type outlined by Zou.

Sybesma originally treats V₁-V₂ forms and V₁-de V₂ resultatives such as (31) and (29) as parallel and suggests that a functional head 'Ext(ent)P' present in the structure always must be filled with overt phonetic material. This is argued to be possible in either of two ways—if the morpheme *de* is present, it occurs in Ext^0 and a lower V$_2$ will remain *in situ* as in (33). If *de* is not present, the V$_2$ will be forced to raise to provide Ext^0 with overt material as in (34):

(33) xi [$_{ExtP}$ -de [$_{VP2}$ yifu   ganjing]]
    wash   DE   clothes   clean

(34) xi [$_{ExtP}$ ganjing$_i$ [$_{VP2}$ yifu   t$_i$]]
    wash   clean   clothes

The raising in (34) can therefore be taken to be responsible for the surface V$_1$-V$_2$ adjacency. However, later on in the development of the account of RVCs, Sybesma concedes that V$_1$-V$_2$ forms and V$_1$-de V$_2$ resultatives have different structures and that an ExtP is not projected in the former RVC type. Consequently the V$_2$ raising is left without any motivation in this account (also as noted in Zou's analysis), and as this is clearly a critical component of the syntactic approach, it is quite unsatisfactory if it cannot in fact be motivated in any way and is only assumed in order to capture the linear sequence of elements. Given that V$_2$ elements such as *ganjing* 'clean' are clearly not clitics, the hypothetical raising can obviously not be triggered by phonological reasons either.

Secondly, a conceivable problem for both Zou and Sybesma concerns the occurrence of the aspectual morpheme *le* following V1-V2 sequences as in (35).

(35) Baoyu xi-ganjing-le   yifu le.
    Baoyu wash-clean-LE clothes LE
    'Baoyu has washed the clothes clean.'

Zou assumes that *le* is an aspectual morpheme located in Infl. This being so, Zou is forced to suggest that V$_2$ first raises up to V$_1$, and then the V$_1$-V$_2$ complex raises higher to Infl where *le* is then attached. However, if the V$_1$-V$_2$-le sequence overtly raises to Infl, then VP adverbs should be found to follow such sequences. This is not what occurs, and as shown in (36), VP-adverbs occur to the left of verbs carrying *le*. Such a pattern clearly argues against an analysis of overt verb raising to Infl.

(36) ta manmarde xi-ganjing-le   yifu.
    he slowly   wash-clean-LE clothes
    'He slowly washed clean the clothes.'

A rather different *le*-related problem occurs in Sybesma (1999). Sybesma states that one of the explicit goals of his own investigation into resultatives is to provide an account of the V$_1$-V$_2$-*le* linear word order i.e., why one finds this order and not any other such as *[V$_1$-le-V$_2$], etc (p.67). Approaching this issue, Sybesma suggests that *-le* is a type of V$_2$ element which heads the VP-internal small clause structure shown in (32). Such a treatment of verbal *le* and RVCs consequently avoids the problem noted for Zou's approach, namely that V_1-V_2-le sequences linearly *follow* VP-adverbs. However, the actual V_1-V_2-le ordering itself is actually *not* derived in any particularly straightforward way as a result of the underlying structure posited in (32). As seen in (32), first the V_2 has to raise and *left*-adjoin to *le* and then this unit has to raise and *right*-adjoin to the V_1. In such a derivation there is no obvious reason why verb-raising in RVCs should result in attachment to different sides of the target raised to (i.e., to the left-side in the first case and to the right-side in the second), and it seems that the choice is made purely in order to mirror the final surface form. Sybesma indeed concedes that:

> If we were to strictly follow Kayne (1994), an underlying structure like (32) [my numbering] would lead to Y-*le*-V [i.e., **ganjing-le-xi* = V_2-le-V_1]. It seems to be the case that in order to derive the right surface order we need to stipulate that in the lexicon it is somehow determined and recorded that *le* is a suffix: it has to come last. (p.76)

Consequently it seems that a syntactic analysis which was designed to account for the word order by positing an underlying structure which would give rise to this is actually unable to output more complex surface form involving *-le*, and a stipulation is required in order to re-convert the output of the syntactic derivation into the attested linear sequence. Furthermore, it should not be possible for the notion 'suffix' to be legitimately employed here; if an element is classified as a suffix, this signifies that it attaches in the lexicon and not within the syntax. In short there seems to be no straightforward way to ensure that both V_2 and *le* attach to V_1 in the syntax and have this attachment mirror the surface order if an underlying order such as (32) is assumed. It should be also noted that the same ordering problem occurs in Zou's account. As mentioned above, Zou is forced to evoke an independent linearization principle which will regularly 'correct' a number of V_1-V_2 orders outputted by the syntax which do not correspond to the surface order found (e.g., correct *lei-zhui* 'tired-chase' to *zhui-lei* 'chase-tired'). The goal of capturing the linear ordering of V_1-V_2-le sequences via a syntactic approach therefore turns out to be unexpectedly difficult.

The small clause account of RVCs would also seem to go against a rather common assumption held about lexical and functional elements, that the latter occur in a syntactic superstructure which dominates a lexical projection (e.g., Grimshaw 1991). The small clause approach to resultatives in Chinese would however seem to be building functional categories into positions which are actually under and dominated by the lexical predicate VP. If one takes the clear aspectual nature and contribution of the V_2 and also *le* in particular to reflect a functional role, one might expect these elements to correspond to functional heads located *above* rather than below the VP. Nevertheless, in (32) *le* is built in as a functional-type head *below* the lexical predicate V_1. Related to this, if one takes the position that V_2 and *le* are *not* related to aspectual heads projected higher than the VP, then it is difficult to explain the co-occurrence restrictions which are found between V_2, *le* and aspectual heads which do occur higher than VP in aspectual projections, as e.g., in (37) adapted from Sybesma (1999), where *le* cannot co-occur with the pre-VP aspectual head *zhengzai* (I return to this point later on):

(37) wo zhengzai ca-gan-(*le) boli.
I ASP-PROG wipe-dry LE glass
'I am just wiping the glass dry.'

A fourth potential objection to the proposed small clause analysis of RVCs concerns the conclusion that there is no direct theta relation between V_1 and the NP which might intuitively seem to be its object, i.e., that there is no theta relation between *xi* 'wash' and *yifu* 'clothes' in (31/32). Supposing the NP occurring after the V_1-V_2 unit were to relate to V_1 only via some rather loose pragmatic inferencing, as noted above, rather than stand in a verb-object relation, then one might expect all kinds of interpretations to be possible which do not in fact occur. For example, it is not clear why sentences such as (38) would be ill-formed when compared with (39):

(38) *Lisi ba Zhangsan   jiao-xing-le Baoyu.
Lisi BA Zhangsan call-awake-LE Baoyu
Intended: 'Lisi called Zhangsan and Baoyu awoke as a result of this.'

(39) Lisi jiao-xing-le Baoyu.
Lisi call-awake-LE Baoyu
'Lisi called and Baoyu awoke as a result of this.'

The small clause hypothesis predicts that (38) should have the following interpretation: 'Baoyu resulted in being awake because of a calling event.' In the absence of *ba Zhangsan* as in (39) it is suggested that we pragmatically *infer* that Baoyu was actually the object of the calling event as a natural salient interpretation. However, if a third NP is introduced in a *ba*-NP form or possibly as a sentence-initial topic as in (40) it is expected that this NP could be taken to be the pragmatically inferred object of the scolding action if this could result in a coherent interpretation (for example if Zhangsan was in the same house that Baoyu was sleeping in and Lisi's calling of Zhangsan could wake up Baoyu). The fact that such an interpretation is unavailable suggests that the NP following V_1-V_2 is the object of V_1 in a strict syntactic way.[6]

(40) *Zhangsan ne, Lisi jiao-xing-le Baoyu.
Zhangsan TOP, Lisi call-awake-LE Baoyu
Intended: 'Lisi called Zhangsan and Baoyu awoke as a result of this.'

RESULTATIVE CONSTRUCTIONS

A final, important general criticism of the small clause analysis of resultatives is that very often there is in fact no clear predication relation between the hypothetical small clause head/V_2 and the 'object' NP. This is true for both English and Chinese. For example, consider (41) and (42) below:

(41) John looked [$_{SC}$ [$_{NP}$ the reference] up].

(42) Mary beat [$_{SC}$ [$_{NP}$ Peter] stupid].

The small clause analysis predicts the following interpretations for these sentences:

(43) *interpretation of (41)*:
The reference is up as a result of a looking event carried out by John.

(44) *interpretation of (42)*:
Peter is stupid because of a beating event carried out by Mary.

However, it is meaningless to say 'the reference is up', and the interpretation of (42) is *not* that Peter is stupid after a beating event. Basically 'up' and 'stupid' only convey the meaning they do *through combination with the V_1* 'look' and 'beat' and there is no isolated predication relation between the particle/adjective and the 'object' NP. The small clause analysis clearly leads one to expect that the 'object' NP and the following particle/adjective should be able to stand in a regular predication (together with a form of the copula to carry tense/agreement) without the need for a higher secondary predicate, yet this is not so. Either the result is meaningless ('*The reference is up.') or the output does not mirror the actual interpretation of a sentence when added to a higher predicate (i.e., (42) does not mean [John is stupid] + [this state terminates a beating event]; 'stupid' only has its non-literal meaning 'badly-hurt' when combined with 'beat'—for example, one cannot point to someone after they have been beaten and simply say: 'He is stupid now.'). The same is true of many examples of V_1-V_2 resultatives in Chinese; although (45) is fine, it would not seem to result from combining the parts in (46):

(45) wo   liu-zhu-le   ta.
I   detain-live/fix-LE he
'I stopped him (I made him stay).'

(46) [ta zhu-le = he lived/was fixed] + [this was a result of a detaining event]

As in many other cases, *zhu* in (45) can not have its literal meaning 'to live' and can only have the non-literal meaning of being motionless precisely when combined with another verb. For example, one cannot paraphrase (45) with (47):

177

CHAPTER 5

(47) wo liu-le ta. *jieguo ta jiu zhu-le.
 I detain-LE him result he then live/fix-LE
 'I detained him. As a result he lived/was fixed.'

Similarly (48) does *not* mean: [We talked] + [the state that [Christmas arrived] terminated this talking event], that is, it does not mean we talked until Christmas. However, such an interpretation is what is expected from a small clause underlying structure such as (49):

(48) women tan-dao-le shengdanjie.
 we talk-arrive-LE Christmas
 'We talked about Christmas.'

(49) women tan [-le shengdanjie dao].
 we talk LE Christmas arrive

With other V_2 elements if one attempts to isolate the object NP and the V_2 into a single sentence predication, the result is unacceptable in any reading as in (50) and (51).

(50) a. ta zhao-zhao-le nei-ben shu.
     he search-catch-LE that-CL book
     'He managed to find that book.'
   b. *nei-ben-shu zhao-le.
     that-CL-book catch-LE
     '???'

(51) a. ta xianzai zhu-jin-le xin-fangzi.
     he now live-enter-LE new-house
     'He has now moved into the new house.'
   b. *xin-fangzi jin-le.
     new-house enter-LE
     '???'

With intransitive V_1 elements, it is suggested in Sybesma (1999) that the surface subject originates as the subject of the small clause and is predicated of by the V_2, shown in (52) and (53).

(52) pao [$_{sc}$ ta lei-le] → ta pao-lei-le.
   run he tired-LE he run-tired-LE
     'He got tired as a result of running.'

(53) wan [$_{sc}$ ta ni-le] → ta wan-ni-le.
   play he bored-LE he play-bored-LE
     'He got bored of playing.'

178

However in other examples, isolation of the V₂ and such a subject NP often results in a quite different meaning. As shown below, the meaning of the sentence in (54a) does not indicate that the subject originates from the small clause as schematized in (54b), since the result of being afraid is not that the NP *women* 'we' end up dying. The isolation of the subject and V₂ and the subject also often results in a quite unacceptable forms, as shown in (55):

(54) a. women dou pa-si-le.
    we   all fear-die-LE
    'We were all scared to death.'
  b. [women si-le = we died] + [this was a result of a fearing event]

(55) a. ta zou-kai-le.
    he walk-open-LE
    'He walked away. (!He got open as a result of walking.)'
  b. *ta kai-le.
    he open-LE
    '???'

The compositional account of resultatives in which the meaning of a small clause encoding a predication relation is added to the meaning of a higher verb cannot be effectively maintained, it would seem. Either the small clause often has no meaning on its own or its meaning may be quite different from the interpretation found in complex V₁-V₂ sequences.[7]

It should be noted that though the counter-examples presented here are mostly "phase resultatives" of some sort, they nevertheless constitute legitimate arguments to the small-clause analysis, as the small-clause analysis is also intended to apply to resultatives with phase V₂ elements. It is also natural that both phase and descriptive resultatives should be represented with the same underlying structure given the fact that literal V₂s and phase V₂s both contribute a telic bound to the activity and significantly never co-occur, as shown in (56) and (57):

(56) *ta xi-ganjing-wan   yifu le.
    he wash-clean-finish clothes LE
    intended: 'He finished washing the clothes clean.'

(57) *ta xi-wan-ganjing   yifu le.
    he wash-finish-clean clothes LE
    intended: 'He finished washing the clothes clean.'

Historical facts also point in the same direction. First literal V₂s appeared in [V₁ object V₂] resultatives during Qin/Han Dynasties, then phase V₂s came to appear in the V₂ position of the same structure during the Wei/Jin/Northern and Southern Dynasties (G. Wu 1999), and finally both literal V₂s and phase V₂s collectively underwent their repositioning to V_1 in the Song Dynasty (C. Li and Y. Shi 1997). The fact that both phase and literal V_2 elements patterned in the same way in this historical re-positioning is good evidence that all V_2s came to be licensed and interpreted very much in the same way.

5.2 An Alternative Analysis: V_2 as Aspect

5.2.1 Telicity and Non-predication

Having seen how a syntactic account of RVCs based on VP-shells or small clause structures faces a number of potential problems and objections, I will now attempt to develop an alternative account driven largely by the following three key observations concerning RVCs:

(58) **Lack of necessary predication between V_2 and NP 'object'**
As noted above in 5.1.4, it is not true that there is always a predication relation between the V_2 and the post-V_1-V_2 'object' NP in RVCs.

(59) **Telic contribution of V_2**
As well-noted in the literature (e.g., Li and Thompson 1981), the V_2 in a V_1-V_2 unit makes a dynamic event telic and aspectually bounded.

(60) **Historical re-positioning of V_2**
Historically sequences of [V_1 Object V_2] changed to [V_1-V_2 Object] as the V_2 re-positioned itself right-adjacent to V_1

I will suggest that these three important properties of Chinese RVCs are intimately connected and combine to result in a single analysis of RVCs. The core claim of the analysis will be that the V_2 in RVCs first underwent reanalysis to become an Aspectual head and then subsequently reanalyzed further as a suffixal instantiation of Aspect attached to the preceding V_1. In order to arrive at this synchronic analysis of RVCs will involve showing how (58-60) are connected to each other and how they have diachronically conspired to produce the V_1-V_2 forms of modern Mandarin.

Property (59), that the addition of V_2 to a dynamic V_1 results in a telic predicate, is so well-established that it here requires no real further qualification. Later on in chapter 6, I will return to consider in more detail how the aspectual domain may be divided into different sub-types, viewpoint and situational aspect (basically following Smith 1997).

Property (58) concerning predication of V_2 and the 'object' NP is very important and so can usefully be stressed again. What has been pointed out above in 5.1.4 is that there are many V_1-V_2 sequences in which the V_2 does *not* predicate of the following NP in any kind of normal way. It should be remembered that the small clause analysis of resultatives suggests that V₂ does indeed predicate directly of the 'object' NP encoding a state which terminates the activity of the V₁. Syntactically and semantically if the V₂-object NP relation is one of genuine predication used to represent the end of some activity, there is no good reason why it should not be possible to isolate this predication from the activity verb and have it stand in a syntactically independent form. However, as illustrated earlier, this is frequently not at all possible, leading to the conclusion that V₂ and the object NP do not have to be licensed by standing in any predication relation.

Essentially with a whole range of V₂ elements, many of which are categorized as phase V₂s, there is clearly no direct predication relation between the V₂ and the object NP and the interpretation of the RVC does not arise from first independently computing the meaning of a small clause and then combining this pragmatically with the action depicted by the main V₁, as is suggested in the small clause approach. Instead it would seem that a large number of commonly occurring V₂s have particular meanings which are built into the meaning of a sentence in some other way. Instructional textbooks tend to list these V₂s as characterizing the whole of particular *actions* rather than particular object-types, as shown in (61) for example:

(61)	verb	literal meaning	meaning as V₂
	dao	arrive	indicates the continuation of an action up a certain point of time
	cuo	be wrong	to carry out an action incorrectly
	zhao	*arrive (no longer in use as a verb alone)	completion or attainment of an action

It is also revealing that pedagogical textbooks frequently list the V₁ types that may typically occur with the V₂, this indicating that the close selectional relation which the V₂ has is to the type of V₁ it is combined with rather then any NP type it might predicate of. The list extract in (62) is from T'ung and Pollard (1982):

(62)	V₂ frequently occurs with:	V₁
	-jian (sensory perception)	kan 'look', peng 'collide',...
	-kai (detachment)	da 'hit', la 'pull',...
	-zhao (attainment)	zhao 'search', shui 'sleep',...
	-hui (learned)	xue 'learn/study'

The important conclusion I wish to draw from all of the above is that although it is *possible* that many V₂ elements could be analyzed as predicating of the 'object' NP in RVCs if a small clause analysis were to be adopted, there are also numerous cases where such a predication relation does not and could *not* exist between the V₂ and the object NP. This being the case, at least these

CHAPTER 5

V_2 elements must be licensed in the V_1-V_2 structure in some other way and consequently *not* in a small clause predication. What I will argue for in future sections is that the mode of licensing which is relevant for the above phase V_2s is also actually made use of by all other V_2 types as well, even those which might seem to have more literal predicative interpretations.

5.2.2 The Historical Re-positioning of V_2 in RVCs: Reanalysis and Aspect

We now come to the third property (60) listed above in 5.2.1—the observation that historically [V_1 Object V_2] sequences converted into [V_1 V_2 Object] forms between the Song and Tang dynasty period. Here I will propose and develop a syntactic account of the change which suggests that there were actually two critical cycles of reanalysis in resultative structures responsible for the change, both importantly relating to the category of aspect. In doing so I will show how properties (58) and (59) above are critically relevant to the re-positioning of V_2, i.e., property (60). I will also how the account of *shi-de* forms in chapter four allows for useful and important insights into structural aspects of the reanalysis that will be argued for.

In the present section I intend to concentrate on the first cycle of hypothetical reanalysis and focus on the importance of phase V_2s in early resultative constructions. Considering the earliest RVCs with [V_1 Object V_2] sequences, it would seem that V_2 was first instantiated by verbs which did indeed have a close selectional relation with the object and seemed to stand in more of a literal than a 'metaphorical' predication-type relation with it. Such verbs I will henceforth refer to as 'literal V_2s and contrast them with phase V_2s which do not have any literal predication relation with the object. Sentences (63) and (64) below contain examples of RVCs with literal V_2s (*fensui* 'shatter' in 63, *luo* 'fall' in 64), whereas (65) and (66) are two examples of phase V_2s both meaning 'finish' (*jin* and *bi*):

(63) shu ri zhong, guo zhen bo <u>fensui</u>, zidi jie
several day within, indeed shake cypress shatter, children all chengqing.
rejoince
'In several days, it indeed shook the cypress tree and broke it into pieces, so the children were all overjoyed.'
Shi: shujie [The World: magic arts], cited in C. Li and Y. Shi (1997)

(64) lieshi   bao   shi   er xing,   suiji   da qi chi <u>luo</u>.
martyr embrace rock and run, immediately hit his teeth fall
'The martyr ran holding the rock, but immediately the rock knocked his teeth out.'
Wu Zixu's narrative literature [Liu Jiang], cited in C. Li and Y. Shi (1997)

(65) Daozhen shi tun <u>jin</u>,   liao   bu   xie.
Daozhen eat pig finish, completely NEG thank
'Daozhen ate and finished the pork, but he did not show any gratitude.'
Shi: rendan [The World: wild behaviors], cited in C. Li and Y. Shi (1997)

(66) Wang yin jiu <u>bi</u>, yin de zi jie qu.
Wang drink wine finish, then happy self relieve go.
'Wang drank and finished the wine, and then he was happy and relieved, and went away.'
Shi: fangzheng [The World: the righteous], cited in C. Li and Y. Shi (1997)

As G. Wu (1999) notes, phase V_2s appear later than literal V_2s in [V_1 Object V_2] sequences:

> As early as in Qin and Han Chinese already developed the 'V(O)+complement' structure. The "V(O)+phase complement" structure emerged during the Wei, Jin and Northern and Southern Dynasties. (p.22)

Given that phase V_2s are generally seen as being more functional in application than the literal V_2s, this is indeed what one would expect, with more literal lexical elements preceding the use of more functional elements in a structure. This emergence of phase V_2s has, furthermore, very important consequences, as will shortly be explained. First however, we need to consider the structural status of literal V_2s in the [V_1 Object V_2] sequences.

In section 5.1.4 it was argued that V_2 elements in present-day Chinese RVCs are not licensed by any predication relation with the 'object' NP. However, although the various reasons given there showed this to be a valid conclusion for modern Chinese V_1-V_2 forms, it might not be unnatural to suggest that *fully literal* early resultative sequences of [V_1 Object V_2] did in fact encode some predicational relation between the Object and the V_2, and that in this early stage the V_2 was licensed in the resultative structure precisely because of this predicational relation. If this is so, a technical question arises as to how such a predicational relation might have been syntactically encoded.

One possibility is to simply assume the small clause structure argued for by Hoekstra (1992) and Sybesma (1999), repeated below as (67):

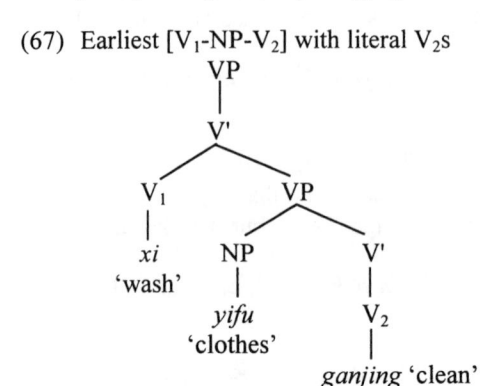

(67) Earliest [V$_1$-NP-V$_2$] with literal V$_2$s

```
              VP
              |
              V'
             / \
           V₁   VP
           |   /  \
          xi  NP   V'
         'wash' |   |
              yifu  V₂
            'clothes' |
                   ganjing 'clean'
```

However, in 5.1.4 it was noted that such a structure has the possibly unattractive aspect to it that there is no direct theta relation between the V$_1$ *xi* 'wash' and the 'object' NP *yifu* 'clothes' which somehow feels rather counter-intuitive. We have seen that in [V$_1$-de NP V$_2$] type resultatives where the linear sequencing resembles the early Chinese [V$_1$ Object V$_2$] RVCs, the post-V$_1$ NP behaves as if it is an object of the V$_1$ rather than just in a following predication with the V$_2$. Yafei Li (1998) has suggested that in the modern [V$_1$-de NP V$_2$] resultatives the overt object NP is linked to the V$_2$ via a co-indexed *pro* which itself occurs in the predication with V$_2$, and we can adopt this suggestion for the early [V$_1$ NP V$_2$] resultatives with literal V$_2$s. Allowing for a co-indexed *pro* to mediate the relation between the overt NP object and the early literal V$_2$ would then permit a rather different small clause structure as in (68). Here the overt NP being truly the object of the V$_1$ and the small clause being analyzed as an optional adjunct:

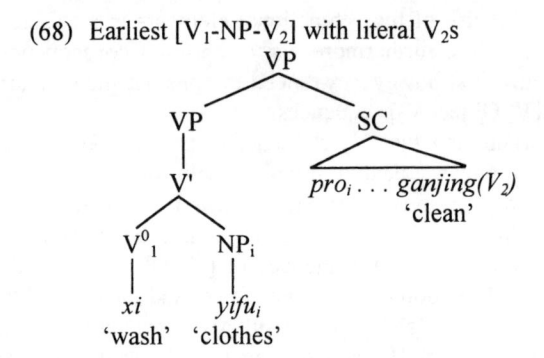

(68) Earliest [V$_1$-NP-V$_2$] with literal V$_2$s

```
              VP
             /   \
           VP     SC
           |     /  \
           V'  pro_i ... ganjing(V₂)
          / \        'clean'
        V⁰₁  NP_i
         |    |
        xi  yifu_i
       'wash' 'clothes'
```

If it is objected that the object NP$_i$ will not c-command the *pro* and that this is necessary for co-reference, an alternative possibility might be to assume a VP-shell structure such as (69) with the NP 'object' base-generated in the lower SpecVP c-commanding the co-referential *pro* in the small clause which is here analyzed as a complement. The verb would then be taken to undergo overt raising to v^0.[8]

(69) Earliest [V$_1$-NP-V$_2$] with literal V$_2$s

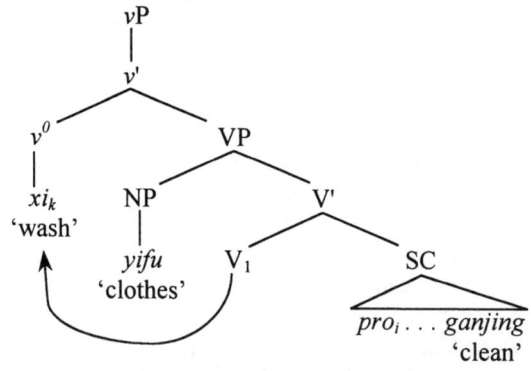

```
              vP
              |
              v'
           /     \
         v⁰       VP
         |      /    \
        xi_k   NP     V'
       'wash'  |    /    \
              yifu  V₁    SC
            'clothes'    /  \
                      pro_i ... ganjing
                              'clean'
```

Without further discussion I will simply assume here that one of these possibilities is correct and that there is indeed an early structure which can accommodate both the overt NP as a genuine object of the V$_1$ and a small clause with a *pro* being predicated of by V$_2$. A similar structure must indeed be available to account for simple sequences such as (70) in which both an overt object NP occurs and a resultative clause with a co-referential NP subject:

(70) I pushed John$_1$ so that he$_1$ fell.[9]

What should be stressed here as important is the assumption that the most natural analysis of literal V$_2$ in early [V$_1$ NP V$_2$] sequences is that it was indeed initially licensed via predicating of the object, with this most likely being effected indirectly through the presence of a co-referential *pro*.

Following the establishment of literal V$_2$ in [V$_1$ NP V$_2$], one next finds the introduction of phase V$_2$s in [V$_1$ NP V$_2$] sequences and this is highly significant. As argued in 5.1.4, phase V$_2$ elements do *not* predicate of the object NP in RVCs. Consequently, a key, important question is how phase V$_2$s could have come to be licensed in such structures? If the early occurrence of literal V$_2$s in [V$_1$ NP V$_2$] was naturally legitimized via the predication relation they bore with the object NP but phase V$_2$s are not interpreted in the same way (i.e., as predicating of the object), then some other means of legitimization must have become available to allow such elements into the early [V$_1$ NP V$_2$] structure. Here I would like to suggest that the emergence of phase-type verbs in the V$_2$ position is the result of a first important stage in reanalysis which re-oriented the resultative construction in a particular way, subsequently allowing in certain V$_2$ elements not instantiating any predication relation with the object

185

NP. Critical here, I suggest, was property (62), that all V_2 elements (whether phase or literal) serve to provide a telic aspectual bound to the action depicted by V_1 and the object. Prior to the occurrence of phase verbs as V_2s, all V_2 elements can be said to have contributed two discrete properties in early [V_1 NP V_2] resultatives:

(71) a. (Literal) V_2s lexically encoded the type of result which terminated the event (e.g., the clothes come to be in a clean state after being washed).
b. All V_2s functionally provided a telic bound to the event of the V_1.

Intuitively, the important change which occurred in RVCs can be suggested to be that after some time V_2s could be licensed in resultative constructions by providing simply property (b) and not necessarily property (a) as well. Phase V_2s which do not predicate of the object NP and consequently do not describe the result state of the object can therefore be said to have become licensed in virtue of providing property (b) alone.

If a V_2 comes to no longer predicate of an object inside the VP but instead provides a more general telic bound to the whole predicate signaling completion of an action, it can be argued that in terms of scope and configurationality the V_2 essentially becomes interpreted as applying its function to the *entire VP* rather than just a sub-part of it (i.e., just the object). If this is correct, a question which naturally arises now is how could such a potential change effect itself structurally in RVCs? Here I believe is precisely where the account of changes in the *shi-de* construction developed in chapter four is now potentially very helpful and enlightening and there is indeed a remarkable parallelism in the diachronic development of *shi-de* forms and RVCs. In order to make this parallelism clear, I will now make a short backtrack through the conclusions of chapter four and point out some of the surface similarity of *shi-de* constructions and RVCs.

As noted at the beginning of this chapter, there is an obvious similarity in the way that *shi-de* forms and RVCs have shown changes in linear order. In both constructions a sequence of [V Object X] changes into a sequence [V X Object] with the element X representing *de* in *shi-de* constructions and a V_2 in RVCs; in both cases it also seems to be the case that the element X re-positions itself leftwards, right-adjacent to the main verb, rather than there being any rightward object movement. Considering *shi-de* forms it was argued that *de* undergoes reanalysis from category D to category T and that sentences such as (72) have a structure such as (73):

(72) wo shi zuotian lai de.
I SHI yesterday come DE
'It was yesterday that I came.'

(73)

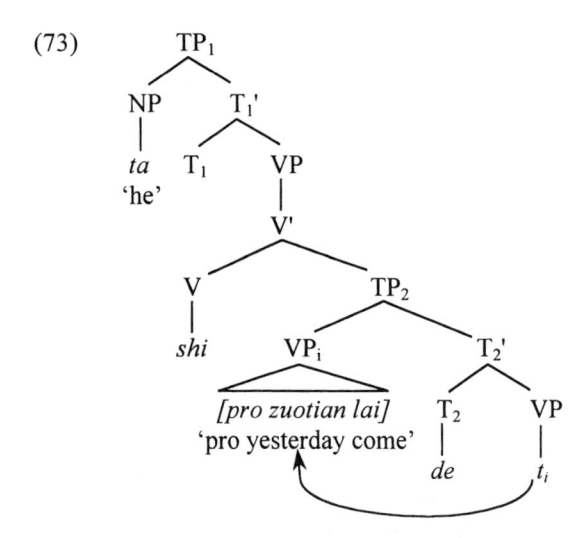

```
           TP₁
          /  \
        NP    T₁'
        |    /  \
        ta  T₁   VP
       'he'     |
                V'
               /  \
              V    TP₂
              |   /  \
             shi VPᵢ   T₂'
                 |    /  \
           [pro zuotian lai] T₂  VP
           'pro yesterday come' |   |
                               de   tᵢ
```

Where the element *de* occurs between the verb and its object as in (74) it was argued that the reanalyzed tense head *de* raises to the verb and cliticizes to it, essentially becoming a tense suffix attached to the verb as is found in many other languages:

(74) wo shi zuotian mai-[de]ᵢ piao tᵢ
     I SHI yesterday buy-DE ticket
     'It was yesterday that I bought the ticket.'

If one considers again the structure and derivation in (73), it was suggested that the VP complement of T⁰ undergoes raising from its base-generated position to the right of *de* up to the SpecTP position. Such raising was motivated on the grounds that *de* is derived from the D⁰ element *de* and D⁰ *de* was argued to trigger raising of an IP to its Spec for phonological support (see chapters 3 and 4).

Such a structure now provides the model necessary to understand the V₂ change in RVCs. What we have arguably found with *de* is a structure in which a functional head T⁰ has its sole argument occurring rather exceptionally in its leftward Spec position. The interpretation of such a structure is that T applies its functional tense value to the VP located in its specifier position. Turning now to early [V₁ NP V₂] resultatives, we have argued that the emergence of phase-type verbs in the V₂ position indicates that after a certain time resultative V₂ elements could be licensed by simply providing a general telic bounding of the situation described in the predicate VP rather than necessarily also providing a predication onto the object of V₁. It was then suggested that this change points to a significant change in scope of the V₂ from being a function applied just to the object NP to being a function applied to the whole VP. The general telic completives of this type are therefore interpreted as functional elements which essentially take entire VPs as their arguments. The question we then raised was how it could be possible for such a semantic relation to be syntactically encoded in [V₁ Object V₂] forms. Now having briefly re-examined the *shi-de* construction, we have a model and precedent on hand which can suggest what the critical syntactic re-organization in RVCs might have been. I would here like to propose that the first important change which introduced phase V₂s into the [V₁ Object V₂] resultatives was that the V₂ position instantiated by phase-type verbs became re-interpreted as a functional Aspect head projecting a single argument VP in a leftward specifier position as in (75), precisely on a par with *de* as T⁰ having a VP in its leftward specifier:

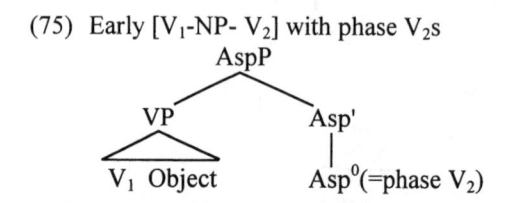

(75) Early [V₁-NP- V₂] with phase V₂s

```
         AspP
        /    \
      VP     Asp'
     /  \     |
   V₁  Object Asp⁰(=phase V₂)
```

The development of phase V₂s into a predicate-final functional projection is then suggested to be very similar indeed to the ongoing development of *de* into Tense. Shortly I will turn to examine the actual re-positioning of the phase-V₂ Aspect-head and suggest that this second major change in RVCs also closely resembles the re-positioning of *de* as Tense. Just as *de* was argued to re-position itself after its reanalysis as a Tense-head and attach itself leftwards to the main verb of the predicate, the re-positioning of V₂ elements to attach to V₁ in RVCs will be suggested to have occurred as a later direct consequence of the first stage of reanalysis outlined here, V₂ elements essentially becoming re-interpreted as aspectual suffixes in the same way that *de* is en route to becoming a new tense suffix. Precisely how (and also more explicitly why) this second stage of re-structuring in RVCs takes place will be considered in greater detail in a later section.

Returning to (75) above and focusing on phase V₂s, it can be noted that such a structure can indeed be argued to accurately represent the relation between V₂, V₁ and the object, and that V₂ in fact *selects* for V₁ and the object as its (VP) argument.[10] One should remember that diachronically from what might appear to be a fully open set of possible V₂ elements there emerged a more specialized and restricted/closed sub-set of phase V₂s. These phase V₂s do not predicate directly of the object but instead are classed as being appropriate for certain *classes* of situations. Each member of the phase V₂ set is interpreted as applying to a different large set of situation-types rather than specific object types and this is precisely why textbooks commonly include lists of the V₁ verbs which are appropriately used with each V₂, that is, the V₂ indeed *selects* for the VP and its V₁ head rather than having any direct relation to the object of that V₁. Such a selection relation is exactly what is represented in (75)—the V₂-Aspect-head selects the VP headed by V₁ as its sole argument, projected like an unergative verb projects its single NP argument in a leftward Spec position. A selection relation of this type also corresponds to the standard relation understood to exist between a functional element and its argument, and as types of phase V₂s are elements which have all *generalized* their applicability (to a wide array of events), this generalization would seem to clearly characterize them as functional elements requiring an argument to apply their function to. Finally, although one finds that there are in fact multiple potential overt instantiations of essentially the same completive Aspect-head rather than simply a unique morpheme (as might be the case in other functional heads such as Tense), it can be noted that elsewhere there are cases of clear functional elements which have multiple instantiations. One good example here is the nominal classifier system found in Asian languages, where each member of a potentially large classifier set functionally selects for a different range of complement types (and in this sense classifiers are rather similar to the V₂ aspectual completives, the latter 'classifying' different situations according to telicity).

Before closing this section and continuing to examine how literal V₂s fit into the picture of change sketched out above, I would briefly like to mention that there is also certain evidence from tone sandhi phenomena that phase V₂s have a functional rather than a lexical status, as suggested here. In Shanghainese (Selkirk and Shen 1999) one finds that tone sandhi clearly differentiates between lexical and functional elements in an interesting way. Essentially a phenomenon of 'tone-spreading' begins at the first syllable of a lexical word and continues (spreading) throughout all following syllables until a second lexical element is met. Functional elements are distinguished from lexical elements in that they do not constitute independent tone sandhi domains and simply undergo the spreading initiated by a preceding lexical syllable (regardless of their syntactic relation to the preceding lexical element). What is relevant here is the fact that V₂s such as *taw* (=Mandarin *dao* 'arrive') in (76) are treated as if they are functional and not lexical elements, undergoing tone-spreading from the preceding lexical syllable and not instantiating a new tone sandhi domain:

(76) (MH MH) (LH HL)   (M H) (L H)
     tsou taw 'noetsiN → tsou taw 'noetsiN
     'walk to Nanjing'

In the southern Wu dialect of Wenzhou reported in Chen (2000) the same basic phenomena also occur. Chen presents the following example and notes that the tone of the V₂ *dao* 'arrive/to' is deleted as with all functional elements and *dao* receives a tone spread from the preceding lexical syllable. In Chen's notation the material between slash brackets indicates a tone sandhi domain; the inclusion of *dao* in the tone sandhi domain initiated by the preceding lexical V₁ element *la* 'pull' indicates that *dao* is interpreted as being a functional element rather than a lexical element:[11]

CHAPTER 5

(77) / ba sanlunche / la dao / menkou /
 BA tricycle   pull arrive gate
 'Pull the tricycle to the gate.'

5.2.3 Literal V_2 and Reanalysis

Above I have largely been concerned with the reanalysis of phase-type V_2 elements which do not predicate of the 'object' NP in [V_1 object V_2] sequences. It was first suggested that early *literal* V_2 elements supplied two discrete properties in resultative constructions: (a) a characterization of the result state of the NP object of the main verb, and (b) a general telic bounding of the predicate. It was proposed that the emergence of V_2 elements which do not provide property (a) is indication that at some stage providing simply property (b) came to be sufficient to be licensed as a V_2 in resultatives, and that V_2 elements which had no direct relation to the object NP but supplied a more general telic bound to the predicate became reanalyzed as being base-generated in an aspectual head Asp^0 with a single selected VP argument projected in its Spec position. The obvious question which now arises concerns the status of other *literal* V_2s in [V_1 Ob V_2] sequences and whether literal V_2s occurred in Asp^0 or continued to be base-generated and licensed in small clause type predication structures. Note that the suggestion that phase-type V_2s occur in Asp^0 does not exclude the possibility that literal V_2s might indeed have continued to be base-generated and licensed in a predication relation with the object and that there could in fact have been two different resultative structures (for literal V_2s and phase V_2s) present in the language. Shortly I will however argue against such a view and suggest that literal V_2s also underwent reanalysis and came to be base-generated in the same Asp^0 and that it was an important change in focus on the critical licensing properties of literal V_2 which preceded and allowed for the occurrence of phase V_2s. I will also suggest that the fact that both phase and literal V_2 elements collectively underwent re-positioning to V_1 during the Song dynasty (C. Li and Y. Shi 1997) is strong evidence that all V_2s came to be licensed and interpreted very much in the same way, therefore causing all V_2s to undergo a shift over the object from Asp^0 to V_1.

Initially there might appear to be many objections to any suggestion that literal V_2s might also occur in Asp^0. As literal V_2s could quite naturally be analyzed as occurring in some kind of predication relation with the object and are indeed assumed to have come from such a source, it could simply be assumed that they continue to be licensed in such structures. Secondly, V_2s might seem to provide key information characterizing the type of result-state the object comes to be in as a result of the action of V_1, and it might be natural to assume that lexical descriptive information of this type is presented in some kind of predication structure rather than with the V_2 occurring as a *functional* element in an aspectual head. Thirdly, and connected to the latter point, the literal V_2 elements might seem to be a fully open class with essentially any predicate being potentially available as a V_2 result. If this is so, it might again seem to argue against literal V_2 status as a functional head, as functional heads are characteristically instantiated by a generally small closed class of elements. Despite the obvious objections to an analysis of literal V_2 as instantiating aspect however, I will now argue that literal V_2s were indeed generated in a clause-final aspect-head even in early Chinese, and attempt to show how all of the above-mentioned objections can in fact be given satisfactory explanations while maintaining an analysis of all V_2s as Asp. First I will begin though with one of the positive rather simple reasons for assuming that early literal V_2 must have come to instantiate Asp.

Considering again how phase-type V_2s came to occur as Asp, it was earlier suggested rather informally that literal V_2 elements provided two properties—(a) a description of the result state of the object and (b) a telic bound—and that at some stage elements came to be licensed as legitimate V_2s by simply providing property (b) (i.e., the occurrence of phase V_2s). What this change can be argued to indicate a little more formally is that it must have *first* been possible for literal V_2s to be licensed by just providing property (b) *before* phase V_2s could then also make use of this less restrictive licensing option and occur in [V_1 obj V_2] resultatives. One can assume that phase V_2s indeed came to be possible in [V_1 obj V_2] resultatives precisely because earlier literal V_2s were optionally licensed in the V_2 position *solely* in virtue of providing property (b). Once literal V_2s could be licensed primarily via supplying just property (b), this then allowed for other phase-type elements which did not provide property (a) also to occur as V_2s. Thus sequentially it can be suggested that phase V_2s could really only have been permitted into the [V_1 obj V_2] structure once other earlier literal V_2s were re-valued in terms of their contribution to the construction. The hypothesized transition can be schematized as follows:

(78) Step 1:
    a. Only literal V_2s occur in early [V_1 obj V_2] resultatives.
    b. Literal V_2s provide both properties (a) predication of the object, and (b) addition of a telic bound.
    c. Literal V_2s are licensed primarily due to property (a).
    d. At this point V_2 elements which do not predicate of the object (i.e., phase V_2s) do not occur in [V_1 obj V_2] resultatives, and the literal V2s is predicated of the object.

(79) Step 2:
Literal V_2s which still provide both properties (a) and (b) come to be optionally licensed just in virtue of property (b), in which case the literal V_2s are analyzed as Asp.

CHAPTER 5

(80) Step 3:
Licensing simply in virtue of property (b) allows in phase-type V_2s which do not supply property (a) at all to also occur in early [V_1 obj V_2] resultatives.

Such a course of development indicates that clause-final Asp would have in fact first been created by an initial reanalysis of literal V_2s into Asp. I will now go on to suggest that this reanalysis occurred due to a simple switch in focus in early resultatives.

Cross-linguistically, it might seem that both properties (a) and (b) above are regularly present in resultative constructions. Reflecting on their frequent co-occurrence one might also initially assume that they are equally weighted in terms of relative importance and that the lexical information provided on the result state of the object is necessarily as important and highly valued as the bounding effect which occurs. However, it is in fact quite possible that there actually is a critical *imbalance* in the relationship between the two properties and that one of the two properties is, or becomes, more highly valued than the other. For example, it is possible that the lexical descriptive property (a) is of more importance in English 'so that' resultative forms and that the focus of interest largely falls on the characterization of the result-state, with the bounding effect (property b) being more of a secondary pragmatic bi-product:

(81) Mary laughed at John so much that he became embarrassed.

In (81) the emphasis is clearly felt to be on describing the type of result state ('embarrassed') rather than focusing simply the completion of an activity (i.e., the termination of laughing). In 'so that' type resultatives it would therefore seem that there is an obvious imbalance between property (a) and property (b) and that the latter is of greater importance. In other cases it is not unlikely that an imbalance might swing in the opposite direction and the telic bounding property might become of greater focus than the actual description of the type of result-state. This is precisely what I would like to suggest has occurred in Chinese resultatives. From an earlier stage where the descriptive property (a) was clearly important and necessary for an element to occur as a V_2, later on the emphasis in resultatives switched to the bounding property (b) and simple completion of an event. In this regard, it has often been noted that the V_2 in RVCs does indeed carry a special focus in the construction, for example Li and Thompson (1981, p.57) state that "the primary communicative function of an RVC is to comment on whether the *result* of an action did or did not, can or cannot, take place." Thus the emphasis is suggested to be on whether an action is completed, and not so strongly on the characterization of the type of completion. Furthermore, it is often rather clear from the consideration of a V_1-V_2 combination that if there is indeed a focus on V_2 then it can only be emphasizing the completion rather than the type of result state. For example, if the V_1-V_2 sequence *xi-ganjing (yifu)* is used as in (82a) below, the emphasis is on completion and not on contrasting the result-state of being clean with other potential result-states. Most speakers agree that the interpretation of (82a) is similar to (82b), in the latter case the V_2 indicates the end point, instead of the result state (clean or not), of the washing event.

(82) a. ta ba yifu   xi-ganjing le.
         she BA clothes wash-clean LE
         'She washed the clothes clean.'
     b. ta ba yifu   xi-hao   le.
         she BA clothes wash-well   LE
         'She finished washing the clothes.'

Basically (and this point will be returned to shortly), with a V_1 such as *xi* 'wash' there is almost no choice in what one could use or expect to hear as a V_2 element, and *ganjing* 'clean' or *hao* 'well' is indeed neutrally anticipated as the result state V_2 rather than any other element. As the characterization of the result state by means of *ganjing* 'clean' is then neither unexpected nor in real contrast with other states which could have resulted from a washing action, it is not its lexical content which is really focused here but simply the telic bound of completeness which it marks through its occurrence in the V_2 position. When the particular type of V_2 is almost predicted by the type of V_1 like this, it is then very clear that the bounding effect is the important emphasized contribution of the V_2, and the lexical characterization of the result-state is far less focused and in some sense almost redundant (i.e., there is basically no other state that clothes could naturally be expected to be in after having been washed to completion).

The suggestion is then once more that an imbalance arose in the relative importance of properties (a) and (b) in Chinese resultatives. Consequently, from being a resultative construction in which the lexical description of the result-state was both clearly very important and necessary (hence only literal V_2s predicating of the object could occur), the V_2 is suggested to have later come to be valued primarily for its bounding function, with property (b) being the identifying and licensing characteristic of any V_2. Formally V_2 is therefore suggested to have come to be interpreted as more of a functional element providing primarily a telic bound to the predicate and so being licensed as a VP-operator selecting the entire predicate as its argument. Syntactically, the hypothesized switch of early literal V_2s to a predominantly functional role selecting and applying to the VP can then be argued to have given rise to a predicate-final Aspect projection, with V_2 elements being base-generated in the Asp^0 head position. Following the creation of the Aspect projection, any type of V_2 which could provide property (b) could then legitimately occur licensed in resultatives, and this can be argued to have allowed in phase-type V_2s which only supply property (b). Possibly there may also have been a period when both the new Aspect-functional structure and the older V_2 predicational small clause structure may have continued to co-exist in resultatives, but importantly a good many literal V_2s must have been re-interpreted in terms of providing primarily a telic bounding function for the creation of the aspect projection (and the subsequent appearance of phase V_2s) to have occurred.

5.2.4 Responses to Apparent Objections

Although I believe that there is no other good formal explanation for how non-literal phase V_2s could have come to be licensed in resultatives, there might appear to be many potential objections to the proposal that literal V_2s also occur in Asp^0. As literal V_2s could quite naturally be analyzed as occurring in some kind of predication relation with the object and are indeed assumed to have come from such a source, it could simply be assumed that they continue to be licensed in such structures. Secondly, V_2s might seem to provide key information characterizing the type of result-state the object comes to be in as a result of the action of V_1, and it might be natural to assume that lexical descriptive information of this type is presented in some kind of predication structure rather than with the V_2 occurring as a *functional* element in an aspectual head. Thirdly, the literal V_2 elements might appear to be a fully open class with any predicate potentially being available as a V_2 result. If this is so, it might again seem to argue against functional head for literal V_2s, as functional heads are characteristically instantiated by a small, closed classes of elements. However, here I will attempt to show how all of the above-mentioned objections can in fact be given satisfactory explanations which strengthen the analysis of all V_2s as Asp.

Let us first consider the assumption that functional heads/categories are instantiated by a small, closed set of items. While this may quite often be the case, it is however certainly not always so, and there is furthermore nothing a priori which requires that a functional projection be instantiated by a closed and highly reduced set of elements. One example of a functional category which is instantiated by a significantly large membership of overt elements is the classifier/CL projected DPs, with the languages of Southeast Asia having particularly abundant classifier systems. Note that within such classifier systems there are classifiers which may be used with only a single type of noun, this being similar to English 'a pack of lions', a 'school of dolphins', a 'murder of crows' and 'a gaggle of geese', where 'pack', 'school', 'murder', etc. can only be applied to 'lions', 'dolphins' and 'crows' respectively. A result of this is that classifier systems may potentially be very large with different classifiers corresponding to all the different feature combinations that a particular language chooses to distinguish in its nouns (i.e., +/-flat, +/-long, etc.). In Thai, for example, it is assumed that there may be over 400 distinct classifier elements. Consequently the hypothetical objection that literal V_2s might not instantiate a functional head because they come from a large, apparently open-ended class is not in fact really a potentially strong or legitimate criticism.

Related to the size of the set of morphemes which instantiate a functional head, it is natural to conclude that the membership of such a set is often small because functional elements may simply have a functional specification and no additional lexical content, and that a single element with such a functional specification will therefore be sufficient to encode the necessary function in the head. However, it has often been observed that when elements grammaticalize as functional elements they do not in fact immediately lose all lexical content and indeed may continue to show even strong traces of earlier lexical content for a considerable time (see e.g., Bybee, Perkins and Pagliuca 1994). As is suggested to be the case here in RVCs, what may often happen in grammaticalization is that there occurs a significant shift in emphasis with the continued use of an element. Initially an element has a predominantly lexical descriptive role, which may also give rise to other semi-functional pragmatic inferences as an accidental bi-product. Later on this may change to a state in which the functional value of the element becomes most highly valued and the element comes to be predominantly functional. When this happens, the element grammaticalizing does not necessarily lose its lexical content; instead there is simply a switch in focus to the mainly functional role it plays. Consequently there is no reason why there should not exist a set of functional elements, such as the V_2 set, which are legitimized as functional heads but also have clearly lexical content as well.

In grammaticalization situations, often one element from a larger set may become more widely used and general in its application (the phenomenon of '*generalization*', Hopper and Traugott 1993), with the result that other members of the set occur less frequently and eventually disappear. One might therefore possibly not expect for such a large V_2 set to exist as functional heads without such generalization occurring. In fact, as will be seen in chapter 6, it is quite possibly true that verbal *le* may indeed be just such a generalized completive marker occurring with a range of verbs, and therefore that there has been generalization in the completive aspect group. If this is in fact so, one might expect, incorrectly, that the other V_2 elements would no longer be used as instantiations of this aspectual function/category. However, I believe that there is actually a potentially good explanation for why this has not taken place. We have noted that there is commonly felt to be emphasis on the completion of the event in a resultative construction. If this emphasis requires further stressing, it will only be possible to do this with a V_2 which has the phonetic strength to carry stress and which has not undergone the phonetic reduction that has occurred with *le*. Therefore the continued use of a range of V_2s alongside the more general completive *le* may well be due to phonological reasons and the focus properties of the construction.[12] Furthermore, if one turns again to classifier systems such as that in Mandarin Chinese, one finds that alongside a large set of classifiers which are appropriate for subsets of nouns, there may also be a very general classifier—in Mandarin the element *ge*. Consequently it is indeed possible for a generalized functional element to co-exist with a

CHAPTER 5

second set of more specialized alternative forms, and the existence of a generalized functional head does not necessarily mean that other more specialized instantiations will automatically cease being used.

Before leaving the general topic of functional heads being commonly taken to correspond to closed sets of elements, I would like to make one further very relevant point. There is a common assumption that because literal V$_2$ elements provide descriptions of the result state in RVCs, the set of such literal V$_2$ elements is fully open and hence very large, allowing for the description of a full range of result states. Such an assumption is however actually not true when one comes to probe matters a little further, and there are various works which point out that result-state predicates are in fact often more restricted than generally thought (see e.g., Lüdeling 1997). Essentially what one often finds in resultative constructions is that there is a strong preference for V$_2$-type result-state predicates to represent *canonical results*, or results which are frequently expected given the content of V$_1$. For example, as was noted above, with a V$_1$ such as *xi* 'wash' the type of result *ganjing* 'clean' is heavily predicted and expected, and it is difficult to imagine what other kind of predicate could occur as V$_2$. Elsewhere one finds very naturally co-occurring V$_1$-V$_2$ pairs such as those listed in (83):

(83) *kuo-da*   expand-big
 da-ying fight-win
 qi-lei   ride-tired
 yong-guan use X until one is used to X

In all cases the V$_2$ represents a largely canonical or expected result. In certain cases there may be a small number of alternate possibilities; for example, alongside *da-ying* 'fight-win' there is also *da-bai* 'fight-lose', but by and large the V$_2$ is frequently predicted to a considerable extent by the V$_1$ and actually not as open a choice as might be imagined. Such restrictions have been noted to occur in resultatives in English, German and many other languages. For example, Lüdeling (1997) points out that only certain result-state predicates seem possible in a considerable number of cases, as illustrated in (84-88) below:

(84) a. He laughed himself insane.
 b. *He laughed me happy.
 c. *He cried me sad.

(85) He ran me tired/*exhausted.

(86) Sally painted the door red/*beautiful.

(87) We laughed the speaker off the stage/*embarrassed.

(88) Robert ran clear of the door/away/*exhausted.

In many cases it might seem that the result described by the secondary predicate is best when it is the most general canonical description of what might be expected as a result given the action of the main verb. For example, in (85) 'tired' is fine where 'exhausted' is unacceptable; as 'exhausted' is simply a more explicit characterization of being 'tired', it seems that the simplest and most general descriptive form is preferred over more explicit less common forms.[13] In (86) too, the action of painting leads one to expect a color result state and it is found that a non-color result state such as 'beautiful' is unacceptable. Elsewhere the result states have the feeling of being idiomatic and also not open, as for example in (84) and (87).

What this indicates is that the set of result state predicates is not as wide open as often assumed. The preference for canonical results encoded by general and commonly-occurring predicates also suggests, as before, that the primary function of result state predicates in many resultative constructions is indeed to supply a telic bound to an event rather than to focus on the description of the result state. Where a non-canonical result state predicate occurs this will tend to attract the focus away from the emphasis on completion and so there will be two competing focal points, resulting in the oddity felt in many RVCs. The idiomatic nature of many resultatives also suggests that the result state may be so commonly expected from application of the V_1 that the result state and the V_1 become a quasi-lexical unit.

Similar patterns can also be discerned in Chinese, and not all V_1-V_2 pairs are felt to be well-formed. For example, (89-91) below are all felt to be either quite unacceptable or rather odd:

(89) ??ta xiao-le-le wo.
    he laugh-happy-LE me
    intended: 'He laughed and as a result I became happy.'

(90) ?*ta (shuo gushi) shuo-ku-le wo.
    he say story say-cry-LE me
    intended: 'He told a story which made me cry.'

(91) *ta ku-beishang-le wo.
    he cry-sad-LE me
    intended: 'He cried so that I became sad.'

(92) *ta xi-ganganjingjing yifu.
    he wash-clean clothes
    intended 'He washed clean the clothes.'

Note that I have suggested that the focus is on the completion of the event in V_1-V_2 resultatives rather than on the description of the result state, and that this imbalance in favor of property (b) is what has resulted in V_2 elements being interpreted as Asp. I also suggested that this imbalance might not necessarily be present in other resultative constructions which could quite possibly value property (a) more highly than property (b). This would seem to be true of the English 'so-that' resultative already mentioned, and also Chinese [V$_1$-de NP V$_2$] forms. Because the V$_2$ must encode a genuine independent description of the result state, one finds that only genuinely predicative V$_2$ elements may occur in such forms. As expected, English resultative particles and Chinese phase V$_2$s which do not predicate of the object may not occur in such resultatives:

(93) a. *I looked (at) the number so that it was up.
b. I looked the number up.

(94) a. *I threw him so that he was out.
b. I threw him out.

(95) a. *wo kan-de shu wan le.
I look-DE book finish LE
intended: 'I finished reading the books.'
b. wo kan-wan-le shu le.
I look-finish-LE book LE
'I finished reading the books.'

(96) a. *wo mai-de shu dao le.
I buy-DE book arrive LE
intended: 'I managed to buy the book.'
b. wo mai-dao-le shu le.
I buy-arrive-LE book LE
'I managed to buy the book.'

(97) a. *wo zhao-de shu zhao le.
I search-DE book arrive LE
intended: 'I searched and found the books.'
b. wo zhao-zhao-le shu le.
I search-arrive-LE book LE
'I searched and found the books.'

This ungrammaticality frequently found when one attempts to convert a V$_1$-V$_2$ RVC into a corresponding [V$_1$-de NP V$_2$] resultative strongly confirms both that phase V$_2$s do not predicate of the object in V$_1$-V$_2$ RVCs (as they cannot be predicated of the same NP in [V$_1$-de NP V$_2$] resultatives), and that phase V$_2$s are consequently not licensed in V$_1$-V$_2$ RVCs in virtue of any predication relation with the object but rather for their pure bounding effect.

[V$_1$-de NP V$_2$] resultatives consequently require a genuine predication relation onto the NP preceding V$_2$ and so can may be considered to require and possibly highly value property (b). This contrasts with V$_1$-V$_2$ RVCs which focus property (a) and do not require property (b) with V_2s. Given this potential difference in focus and orientation between the two resultative constructions, one might wonder if those V_2 elements which cannot occur in V_1-V_2 RVCs might possibly be acceptable in [V_1-de NP V_2] resultatives, and interestingly this turns out to be so. Examples in (98-101) are [V_1-de NP V_2] equivalents to the unacceptable/marginal V_1-V_2 RVCs in (89-92) and are all fully well-formed.

(98) ta xiao-de wo hen le.
he laugh-DE I very happy
'He laughed and as a result I became happy.'

(99) ta (shuo gushi) shuo-de wo ku-le.
he say story say-DE I cry-LE
'He told a story which made me cry.'

(100) ta ku-de wo hen beishang.
he cry-DE I very sad
'He cried so that I became sad.'

(101) ta xi-de yifu gan-gan-jing-jing.
he wash-DE clothes clean
'He washed the clothes and the clothes became very clean.'

What all the above demonstrates is that V_2 elements are actually be more restricted than commonly imagined in V_1-V_2 RVCs and this is not because of any inherent semantic incompatibility between a particular result state and a main event verb V_1 (as these V_2s may co-occur in a different type of resultative with the same V_1s), but rather because of the focus of the V_1-V_2 RVC. V_1-V_2 RVCs are *primarily* oriented around bounding the activity rather describing the result state and hence frequently occurring, predictable, canonical result type predicates are naturally preferred because they result in the least distraction away from the focus on completion. Consequently the potential objection to a functional analysis of V_2 elements that they constitute a fully open class cannot be made and a comparison of the two resultative constructions (V_1-V_2 and V_1-de V_2) actually supports the treatment of V_2 in the former as a primarily functional operator.[14, 15]

So, to briefly summarize, in this section I have suggested that a significant change occurred in the underlying structure of early V_1 Ob V_2 sequences. From an original form in which V_2 occurred licensed as a genuine secondary predicate, the V_2 underwent re-interpretation as instantiating an aspectual head which encodes a telic bound on the event depicted by the V_1 and its object. Such a change was suggested to have been the result of a change in focus of the resultative construction. An increase in the focus on the pure bounding property of V_2 later allowed phase V_2s with no direct predicational relation with the object NP to also occur in early V_1 Ob V_2 sequences. The syntactic realization of this change was argued to be that V_2 became base-generated in a discrete Asp-head selecting VP as its argument projected in a leftward specifier position. Finally I reflected on certain potential objections to the claim that V_2 instantiates Asp and attempted to show that a functional analysis of V_2 elements can in fact be maintained. Having established the V_2-as-Asp proposal and showed how it is able to offer a clear potential insight into the early development of resultatives, I will now proceed to examine a second significant change in Chinese resultatives: the re-positioning of V_2 to a position right-adjacent to V_1. I will offer an account of how and why this important re-structuring took place and suggest that the change should be similarly attributed to the functional-aspectual properties instantiated by V_2.

5.3 V_2 Re-positioning and Directionality

According to G. Wu (1999) and C. Li and Y. Shi (1997), V_1 NP$_{object}$ V_2 resultatives largely changed into V_1-V_2 NP$_{object}$ forms around the time of the Song dynasty (960-1279), possibly having first appeared during the Tang dynasty (Mei 1981). Certainly V_1-V_2 Ob sequences are taken to be the only acceptable forms from the time of the Song dynasty onwards. The linear re-positioning of V_2 over the object to become right-adjacent to V_1 is represented again in (102):

(102) V_1 NP$_{object}$ V_2 → V_1 V_2 NP$_{object}$

First of all it should be noted that the later forms do not seem to have resulted from earlier sequences via any Heavy NP Shift type operation which post-poses heavy objects. It is fairly clear that even light object NPs occurred after V_2 in the new order and so the change is much more likely to have resulted from a re-positioning of the V_2 and possibly movement of the V_2 to V_1. The critical question in need of answering therefore is what actually triggered this re-positioning and what this might then be able to tell us about the synchronic structure of V_1-V_2 forms?[16] Both the syntactic accounts of Chinese RVCs we have reviewed assume that there is indeed movement of V_2 to V_1 still actively occurring in the underlying syntax, and hence that the historical source continues to be present in the base-generated structure of RVCs; however neither account offers any understanding of what might actually cause the movement of V_2 to V_1. In Yafei Li's lexical approach by way of contrast, reference is simply not made to the earlier [V_1 Ob V_2] forms and there is consequently no attempt to explain how syntactically created [V_1 Ob V_2] sequences might later come to be formed as V_1-V_2 compounds in the lexicon. The development of the modern [V_1 V_2 object] forms from [V_1 Ob V_2] sequences therefore remains as an interesting puzzle.

5.3.1 Arguments Against a Phonological Explanation

One possible mode of explanation for the change to V_1-V_2 forms which might initially be entertained, but which I will argue against, is that the re-positioning could have occurred for *phonological* reasons. Earlier in the introduction it was noted that the change in RVCs and with verbal *le/liao* might seem to resemble the change in *shi-de* forms in that an initial sequence of a main verb, an object and some sentence-final element X (where X=*de, liao,* V_2) undergoes re-ordering to [V X Object]. With *de* it was pointed out that the change in position arguably resulted from *de* as a clitic targeting the verb as its new phonological host following earlier syntactic reanalysis as a tense element. Considering the V_2s in RVCs however, it is not possible to argue that such elements moved to attach to the main verb V_1 in any parallel way because the V_2 series do not show obvious signs of being clitics. Both phase V_2s such as *wan* 'finish', *dao* 'attain', *zhu* 'hold', and non-phase V_2s such as *ganjing* 'clean', *lei* 'tired', etc. seem to occur quite unreduced in phonological shape when occurring in V_1-V_2 pairs. It would therefore be somewhat implausible to attempt to treat such elements as clitics. Furthermore, as will be shown in a later section, there is also good evidence that verbal *le* only underwent reduction from its full pronunciation as *liao* to its present *le* form *after* it had moved adjacent to the V_1 and so this re-positioning can similarly not have been caused by any cliticization targeting V_1.

There is however also a second way in which one might attempt to explain the V_2 re-positioning in phonological terms. Although it is unlikely that clitic-like phonological dependency in the V_2 alone was responsible for V_2 movement to V_1, there is a possibility that some rather more subtle phonological deficiency in the V_1 could have resulted in the attraction of V_2 to the V_1. It has long been noted that Chinese early on developed an increased tendency for bi-syllabic compound-type elements in places where mono-syllabic forms had previously often occurred, and frequently-given explanations for this increase in bi-syllabicity relate it to some other process of phonological decay. A number of researchers (e.g., Karlgren 1923, Wang 1980, Norman 1988) have pointed to the fact that Chinese underwent a large-scale simplification in its syllable structure from being (C)(C)V(C)(C) to (C)V(C) and noted that the immediate decrease in the number of contrasting syllables available led to an increase in ambiguity among mono-syllabic words. It is suggested that in order to compensate for this increased ambiguity, many earlier monosyllabic words came to be bi-syllabic, with the addition of a second syllable serving to disambiguate otherwise similar mono-syllabic words. A more recent and interesting treatment of the increase in bi-syllabic words along the same basic lines is found in Feng (1998). Feng agrees that the increase in bi-syllabic words in Old Chinese was most likely due to the simplification of the syllable structure, but argues against the view that it was increased ambiguity which caused the growth of bi-syllabicism. Instead it is argued that simplification of the syllable structure led to the occurrence of a changed prosodic structure in which new mono-syllabic elements may no longer have been heavy enough to form minimal independent prosodic units/feet. Feng claims that consequently the new prosodic system required that a prosodic foot be formed by not just one but two syllables, this leading directly to the increase in new bi-syllabic words.

Either the more traditional view relating to ambiguity or that proposed by Feng could clearly be used to attempt to account for the change in RVCs and the re-positioning of V_2 adjacent to V_1. It has also been suggested that monosyllabic V_1 verbs may have become either too potentially ambiguous or have been prosodically too light to stand on their own and that re-positioning of the V_2 adjacent to V_1 would have served as a means to overcome this deficiency, creating unambiguous phonologically legitimate bi-syllabic resultative compounds (as proposed in Frank Li (in prep). Note that similarly ambiguous or phonologically weak mono-syllabic V_2 elements would also have arguably benefited from such a re-positioning.

Despite the possibility of a phonological account of the creation of V_1-V_2 forms however, there are several reasons to be suspicious of such a mode of explanation. First of all, if main verbs essentially became either too ambiguous or prosodically too light to stand alone and unsupported, it is not clear why a resultative V_2 and not other elements should have necessarily been selected as the means to overcome such a phonological deficiency. If mono-syllabic main verbs became too light or ambiguous on their own, one might expect that the NP *object* of the verb could have been re-phrased together with the verb to create a prosodic unit with enough weight to stand alone. It is certainly true that a significant number of verb-object compounds do exist in Chinese so one might expect verb-object re-phrasing to have been the most naturally available solution to overcome any phonological weakness in a monosyllabic verb. The presence of the object with the main verb would have also arguably overcome any ambiguity present. Another option which could have been made use of would have been to add a second verb with a similar meaning to the first, resulting in sequences such as 'hit-strike', 'look-watch' or 'think-reflect'. Such a 'strengthening/disambiguating' strategy may seem to have been made use of with nouns (e.g., *dao-lu* 'way-path') so could have been a natural means to strengthen/disambiguate verbs as well. Nevertheless one finds that instead of these options it is a specifically resultative V_2 which becomes added to the main verb and the obvious potential for the object of a verb to strengthen it seems to have been ignored, which is rather puzzling. If one reflects on the fact that [V_1 Object V_2] sequences became [V_1 V_2 Object], it is not at all clear why the presence of the object as a second mono-syllable adjacent to the V_1 could not have been enough to support it and the V_1 specifically required the re-positioning of the V_2 to provide it an extra syllable. One would not expect any purely phonological deficiency to be so semantically selective.

Furthermore if monosyllabic elements became too weak to stand as legitimate prosodic units in Old Chinese and this triggered the creation of V_1-

V_2 forms, one would expect to find the necessary presence of bi-syllabic units throughout the language; however, singular pronouns and a large number of adverbs did not obligatorily add on second supporting syllables. As the suggested dramatic change in phonological structure should have affected all phonological units in the same blind way, the particular increase of V_1-V_2 resultative forms tends to stand out as somewhat odd. Note also that it is indeed phonologically legitimate for mono-syllabic verbs to stand licensed in sequences of [V_1 Object V_2] in Chinese if they have a non-resultative purpose interpretation, as shown in (103). This again indicates that there is nothing ill-formed in such strings from a phonological point of view:

(103) (wo qu) [$_{VP}$ [$_{V1}$ mai] [$_{OBJ}$ dongxi] [$_{V2}$ chi]].
      I   go   buy   things   eat
      'I am going to buy something to eat.'

A third reason to be wary of any claim that a change in the prosodic structure directly triggered the re-positioning of V_2 to V_1 is that dramatic phonological change of this type (i.e., movement of V_2 over the object to V_1) in general tends to *follow* on from some underlying syntactic change rather than precede and bring about new syntactic forms/changes (see e.g., Harris and Campbell 1995). Consequently, if there are phonological changes in V_1-V_2-NP resultatives, they are perhaps expected to have occurred *after* the repositioning of V_2 and not trigger the repositioning of V_2.

Finally, and perhaps most significantly, there is a telling and important time difference between the suggested rise of bi-syllabicity in Chinese and the formation of V_1-V_2 resultatives. Packard (1998), Feng (1998) and others report that the noted shift from mono-syllabic to bi-syllabic words began at some time during the Zhou dynasty around 1000-700 BC, and that this turned into a sharp increase in bi-syllabic words during the Han dynasty (206 BC–220 AD). Feng argues that the prosodic changes responsible for the increase in bi-syllabicity also largely occurred around the Han period. This being so, if V_1-V_2 forms did result from the need for mono-syllabic main verbs like other mono-syllabic elements to be supported by a second syllable, one would clearly expect that V_1-V_2 resultatives would have been formed at the time when other mono-syllabic elements became bi-syllabic—i.e., during the Han period. However, it is well-reported that the critical change from [V_1 Object V_2] to [V_1-V_2 Object] resultatives only came about in the Tang dynasty (618-907 AD) and that [V_1-V_2 Object] only fully replaced [V_1 Object V_2] sequences in the Song dynasty (960-1279 AD) which is well over 700 years later than the Han period and the time of the suggested change in prosodic/syllable structure. This seems to cast in serious doubt any possibility that early phonological changes leading to necessary bi-syllabism were the trigger for the change from [V_1 Object V_2] to [V_1-V_2 Object]. It seems that [V_1 Object V_2] forms in fact existed quite legitimately for many centuries after the general switch to bi-syllabic forms in the Han period, and therefore that the change to V_1-V_2 resultatives must have some other non-phonological trigger and explanation.

5.3.2 V_2 Elements as Verbal Suffixes

One important aspect of the approach towards RVCs being developed here has been to highlight the obvious parallels with ongoing changes in the *shi-de* construction. In both RVCs and *shi-de* forms a sentence-final element (V_1/*de*) appears to re-position itself over the object, targeting the main verb, and settles in a position right-adjacent to the verb as in (104):

(104) a. V_1 Ob V_2 → V_1 V_2 Ob
　　 b. V Ob de → V de Ob

Such striking similarity in the change in both constructions suggests that a common re-structuring process may perhaps be responsible for both the earlier RVC change and the present reanalysis in *shi-de* forms. Considering how we approached the latter construction in chapter four, we first noted the positional change occurring with *de* and then worked our way forward to various claims about restructuring in *shi-de* forms. Observing from a range of data that *de* appears to be developing into a verbal suffix of some kind, the chapter reflected on the kind of verbal suffix this was likely to be, and came to the conclusion that *de* is undergoing reanalysis as a past tense morpheme suffixed to the verb.

Supposing now that the linear re-positioning in RVCs and *shi-de* forms does indeed reflect a common restructuring process and that sentence-final V_2 elements in RVCs targeted the verb in the same essential way that *de* is currently doing, the natural conclusion to make would be that resultative V_2 elements in the Tang/Song dynasty underwent reanalysis as verbal suffixes. Having furthermore spent time clearly motivating an earlier reanalysis of V_2 elements as heads of an Aspect phrase, the parallel with *de* might really seem to become very clear and in both cases a functional head with a verb-related meaning would be re-analyzing as a verbal suffix, (past) tense in the case of *de*, completive aspect in the case of V_2 elements in RVCs. It is also cross-linguistically highly common for tense and aspect to be encoded via suffixes on a verb, and so the suggestion that V_2 elements reanalyzed as aspect markers would have become verbal suffixes seems natural from a general cross-linguistic perspective too.

However, despite the intuition that suffixation of V_2 elements as Aspect markers is both generally plausible as an ultimate description of V_1-V_2 pairs and that such a change is also specifically motivated by the parallels with *de*, there is nevertheless still much to explain here. First of all, as mentioned earlier, V_2 elements are phonologically not obviously reduced or weakened, and so in this regard not so immediately like suffixes. Secondly, it is also not fully obvious that re-positioning of the V_2 to V_1 was actually the result of *movement* of the V_2 to V_1, as might be initially assumed. Thirdly, although movement of *de* to the verb is possibly consistent with *de* becoming a tense suffix, it does not really *explain* this movement. It should be remembered that evidence was presented indicating that sequentially *de* first undergoes reanalysis in its sentence-final position and then raises up to the verb; having successfully reanalyzed as tense, it is not entirely clear why *de* should then subsequently need to raise to the verb. Noting that *de* is a clitic element, it could be suggested that this simply reflects a re-alignment of what its target host element is specified to be. That is, as an enclitic *de* has to target some phonological host for support, and if it encodes a classically verbal property such as tense then it may be natural for it to specify the verb as its target-host. Such a clitic-based explanation is however unavailable for the V_2 re-positioning for the noted reason that V_2 elements are not obviously clitic-like. Quite generally then there is a significant difficulty in understanding why V_2 should have raised to V_1. Remember that the analysis developed so far has argued that V_2 elements were first reanalyzed as instantiating a sentence-final Aspect head, and critically it was argued that as such aspectual heads the V_2-Asp elements became operators which apply their function to entire VP predicates. Such scope over the VP was therefore taken to be encoded by V_2-Asp selecting VP as its (sole) argument and projecting this in its specifier position. Given therefore that such a configuration with V_2 in the head of AspP naturally corresponds to the scope and selection relation between V_2 and the VP, the obvious question in need of an answer is why V_2 would re-position itself and adjoin instead to the V_1-head. Such a re-adjustment might seem to represent a *decrease* in its scope, with V_2 c-commanding and having scope only over V_1 rather than the whole VP. A similar criticism could be possibly made of the encliticization of *de* to V^0—tense is an operator which takes a predicate as its argument and this is naturally represented in the structure with *de* in T^0 and the VP (raised overtly) in its specifier. If *de* re-positions to adjoin to V^0 this might again seem to represent a decrease in its scope to just the V^0, so there is clearly much to be accounted for here.

5.3.3 *V_2 Elements Do Not Undergo Raising to V_1*

In what follows I will argue that the surface re-positioning of V_2 to V_1 did indeed directly result from the aspectual properties of V_2 as Asp, and does also represent the process of V_2-Asp turning into a verbal suffix. However, I will claim that this re-positioning did not occur as the result of any movement of V_2 to V_1 but arose due to natural V_1-V_2 adjacency. It will be suggested that due to focus being on the V_2 representing completion in RVCs, the object in RVCs is frequently old information and therefore either fronted to a pre-verbal position or phonetically null (a *pro*), resulting in V_2 being quite naturally adjacent to V_1 in linear terms, and only infrequently separated from V_1 by the object. Such natural and frequent V_1-V_2 adjacency is then suggested to have led speakers to reanalyze the V_2-Asp in V_1-V_2 pairs as an aspectual suffix attached to V_1 in the lexicon. The critical motivation for such a reanalysis is argued to be *directionality*, and that re-analyzing V_2-Asp as a suffix resulted in speakers constructing an analysis in which the suffix V_2-Asp is licensed at LF by a higher AspP generated to the *left* of VP, with VP as its *complement*. Such reanalysis has the potential to re-align the AspP in synchronization with the general head-initial direction of selection in Mandarin Chinese. Prior to this the earlier sentence-final AspP is suggested to have grammaticalized in a way which was in disharmony with the canonical direction of functional selection, and re-interpretation of V_2-Asp as a suffix represents a natural correction made by speakers having a default head-initial parameter setting in their language.

An important assumption made in the approach here is that there is constant pressure towards uniformity in the directionality of selection in a language and that languages are indeed canonically either head-initial or head-final. Such a view of directionality is essentially present from the time of Greenberg (1963) through other early typological work in Lehmann (1973), Vennemann (1974), Hawkins (1979) and continued on in Chomsky (1981) and other more recent work. At least among the earlier typologists, the view is also commonly held that if a language somehow exhibits a structure which goes against the basic directionality of selection in a language, there will be a general pressure for the language to re-align such a structure in harmony with the canonical direction of selection. Vennemann (1973) talks of a Principle of Natural Serialization as a force which operates to restore consistency in languages which become 'inconsistent' (i.e., not uniformly head-initial or head-final) as the result of external influence or disruptive language-internal change. Lehmann (1973) also argues that if inconsistency creeps into a language then there will be pressure for this inconsistency to be corrected, and Hawkins (1979) proposes that a Principle of Cross-Category Harmony will similarly lead to languages re-aligning any non-uniform directionality. Commenting on the above proposals, Mallinson and Blake (1981, p.417) point out that correction of this type may be explained in terms of natural economy, and that it leads to a reduction in category/word-specific rules: "A disharmonic language requires more category-particular ordering rules and thus the grammar of such a language is more complex." Descriptively then, much research has shown that languages do tend to follow either a consistent head-initial or head-final ordering and that there would seem to be internal pressure for all categories to conform to the basic directionality present in a language.[17]

The sentence-final Aspect projection argued to have arisen in Chinese as a natural result of V_2 elements being reanalyzed as instantiating completive aspect can now be suggested to be in potential conflict with the general directionality of functional/complement selection in Chinese. When the sentence-final AspP was initially proposed, we took as a model the structure assumed for *de* in the TP after reanalysis, and suggested that the argument VP selected by V_2-Asp is projected in the SpecAspP position. The parallel pointed to with TP headed by *de* was that the predicate complement of T⁰-*de* becomes raised into SpecTP. It therefore seemed to be a reasonable suggestion that the predicate complement of V₂-Asp might similarly simply occur in a Spec position, likening this in essence to unergative intransitive verbs which are taken to project their sole argument NP in a specifier position. However, I would now like to argue that such a suggestion needs to be re-assessed and that the label 'specifier' here is actually rather deceptive. Consider again the basic structure which has been proposed for AspP:

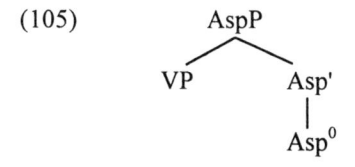

(105)
```
        AspP
       /    \
      VP    Asp'
             |
            Asp⁰
```

What needs to be reflected on is the way in which the term 'specifier' is understood and the way in which a specifier is licensed in the projection of a head. Canonically it might seem that a specifier has the following general properties:

(106) Specifier properties
    a. a specifier is an XP position
    b. the XP in the Spec position is either directly selected by the Y⁰-head of YP if base-generated there, or agrees with the Y⁰-head if moved to the Spec position.
    c. the specifier closes off the YP
    d. the specifier is built into the YP *after* the complement of Y⁰ is combined with Y⁰.

Complements have the general properties in (107):

(107) Complement properties
    a. a complement is an XP
    b. the XP is directly selected by the Y⁰
    c. the complement is combined with its selecting head Y⁰ as the first branching sister of Y⁰.

Abstracting away from the issue directionality in the projection of specifiers and complements, it might seem that in one sense a specifier is only really different from a complement in virtue of being built into a projection critically *after* the complement of the head has been combined with the head. Both specifiers and complements are maximal projections commonly selected by the head of a projection; the specifier simply happens to be inserted into the structure at a point later than the complement. While such an ordering relation does indeed result in a clear hierarchical difference when both complements and specifiers are projected as in (108) (assuming a Spec-initial complement-final pattern for illustration), if a head were not to project any complement, the difference between a specifier and a complement becomes less obvious. If indeed one follows assumptions commonly-made in recent work that a node is not projected unless it is genuinely branching (i.e., there should be no vacuous non-branching nodes—see Chomsky 1995a and references therein), then configurationally the difference between complements and specifiers reduces further, as illustrated in (109):

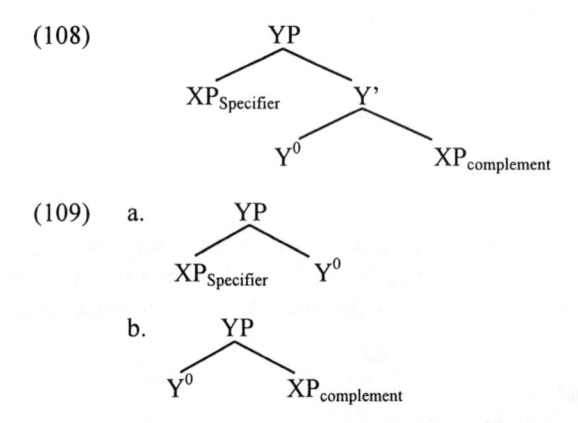

(108)   YP
          / \
   XP$_{Specifier}$ Y'
                     / \
                   Y^0 XP$_{complement}$

(109) a.   YP
             / \
      XP$_{Specifier}$ Y^0

      b.   YP
             / \
           Y^0 XP$_{complement}$

Now, considering the structure for AspP in (105), Asp^0 is a head which is suggested to have a specifier which hosts the single argument of Asp^0 (the VP) and will therefore never have a complement branching off Asp' to its right. If the Asp' node should therefore not be projected (due the no vacuous branching nodes constraint), (105) should instead actually be represented as (110):

(110)   AspP
          / \
        VP   Asp^0

I would now like to suggest that in such a structure, where the head Asp^0 importantly *never* projects any complement XP off an intermediate Asp' level, that the leftward branching XP (i.e., the VP) can no longer be determined as a specifier but is instead itself interpreted as a *leftward-branching* complement. In other words, one might suppose that a specifier is a relation which may possibly depend on the potential existence of a complement XP, so that an element can only be functionally determined as a specifier if there may also occur a hierarchically lower complement XP. Here in the AspP projection, the VP is essentially so similar to a complement of Asp^0 that although we have been referring to it as a specifier, in fact in the structure in (110) it actually gets interpreted as a complement. Note that the structure in (108) and (109) had two particular models: (a) *de* with VP in SpecTP, and (b) unergative intransitive verbs. In case (a) the VP was originally raised to SpecTP from a regular complement position and so T^0 did have a complement (therefore a VP to the

RESULTATIVE CONSTRUCTIONS

left of the T head can be determined as a legitimate specifier). In case (b) it might be assumed that unergative verbs have a structure such as (111a), assuming English as the relevant language here. If a no vacuous non-branching nodes constraint is adopted, this should then be represented as (111b):

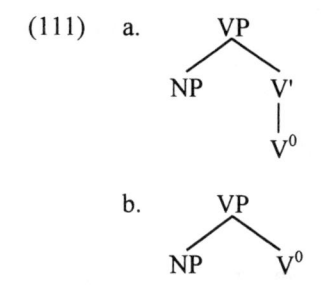

(111) a.
```
        VP
       /  \
      NP   V'
           |
           V⁰
```

b.
```
        VP
       /  \
      NP   V⁰
```

In (111b) this should mean that the NP cannot be determined as a specifier and should instead be interpreted as a complement, making it an exceptional head-final structure in a language such as English. However, in recent work (e.g., Hale and Keyser 1993) it has been argued that unergative intransitive verbs do in fact have complement NPs in addition to specifier subjects. One may either assume that unergative verbs have null cognate object type complements so that an example such as: 'John sighed' is interpreted as: 'John sighed a sigh', or it may be suggested that 'John sighed.' is possibly derived via incorporation of the N⁰ head of an object NP 'sigh' into V⁰, represented as (112) and (113) respectively:

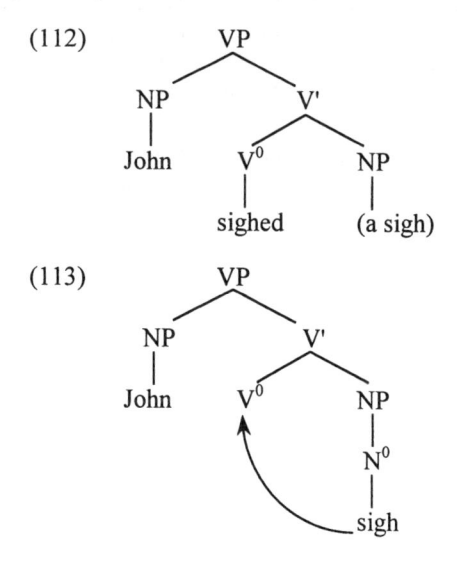

(112)
```
            VP
           /  \
          NP   V'
          |   /  \
         John V⁰  NP
              |   |
            sighed (a sigh)
```

(113)
```
            VP
           /  \
          NP   V'
          |   /  \
         John V⁰  NP
                  |
                  N⁰
                  |
                 sigh
```

CHAPTER 5

In either case there would be no head-final structure as the subject NP could be legitimately determined as a specifier due to the existence of the complement NP.

Returning to Chinese (110) now, I would like to maintain that such a structure is indeed interpreted as being head-final, with the VP failing to be determined as a specifier and instead being interpreted as a leftward projected complement. Having argued in chapter three that Chinese is essentially a head-initial language, and having noted in this section that languages will tend to be either head-initial or head-final wherever possible, the grammaticalized AspP clearly goes against the general headedness and directionality of complement selection in Chinese. Assuming there to be pressure towards a uniform directionality of headedness, one might naturally imagine that structures such as (110) would then be under pressure to be reanalyzed in a way conforming to the head-initial parameter if the opportunity for this arose. I will now attempt to argue that such directionality considerations are exactly what motivated the re-positioning of V_2 to V_1 and show how re-alignment of the structure in a head-initial way was indeed able to take place.

In a Minimalist (Chomsky 1993, 1995b) approach to morpho-syntax, X^0-level functional morphemes which correspond to syntactic head positions are taken to be base-generated either as independent word-level elements actually in the relevant head positions or alternatively as affixes attached to other (generally) lexical X^0-level elements. If an element is base-generated as an affix on a lexical head but instantiates a functional category (such as for example tense), it is assumed that the element (or the formal features it carries) will undergo raising from the base-generated lexical head position to a relevant higher functional head position to be licensed at some point in the derivation. Concretely this allows for three possibilities, illustrated in (114-116). Considering here the example of a functional morpheme instantiating tense and how it occurs and is licensed in syntactic structure, if the tense morpheme is a free-standing word, it may be base-generated separately from the verb and directly in the tense head T^0 as in (114). It will therefore be licensed directly in this base-generated position. (114) is modeled on an SVO language with overt subject raising:

(114)

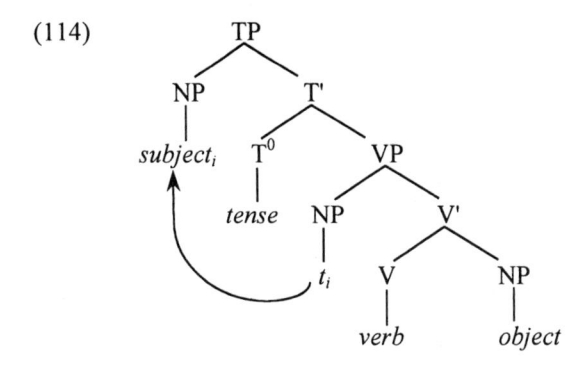

```
                    TP
                  /    \
                NP      T'
                |      /  \
            subject_i T⁰   VP
                     |    /  \
                   tense NP   V'
                         |   /  \
                        t_i  V   NP
                             |    |
                            verb object
```

A second possibility is if the tense morpheme is an affix, it will be base-generated attached to the verb in the lexicon and then inserted together with the verb in V^0. If the licensing of tense has to be effected in the overt pre-Spell-Out syntax in a language, this will then trigger overt raising of the verb-tense combination to T^0 as in (115):

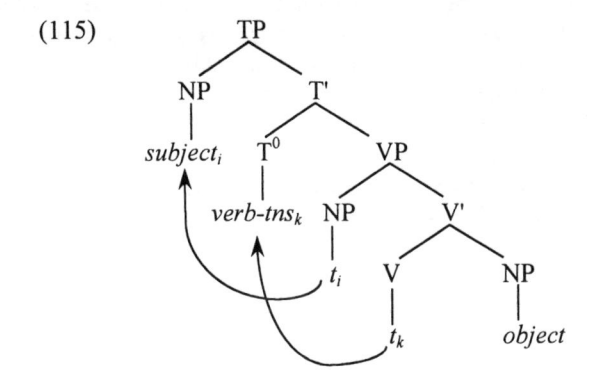

(115)

```
                        TP
                      /    \
                    NP      T'
                    |      /  \
                subject_i T⁰   VP
                          |   /  \
                   verb-tns_k NP  V'
                              |  /  \
                             t_i V   NP
                                 |    |
                                t_k  object
```

The third possibility occurs when the tense morpheme is base-generated as an affix on the verb but licensing of tense does not have to be effected in the overt syntax. Here it is assumed that the verb+tense affix (or the formal features present in the tense morpheme) will undergo covert post-Spell-Out raising to T^0 to be licensed/feature-checked at some point prior to LF. The structure in (116) represents the Spell-Out structure of this possibility with the verb and its tense affix still *in situ* in V^0. Raising of the verb-tns combination to T^0 will occur later at LF:

(116)

```
            TP
           /  \
         NP    T'
         |    /  \
      subjectᵢ T⁰  VP
         ↑        /  \
         |       NP   V'
         |       |   /  \
         |       tᵢ  V   NP
         |           |    |
         |_____verb-tns object
```

Returning now to Chinese RVCs, the analysis of V_2-Asp elements as occurring base-generated in a sentence-final Asp^0 essentially corresponds to the situation in (114)—the functional morpheme occurs as a free-standing word directly in the relevant licensing functional head, and this has been argued to lead to interpretation as a head-final structure in disharmony with the head-initial parameter-setting in Chinese. Supposing however it were to be possible for V_2-Asp elements to be somehow re-interpreted as aspectual suffixes attached to the V_1 in the lexicon, it could then be assumed that the V_1-Asp unit is inserted directly into V^0. Due to the occrrence of the V_1-Asp unit to the right of VP-type adverbials such as *manmarde* 'slowly' (as below in 117), it would then be assumed that the aspectual suffix is licensed later at LF, this corresponding in essence to the third possibility above where tense is licensed by LF-raising of the *verb-tns* unit to T^0 in (116).

(117) ta manmarde xi-ganjing-le yifu.
 he slowly wash-clean-LE clothes
 'He slowly washed clean the clothes.'

Significantly it then becomes possible to assume that the AspP projection which will license the aspectual suffix at LF in fact occurs as a fully regular head-initial functional projection selecting its VP argument in the canonical rightward direction. This is represented in the Spell-Out structure (118). It is assumed that the V_1-Asp unit (or the formal features of the Asp-suffix) will then at LF undergo raising up to the licensing Asp^0-head (and maybe also higher to T^0), this now being represented by a broken line in (118). TP is included in the structure in order to place the subject; I return to consider the status and instantiation of TP and other higher functional projections in chapter 6. Note that I also do not include verbal *le* here as this is examined in depth in chapter 6.

RESULTATIVE CONSTRUCTIONS

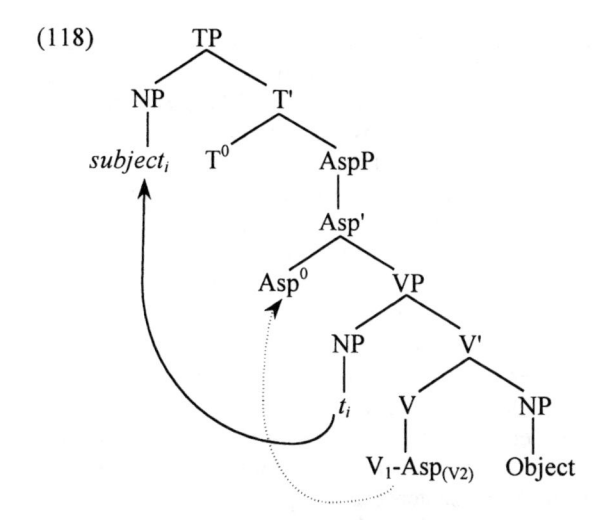

(118) [tree diagram: TP dominating NP (subject$_i$) and T'; T' dominating T^0 and AspP; AspP dominating Asp'; Asp' dominating Asp^0 and VP; VP dominating NP (t_i) and V'; V' dominating V (V$_1$-Asp$_{(V2)}$) and NP (Object); with arrows showing movement of subject and V-to-Asp raising]

The structure in (118) if instantiated with lexical items would result in (120) corresponding to the simple string in (119):

(119) (yaoshi) wo kan-wan shu,...
     (if)   I look-finish book
     'If I finish reading the book,...'

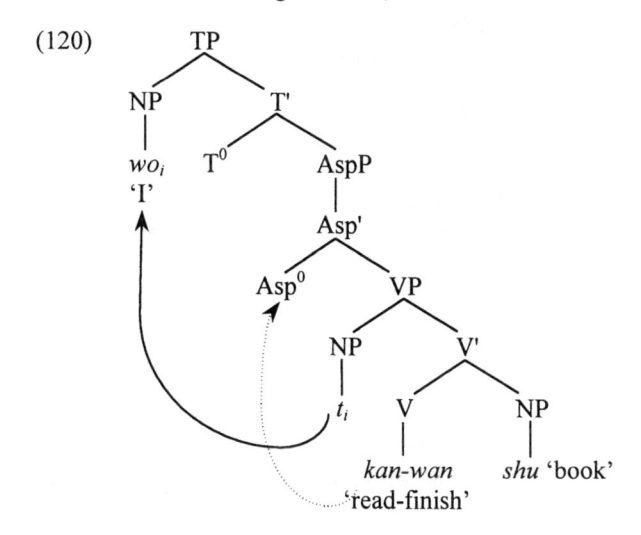

(120) [tree diagram: TP dominating NP (wo$_i$ 'I') and T'; T' dominating T^0 and AspP; AspP dominating Asp'; Asp' dominating Asp^0 and VP; VP dominating NP (t_i) and V'; V' dominating V (kan-wan 'read-finish') and NP (shu 'book'); with arrows showing movement]

Importantly then, reanalysis of V$_2$-Asp as a suffix attached to V$_1$ in the lexicon and licensed via LF raising to Asp^0 would critically allow for the grammaticalized sentence-final AspP to be re-interpreted as a regular harmonic head-initial structure. I will now suggest that certain aspects of the resultative

213

construction conspiring with general properties of Chinese in fact made such a reanalysis of the V_2-Asp as a suffix very easy to arrive at.

Earlier it was suggested that an important aspect of the earlier reanalysis of V_2 as completive aspect occurring in Asp^0 was that the focus in RVCs came to be squarely centered on the completion of the event represented by V_2. Such emphasis on the V_2 has been frequently pointed out (e.g., in Li and Thompson 1981) and, as noted earlier, may well have arisen naturally due to the sentence-final position of V_2 in early Chinese, sentence-final position attracting a natural focus. Now, if the V_2 element does indeed encode the focus in RVCs, this will have as consequence that the object of the verb will normally not be taken to be in focus. This will in turn mean that the object in RVCs will frequently be old and given information rather than represent a newly introduced NP (which, being new information, would constitute a focus). Consequently, commonly being old information, the object of the verb will often be represented either pronominally and hence normally by a phonetically null *pro* element in Chinese, or as a topic fronted to a sentence-initial position. It is also suggested in C. Li and Y. Shi (1998) that many V_1-O-V_2 occurrences in the Song dynasty were later replaced by verb-copying, *ba*-preposing of the object and object topicalization in order to prevent the intervention of the object between V_1 and V_2. We can represent these instances abstractly in (121).

(121) a.   Subject V_1 (pro) V_2
     b.   Subject V_1 O V_1 V_2
     c.   Subject ba-O V_1 V_2
     d. Topic$_i$ Subject V_1 (t_i) V_2

The result of such representation of the object in earlier [V_1 Object V_2] sequences will be that the V_1 and the V_2 are effectively heard linearly adjacent to each other. It can now be suggested that such frequently occurring linear adjacency of V_1 and V_2 would naturally allow for V_2 to be reanalyzed as a suffix attached to V_1 rather than being taken as base-generated in an independent head position. Consequently, suitable conditions for a reanalysis of V_2 in a way which would automatically permit a head-initial re-alignment of AspP were indeed arguably quite naturally available in the language. I would therefore like to suggest that general pressure for uniformity in the direction of selection combined with frequent occurrence of linearly adjacent V_1-V_2 led speakers in the late-Tang and Song periods to reanalyze V_2-Asp as a suffix on V_1 in the way outlined. These speakers may then have formally reinforced the reanalysis by themselves producing new RVCs with objects occurring *in situ* in post-V_2 positions. In other words, speakers during the period of change can be suggested to have had frequent input of forms with objects either in pre-verbal position or phonetically null and from such data reanalyzed the V_1-V_{2Asp} linear sequences as verb-suffix units occurring in V^0. Following this, such speakers with a reanalyzed interpretation of $V_{2\text{-Asp}}$ as a suffix would have then deduced that if an object were to be both overt and *in situ*, then it should occur *following* the V_1-Asp unit. Such a hypothetical process of reanalysis would then eventually have led the new generations of speakers to produce forms with overt objects following V_1-V_{2Asp} units.[18]

Note that in such an analysis one does not in fact need to assume that any movement of V_2 over the object to V_1 ever actually occurred and the whole sequence of change is simply the result of different generations of speakers re-analyzing what they hear in rather different ways. Whereas it was noted that the 'movement' of V_2 to V_1 largely remains unexplained in other syntactic accounts of RVCs, here with the suggestions made above and following careful justification of each step of the argumentation it has finally been possible to reach a rather natural explanation of the critical re-positioning of V_2. The suggested account therefore achieves the important joint goals set out earlier in section 5.1 of explaining both the historical re-positioning of V_2 and the current syntactic status of V_1-V_2 RVCs, and doing this in a way which links the two together in a principled and natural way. The analysis now developed has taken the three properties of RVCs identified as critical in section 5.2.1, notably (a) the lack of necessary predication between V_2 and the NP 'object', (b) the telic bounding property of V_2, and (c) the historical re-positioning of V_2, and suggested how these interact in important ways to result in the present day V_1-V_2 resultative. It has been suggested that there were in fact two stages to the reanalysis process. First, increased focus on the completive function of V_2 led to its reanalysis as instantiating a sentence-final Aspect head and allowed in non-predicative phase V_2 elements. Later, V_2 was reanalyzed as an aspectual suffix attached to V_1 in the lexicon and raised to Asp^0 for licensing in the covert syntax, this being fully in line with recent Minimalist assumptions concerning morpho-syntax.

In such an analysis with V_{2Asp} added to V_1 in the lexicon and inserted together as a unit in V^0, the V_1-V_2 pairs are essentially formed rather like complex-predicates, as a single verbal element combining the properties of two discrete morphemes, the main activity verb and the aspectual V_2 element. Consequently it is now fairly straightforward to suggest that any predicational properties which the V_{2Asp} might have in addition to its critical aspectual function may be simply added to those of the main V_1. If there are lexical descriptive properties inherent in the V_{2Asp} which apply to the object (as with 'literal' V_2s), then these can be applied to the object in a natural way from within V^0. Given that there are possibly a range of restrictions on the ways that V_1-V_2 pairs may be interpreted, I would now like to suggest that Yafei Li's (1990) rather successful lexical account of the way the predicational structure of V_1 and V_2 is merged together may now be adopted and taken up into the present analysis which takes V_2 to be *primarily* a functional aspectual element with *possible* additional lexical content/contribution. As noted earlier and stressed several times, there are numerous V_{2Asp} elements which are *purely* functional and it was suggested that the V_{2Asp} group is syntactically licensed in virtue of its functional contribution. Consequently V_{2Asp} elements will not necessarily have to contribute any descriptive properties in V_1-V_{2Asp} pairs—any lexical/descriptive properties which are present may be interpreted subject to the set of constraints presented in Yafei Li (1990), but all of the V_{2Asp} group will be formally licensed by the aspectual contribution.[19]

5.4 Consequences Related to Other Structures

Above in section 5.2 and 5.3 it has been suggested that in certain circumstances structures might in fact naturally grammaticalize in a way which is ultimately in conflict with the general direction of selection in a language. It was also suggested that in such cases there will be pressure for these structures to be reanalyzed in a way which does conform with head-parameter setting in the language. As part of the argumentation here, it was proposed that elements may become functionally determined as specifiers only if there is a hierarchically lower complement present, and in the absence of such a complement the 'specifier' may instead become functionally determined as a complement itself. If this element then branches in a direction which does not coincide with the general direction of complement selection, the result will be that the structure constitutes an exception to the general headedness directionality in a language and will be under pressure to undergo reanalysis. Reflecting on this idea of functional determination of the specifier relation, one might now reconsider certain other cases which could seem to be counter-examples to such a proposal. Although we noted that unergative verbs may be analyzed as having null cognate objects (or to arise via N-incorporation into V^0 and hence derivationally have a complement position present), one might wonder about the structures projected with relative clause *de* and the Taiwanese complementizer *kong* considered in chapter 3; in both such cases there is a large predicate-like element in the 'specifier' of a functional head (D^0 and C^0 respectively) and so they might seem to be similar to the AspP case where the predicate VP occurs in 'Spec'-AspP. However, in relative clauses the D^0 head does indeed have a complement—the CP—and so the leftward IP is in fact legitimately licensed as occurring in a specifier position. In the case of *kong*, the IP predicate in its Spec is raised to this position from a regular rightward complement position, so again the Spec position is legitimately licensed (in virtue of the existence of the lower complement position). What the potential constraint might seem instead to class as exceptional and therefore under pressure to be reanalyzed is structures in Chinese in which a predicate element is base-generated in the 'Spec' of a functional head which has no other complement. Here one might think of sentential *le*—if the predicate argument of *le* is base-generated to its left and *le* has no other complement then the predicate will be determined as a left-branching complement rather than a specifier. However, in footnote 12 it was pointed out that there may be prosodic stress-related evidence indicating that the predicate is actually raised to its surface position from an underlying position as a rightward complement, and so this case might also not be an exceptional left-branching structure.

One last non-Chinese case I would like to consider briefly here is that of N^0 elements, and I believe that the hypothetical constraint on specifier determination might possibly offer some insight into a hitherto unsolved puzzle. Specifically one might wonder whether it is possible for nouns to project an external argument in a specifier position but not a complement. In a language such as English where specifiers branch to the left and complements branch to the right this would result in an exceptional structure—the 'specifier' would be determined as a left-branching complement. In this regard, Grimshaw (1990) suggests that only process nominals have a genuine argument structure with external 'subject' arguments and internal complements, and furthermore that the projection of this argument structure is largely optional. What is of particular interest and relevance here is the observation Grimshaw makes that the external subject argument of process nominals may *only* be projected if the internal complement argument also co-occurs and that whereas (122) is fine, (123) with 'John' being interpreted as the agent of the 'examination' is not. Note that the adjective 'continual' is used to ensure the process nominal interpretation:

(122) John's continual examination of the patients impresses everyone.

(123) (*)John's continual examination impresses everyone.
(*) = ungrammtical if 'John' is Agent, only acceptable if 'John' is Patient

This interesting fact about the interpretation of process nominals has arguably not been explained in any non-stipulative way since Grimshaw's original observations. However, given what has been suggested above it is actually predicted that (123) should be exceptional with 'John' being interpreted as the external argument of the noun. For 'John' to be interpreted as the external argument it would have to be base-generated in Spec of NP (and then raised to Spec of DP for case). However, if the complement patient NP 'patients' is not projected, the result will be that the subject in NP Spec position will be determined as an exceptional leftward complement. This exceptionality may then explain why (123) is commonly felt to be bad. What is also of interest is that there *is* in fact a legitimate (although not immediately obvious) interpretation of (123). If 'John' is interpreted not as the external *agent* but instead as the *patient complement* of the 'examination', (123) is relatively acceptable (although perhaps not an immediately obvious interpretation). This is quite possibly a consequence of the 'Spec' position functionally being determined as a complement position in the absence of a true rightward branching complement—the NP base-generated in this position actually does get interpreted as if it were the complement of the N^0-head.

Finally, another general aspect of the account has been to show how suffixation may come about in an SVO type language. Typologically suffixation is extremely common in head-final SOV-type languages and much less frequently found in SVO type languages (see e.g., Greenberg 1963, Dryer 1992). This imbalance is generally explained by the way suffixes naturally arise in SOV-type languages. Most commonly verbal suffixes are grammaticalized functional morphemes which originated as independent verbs embedding a clausal complement (which they applied their particular function to). For example, causative suffixes often arise when an embedding verb encoding causation such as 'make/do' reduces and becomes dependent on the main lexical verb in its clausal complement. Such a grammaticalization process is both common and natural in SOV languages for the reason that the lexical verb of the subordinate clause and the functional verb of the higher clause occur linearly adjacent to each other, as seen in (124) (using English words for simplicity; see Mallinson and Blake 1981 for details). (124) is intended to mean: 'John made Mary leave.':

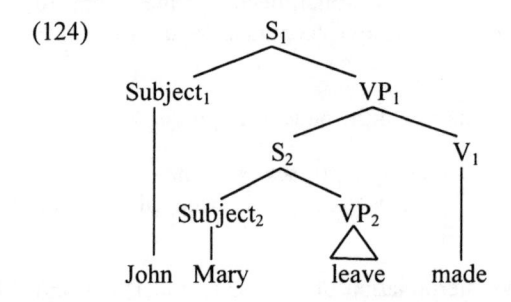

(124)

```
                S₁
              /    \
      Subject₁     VP₁
         |       /    \
         |      S₂     V₁
         |    /   \     |
         | Subject₂ VP₂ |
         |    |     △  |
        John Mary leave made
```

Such adjacency between the lexical verb of the lower clause and the functional embedding verb of the higher clause together with the phonetic reduction frequently accompanying grammaticalization of a functional element naturally results in the V_1 becoming phonologically dependent on the verb in VP_2 and reanalyzed as a suffix attached to the verb in VP_2.

With SVO-type languages there is no such adjacency between a matrix verb and the verb of its complement clause[20], as seen in (125):

RESULTATIVE CONSTRUCTIONS

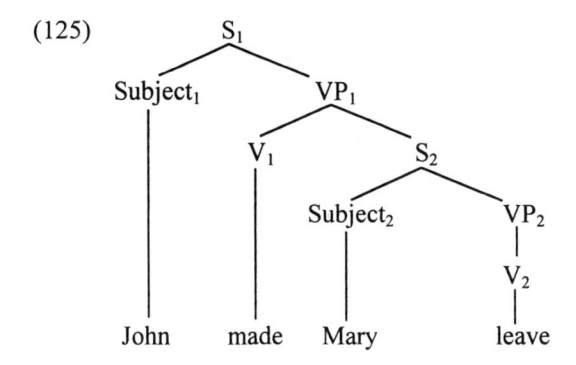

(125)

```
           S₁
          /  \
    Subject₁  VP₁
              /  \
             V₁   S₂
                 /  \
            Subject₂  VP₂
                       |
                       V₂

     John   made   Mary   leave
```

Consequently the conditions for natural reanalysis of a higher embedding functional type verb as a suffix attached to a lower lexical verb are absent from SVO type languages. The existence of the limited suffixation which does occur in such languages therefore needs some different explanation. Here a commonly adopted approach has been to suggest that suffixation in SVO languages must actually have arisen at a time when the language in question was SOV in its basic word order, and the existence of suffixation in SVO languages is even suggested to be evidence that such languages must have been SOV at some earlier point—see e.g., Givón (1971). However, while such a theory may be justified for west European languages with earlier SOV forms and their origins in Latin, it is contentious for languages such as the Bantu group which otherwise show no real convincing signs of ever having been SOV. One clear result of the current chapter has been to show precisely how and why suffixation might in fact also arise in SVO type languages, and the analysis developed therefore now allows for potential insights into directionality and suffixation in other head-initial languages.

5.5 English Resultatives: a Speculation

Finally before continuing on in next chapter to consider the nature of verbal *le* and its relation to resultative sequences in chapter 6, I would like to add certain thoughts about the structure of resultatives such as (126) in English:

(126) John ate the apple up. [V-Obj-Prt]

English resultatives appear to show a number of similarities with Chinese RVCs. First of all there are resultatives in which the element following the object of main verb is an adjective which seems to predicate rather literally of the object in some way, as in (127), and there are also resultatives in which a particle occurs and there is no literal predication relation between this element and the object NP, as illustrated in (128). This split resembles the distinction noted between literal and phase/non-literal V_2 elements in Chinese RVCs:

CHAPTER 5

(127) a. John washed the plates clean. The plates are now clean.
b. Mary painted the door purple. The door is now purple.

(128) [V-Obj-Prt]:
a. John ate the apple up. *The apple is now up.
b. John looked the article over. *The article is now over.
c. He thought the problem through. *The problem is now through.
d. He dried the socks out. *The socks are out.

Secondly it has been noted that there are two distinct orders possible with verb-particle resultatives; alongside the [V Object Prt] order in (128) it is possible to use a [V Prt Object] order as in (129):

(129) [V-Prt-Obj]:
a. John ate up the apple.
b. John looked over the article.
c. He thought through the problem.
d. He dried out the socks.

These two orders possible with V-Prt pairings seem to resemble the past and present orderings of V_1 and V_2 in Chinese RVCs, with the [V Object Prt] appearing like the original [V_1 Object V_2] Chinese type and the [V Prt Object] alternate possibly resembling current Chinese [V_1-V_2 Object] forms, as schematized in (130) and (131).

(130) a. Old Chinese $\quad$ V_1 OB V_2
b. English (i) $\quad$ V OB Prt

(131) a. Mod. Chinese $\quad$ V_1 V_2 OB
b. English (ii) $\quad$ V Prt OB

It should be noted that this second [V Prt Object] ordering is perfectly natural with verb-particle pairs, but often rather odd and unacceptable with verb + literal adjective sequences:

(132) a. ??He painted purple the door.
b. ??/*He rode tired the horse.

For this reason I will here restrict my attention to verb + particle pairs, which seem to show more of the patterning found in Chinese RVCs. Such English verb-particle sequences have indeed been studied by numerous investigators, e.g., Curme (1914), Kennedy (1920), Visser (1963), Kayne (1984), Johnson (1991), Hoekstra (1992), den Dikken (1995) and Collins and Thrainsson (1996) among many others, and a variety of different analyses have been proposed (which I will not review here for obvious reasons of space). Now that the present chapter has developed an analysis of Chinese RVCs, and given the apparent similarities with English verb-particle resultatives, it is natural to wonder whether the account of Chinese might allow for some further new insight into English verb-particle sequences.

Supposing that English verb-particle forms were indeed to be syntactically equivalent to Chinese RVCs, the particle would essentially be the equivalent of the Chinese V_{2Asp}. The [V Object Prt] sequences might be analyzed as having an underlying structure in which the particle instantiates a completive aspect head Asp^0 with the [verb + object] as a VP projected in Spec of AspP. Other [V Prt Object] forms if directly paralleling the analysis of Chinese might then have resulted from reanalysis of the particle as an aspectual suffix attached to the main verb and licensed by a higher AspP via LF raising, precisely as outlined for Chinese.

Such an analysis cannot however be correct for English, I believe, for two simple reasons. First of all, supposing the particle were to be interpreted as an aspectual suffix in [V Prt Obj] forms, this would result in a morphological sequence in (133):

(133) [verb-stem + tense-suffix + aspect-suffix]
     look-   -ed   over   (the article)
     dry-   -ed   out   (the socks)

Such a sequencing would seem to go against the cross-linguistic patterning commonly observed that aspectual morphemes occur closer to the verb stem than tense morphemes. This cross-linguistic patterning corresponds to the assumption that tense projections are structurally higher than aspect projections and that the highest functional projections relate to affixes which are farthest away from the verb stem (essentially Baker's 1985 Mirror Principle). If Tense is universally ordered higher than Aspect in syntactic structure and if the Mirror Principle (or a Minimalist equivalent) is a universally valid constraint then one should always find the affix order in (134):

(134) expected order following the Mirror Principle
     *look-over-ed = V-Asp-Tns
     *dry-out-ed   = V-Asp-Tns

Secondly, conversion of [V_1 Object V_{2Asp}] forms into [V_1-V_{2Asp} Object] sequences in Chinese is suggested to have resulted from V_1 V_2 adjacency arising naturally through frequent topicalization of an old/definite object and the occurrence of *pro* in object position. As English does not obviously have *pro* in regular object position nor topicalization to the same frequent extent as in Chinese, it might seem that this natural route of change would not be open to English verb-particle structures.

If this is so, it is natural to ask where the English alternation comes from and how it might relate to Chinese RVCs, as there are clear surface similarities. Here I suggest that a potential solution is to be found in considering an

CHAPTER 5

additional piece of extremely interesting and revealing historical information which is curiously ignored in most recent analyses of verb-particle constructions. Abundant evidence from Old English recorded in Curme (1914), Kennedy (1920) and Visser (1963-1973) indicates that there was in fact much earlier a *third* alternative ordering of verb, particle and object, in which the particle actually *precedes* the verb as in (135):

(135) English "type (iii)" resultatives:
     particle – verb – object

In fact a fourth variant of this was also apparently possible, with the object preceding both the particle and the verb, as in (136):

(136) Type (iii) variant
     object – particle – verb

Thus there were equivalents to forms such as:

(137) a. X out dried the-clothes
    b. X the-clothes out dried

(138) a. X up ate the-food
    b. X the-food up ate

Certain researchers such as Curme (1914) and Kennedy (1920) suggest that such forms were in fact more common than equivalents in which the object and the particle follow the verb (128) and (129). They also argue that these forms with the particle critically preceding the verb were earlier than the forms with the particle following the verb.

Such an early order in which the particle occurs before the verb is interesting and revealing. If the particle occurs to the left of the verb it could be suggested that the particle is actually in some functional head higher than the VP, hence quite naturally in a (completive) Aspect head. Such a possibility is indeed quite likely to be correct for verb-particle resultatives which occur in the Kartvelian languages as reported by Harris and Campbell (1995). There it is noted that in Svan there are particles which occur either following the verb as in (139), or alternatively preceding it as in (140). Interestingly when the particles precede the verb they are clearly not prefixed or cliticized to the verb for two reasons. First of all an adverb such as *ud* 'again' may intervene between the particle and the verb as in (141):

(139) acad   sga.
     s/he-go inside
     'S/he went inside.'

(140) sga acad.
 in s/he-go
 'S/he went inside.'

(141) sga ud etqarix yerbats.
 in again they-implore God-DAT
 '... again they implore God.'

Secondly, the particles may occur standing alone and unsupported as (affirmative) answers to yes/no questions, as in (142) with the particle *ka* 'out':

(142) ka acad ma? → answer: ka.
 out s/he-go Q   out
 'Did s/he go out?'   'Yes.'

This suggests that such elements are neither raised from some lower position and cliticized to the front of the verb, nor base-generated as verbal prefixes, as if they were clitics/prefixes they should not be able to stand alone without the verb or be separated from the verb by adverbs. The patterning rather suggests that such elements are instead free-standing heads occurring base-generated in some functional head dominating the VP, hence naturally in an Aspect head. Furthermore, it is a common characteristic across a wide range of languages (including Chinese, Thai, Vietnamese, etc.) that yes/no questions are answered in the affirmative with the highest verbal element in a sentence (hence a modal if present, otherwise the main clause lexical verb, see Simpson 2001). This might again seem to indicate that the particles in Svan and other Kartvelian languages are indeed independent heads in a verb-related functional projection dominating VP—as the hierarchically highest 'verbal' elements present they are used as answer-forms instead of the main verb which is lower down in the structure.

Returning back to English, if it is true that forms with the particle preceding the verb are indeed older and were more frequent than present-day forms in which the particle (and the object) follows the verb, then it is reasonable to suggest that the present-day forms may well have derived from the earlier particle-verb sequences. (143b) and (143c) should then be both derived from (137a) in some way:

(143) a. (Obj) Prt V (Obj) = (the-clothes) out dried (the-clothes)
      b. V Obj Prt   = dried the-clothes out
      c. V Prt Obj   = dried out the-clothes

That is, type (iii) forms schematized in (144) historically developed into the present type (i) and type (ii).

CHAPTER 5

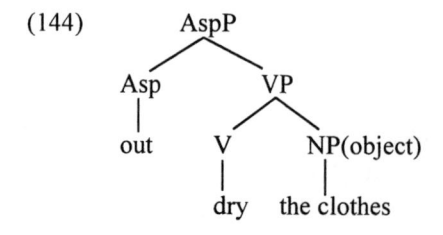

(144)
```
        AspP
       /    \
      Asp    VP
       |    /  \
      out  V   NP(object)
           |    |
          dry  the clothes
```

Various possibilities suggest themselves. Certainly it would seem that one needs to allow for object-shift to play a role (as in fact assumed in Johnson (1991), as it is clear that the object may occur in two independent positions in (143a). In addition to this one might perhaps then make the assumption that the particle is indeed in Asp^0, and not just in (143a) but in (143b) and (143c) as well. In (143a) both the particle and the verb would be in their base-generated positions in Asp^0 and V^0 respectively. (143c) would then be derived from an underlying sequence [Prt V Obj] by raising the verb to some higher position above completive Asp as in (145). (143b) would result from similar raising of the verb combined with object-shift to Spec-AspP, as in (146):

(145) V_i [$_{Asp}$ Prt [$_{VP}$ t_i Obj]] = dried$_i$ out t_i the-clothes

(146) V_i [$_{AspP}$ Obj$_k$ [$_{Asp}$ Prt [$_{VP}$ t_i t_k]]] = dried$_i$ the-clothes$_k$ out t_i t_k

However, if the particle is in fact in Asp^0, it might be objected here that movement of the verb to a higher head-position would violate the Head Movement Constraint (HMC), being head-movement from a lower V^0 over a filled Asp^0 to some higher X^0. An alternative might therefore be to propose that the particle is actually an aspectual-prefix attached to the verb in the lexicon and inserted into V^0. In a way similar to Johnson (1991) it can then be suggested that when the verb raises it strands the aspectual particle in V^0 and then moves on higher. This would not result in any HMC violation and would essentially be a treatment of particle stranding similar to that commonly adopted for particle-verb separation in German V2 clauses. As shown in the following, whereas the German particle and verb occur together in V^0 in (147), when the verb raises to C^0 in V2 clauses, it strands the particle in V^0 (or possibly some other higher head), as in (148):

(147) [$_{CP}$ Johann [$_C$ will [$_{IP}$ die Tür aufmachen]]].
        Johann wants   the door open-make
   'Johann wants to open the door.'

(148) [$_{CP}$ Johann [$_C$ macht$_1$ [$_{IP}$ die Tür auf-t$_i$]]].
   Johann   makes   the door open
   'Johann opens the door.'

In such an approach to English, the particle as a stranded aspectual prefix would then undergo raising to Asp at LF for licensing/feature-checking. A further variant of such an approach would be to suggest that the verb + particle prefix first raise together to Asp^0 and the particle is stranded there when the verb moves to a higher head.

Either way, understanding the particle as an aspectual prefix added in the lexicon in a way similar to the analysis of Chinese allows for a plausible account of resultative verb-particle structures which has historical support and is able to make good sense of the third type of patterning noted where the particle precedes the verb. This third patterning is curiously ignored in recent treatments of particle-verb forms and has led to an emphasis on analyses in which the particle is taken to predicate of the object, e.g., Hoekstra (1992), Collins and Thrainsson (1996). As noted in (128) there are clear problems with such predication-based analyses, problems which an alternative aspect-based approach is able to avoid.[21] Furthermore, if historically later [V-Object-Prt] sequences such as [dry the-clothes out] are actually derived via verb-movement and object-shift from earlier structures in which the particle was a verbal prefix, then syntactically there is no predication relation between the particle and the NP 'the clothes'—the NP in such sequences is in a derived hence non-theta position and is consequently not the subject of any (small) clause type predication. The 'predication' structure seen in the linear sequence of NP followed by particle in [dry [$_{NP}$ *the clothes*] *out*] is actually a derivational illusion resulting from a combination of raising operations and is not a primitive theta relation. Finally, the conclusion that particle elements in both English and the Kartvelian languages (among others) are either verbal affixes or base-generated in a pre-verbal Asp-head would seem to add support to suggestions here that similar resultative V$_2$ elements in Chinese are also affixal instantiations of completive Asp. Further careful historical research is certainly required, but generally the analysis of resultative elements as being potentially reanalyzed instantiations of Aspect would seem to open up a number of interesting cross-linguistic possibilities.

5.6 Summary

Before continuing on to examine the diachronic and synchronic patterning of verbal *le* and how it may or may not relate to the changes which have taken place in RVCs, I now provide a short summary of the main conclusions of this chapter.

The chapter began as an investigation of the apparent diachronic re-positioning of V$_2$ elements to a position right-adjacent to the main verb V$_1$ and

CHAPTER 5

how an understanding of this historical change might shed better light on the current syntactic status of V_1-V_2 resultative sequences. Reviewing first previous syntactic approaches to V_1-V_2 composition, I pointed out a number of unsatisfactory aspects in analyses which assume that V_2 elements must synchronically undergo raising to the V_1 and instead attempted to develop an alternative approach, critically linking the diachronic word order change to an increase in focus on the telic contribution of V_2 and the lack of a necessary predication relation existing between V_2 and the object of V_1. Suggesting that V_2 elements became reanalyzed as instantiating a sentence-final aspectual head, this allowed for an explanation of why it was that phase-type V_2 elements could occur licensed in such positions with no necessary predicational relation to the object of V_1. Subsequently considering the actual re-ordering of V_2 elements right-adjacent to the V_1, it was argued that this actually did not result from any movement of V_2 but instead occurred as an instance of re-structuring when both the fronting of objects and the occurrence of objects in null pronominal form would have given rise to natural instances of V_1 V_2 adjacency. In such re-structuring it was suggested that the V_2 aspectual head became reanalyzed as an aspectual suffix taken to be combined with V_1 in the lexicon. Trying then to make sense of why such a reanalysis might have actually taken place, it was ultimately argued that re-structuring of this type would have allowed for a non-canonical head-final structure to be naturally reanalyzed as head-initial, and hence that *directionality* can be suggested to have been the critical force behind the second stage in the reanalysis and the physical 're-positioning' of V_2 adjacent to V_1. Finally, it was noted that the occurrence of suffixation in head-initial languages is typologically much less common than in head-final languages for certain fairly simple reasons relating to the linear ordering of elements in SOV-type languages. A significant general conclusion of the chapter has therefore also been to provide a principled explanation of just how and why less frequent instances of suffixation in head-initial languages might in fact possibly develop.

Notes

[1] Note that since the Wei, Jin and Northern and Southern Dynasties there had been other V-V structures consisting in the sequence of V_1-V_2-Object, such as (i) below, where both V_1 and V_2 were originally used as transitive verbs and in these V_1-V_2 sequences occur sharing the same object following both verbs. Such sequences also commonly allowed for the insertion of a coordinator (for example, *er* 'and') between the two verbs, as in example (ii). Historically such structures never underwent any re-positioning of the object, unlike the RVCs examined in this chapter, and can be suggested to have originated from rather different co-ordinate structures, as indeed argued in C. Li and Y. Shi (1998). As a result they will not be considered here in the chapter. Examples below are from C. Li and Y. Shi (1998).

(i) kai-tong daolu, wu you zhangai.
    open-through road NEG have obstacle
    'Open the road and make them free of obstacles.'

(ii) bao zi hou ji er sha zhi.
    leopard from behind attack and kill it
    'The leopard attacked and killed it from behind.'

[2] Note that until verbal *le* is properly re-examined in chapter 6 I will simply gloss it as 'LE' in the examples.

[3] Yafei Li admits that a VP headed by V_2 could occur as an optional adjunct adjoined to VP_1, but adds that head-movement from V_2^0 to V_1^0 should then violate constraints such as Subjacency/the ECP. Consequently, the only syntactic representation one should potentially consider as a competitor to the lexical compounding approach should be one in which V_2 indeed heads a VP selected by V_1 (hence not constituting a barrier to raising).

[4] Note that the small clause here is a VP (assuming *ganjing* 'be-clean' to be a stative verb) but that it could in principle be some other categorial type, e.g., a PP, as argued in Hoekstra (1992).

[5] Later in his analysis Sybesma points out that there are however also significant differences between simple V_1-V_2 forms and the [V_1-de NP V_2] type of resultative which suggests that they are not derived from a single underlying structure.

[6] Such a conclusion is in fact also suggested by Yafei Li (1998) for the similar [V_1-de NP V_2] resultative type. Li notes that when V_1-de is intransitive, it is possible to topicalize an NP in the sequence which follows V_1-de as in (i)

(i) Zhangsan ku-de [shenme huor]$_i$ Lisi dou bu xiang gan t$_i$.
    Zhangsan cried-DE any work Lisi all NEG want do
    'Zhangsan cried to the extent that Lisi didn't want to do any work.'

However, when V_1 is transitive, it is not possible to topicalize an NP in the same way. This is taken to indicate that the NP *Lisi* is indeed the direct object of V_1 (and a *pro* co-referential with the object occurs as the subject of the lower clause) and so may not be preceded by a topic from a lower clause:

(ii) *Zhangsan kua-de [shenme huor]$_i$ Lisi dou bu xiang gan t$_i$.
    Zhangsan praised-DE any work Lisi all NEG want do
    Intended: 'Zhangsan praised Lisi to the extent that she didn't want to do any work.'

The same conclusion is reached on the basis of prosodic facts. If a pause is created directly after V_1-de via the insertion of a particle *ya*, then this is acceptable only in the intransitive case with *ku-de* 'cried' and not with the transitive *kua-de* 'praised', indicating that the NP *Lisi* is again the object of a transitive V_1 and cannot be separated from it. Although there are certain differences between V_1-V_2-NP forms and V_1-de NP V_2 resultatives, it is interesting that when the NP occurs between a transitive V_1 and V_2 it clearly does behave like the object of V_1, contra Sybesma's analysis of such forms.

CHAPTER 5

[7] Relating to the small clause 'issue' and the potential predication relation between the V_2 and the object which it might encode, patterns of adverbial modification may indicate that there is actually a significant difference in (underlying) structure between English resultatives and Chinese V_1-V_2 resultatives, contra the assumption made in Sybesma (1999). Although adverbial modification of the secondary predicate in English resultatives is not common, it can occur with time adverbials as shown in (i):

    (i) John brushed [the table clean of dust for five minutes].
        (and then it got dusty again).

In (i) the duration phrase can be understood to modify just the state [the table clean of dust] and not the action of 'brushing.' In Chinese [V_1-de NP V_2] resultatives, the same kind of modification is also possible:

    (ii) wo qi-de ma lei-le liang-ge zhongtou.
        I ride-DE horse tired-LE two-CL hour
        'I rose the horse so that it got tired for two hours.'

However, parallel modification is significantly *not* possible in V_1-V_2 resultatives:

    (iii) *wo qi-lei-le ma liang-ge zhongtou.
        I ride-tired-LE horse two-CL hour
        Intended: 'I rose the horse so that it got tired for two hours.'

What this would seem to indicate is that adverbial modification of this kind is possible when an NP and a predicate occur in a single predicational-type sequence as in (ii) *ma-lei-le* or (i) 'the table clean of dust' and not possible when the potential predicate V_2 occurs bound to another predicate V_1 in a single unit as in (iii). Supposing that V_1-V_2 resultatives were to have an underlying structure in which there was a small clause-type predicational sequence, one would expect similar adverbial modification to be available. As examples like (iii) are however unacceptable, the natural conclusion may again be that they are not derived from structures encoding a small clause predication.

[8] A third possibility with a ternary branching structure would be to have both the object NP and the small clause projected off the same complement node, this allowing for c-command between the object NP and a pro in the small clause.

[9] Some structure of this type must also be available for resultatives in Korean as reported in Soonwon Kim and Maling (1997). Case marking in Korean RVCs is particularly revealing. If the main activity verb is intransitive, the NP 'subject' of the result sequence surfaces in nominative case, as in (i) and (ii):

    (i) Robin-i paykkop-i ppacki-key wus-ess-ta.
        Robin-NOM belly-NOM come.out-KEY laugh-PAST-DEC
        'Robin laughed his belly out.'

    (ii) Chris-ka palpatak-i talh-key talli-ess-ta.
        Chris-NOM feet-NOM worn-KEY run-PAST-DEC
        'Chris ran his feet sore.'

However, if the main event verb is transitive, the NP 'subject' of the result predication occurs in accusative case:

(iii) Robin-i   soy-lul   ttukep-key talkwu-ess-ta.
Robin-NOM metal-ACC hot-KEY heat-PAST-DEC
'Robin heated the metal hot.'

Soonwon Kim and Maling suggest that -*key* is an inflectional element which assigns nominative case to the subject of the result clause. Because -*key* is also present in (iii) nominative case must also be available and assigned in (iii). As the overt NP *soy-lul* 'metal' however surfaces in accusative, it must be assumed that a *pro* subject occurs in the result clause in (iii) receiving the nominative case, and that the overt NP *soy-lul* originates in the main clause, being assigned accusative there. It is not possible to suggest that *soy-lul* somehow originates in the lower result clause and skips the subject position avoiding nominative case to explain the fact that it surfaces with accusative. Subject case-positions cannot simply be skipped over as (iv) below shows:

(iv) *John mentioned him$_i$ [(that) t$_i$ arrived].

Consequently UG must indeed in some way make available structures in which a transitive verb has a genuine NP object and also allows for the projection of a result clause with a co-referential *pro* subject.

[10] Note that Korean has V_1-V_2 sequences and that aspectual completion is frequently expressed by a V_2 *peli-ta* which literally occurs as a verb meaning 'to throw away.' What is important to note is that this V_2 has clearly grammaticalized and been reanalyzed as a functional head which is structurally higher than the V_1 and its object, just as has been suggested here in Chinese. In the Korean V_1-V_2 resultative/completive sequence, V_1 occurs with its object in a structurally subordinate VP marked with the particle -*e* and the V_2 occurs as the higher verb inflected for tense and declarative-marking, as illustrated in (i):

(i) ku-nun sihem-ul phokiha-e   peli-ess-ta.
he-TOP exam-ACC give-up-E throw-away-TNS-DEC
'John just gave up on the test.'   (Lee 1993)

[11] Note that if no lexical material occurs to the left of a functional element it may be phrased with the lexical element to its right, this occurring here with *ba*.

[12] This phenomenon shows through when one considers the position of the verbal complex. If no object follows the V_1-V_2 pair (as e.g., in a *ba*-construction) and the V_2 is then sentence-final, the V_2 will normally carry a focus stress. In such a situation, it is more common to find a completive V_2 with the phonetic strength to carry this stress rather than the general completive *le*.

(i) wo ba shu   kan-<u>wan</u>-le/??kan-<u>le</u>.
I   BA book look-finish-LE/look-LE
'I finished reading the book.'

(ii) nei-ben-shu wo kan-<u>wan</u>-le/?kan-<u>le</u>.
that-CL-book I look-finish-LE/look-LE
'I finished reading the book.'

Elsewhere when an object follows the V_1-V_2 pair and the object can absorb any sentence-final stress, *le* occurs quite freely (and verbal completive *le* is possibly more common than other V_2 completives in such non-emphatic positions):

229

CHAPTER 5

(iii) wo kan-<u>wan</u>/kan-<u>le</u> liang-ben shu le.
I look-finish/look-LE two-CL book LE
'I read two books.'

Note interestingly that it is technically incorrect to classify the relevant stress as being sentence-final because it actually occurs on the element preceding sentence *le*. If one assumes that sentence *le* is a sentential operator and therefore in some structurally high position, the stress can therefore more accurately be classed as occurring on the most deeply-embedded element—the object in (iii) and the V_2 in (i) and (ii). Such a conclusion clearly raises interesting questions about the position of sentence *le* and when the stressing rule applies (i.e., is the sequence to the left of sentence *le* possibly raised there to Spec-*le* from a rightward complement position, and does the stress rule apply to the sequence before raising?).

[13] The preference for canonical, commonly occurring general forms such as 'tired' rather than 'exhausted' in resultative constructions focused on completion can be linked with the common preference for generality found in grammaticalization. In Bybee, Perkins and Pagliuca (1994) and elsewhere it is noted that it is standardly more general verbs such as 'come' or 'go' which tend to grammaticalize as functional tense and aspect elements rather than semantically related but more specific manner of motion verbs such as 'amble', 'wander', 'stroll', etc. The general forms allow more easily for focus to fall on the particular abstract tense/aspect *function* they encode, whereas more specific descriptive verbs have stronger lexical content which may distract attention away from their use as primarily functional elements.

[14] A further observation that also indicates that V_2s may frequently be highly predictable and hence not fully open is that it is very difficult to stress a V_2 and understand this as *contrastive*. This is because it is simply often difficult to imagine what the V_2 might contrast with, i.e., what other possible outcomes application of the V_1 to the object could result in:

(i) ?*wo ba yifu   xi-GANJING le, bushi HONG le.
I BA clothes wash-clean LE, not   red   LE
?*'I washed the clothes CLEAN, not RED.'

Furthermore, in German resultatives (see Lüdeling 1997) focus-topicalization patterns show that V_2-equivalent type elements are often not really new information but actually rather predictable. In (ii) below it is seen that the adjective *kaputt* 'broken' can appear fronted in a simple sentence licensed by encoding new information in the focus-topic position:

(ii) Kaputt ist die Tür.
broken is the door
'The door is broken.'

However, when *kaputt* occurs in the resultative adjective-verb pairing *kaputt-schlagen* 'hit-broken' it can only occur in the fronted position if it is emphasized by an additional intensifier such as *ganz* 'quite' or *völlig* 'completely' as shown in (iii). This indicates that when it occurs in a resultative the adjective does not encode information about a new state in the same way that it does in (ii) and is instead licensed *primarily* as a telic bounding element. Only if further intensification is added to the adjective can it therefore be licensed in the focus-topic position:

(iii) *(Ganz/völlig) kaputt hat Max die Tür geschlagen.
quite/completely broken has Max the door hit
'Max completely smashed the door.'

[15] Having argued at length that V_2 elements are licensed in RVCs in virtue of providing the general bounding property (71b), I have not discussed how any lexical descriptive content they may have comes to be interpreted. There are a couple of points and possible suggestions which can be made here. First of all, it has been noted that many functional elements do also have clear lexical content; if these elements are however licensed as primarily functional and therefore base-generated in functional heads, it must be assumed that any lexical content they have may be built into the structure from their position of origin in the functional head. Such an assumption may now also be made for V_2 elements argued to be base-generated in Asp and the lexical content of literal V_2s may be interpreted from within the functional head Asp. Note also that V_2-Asp is taken to select for the VP and hence the type of situation represented by the VP. The frequent interpretation that the object in the VP has the result state property represented by V_2 may then be a function of V_2 selecting for the situation in which that object is affected (e.g., a 'washing' event is one which can be selected by a V_2-Asp 'clean', and the object of the washing may then naturally be interpreted as having such a result state property). In some way the selection relation here is similar to that existing between classifiers and nouns; just as a classifier is sensitive to certain features of a range of nouns (e.g., +round), V_2s may classify situation types according to their potential natural outcomes, and in both classifier and V_2-Asp case this translates into a selection relation. There is also a possible similarity here to the idea of 'pragmatic association' proposed in Kayne (1985) and taken up in Sybesma (1999) in a different way from the proposal here. It can be suggested that if there is a washing event involving an object and this is terminated by some clean state, then it is just pragmatically natural to associate the object with that clean state. Another alternative might be to make use of Borer's (1994) idea that objects check case in the Spec of a telic aspectual head and suggest that at LF the object raises to an outer SpecAsp to check its case and at the same time is predicated of by the V_2 in Asp. This would be similar to analyses of *tough*-movement in which the surface subject is raised from object position and predicated of by the entire *tough*-predicate when in its raised position (see e.g., Brody 1994):

(i) John$_i$ [is easy to please t$_i$].

Because the V_2-Asp is licensed in virtue of its functional-aspectual property (71b), such predication would not be forced to occur and phase V_2s would not have to predicate of the object (in contrast to small clause analyses in which the V_2 is licensed precisely as a predicate and therefore must predicate of the object in order to be legitimized). As we will shortly see, the situation is clearer in V_1-V_2 pairs after the second stage of reanalysis and so I will not discuss this further here.

[16] As noted earlier, there are certain obvious parallels between Chinese RVCs and English verb-particle forms. In the latter there are currently two orders available, which might seem to reflect the two historical orders in Chinese. In (i) the particle follows the object, whereas in (ii) the particle occurs preceding the object and adjacent to the verb:

(i) John found the information out.
   [$_{VP}$ V Object Prt] similar to early Chinese [V_1 Obj V_2]
(ii) John found out the information.
   [$_{VP}$ V Prt Object] similar to later Chinese [V_1 V_2 Obj]

It is pointed out in Johnson (1991) that the variant in (ii) is also not produced by any Heavy NP Shift operation as the object can be significantly lighter than in regular Heavy NP Shift examples. For example, simple NPs can normally not be extraposed in potential HNPS forms such as (iiia), yet bare NPs do easily occur following particles in verb-particle sequences:

(iii) a. *John painted t$_i$ red the door$_i$.
     b. John painted t$_i$ red all the doors which face northwards$_i$.

[17] An interesting case here is Amharic as reported by Comrie (1989). Amharic having originated as a classically head-initial Semitic language, migration of the Amharic-speaking people to a head-final Cushitic-speaking area resulted in change in many of the basic orderings, due to the external influence of the Cushitic languages. Pressure for uniformity has now led Amharic to become head-final in just about all its category types, preposition-NP ordering being the sole residue of the earlier head-initial order.

[18] It should be noted that (rather unsurprisingly) reference to certain resultative V_2 elements as suffixes has in fact been made elsewhere, though largely without much justification. For example, Smith (1997) simply states that: 'Mandarin marks the distinction between telic and atelic verb constellations with verb suffixes known as Resultative Complements.' (p.43). There is no further qualification of use of the term suffix, nor any discussion of whether it is intended to refer to just phases or more literal V_2s as well. In Starosta, Kuiper, Ng and Wu (1998) there is also suggestion that certain phase-type V_2 elements may be considered to be suffixes on the grounds that they are not elements which encode literal predication on any NP (precisely as argued here). However, there is no proposal that any unifying property (such as telicity/aspect) might possibly link these elements together as a single functional group and so the conclusion is simply that any non-predicating V_2 should by default be classed as a suffix. The critical question of why literal V_2s might pattern syntactically in the same way as phase V_2s is also not touched upon. Here the attempt has been made to develop a unified treatment of literal and phase V_2s both from a historic and a synchronic point of view and provide a principled account of precisely why the modern structures may exist as they do. For further general discussion of the possibility that V_2 elements in the V_1-V_2-Object sequences may be aspectual verbs, see Wang (1990) and Mei (1994).

[19] Note that Wang (1990) and Mei (1994) also suggest that wherever a V_2 element from an earlier V1-Obj-V2 form occurs re-positioned before the object in a new V_1-V_2-Obj sequence, this V_2 element is an aspectual morpheme. The present analysis attempts to provide a principled explanation for exactly how such a reanalysis may have taken place. In view of the fact that V_2 elements could occur in V_1-Obj-V_2 sequences without there being any predication relation between V_2 and the object, such patterns strongly suggest that V_2 elements grammaticalized as functional aspect heads in final position prior to re-positioning and suffixation to V_1. The latter re-positioning of V_2 in the present analysis occurred as a direct result of the reanalysis of V_2 as a functional category in final position. In this sense the *surface reflex* of reanalysis, i.e.,

suffixation of V_2 to V_1, consequently occurs *after* the underlying syntactic reanalysis. Such a sequencing of surface reflex following initial reanalysis is suggested to be quite common in diachronic change (see Harris and Campbell 1995).

[20] Unless of course the Subject$_2$ comes to be positioned after V_2 in a PP as in causatives in certain Romance languages:

    (i)   Jean a fait manger les pommes à Marie.   (French)
           Jean has made eat   the apples   to Marie
           'Jean made Marie eat the apples.'   (p.c., Lina Choueiri)

[21] The aspect-based approach proposed here is most similar to the account argued for in Johnson (1991). However, Johnson treats the particles as unclassified lexical suffixes on the verb and makes no connection to aspectual characteristics. Treatment of the particles as suffixes in English can also be suggested to run into a number of difficulties concerning the generation and licensing of the tense suffix which appears attached inside the particle (see Collins and Thrainsson 1996 for relevant criticism here).

6

VERBAL *LE*
ASPECT AND TENSE

6.0 Introduction

In this chapter I turn to verbal *le* and consider how the re-positioning of *le/liao* relative to the main verb and its object relates to parallel changes observed in resultative constructions. Suggesting first that *le/liao* historically underwent structural reanalysis as completive aspect similar to other V_2 elements in RVCs, I then concentrate on the synchronic status of verbal *le* and argue that a particular process of upwards grammaticalization in the functional structure dominating VP has resulted in verbal *le* currently being a morpheme which may actually instantiate three discrete functional heads—completive aspect, perfective aspect and also, more controversially, past tense. The chapter attempts to show that Smith's (1997) two-tiered system of situational and viewpoint aspect provides an insightful model for understanding the roles played by different functional suffixes on the verb, and argues for the possibility that functional morphemes undergoing change may naturally instantiate more than just a single functional head in any extended functional sequence. The central conclusion of the chapter that affixal elements undergo grammaticalization and reanalysis in a way which significantly parallels the movement-dependent reanalysis of free-standing morphemes is also argued to provide good evidence in favor of the Minimalist hypothesis that affixes are licensed via raising to a higher functional head, and that this raising may take place either overtly or covertly at the level of LF.

6.1 The Re-positioning of *Le/Liao*

Historically it is well documented that modern day verbal *le* in fact originated as the full verb *liao* meaning 'to finish' in a sentence-final position and then later re-positioned itself right-adjacent to the main descriptive verb. Where the main verb is transitive with an object NP, this re-positioning is particularly obvious, as schematized in (1):

(1) a. V Object *liao/le* → b. V *liao/le* Object

The change from (1a) to (1b) is reported to have taken place primarily during the Song dynasty (960-1279) (see for example Mei 1981, Z. Shi 1988, and G. Wu 1999). The obvious question, as with V_2 re-positioning in RVCs, is why such re-positioning should have taken place. One possibility which might be considered is that the change occurred for phonological reasons. It is clear that modern day verbal *le* is phonologically much reduced from its earlier full form *liao* and is now fully dependent on the verb to its left. It might therefore be suggested that *liao* first reduced to a clitic-form *le* and then raised to the verb to encliticize to it as a suitable host element. However, such a possibility can in fact be rather quickly dismissed. In a very informative paper G. Wu (1999) shows that there is good evidence that *liao* first re-positioned itself right-adjacent to the verb and only much later underwent reduction to *le*. Among other evidence for this conclusion is a particularly telling argument from Korean. In the Korean textbook of Mandarin Chinese called the *Chunggan Nogoltae* written in 1795, the element corresponding to modern day verbal *le* is transcribed as having a pronounciation equivalent to *liao* not *le*. Verbal *le* then still had its original shape *liao* at least until the end of the 18th century, five hundred years after it underwent its positional change. Consequently such re-positioning cannot be ascribed to any phonological clitic-like properties of *le* triggering movement of *le* to the verb.

Fully in line with suggestions made in a number of works (e.g., Mei 1981, Z. Shi 1988, G. Wu 1999, Sybesma 1999), I would instead like to assume that the re-positioning of *liao/le* was actually just one instance of the general phenomenon of V_2 re-positioning which occurred in resultative constructions. It has been frequently noted that the change in *liao*'s position essentially coincided with the re-positioning of V_2 elements in RVCs which is suggested to have occurred around the time of the Song dynasty (probably preceded by its beginning emergence in the Tang dynasty), precisely when *liao* also underwent its positional change. G. Wu (1999) writes that:

> The "V(O)+phase complement" structure emerged during the Wei, Jin and the Northern and Southern Dynasties, and changed into the "V+phase complement (O)" structure around Song. (p.22)

It is therefore commonly suggested that the re-positioning of *liao* may be thought of as having been strongly influenced by V_2 re-positioning in RVCs and might even be considered to be a further occurrence of the general change in RVC word order. G. Wu (1999) continues:

> . . . the grammaticalization of *liao* coincides with the development of the "verb resultative complement" structure and the formation of resultative verb compounds in the language. In other words, the grammaticalization of *liao* is actually a part of the process. (p.23)

CHAPTER 6

The original element *liao* did indeed also have the meaning of a typical resultative phase-type V_2 'to finish' and can therefore be taken to have signaled simple completion much in the same way as other V_2 elements such as *wan* 'to finish' do. I would therefore now like to simply assume that *liao* originally occurred in the sentence-final completive Asp^0 and then later underwent 're-positioning' to be right-adjacent to the verb for the same reasons suggested to underlie the re-positioning of RVC V_2 elements in general, i.e., *liao* became reanalyzed as an aspectual suffix on the V_1 in order that the head-final AspP could be re-interpreted as being head-initial instead. Only much later on *liao* would then have phonologically reduced to its present pronunciation as *le*.

This much concerning verbal le is not so new in terms of the basic underlying conclusion that *liao/le* was originally just one of the general phase-V_2 group in RVCs. The mechanism which led to its re-positioning is also taken to be essentially the same as that which occurred with other V_2s. What is now of greater interest with verbal *le* is the possibility that *le* has in fact undergone further significant development from being just a simple completive aspect marker to encode other higher functions as well. I will therefore spend the rest of this chapter considering what kind of formal syntactic structures might correspond to the interpretations instantiated by modern day verbal *le* and how diachronic development might have also given rise to such structures, i.e., what mechanisms might lead to the changes observed.

6.1.1 The Current Status of Verbal Le and Completive Aspect

Given the fact that liao had the typical completive-type meaning of other V2 elements and that it underwent re-positioning at the same basic period as other V2s it would seem to be fairly natural and straightforward to treat it as a simple V2 as suggested here and also by various other investigators. In the present approach proposed in chapter 5, this consequently means assuming that it was first generated in the sentence-final completive Asp^0 and then together with the other V2s reanalyzed as a verbal suffix licensed by a higher 're-aligned' completive AspP at LF, as represented in (2):

(2)

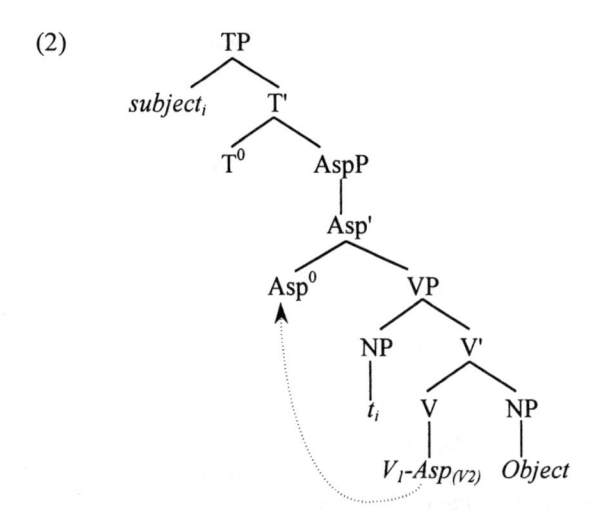

```
            TP
           /  \
    subjectᵢ   T'
              /  \
            T⁰   AspP
                  |
                 Asp'
                 /  \
               Asp⁰  VP
                ⬆   /  \
                   NP   V'
                   |   /  \
                   tᵢ  V   NP
                       |    |
                  V₁-Asp₍V2₎ Object
```

Now, although it can be maintained that such an analysis has good motivation as a *diachronic* account of the origin and re-positioning of *liao/le*, there is also evidence indicating that *synchronically* verbal *le* in fact may not have exactly the same status as other members of the V₂ set and that *le* may therefore have undergone some further syntactic change since its initial reanalysis.

One rather simple but strong piece of evidence that *le* is currently different from other V₂ aspect suffixes is that *le* may occur as a suffix *in addition* to a second regular V₂ suffix of either 'literal' or phase type, as shown in (3) and (4) below. Such examples contrast with (5) and (6) where *le* occurs just with a bare V₁:

(3) ta xi-ganjing-le suoyoude yifu.
    he wash-clean-LE all clothes
    'He washed all the clothes clean.'

(4) wo yijing kan-wan-le san-ben shu le[1].
    I already look-finish-LE three-CL book LE
    'I already finished reading three books.'

(5) wo yijing chi-le fan le.
    I already eat-LE rice LE
    'I've already eaten.'

(6) ta zuotian qu-le Beijing.
    he yesterday go-LE Beijing
    'He went to Beijing yesterday.'

In (3) and (4) it is clear that *ganjing* 'be-clean' and *wan* 'be-finished' are in the regular V₂ position signaling completion of the action and can be therefore

237

CHAPTER 6

taken to instantiate completive aspect, raising to and being licensed by Asp^0 at LF. This being so, the *le* which occurs outside the V$_{2Asp}$ must be taken to encode some other function here.

A second reason to believe that *le* is at least in some of its occurrences not licensed as completive aspect is that *le* is also frequently found with *achievement* predicates which represent instantaneous events with no extension over time. Typical V$_2$ completive verbs/suffixes occur with V$_1$ elements which represent *activities* which do occur over a period of time; the V$_{2Asp}$ suffix marks the end-point of the activity and signals completion of the action. In contrast to activities (such as 'run', 'wash', 'read', etc.) or accomplishments (such as 'draw a circle', 'walk to school', etc.), achievement predicates such as 'arrive', 'recognize someone' and 'die' are commonly interpreted as referring to events which are instantaneous and do not take any time. Consequently such predicates are normally quite unnatural with expressions of completion which require that the predicate express an action which naturally extends over a period of time before it is completed. Examples in (7)-(9) below have achievement predicates whereas those in (10)-(11) have an activity and an accomplishment predicate:[2]

(7)   */??John finished recognizing Mary.

(8)   */??Mary finished arriving.

(9)   */??Bill finished dying.

(10) John finished reading.

(11) John finished drawing the circle.

In Chinese one finds that *le* is highly natural with all of the achievement class and no special context is required for use of *le* with achievement verbs, i.e., they are still interpreted as representing instantaneous actions/events. This indicates that *le* in such instances cannot be expressing *completion* but some other function. (12) and (13) are examples with clear achievement predicates:

(12) ta ba-dian jiu   dao-le   huo-che-zhan le.
      he 8-o'clock then arrive-LE train station LE
      'At 8 o'clock he already arrived at the train station.'

(13) shoushang-de ren dang-zhong, huran   si-le   liang-ge ren.
      injured-DE   people among   suddenly die-LE two-CL people
      'Among the injured, suddenly another two people died.'

It should be noted that such predicates are completely unacceptable with other general V$_{2Asp}$ completive suffixes such as *wan* 'finish' confirming that they are interpreted as instantaneous actions and that they are consequently incompatible with a V_2 which expresses (general) completion:

(14) *ta zuotian si-wan-le.
he yesterday die-finish-LE
literally: ??'He has finished dying yesterday.'

(15) *tamen gangcai zhongyu dao-wan-le huo-che-zhan.
they just now finally arrive-finish-LE train-station
literally: *'Just now they finally finished arriving at the train station.'

It can therefore be concluded that *le* may express some function which is clearly distinct from simple completion. The question now is what exactly is this function of *le*? In order to approach the issue I will now present a brief overview of Smith's two-tiered theory of aspect and show how it provides a rather natural answer to the question of *le*'s role in examples such as (3)/(4) and (12)/(13). Anticipating the results somewhat, it will be suggested that *le* here encodes perfective aspect as is in fact suggested in various other descriptive approaches such as Li and Thompson (1981), though the notion of perfective aspect which will be adopted here is somewhat different from that assumed in works such as Bybee, Perkins and Pagliuca (1994). Syntactically it will be suggested that this perfective aspect is structurally distinct from completive aspect, with both types of aspect being represented by discrete functional heads/projections. Incorporating certain insights in Sybesma (1999) and others it will subsequently be argued that *le* is in fact able to encode both completive and perfective aspect with a number of verbs and that it is the natural grammaticalization of completive *le* with these verbs to a structurally higher aspect head as a result of LF movement which allows for its current generalized use as a perfective.

6.1.2 Smith (1997): Two Different Types of Aspect

Smith (1997) convincingly argues that the commonly used term 'aspect' in fact refers to two quite different types of properties, which she then describes as 'situational aspect' and 'viewpoint aspect.' Situational aspect is suggested to be an inherent property of predicates and refers to the basic types of situations represented by a predicate—the Aktionsart of a predicate in more traditional terminology. As proposed in Vendler (1957) and frequently assumed in other works, situations described by predicates may essentially be classified according to three parameters: (a) whether they are aspectually bounded/telic or not, (b) whether they are instantaneous or have extension over time, and (c) whether they are dynamic or not. The cross-classification of such properties is commonly taken to result four basic situation types, as in (16):

(16) Situation Types:

Situation	examples	properties
stative	be happy, be hungry	-dynamic, -instantaneous, -telic
activity	run, talk	+dynamic, -instantaneous, -telic
accomplishment	draw a circle, run to X	+dynamic, -instantaneous, +telic
achievement	arrive, recognize X	+dynamic, +instantaneous, +telic

Viewpoint aspect, by way of contrast, is suggested to encode how one views any of the above situation types on a particular occasion. Following earlier work such as Comrie (1976) it is noted that it is possible for a single basic situation type to be linguistically presented in different ways, this corresponding to different perspectives or 'viewpoints' on the event/situation. If one assumes that events and situations potentially may have initial points, end points and internal stages as represented in (17) with a sequence of points, viewpoint aspect is suggested to allow for focusing on these properties in two common ways:[3]

(17) Potential Event Type
Initial Point.......... (internal stages).......... End Point

Imperfective viewpoint aspect is suggested to focus just the internal parts/stages of a situation, and does not include either any initial or final endpoint in its focus/presentation. In English, the *be...-ing* form is the standard imperfective aspect; this focuses attention on the internal progression of the situation rather than any initial point or endpoint it may have. Note that viewpoint aspect is a type of aspect which is distinct from the classification of an event in terms of its situation aspect. The imperfective may combine with either an unbounded activity situation type as in (18a) or a bounded accomplishment as in (18b). However, because the imperfective form by definition focuses the internal stages of a situation, it cannot normally be combined with achievement situations which are +instantaneous and have no internal stages, as seen in (17c). Also, in English, the *be...-ing* imperfective does not combine with stative situations because the *be...-ing* imperfective requires a situation which is +dynamic:

(18) Imperfective viewpoint aspect
    a. John is/was running.   imperfective+activity
    b. Mary is/was drawing a circle.   imperfective+accomplishment
    c. *John was recognizing Mary.   imperfective+achievement
    d. *Mary is/was being pretty.   imperfective+stative

Note also that both the imperfective viewpoint aspect and the situation aspect of any event/situation are properties which are independent of the tense property associated with that event/situation, and that tense simply functions to locate an event/situation in time. Because of this independence, the tense associated with an event/situation may clearly be varied while maintaining the viewpoint aspect constant as imperfective, as seen above in (18a/b).

In contrast to imperfective viewpoint aspect, *perfective* viewpoint aspect is argued to focus the whole of a situation and therefore critically include both the initial and the final endpoint of a situation in this focus. In many languages such perfective viewpoint aspect would actually not seem to be expressed by any distinct overt morpheme on the verb; in English. For example, there is no identifiable perfective counterpart to the imperfective *be...-ing* form; rather, it may be suggested that perfective has zero morphological expression and that a verb may come to be interpreted as perfective when it is not marked positively for imperfective viewpoint. Concretely, when a simple past tense form of a verb in *-ed* occurs, it expresses perfective viewpoint in addition to past time location as it importantly contrasts with the combination of past and imperfective which results in *was V-ing:*

(19)   past + perfective + situation/verb
       -ed +   ∅   + walk to the park → (John) walked to the park.

(20)   past + imperfective + situation/verb
       past + be...-ing   + walk to the park → (John) was walking to the park.

As is the case with imperfective viewpoint aspect, perfective aspect is in essence independent of the situation aspect of a predicate and may therefore be combined with events encoding different situation aspects. For example, the following are all taken to encode perfective rather than imperfective aspect (largely due to the contrastive absence of *be...-ing*):

(21)   John walked to the park.   perfective + accomplishment

(22)   John arrived at the park. perfective + achievement

(23)   John walked in the park.   perfective + activity

Consequently it may be argued that there are (at least) three distinct formal properties potentially associated with any predicate—(a) its situation type/aspect, (b) the viewpoint aspect used to present that situation, and (c) its temporal location, i.e., the tense used to locate the situation relative to other events/situations. These three properties might also seem to occur in a natural hierarchical ordering. Compositionally, a situation/event will first be identified and defined in terms of its situation aspect; then the situation will be presented in a particular way, either as a whole with perfective aspect, or with a focus on its internal structure with imperfective aspect. Finally the situation/event so interpreted may be located in time via the use of tense. Such a natural compositional hierarchy among the three properties is also found to be reflected in the linear ordering of tense and aspect elements in many languages. In head-initial languages where tense and aspect markers are instantiated by independent free-standing morphemes rather than by suffixes, it is commonly noted that tense morphemes precede (im)perfective-type morphemes, which in turn precede morphemes relating to situation-type aspect (see Cinque 1999 for a wide range of data and relevant discussion). If one assumes that such unbound morphemes are located in (functional) head positions, in head-initial languages this leads to the conclusion that tense/TP hierarchically dominates perfective aspect which in turn dominates situation aspect, as schematically illustrated in (24):

(24)   TP
        /\
          T'
         / \
       T^0 $AspP_{1=(im)perfective}$
               /\
                 Asp_1'
                / \
           Asp_1^0 $AspP_{2=situation}$
                      /\
                        Asp_2'
                       / \
                  Asp_2^0 VP

A structure such as (24) also naturally encodes the selection relation between viewpoint aspect and situation aspect. For example, above in (18) it was noted that the English imperfective viewpoint aspect *be...-ing* combines only with predicates which have the aspectual situation type of either activity or accomplishment. (Viewpoint) Asp_1^0 can therefore be taken to select for the situation type represented by (situation) $AspP_2$.

The main semantic difference between the viewpoint types argued for by Smith concerns how much of a situation that the viewpoints 'make visible' in any particular instance. As noted, perfectives focus a situation in its entirety and so include the initial and final endpoints of the situation, whereas imperfectives only focus on the internal stages of an event and so exclude the endpoints from the focus. Smith points out that such a difference in the presentation of an event can be clearly observed when one attempts to qualify the description of (im)perfective events with denials and continuative statements. For example, it is possible to combine imperfective aspect with a telic situation (and past tense) to describe a certain situation and then deny the completion of that situation, as in (25):

(25) Mary was walking to school, but she didn't actually get there.

This contrasts with the combination of perfective aspect with a telic situation and past tense to describe the same essential situation. Such a combination does not allow for any denial of the completion of the event:

(26) *Mary walked to school, but she didn't actually get there.

The contrast in (25) and (26) can be given the following explanation. In (26) the use of a perfective viewpoint (i.e., lack of *be...-ing* form) makes both the initial and final endpoints of the event (properties of its situation aspect) naturally 'visible' in the description. When past tense is applied to a telic event whose endpoints are visible and focused by the perfective viewpoint, this consequently results in an interpretation in which both the initial and the final endpoint are interpreted as having been realized. Because the final endpoint of having arrived at the school is therefore understood as having occurred, it is impossible to follow this with a denial that it occurred. In (25) however, due to presentation of the same telic situation with imperfective viewpoint aspect, there is only focus on the internal stages of the event, and while it can be deduced that the initial point must have occurred in order for there to be these internal stages, there is no necessity that the final endpoint also be realized. Semantically the endpoint is simply not made visible in the presentation of a telic situation with an imperfective viewpoint, and consequently it is possible to deny that such an endpoint actually is realized. It should be carefully noted that the relevant factor here is not tense, as (25) and (26) are both given past tense (nor is it situation aspect, as the situation is identical and telic in both cases); it is critically just the viewpoint choice which is responsible for the difference in acceptability. Such simple contrasts again illustrate the conclusion that tense, viewpoint aspect and situation aspect are indeed three essentially independent properties.

The same basic patterning is seen again with attempted statements of continuation.

(27) John was writing the letter an hour ago, and in fact he still is writing it.

(28) *John wrote the letter an hour ago, and in fact he still is writing it.

In (27) use of the imperfective does not make the endpoint visible and so it can be asserted that the endpoint effectively has not occurred. In (28) however, the perfective viewpoint does make the endpoint visible and so when combined with past tense results in an interpretation that the letter-writing was completed and therefore cannot be still continuing.

Given that examples such as (26) and (28) with past tense and perfective viewpoint applying to a telic predicate cannot be followed by any denials of completion, and given also that past tense applied to the same telic situation presented with imperfective aspect does allow for a denial of completion, one can assert the following conclusions, in line with Smith (1997):

(29) a. realized completion is part of the genuine meaning of past tense applied to perfective aspect presenting a telic situation and is not simply a pragmatic inference.
b. perfective viewpoint is critical in effecting the meaning of realized completion, because past tense and a telic predicate otherwise with imperfective aspect do not result in any necessary interpretation of completion.
c. perfective viewpoint does indeed 'exist' in English although not obviously instantiated here by an overt morpheme distinct from past tense.
d. it is necessary to recognize three independent properties which interact with each other in different combinations—tense, viewpoint aspect and situation aspect.

Finally it can be noted that Smith (1997) argues strongly that both types of viewpoint and situation aspect are in fact always present in some form in the linguistic representation of events. It is suggested that the lower situation aspect properties of a predicate can only be semantically interpreted if some kind of viewpoint aspect is applied to make them visible and that this requirement results in the occurrence of viewpoint aspect being necessarily encoded in some way in the descriptions of all events.

6.1.3 Verbal Le and Perfectivity

The above discussion of Smith's well-reasoned two-tiered theory of aspect now allows for a clearer understanding of the status of verbal *le* in V_1-V_2-le forms such as (3) and (4) repeated below:

(3) ta xi-ganjing-le suoyoude yifu.
he wash-clean-LE all clothes
'He washed all the clothes clean.'

(4) wo yijing kan-wan-le san-ben shu le.
I already look-finish-LE three-CL book LE
'I already finished reading three books.'

It was noted that because there is already a V_{2Asp} suffix instantiating completive aspect on the main verb in addition to verbal *le*, then verbal *le* in such instances cannot itself be taken to be completive aspect. Verbal *le* was also seen to occur with achievement verbs with no extension over time and no process to complete, which again disallows an analysis *le* as completive aspect with such verbs. The question therefore naturally arose as to what kind of functional head the verbal *le* suffix might correspond to in V_1-V_2-le forms and with achievement verbs.

If one now adopts Smith's two-tiered model of aspect, a simple answer to this question suggests itself, and verbal *le* can be assumed to instantiate perfective viewpoint aspect here. It can be suggested that corresponding to Smith's viewpoint and situation aspect syntactically there are indeed two independent functional projections encoding aspect precisely as illustrated in the tree in (24), and that whereas Chinese V_2-completive suffixes are licensed by the lower $Asp_{2\text{-situation}}$ head, *le* in V_1-V_2-le forms will be licensed as a perfective suffix by the higher $Asp_{1\text{-viewpoint}}$ head. Such a general assumption not only coincides with traditional views that verbal *le* is a perfective marker, as for example expressed in Li and Thompson (1981) and many other works, but there is also simple evidence from certain co-occurrence restrictions which indicates that *le* is here functioning as an instantiation of perfective aspect. Specifically, the element *zhengzai* is rather clearly a marker of (progressive) imperfective aspect and therefore arguably occurs in the higher $Asp_{1\text{-viewpoint}}$ head. Significantly it is not possible for *zhengzai* to co-occur with a V_1-V_2-le sequence even though *zhengzai* may appear with V_1-V_2 forms, as seen in (30), (31) and (32):

(30) wo zhengzai ca boli ne.
 I ASP-PROG wipe glass NE[4]
 'I am just wiping/cleaning the glass (at the moment).'

(31) wo zhengzai ca-gan boli ne. (Sybesma 1999)
 I ASP-PROG wipe-dry glass NE
 'I am just wiping dry the glass.'

(32) *wo zhengzai ca-gan-le boli ne.
 I ASP-PROG wipe-dry-LE glass NE

In this case, verbal *le* and *zhengzai* are thus in complementary distribution. Assuming *zhengzai* to be in $Asp_{1\text{-viewpoint}}$, this co-occurrence restriction is naturally explained if *le* instantiates perfective aspect and needs to be licensed by the same $Asp_{1\text{-viewpoint}}$ head; the clash of (im)perfective values in *zhengzai* and *le* will simply result in *le* failing to be licensed here. Note that in the current approach it is indeed expected that *zhengzai* and a V_2 element such as *gan* 'dry' will be able to co-occur. *Zhengzai* is argued to be in Asp_1^0 instantiating imperfective viewpoint aspect, while the V_2 *gan* is taken to be a suffix encoding completive aspect and hence licensed by the lower situation aspect head Asp_2^0. The two elements are hence *not* competing for the same aspectual head and so one might indeed expect that they could co-occur. The same is basically true of English where it is possible to combine imperfective aspect *be...-ing* with a meaning of completion/a completive situation:[5]

(33) John is finishing reading the book.

(34) He is looking the reference up/washing the dishes clean.

Another reason for believing that the V_1 and *le* are respectively completive and perfective aspect aside from their interpretation concerns their relative ordering on the V_1 as suffixes. In section 6.1.2 it was noted that in terms of relative scope, viewpoint aspect is naturally higher than situation aspect—viewpoint aspect applies to a predicate which already has a certain aspectual value as +/- telic, +/-durative established by the situation aspect and functions to focus in on some particular aspectual property of the predicate (making its endpoints visible, focusing its internal stages, etc.). Such a hierarchical ordering should normally be reflected in syntactic structure and also here significantly in the ordering of morphemes on a lexical stem. For example, (as pointed out above in 6.1.2) it has been noted that when functional categories such as tense, mood and aspect are instantiated by free-standing lexical elements, these elements seem to consistently occur in a common cross-linguistic ordering and that interestingly, this is precisely the inverse ordering found when the same functional types are represented by suffixes on a lexical stem. Specifically Cinque (1999) observes that in head-initial languages there is a broad ranking of free-standing verb-associated functional elements as in (35):

(35) free-standing morphemes:
epistemic-modality – tense – root-modality – aspect – V

The hierarchical ranking is actually far more refined in Cinque (1999), but (35) can be taken to translate into a functional structure approximately as in (36):

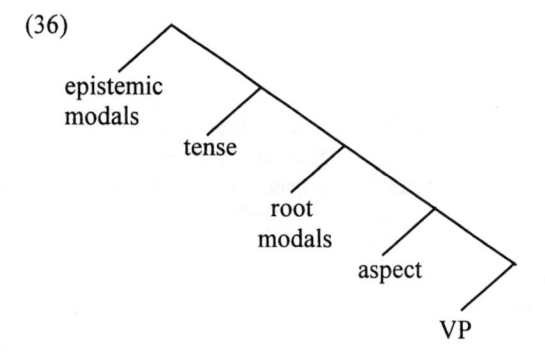

(36)
```
epistemic
modals
      tense
            root
            modals
                  aspect
                        VP
```

What is significant here is that if the elements representing such functional categories are not free morphemes but suffixes instead, they are consistently observed to occur bound to the verb in the inverse linear ordering, as in (37):

(37) Suffixes:
V – aspect – root-modality – tense – epistemic-modality

In Government and Binding theory (GB) this ordering of suffixes in a sequence which is the opposite of the linear ordering of corresponding free-standing functional equivalents has been referred to as the Mirror Principle (Baker 1985). It is suggested that the (suffix) ordering arises due to the movement of a verb (or other lexical category) through the functional heads which dominate it, sequentially attaching the suffixes which are base-generated there. For example, supposing that a verb occurs with suffixes corresponding to aspect and tense and these suffixes are labeled S_1 and S_2 in Asp^0 and T^0, the verb will first move to Asp^0 and attach S_1 and then subsequently raise to T^0 to attach S_2. The final ordering will be V-S_1-S_2 which is the mirror image of the linear ordering of the relevant functional heads:

(38) Movement 1 → V-S_1

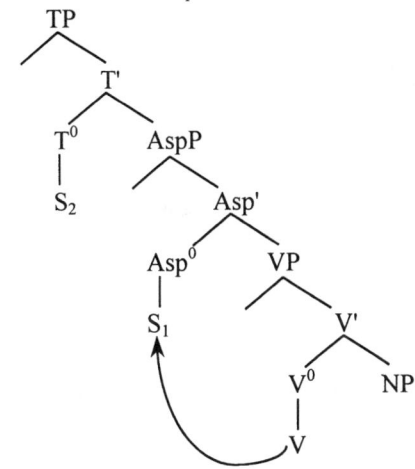

(39) Movement 2 → V-S$_1$-S$_2$

```
         TP
        /  \
           T'
          /  \
        T⁰    AspP
        |   /    \
        S₂       Asp'
               /     \
            Asp⁰      VP
             |       /  \
           [V-S₁]ᵢ        V'
                        /   \
                      V⁰     NP
                      |
                      tᵢ
```

In the Minimalist Program, for a variety of reasons it is assumed that inflectional affixes are actually attached to their stems in the morphological component prior to syntactic insertion in a tree and that they are licensed (checked) via subsequently raising to the relevant functional heads during the course of the syntactic derivation. The Mirror Principle effects are accounted for by assuming that there is an inherent ordering to the checking of all suffixal elements and that inner suffixes adjacent to the lexical stem must be checked before outer suffixes. Given a base-generated sequence of a verb and two suffixes V-S$_1$-S$_2$, suffix S$_1$ will then have to check against a functional head before the S$_2$ suffix can be licensed. Consequently the functional head corresponding to S$_1$ will necessarily need to be lower in the tree than the functional head which licenses S$_2$. Concerning these two frameworks, in chapter 5 I have argued against the overt raising of V⁰ for the attachment of *le*. Recall that in (40) overt raising of V⁰ to *le* in Infl/Asp is argued against by the fact that V-*le* sequences follow VP-adverbs. Therefore it seems that the Minimalist Program in which *le* could be assumed to be a verbal suffix checked at LF would seem to be a naturally more desirable choice to take.

(40) ta manmarde xi-ganjing-le yifu.
 he slowly wash-clean-LE clothes
 'He slowly washed clean the clothes.'

Given the basic Mirror Principle patterning and considering Chinese V$_1$-V$_2$-le sequences, one would now expect that the V$_2$ element as an inner suffix S$_1$ should correspond to a licensing functional head which would be projected lower in the structure than the outer S$_2$ suffix *le*, and this is indeed exactly what it entailed by the relative hierarchical ordering suggested to exist between viewpoint and situational aspect. Above it was noted that viewpoint aspect applies to a predicate which has already been determined for its situation aspect, and that viewpoint aspect is therefore hierarchically superior to situation aspect. In terms of syntactic structure, viewpoint aspect and situation aspect as functional projections in a head-initial language are therefore expected to projected themselves as in (41) (=24):

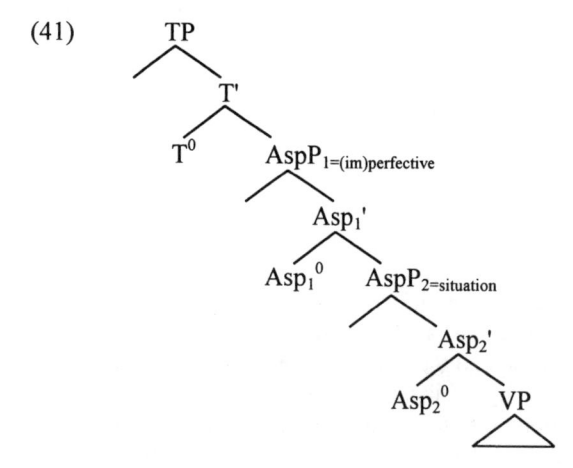

(41)
```
            TP
           /  \
              T'
             /  \
           T⁰    AspP₁₌₍ᵢₘ₎ₚₑᵣfₑcₜᵢᵥₑ
                /    \
                    Asp₁'
                    /   \
                 Asp₁⁰   AspP₂₌ₛᵢₜᵤₐₜᵢₒₙ
                        /    \
                            Asp₂'
                           /    \
                        Asp₂⁰   VP
```

In any sequence of two suffixes relating to viewpoint and situation aspect on a single verb, the inner aspectual suffix should therefore be licensed against the lower $Asp_2^0{}_{situation}$ and the outer aspectual suffix should be licensed by the higher $Asp_1^0{}_{(im)perfective}$. In V_1-V_2-le sequences this is exactly what is suggested to be the case—the inner 'V_2' suffix is argued to be an instantiation of completive (situation) aspect and so should be licensed against Asp_2^0, and the outer le suffix is suggested to be perfective aspect and so should be licensed against the higher Asp_1^0 head. The relative ordering of V_2 and le as suffixes on the V_1 therefore seems to be further good confirmation that le in V_1-V_2-le sequences is indeed occurring as perfective aspect.

A final relevant point supporting treatment of le as perfective aspect which has often been made in the literature is that verb le and the negative form mei(-you) 'Neg-have' would seem to be in simple complementary distribution as seen in (42):

(42) wo mei-you xie(*-le)   xin.
     I NEG-have write(*-LE) letter
     'I didn't write the letter.'

Commonly it has been assumed that mei-you is the combination of negation and perfective aspect (see e.g., Li and Thompson 1981). In a Chomskean approach one may therefore assume that the auxiliary element you is in a perfective aspect head. The complementary distribution of mei(-you) and verbal le consequently has a natural explanation. Assuming that the perfective

249

aspect head maximally checks a single set of perfective aspect features, if *you* and *le* co-occur and both carry perfective aspect features, one of the sets of features will remain unchecked and cause the derivation to crash. In negative perfective aspect sentences the perfective aspect head is occupied by *you* (or alternatively a phonologically null equivalent) and the features are checked in-situ; it is therefore not possible to have a second instantiation of the same aspect type (i.e., *le*).[6, 7]

There are therefore a variety of good reasons indicating both that *le* is representing perfective aspect in the cases reviewed and that formally *le* may be assumed to be licensed as a functional suffix by raising (at LF) to a higher $Asp_{1\text{-perfective}}$ head position which dominates $Asp_{2\text{complective}}$.

6.1.4 Grammaticalization and the Dual Status of Verbal Le

Section 6.1 began with the suggestion that verbal *le* historically was a member of the V_2 set and grammaticalized as an instantiation of complective aspect in sentence-final position just like all the other V_2 elements. This analysis of *le* as a simple V_2 was supported by its literal complective meaning and by the fact that it underwent re-positioning to the V_1 at essentially the same time that other V_2 elements re-positioned themselves adjacent to V_1. Following this however, it has been suggested that verbal *le* should be taken to instantiate perfective aspect rather than complective situation aspect in a number of rather clear synchronic cases. The question now is how to reconcile these two rather different views of *le*.

I would like to suggest that the element *liao/le* did indeed originate as an instantiation of complective aspect as indeed proposed in 6.1, but that since this time *le* has in fact undergone further grammaticalization and reanalysis as perfective aspect, and that both this diachronic development of *le* and its current sometimes ambivalent status can be neatly and naturally captured in a development of the movement-and-reanalysis approach to grammaticalization introduced in chapter two.

6.1.4.1 Parallel grammaticalization of independent X^0-heads and affixes

It may be remembered that the analysis of *ge* in chapter two made use of an idea (suggested in Simpson 1998, Roberts and Rousseau 1999) that grammaticalization may often result from a combination of movement and reanalysis within the functional structure dominating a lexical element. In the case of *ge* it was argued that *ge* originated in Cl^0 but then later became reanalyzed as an instantiation of D^0 following continued raising from Cl^0 to D^0. The process which leads to grammaticalization and category change is then taken to be a sequence of movement to a particular functional head/Spec and then subsequent reanalysis relative to/in that position. Essentially there are three basic stages to the process:

(43) Stages of grammaticalization (for X^0-head elements)[8]
   a. Stage 1: an element α is base-generated and remains throughout the derivation in its position of origin, X^0
   b. Stage 2: α is base-generated in X^0 but then raises up to a second functional head position Y^0 as α is associated with the interpretation of position Y^0
   c. Stage 3: α becomes reanalyzed as being base-generated in Y^0 and no longer is interpreted as instantiating the properties of X^0; consequently a new element β is/can be base-generated in X^0

Trees (44)-(46) show the process of change from stage 1 to stage 3. In stage 1 the element α is simply base-generated in X^0 and remains there. In stage 2 α is base-generated in X^0 but also raises up to the functional head Y^0 and is licensed/checked also against Y^0. In stage 3 α is reanalyzed as being directly base-generated in Y^0 and has effectively grammaticalized as an element which only instantiates a head of type Y^0. A direct consequence of α being reanalyzed as being base-generated in Y^0 is that X^0 may be filled with a new discrete element, here β.

(44) Stage 1

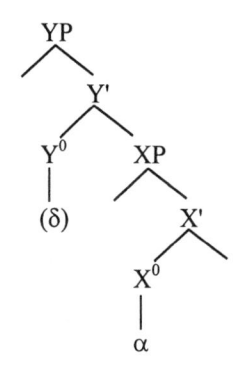

```
        YP
       /  \
          Y'
         /  \
       Y⁰    XP
       |    /  \
      (δ)      X'
              /  \
            X⁰
            |
            α
```

(45) Stage 2

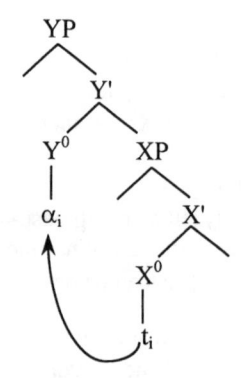

```
        YP
       /  \
          Y'
         /  \
       Y⁰    XP
       |    /  \
       αᵢ        X'
           ↑   /  \
           |  X⁰
           |   |
           └── tᵢ
```

(46) Stage 3

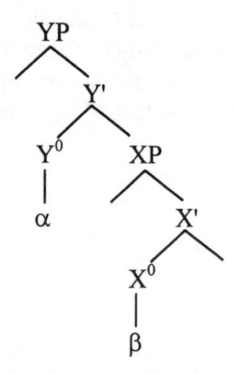

```
        YP
       /  \
          Y'
         /  \
       Y⁰    XP
       |    /  \
       α         X'
              /  \
            X⁰
             |
             β
```

Such an approach to grammaticalization was initially developed to account for category changes occurring with free-standing heads and phrases which also undergo overt positional changes. For example, French *pas* was noted to have undergone raising from canonical object position and then later grammaticalized as a simple marker of negation (Simpson 1998b), the English modal set is commonly taken to occur base-generated in a position higher than lexical verbs having earlier undergone raising from the V⁰ position and grammaticalized in a higher functional head (Lightfoot 1979), and Chinese *ge* was similarly argued to have raised from Cl⁰ to D⁰ and then grammaticalized as a D⁰. If it is assumed that the same essential modes of interpretation should be equally open to both morphologically free and phonologically dependent elements, i.e., affixes, then it might be imagined that the basic underlying process of reanalysis outlined above should also in theory be available with affixal elements, although somewhat different in its surface execution due to the phonological free/bound distinction. Inflectional affixes are indeed interpreted as instantiating functional heads and hence correspond to a genuinely real part of the syntactic structure projected in a tree. It is simply due to their phonologically dependent nature that affixes first require attachment to some host before they can be raised and matched against a relevant syntactic head. Given then that the free/bound distinction is therefore really just a phonological property and is not assumed to correspond to any kind of fundamental semantic difference (i.e., tense as a suffix will not be interpreted differently from tense instantiated by a free-standing morpheme), it would be natural to assume that the re-interpretation of an element as a different functional type should not be restricted to just free-standing morphemes but also occur with morphologically bound elements. Below I therefore now outline exactly how a process of grammaticalization with affixal elements might formally be understood to take place, and then suggest that just such a sequence of change and reanalysis has in fact occurred with Chinese verbal *le*.

In a Minimalist approach to inflectional morphology, affixes are assumed to be licensed not immediately when inserted on their lexical host (e.g., in V^0) but only later on in the derivation when they are raised to the relevant licensing functional head. In this sense they become 'active' only when matched against a particular functional head during the course of movement through the functional structure dominating a lexical element. Grammaticalization and reanalysis of affixes will below essentially be suggested to occur when a particular affix first comes to be 'active' and licensed against a series of two distinct functional heads, and then is interpreted as being actively licensed only against the higher of these heads. The movement and reanalysis sequence found with free morphemes will then also occur with affixes, but with the difference that because affixes are phonologically parasitic on a secondary host throughout the derivation, they may not be simply base-generated independently in a different higher position after an occurrence of reanalysis but will instead be simply re-interpreted as being 'active' and engaged in licensing relations with functional heads during a different progressively higher portion of raising through the functional structure.

In more detail, the following sequence of steps can be suggested to take place in affixal reanalysis. Stage 1 represented in (47) is the simple case of a suffix α attached to a lexical host S raising with S to be licensed against a functional head X^0. The functional head X^0 essentially represents the interpretation given to α (e.g., +past tense), and at an abstract level of analysis it is assumed that a set of features corresponding to the meaning of X^0 (i.e., +past) is lexically added to or built into the overt entity α. The morpheme α is therefore the physical host for a feature-set (i.e., meaning) which corresponds to a parallel specification in the functional head X^0. S and α are base-generated together in the head-position Z^0 and then raise together up to X^0. The lower bracketed (x) following α is a visual specification of the type of functional head that α needs to be matched/checked against. Similarly on the functional head X^0 there is a lower bracketed α indicating that X^0 corresponds to the meaning taken to be instantiated by α. In (47) S-$\alpha_{(x)}$ simply raises up to X^0 and the features carried by α are checked and licensed against those on X^0:

253

(47) Stage 1

$$
\begin{array}{c}
YP \\
\diagup\diagdown \\
Y' \\
\diagup\diagdown \\
Y^0 \quad XP \\
\quad\diagup\diagdown \\
\quad X' \\
\quad\diagup\diagdown \\
X^0_{(\alpha)} \quad ZP \\
\quad\quad\diagup\diagdown \\
\quad\quad Z' \\
\quad\quad\diagup\diagdown \\
\quad\quad Z^0 \\
\quad\quad\mid \\
\quad\quad S\text{-}\alpha_{(x)}
\end{array}
$$

In stage 2 with free-standing morphemes such as *ge* and French *pas* it was argued that *ge/pas* both fulfil two functions. *Ge* in stage 2 instantiates both the Cl^0 head and the D^0 head, and *pas* is both an object DP and an emphatic marker in negative contexts. With affixes it can be assumed that this same kind of multi-functionality may also sometimes occur; in stage 2 of affixal change it can therefore be suggested that a single affix α is able to act as the physical lexical host for two different feature sets. This will essentially result from α being understood to be 'active' and engaged in a checking relation not only against X^0 but also a higher functional head Y^0 as it raises up to Y^0 with the lexical stem S. One may suppose that prior to this change the relevant features on Y^0 would have been checked either by (features on) a phonologically null affix attached to S-α or via the base-generation of a phonologically null head with a feature-set directly in Y^0 (i.e., base-generation of a free-standing head in the Y^0 position). From an initial situation (stage 1) in which features on Y^0 are checked by an element with zero phonological realization and α is interpreted as checking only features on X^0, in stage 2 α comes to be interpreted as being in a licensing relation with both X^0 and Y^0. This dual function stage 2 is represented in (48). As seen, the suffix α is followed by a lower bracket enclosing an ordered sequence of *x* and *y* indicating the functional heads which it is understood as checking against; X^0 and Y^0 also both have lower-bracketed specifications for α encoding the fact that these heads are interpreted as having meanings licensed by the presence of the element α on S:

(48) Stage 2

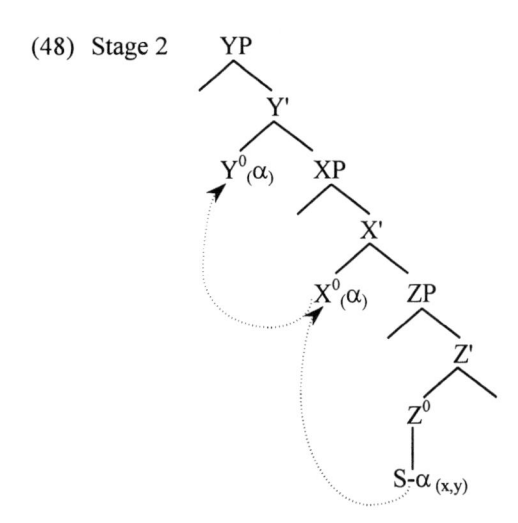

```
        YP
       /  \
         Y'
        /  \
    Y⁰(α)   XP
           /  \
              X'
             /  \
         X⁰(α)   ZP
                /  \
                   Z'
                  /  \
                 Z⁰
                 |
                S-α (x,y)
```

In stage 3 with free-standing morphemes, *ge* and *pas* were argued to have undergone reanalysis as instantiating only the higher position raised to (D⁰ and SpecFocP respectively). In affixal terms, stage 3 will correspond to a situation in which the suffix α in the model here is reanalyzed as only representing the interpretation of the higher head Y^0. Formally, features encoding the meaning of only the functional head Y^0 will be lexically added to α, and during the course of raising the suffix α will only be in an active licensing relation with the higher head Y^0 and not X^0. Reanalysis of free-standing morphemes in a higher position in stage 3 was seen to allow for the original base-generated site to be occupied by another different element (a classifier in the case of *ge*, and an object DP with *pas*). When a suffix such as α undergoes stage 3 reanalysis as only relating to a higher head, this should allow for a new affixal element to be base-generated in the suffixal slot previously occupied by α, or alternatively a phonologically zero affixal element is understood as carrying the relevant features relating to X^0. The above is all represented in the stage 3 tree (49). Note that the suffix α now only has a lower bracket specification for Y^0, and a new suffix β (or a phonologically zero suffix ∅) carries the features which will be licensed against X^0:

(49) Stage 3

$$\begin{array}{c} YP \\ \diagup\diagdown \\ Y' \\ \diagup\diagdown \\ Y^0_{(\alpha)} \quad XP \\ \diagdown \\ X' \\ \diagup\diagdown \\ X^0_{(\beta/\varnothing)} \quad ZP \\ \diagdown \\ Z' \\ \diagup\diagdown \\ Z^0 \\ | \\ S\text{-}\beta_{(x)}/\varnothing_{(x)}\text{-}\alpha_{(y)} \end{array}$$

Note furthermore that the above sequence of change and reanalysis may be taken to apply equally to either overt movement of an element from Z^0 to X^0 to Y^0 or to covert LF raising. In Chomsky (1995) it is suggested that raising at LF only involves purely formal feature-sets, and other semantic-type features are stranded. This perhaps might lead one to assume that LF movement would simply raise an unstructured cluster of features rather than a structured object such as the hypothetical form [S-$\beta_{(x)}/\varnothing_{(x)}$-$\alpha_{(y)}$]. However, there is good reason to believe that what raises at LF cannot in fact be fully unstructured. If ordering and hierarchical structure were absent from the LF-raised feature-sets which correspond to a lexical stem and its affixes, one would not expect to find Mirror Principle type affixal ordering phenomena in languages where movement occurs only at LF. Specifically, supposing a verb were to have tense and aspect suffixes but only raised to Asp^0 and T^0 at LF, if the LF feature-set were to be fully unordered then one might expect that the tense and aspect suffixes would not need to occur in any particular order on the verbal stem and that they would simply be checked when the feature-set raised through the appropriate heads. However, Mirror Principle suffixal ordering phenomena occur in the same way both in languages with overt movement and languages where the raising occurs only at LF. In the case of a verb with tense and aspect suffixes, it is found that aspect suffixes come closer to the verbal stem than tense both when raising of the verb is overt and when it is covert (Baker's 1985 Mirror Principle). What this indicates clearly is that LF raising actually involves an element with as much and effectively the same internal structure as equivalent forms which are raised overtly. In the case of the stage 3 sequence in (49) then, the hypothetical form [S-$\beta_{(x)}/\varnothing_{(x)}$-$\alpha_{(y)}$] will essentially raise with the same internal structuring whether this raising is overt or at LF.

Finally a word should be said about the hierarchical direction of affixal reanalysis. If such a process basically parallels the grammaticalization of free-standing elements, then one would expect that reanalysis should follow the path of movement and only go in an upward direction; specifically one would expect that an affix originally encoding the meaning of a functional head X^0 would possibly allow for reanalysis as relating to a higher head Y^0, but not allow for downward change and reanalysis as relating to a functional head W^0 hierarchically lower than X^0. Careful research on affixal change is obviously first necessary to establish that there is indeed an 'upward' direction to reanalysis with phonologically bound elements, but imagining this to be a likely conclusion one might suggest the following to account for the patterning. It may be suggested that an affix essentially becomes 'active' when it and its host raise up to the head against which the affix is licensed and that before such a point the affix is effectively completely ignored. Having once become 'active' though, it may be possible for the affix to be interpreted as also engaging in a licensing relation with some subsequently higher functional head, especially if this head is otherwise interpreted as being licensed by a phonologically zero affix/form. Reanalysis would then be possible only in an upward direction after an affix had become active in licensing terms, and never in a downward direction—prior to becoming active the affix will simply not be visible for any possibility of re-interpretation. In such a way then affixal reanalysis would also be dependent on the upward direction of movement in a tree.

Turning back to Chinese, I would like to suggest that the hypothetical three-stage process of affixal reanalysis proposed here now allows for a simple and natural explanation of the diachronic patterning and synchronic status of verbal *le*. In sections 6.1.1 above it was argued that there are good reasons to believe that verbal *le* originated as an instantiation of completive aspect; *liao/le* both originated as a verb meaning 'to finish' and hence had the typical lexical meaning of other completive phase V_2s, and *liao/le* underwent re-positioning adjacent to the verb at the same basic time that other V_2s are taken to have re-positioned themselves. In section 6.1.3 however, other evidence has indicated that synchronically verbal *le* appears in many situations to be rather clearly instantiating perfective viewpoint aspect—notably when it occurs in V_1-V_2-le forms and also with achievement predicates. The view of affixal grammaticalization and reanalysis proposed above now allows one to reconcile these apparently conflicting views. I would like to suggest that *le* as a suffix has over time gone through a process of upwards reanalysis, beginning as an instantiation of completive aspect/Asp_2^0 and then becoming re-interpreted as perfective aspect licensed against the structurally higher Asp_1^0. This hypothetical process of grammaticalization is illustrated in (50-52) below.

In stage 1 of the process *le* is taken to be a simple instantiation of completive aspect licensed against Asp_2^0 after raising at LF as in (50) (using the verb *mai* 'to sell' as a verbal stem):

(50) Stage 1 $\quad$ Asp$_1$P$_{((\text{im})\text{perfective})}$

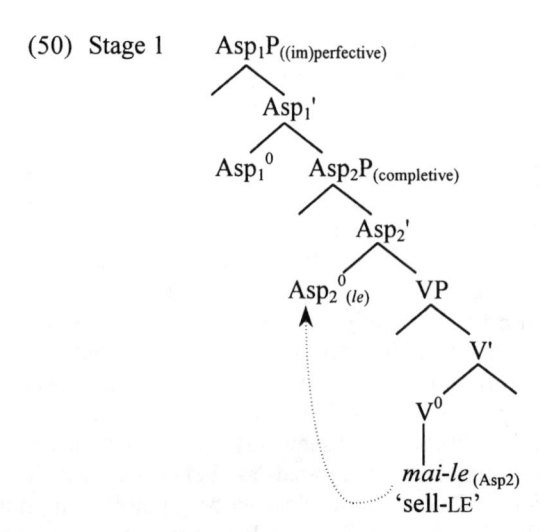

```
            Asp₁P((im)perfective)
           /    \
              Asp₁'
             /    \
          Asp₁⁰   Asp₂P(completive)
                  /    \
                     Asp₂'
                    /    \
                Asp₂⁰(le)  VP
                    ▲        \
                             V'
                              |
                              V⁰
                              |
                          mai-le (Asp2)
                          'sell-LE'
```

In stage 2, *le* is re-interpreted as instantiating not only completive aspect but also perfective aspect, being active in a checking relation not only with Asp$_2^0$ but also the higher Asp$_1^0$, as in (51):

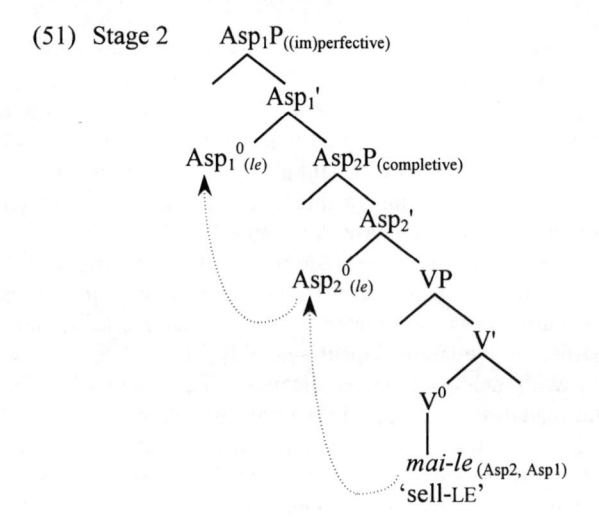

(51) Stage 2 $\quad$ Asp$_1$P$_{((\text{im})\text{perfective})}$

```
            Asp₁P((im)perfective)
           /    \
              Asp₁'
             /    \
        Asp₁⁰(le)  Asp₂P(completive)
           ▲       /    \
                      Asp₂'
                     /    \
                 Asp₂⁰(le)  VP
                     ▲        \
                              V'
                               |
                               V⁰
                               |
                          mai-le (Asp2, Asp1)
                          'sell-LE'
```

In stage 3 of the process, *le* comes to be reanalyzed fully as potentially instantiating only the higher aspect type Asp$_{1\text{perfective}}$. This then allows for a new suffixal instantiation of the lower Asp$_{2\text{completive}}$ to be inserted in the completive aspect position immediately right-adjacent to the verbal stem, as shown in (52) (using the completive suffix *wan* 'be finished'; alternatively completive aspect features might be carried by a suffix with zero phonological realization $\varnothing_{(\text{Asp2})}$):

(52) Stage 3

$$\text{Asp}_1\text{P}_{\text{((im)perfective)}}$$

Asp₁'

Asp₁⁰ (le)   Asp₂P(completive)

Asp₂'

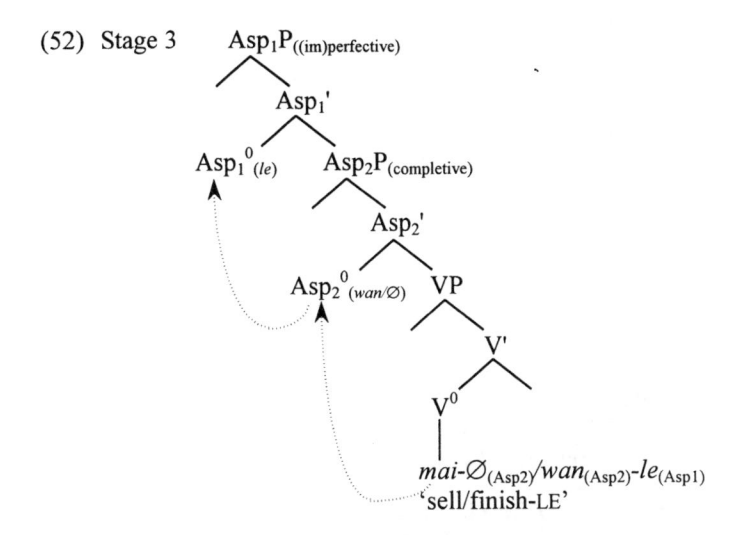

Asp₂⁰ (wan/∅)   VP

V'

V⁰

mai-∅(Asp2)/*wan*(Asp2)-*le*(Asp1)
'sell/finish-LE'

Such a process of upward affixal grammaticalization within the functional structure is able to provide a rather simple account of both the origins of *le/liao* and its current status in V₁-V₂-*le* forms. Having begun as completive aspect, *le* is taken to have grammaticalized further up the functional structure to be re-interpreted as perfective aspect, allowing for its current co-occurrence with clear completive aspect suffixes such as *wan* 'finish'.

6.1.4.2 Current distinctions between completive and perfective *le*: evidence for diachronic development

The suggested diachronic development of *le* modeled in (50-52) might also seem to be supported by certain interesting patterns pointed out in Sybesma (1999) and Lü (1980). In the latter work it is suggested that there are 28 verbs in Modern Chinese which verbal *le* combines with as a V₂ resultative type element similar to other phases.[9] Examples both in Lü (1980) and Sybesma (1999) with verbs such as *mai* 'sell', *guan* 'close', *wang* 'forget', and *chi* 'eat' show that there are distinct contrasts in the patterning of these verbs and other verbs not in the group of 28. Basically the verbs from this 28-verb group can combine with *le* without indicating perfectiveness, although a completive reading of the action verb is intended. For example, it is possible to combine many of the group of 28 with *le* and a higher modality verb such as *xiang* 'think of (doing X)', *keyi* 'be allowed to' or *yao* 'want to', whereas other verbs do not allow this. The examples below are mostly taken from Lü and Sybesma:

CHAPTER 6

(53) ni   bu   ai   ting, keyi guan-le shouyinji.
      you NEG like listen, can close-LE radio
      'If you don't want to listen, you can turn the radio off.'

(54) wo xiang mingtian mai-le nei-liang che.
      I   want tomorrow sell-LE that-CL car
      'I'm thinking of selling off that car tomorrow.'

In (53) and (54) the verbs *guan* 'close' and *mai* 'sell' are members of Lü's group of 28. In (55) and (56) it is seen that verbs such as *xie* 'write' and *kan* 'look at' not in this group do not allow combination with similar modality verbs and *le*:

(55) *wo xiang/yao xie-le   yi-feng xin.
       I want/want write-LE one-CL letter
       intended: 'I want to write a letter.'

(56) *ni yao zhidao, keyi kan-le zhei-ben shu.
       you want know   can look-LE this-CL book
       intended: 'If you want to know (this), you can read this book.'

Sybesma also notes that verbal *le* may combine with verbs such as *wang* 'forget', a member of the group of 28, and the habitual adverb *zongshi* resulting in a completion type reading, but that this kind of combination is again not possible with verbs from outside the group of 28, as seen in (57-58):

(57) wo zongshi wang-le ni-de mingzi.
      I always forget-LE you-DE name
      'I always forget your name.'

(58) *wo zongshi kan-le ta xie de shu.
       I always look-LE he write DE book
       intended: 'I always read the books he writes.'

Note that *le* does not have a perfective meaning in (57), and that (57) describes a situation which is not closed with visible endpoints.

Finally, Sybesma shows that members of the group of 28 may actually co-occur with the negative perfecive element *mei-you* 'Neg-have', which is not at all possible with verbs from outside the group of 28:

(59) wo hai mei-you   mai-le nei-liang-che
      I still NEG-AUX sell-LE that-CL-car
      'I still didn't sell off that car.'

260

(60) *wo hai mei-you xie-le nei-feng xin.
    I still NEG-AUX write-LE that-CL letter
    intended: 'I still didn't write that letter.'

From all this patterning Sybesma concludes that there must indeed be two distinct verbal *le*'s, one which occurs as a phase V₂ element with a restricted group of verbs (the group of 28), and a second element which is fully general in its occurrence. The first of these Sybesma calls 'Endpoint' *le* and the second 'Realization' *le*. Both are treated as small clause predicates base-generated as complements to the main verb V₁. (61) corresponds to a surface string *mai-le che* 'sell-LE car' with *le* occurring as a phase V₂ signaling simple endpoint with one the group of 28 verbs:

(61) Sybesma's Endpoint *le*

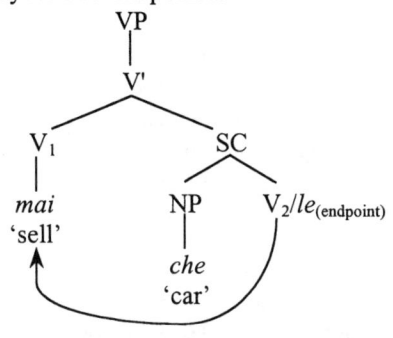

```
            VP
            |
            V'
           / \
         V₁   SC
          |   / \
        mai  NP  V₂/le(endpoint)
       'sell' |
             che
             'car'
```

(62) is the structure suggested by Sybesma to underlie the use of Realization *le* and a surface sequence such as *xie-wan-le shu* 'write-finish-LE book.' Note that here the V₂ *wan* has to raise to left-adjoin to *le* and then the sequence *wan-le* has to raise and right-adjoin to *xie* in order for the word order to match the surface string:

(62) Sybesma's Realization *le*

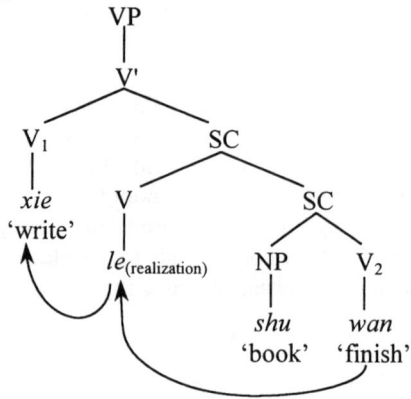

```
            VP
            |
            V'
           / \
         V₁   SC
         |   / \
        xie V   SC
       'write' |  / \
          le(realization) NP  V₂
                    |    |
                   shu  wan
                  'book' 'finish'
```

For a variety of reasons given earlier in chapter 5 I decided to explore an alternative solution to the small clause analysis of RVCs and *le*. One of the general objections to a small clause analysis which was raised, it may be recalled, was that such an analysis appears to build functional categories into positions selected by the main predicate/V inside the lexical VP, contra the common view that verb-related functional projections are expected to be projected above the VP (e.g., Grimshaw 1991). Functional categories (such as for example 'realization') are indeed regularly assumed to be functions which take lexical objects as their arguments rather than the reverse (i.e., lexical elements selecting functions). A further potential objection to a small clause analysis of *le* which can be noted here is that the structure in (62) with realization *le* predicating of a (second) small clause as its subject leads one to expect that it should be possible for *le* to stand alone with this small clause in an isolated predication relation. However, whereas this may sometimes be possible, and (64) corresponding to the hypothetical lower small clause part of (63) is indeed a well-formed string, in other cases this is not at all acceptable, as (66) relating to (65) shows:

(63) ta xi-ganjing-le (suoyoude) yifu.
 he wash-clean-LE all clothes
 'He washed (all) the clothes clean.'

(64) yifu xianzai ganjing-le.
 clothes now clean-LE
 'The clothes are now clean.'

(65) ta kan-wan-le (suoyoude) shu.
 he read-finish-LE all book
 'He finished reading (all) the books.'

(66) *shu xianzai wan-le.
 book now finish-LE
 'The book(s) is/are now finished.'

A further, similar example is (67). Here the small clause analysis will need to assume a structure such as (68) to account for the RVC+*le* string *fang-zai-le* 'put-at-LE'. This however incorrectly leads one to expect that the small clause headed by *le* can be separated from V_1. As shown in (69), V_2 *zai* can clearly be separated from V_1 in (69a). However, (69b) indicates that when *le* is present, *zai-le* has to co-occur with an adjacent V_1 as in (67), otherwise the sentence is ungrammatical.

(67) ta zuihou ba shu fang-zai-le zhuozi-shang.[10]
 he at last BA book put-be-LE table-top
 'At last he put the book on the table.'

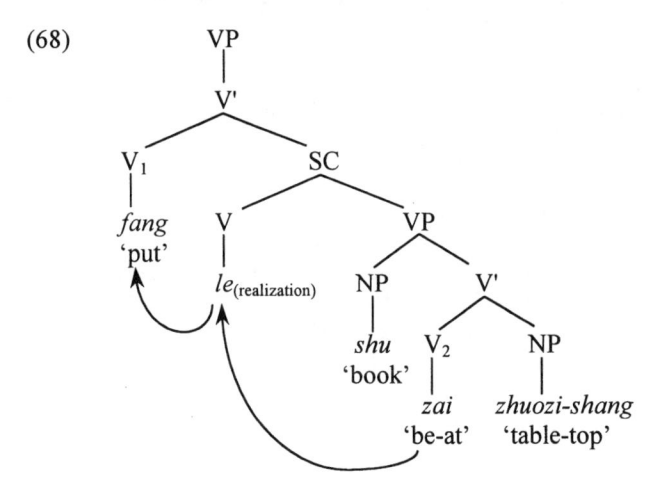

(68)
```
         VP
         |
         V'
        / \
      V₁   SC
      |   / \
    fang V   VP
    'put'|   / \
      le(realization) NP  V'
              |    / \
             shu  V₂  NP
            'book'|   |
                 zai  zhuozi-shang
                'be-at' 'table-top'
```

(69) a. shu zai zhuozi-shang.
 book be-at table-top
 'The book is on the table.'
 b. *shu zai-le zhuozi-shang.
 book be-at-LE table-top

This would therefore seem to confirm that when *le* occurs with a V_1 and a V_2 as in (63), (66) and (67), it is *not* hierarchically lower than the V_1, predicating of a small clause as its subject (as per 62), but rather a higher function applying to the whole [V_1-V_2 NP] as suggested in the perfective aspect analysis put forward here.

The observations made concerning Lü's group of 28 verbs can now be interpreted in a potentially revealing way in the present attempted modeling of the grammaticalization of verbal *le*. Sybesma's interesting insight (following Lü) is that *le* with a restricted set of verbs might seem to function in Modern Mandarin like an instantiation of the V_2 group. If this is true, and *le* can indeed simply instantiate completive aspect with certain verbs, it would seem to substantiate the assumption made on other grounds that verbal *le* indeed originated as a completive aspect suffix. Typically, as mentioned in chapter 5, each member of the V_2 group would seem to be lexically selective and combine with a limited number of V_1 elements. If there is an element *le* which only combines with a particular set of 28 verbs resulting in a completive meaning, this would seem to identify *le* in these cases as really being a canonical (completive aspect) V_2 element. Such a conclusion concerning the synchronic patterning of *le* with a subset of verbs now arguably leads to a strengthening of the grammaticalization account. It can be suggested that after re-positioning adjacent to the main verb V_1, *le* originally was a completive aspect suffix in stage 1 of the reanalysis process represented in (50). At this point in time *le* would have only occurred with a restricted set of V_1 elements just as other V_2 completives did. Later on *le* can be argued to have entered into stage 2 of the grammaticalization process shown in (51) potentially instantiating both completive aspect and perfective aspect. Here I think it is natural to assume that the possibility of a stage 2 interpretation of *le* with certain verbs (i.e., as instantiating completive aspect as well as perfective aspect) would not have necessarily immediately excluded a stage 1 interpretation of *le* as instantiating only completive aspect. In other words it may be assumed that *le* was only optionally interpreted as instantiating both completive and perfective aspect and that both stage 1 and stage 2 type interpretations could actually be available during a single time period (formally, any perfective aspect features present could be added either to *le*, or to some other phonologically null affix so that *le* would be interpreted as only instantiating completive aspect). Such an assumption essentially reflects the intuition that certain types of diachronic change are not effected catastrophically at a single point in time but instead occur over extended periods of time.

The arrival at stage 2 with *le* optionally being interpreted as instantiating perfective aspect/carrying perfective aspect features is however highly significant. It can be argued that once perfective aspect features could be added to *le* with a certain set of verbs, then this option might have also became quite generally available and *le* could have come to be interpreted as encoding perfectivity with a full and wide range of verbs. In the V_2 completive aspect (suffix) position, *le* would have contrasted with a large number of other V_2 elements and so it is not unreasonable to accept that it would be lexically restricted, each V_2 selecting a certain set of situations. However, when in stage 2 optionally instantiating perfective aspect, *le* would not have stood in contrast with other (overt) instantiations of perfective and so it is consequently very natural that it should have become a fully general marker of perfectivity. Furthermore, although completive aspect Asp_2^0 selects directly for a predicate

VP and hence a complement with clear descriptive content, perfective aspect Asp_1^0 selects for an Asp_2P which is essentially just a telic situation and hence far more abstract. It is therefore not surprising that lexical restrictions should occur in the selection relation between the instantiaion of $Asp_{2completive}$ and VP but not between $Asp_{1perfective}$ and Asp_2P and that *le* as a perfective marker should be quite general in its applicability. This point at which *le* may be taken to instantiate just perfective aspect with verbs which do not allow *le* as a simple completive is stage 3 of the process—*le* is available as a pure instantiation of the higher head $Asp_{1perfective}$. The hypothetical sequence of change is partially summarized in (70):

(70) a. *liao* occurs as completive aspect sentence-finally
b. *liao* re-positions adjacent to the verb as a suffix and reduces to *le* still as completive aspect = stage 1; *le* is (assumed to be) lexically restricted as other $V_{2completive}$ elements are
c. *le* can optionally be interpreted as instantiating perfective aspect as well as completive aspect; this possibility corresponds to stage 2. A stage 1 interpretation of *le* with a restricted set of verbs as just instantiating completive aspect is also still possible
d. the possibility that *le* can instantiate perfective aspect initiated with the restricted set of verbs becomes fully general, arguably due to the lack of contrast of perfective *le* with other parallel perfective morphemes. This represents stage 3 of the process.

It is important to stress here that although stage 1-3 of the reanalysis process are taken to be sequentially ordered, the occurrence of a later stage of the process does not necessarily exclude an earlier stage still being available as an interpretation. Thus in order for stage 3 to be reached it is assumed that there was first the possibility of a stage 1 interpretation and later a stage 2 interpretation. However, the possibility of a stage 3 interpretation does not mean that a stage 2 interpretation should necessarily no longer be available. The stage 1-3 interpretations for *le* are listed in (71) below:

(71) a. Stage 1: *le* instantiates only <u>completive</u> aspect.
b. Stage 2: *le* instantiates <u>completive</u> and <u>perfective</u> aspects.
c. Stage 3: *le* instantiates only <u>perfective</u> aspect.

What these stages represent are possibilities—the possibility of associating *le* with a certain type of interpretation. In terms of formal features, stage 2 represents the possibility of adding perfective aspect features to *le* in addition to completive aspect features, and *le* being interpreted as being potentially active in a checking relation with both the lower $Asp_{2completive}$ and the higher $Asp_{1perfective}$. However, in a situation of ongoing reanalysis over time it can be imagined that once a possibility (a new interpretation) becomes available, it does not have to be used in every instance; concretely in terms of the change with *le,* the arrival of the possibility of adding perfective features to *le* (i.e., interpreting *le* as perfective) does not mean that every time that *le* might be used perfective features would have to be added to it in addition to completive aspect features, and not every occurrence of *le* would have to be interpreted as perfective in addition to being completive. Similarly the possibility of a stage 3 interpretation of *le* as instantiating just perfective aspect would not necessarily mean that a stage 2 interpretation should no longer be available with verbs from the group which tolerate *le* as instantiating completive aspect.

What this is intended to suggest in general is that reanalysis of an element of type A as possibly instantiating a second function B does not have to result in the loss of the original A-type interpretation, even though this may in fact even frequently occur over time. In the case of Mandarin *le* I would like to suggest that the patterning highlighted by Sybesma (1999) showing critical differences between Lü's group of 28 verbs and other predicates when combined with *le* indicates that *le* synchronically may still indeed be interpreted with stage 1 status when occurring with members of the group of 28 verbs. When appearing with all other verbs *le* occurs interpreted with its stage 3 meaning of perfectivity alone.

Finally there may be evidence that *le* can also be interpreted as instantiating both completive and perfective aspect with verbs in the group of 28, i.e., stage 2. First of all it is clear that *le* can occur with verbs in this group instantiating just perfective aspect, i.e., stage 3. In (72) below there is an overt completive V$_2$ element occurring in addition to *le* and so *le* must here be instantiating perfective rather than completive aspect:

(72) ta ganggang cai   chi-wan-le   san-tiao yu.
 he just now then eat-finish-LE three-CL fish
 'He just finished eating three fish.'

When *le* occurs without a second distinct completive V$_2$ as in (73) the interpretation is effectively the same as in (72) and all three fish are understood to have been consumed:

(73) ta ganggang cai chi-le san-tiao yu.
 he just now then eat-LE three-CL fish
 'He just ate three fish.'

If completion of the eating of all three fish results from the use of completive aspect, it may consequently be suggested that *le* in (73) also instantiates completive aspect and hence has a stage 2 interpretation.

Summarizing then, it has been argued that *le* has developed over time from an original status as a marker of completive aspect similar to other V$_2$ elements to also instantiate perfective viewpoint aspect. Synchronically it has been suggested that *le* actually has an ambivalent current status and that there is evidence indicating that it may still occur instantiating either stage 1, 2, or 3 of the hypothesized route of diachronic change, this being represented in the table below:

Current potential interpretations of *le*:
a. Stage 1 interpretation: *le* occurs with a restricted group of 28 verbs instantiating just completive aspect.
b. Stage 2 interpretation: *le* occurs with a restricted group of 28 verbs instantiating both completive aspect and perfective aspect.
c. Stage 3 interpretation: *le* occurs as a general instantiation of perfective aspect.

Quite generally in this section I have argued for the significant conclusion that affixes are subject to the same type of (further) grammaticalization and reanalysis that occurs with free-standing morphemes. It was argued that as with the reanalysis of free-standing morphemes, this process of change takes place in a way which importantly parallels the direction of syntactic movement upward in a tree, *le* as a completive aspect suffix coming to be re-interpreted as a perfective aspect suffix licensed by an Asp_1P which is higher in the functional structure than the completive aspect head Asp_2^0. If this conclusion is correct and affixal reanalysis does mirror the reanalysis of free morphemes in relating an element to successively higher functional projections, it is clearly important for two reasons. First of all, it would seem to provide strong evidence in support of the Minimalist assumption that affixes are licensed via *movement* to higher functional heads—specifically, if affixal reanalysis shows parallels to the grammaticalization of free morphemes and the latter occurs as a result of movement to a higher functional position and reanalysis in this position, parallel affixal reanalysis can then also be assumed to result from movement and reanalysis relative to a licensing functional head. Secondly, the particular case of *le* would further seem to substantiate the Minimalist hypothesis that movement for the licensing of functional morphemes/heads (i.e., feature-checking) may frequently take place covertly at LF. As *le* does not appear to occur overtly raised out of V^0, it must be assumed that the movement to Asp_2^0 and Asp_1^0 must occur at some later derivational point hence LF. Considerations of language change and affixal reanalysis such as outlined here can thus be suggested to provide important evidence and arguments in favor of critical Minimalist assumptions concerning the licensing of functional interpretations in syntax.

6.2 Verbal *Le* and Tense

In this last section of the chapter I would like to explore the more contentious possibility that verbal *le* is also currently coming to instantiate *past tense* in Modern Chinese in addition to its other specifications.[11] Such a speculation has been specifically argued against by linguists such as Li and Thompson (1981)

CHAPTER 6

and there would furthermore seem to be a quite wider tacit assumption that *le* cannot be tense. However, here I will attempt to show that not only are there good reasons to support an analysis of *le* as plausibly instantiating tense, there are in fact also good counter-arguments to Li and Thompson's objections to such an analysis. The structure of the section is as follows. First I will outline the evidence and patterning which suggests that *le* may be coming to instantiate past tense. Then I will discuss the relation of aspect to tense, in particular focusing on the notion of perfectivity and argue that the categories tense and perfective must be taken to correspond to discrete syntactic heads, which may however be phonetically instantiated by a single overt morpheme. Subsequently showing how *le* can rather naturally be analyzed as instantiating tense as well as aspect in the model of grammaticalization proposed above, I will then go on to re-examine Li and Thompson's reasons for rejecting an analysis of *le* as tense and provide alternative explanations in each case for the phenomenon discussed by Li and Thompson. Ultimately it will be concluded that a close re-consideration of all the evidence and assumptions concerning the interaction of tense and aspect does indeed support the contention that verbal *le* is now coming to functionally represent tense.

The evidence in favor of an analysis taking *le* to instantiate past tense is simple and quite straightforward. First of all it is well-observed that the use of verbal *le* very frequently coincides with an interpretation of the predicate as having taken place in the past. This simple fact is noted in almost all descriptions of the patterning of *le* and in analyses of *le*'s distribution in experimental studies.[12] Secondly, it can be noted that in non-subordinate contexts *only* a past time interpretation is available when *le* is used (with one potential exception to which I later return). For example, (74) below can only be interpreted as having taken place in the past and neither a present tense nor a future reading is available:

(74) wo zai Beijing canguan-le Gugong.
        I   in Beijing visit-LE   Imperial Palace
        'I visited the Imperial Palace in Beijing.'
        Not: 'I am visiting/will visit/will have visited the Imperial Palace in Beijing.'

In (75) and (76) it is also shown that it is not possible to over-ride the past time reading by providing suitable non past-time adverbials/modal verbs:

(75) *wo mingtian (hui/cai-yao) zai Beijing canguan-le Gugong.
        I   tomorrow (will/then-will) in Beijing visit-LE Imperial Palace
        intended: 'Tomorrow I will visit/will have visited the Imperial Palace.'

268

(76) *wo mei-tian/xianzai gen Zhangsan canguan-le Gugong.
  I   every day/now with Zhangsan visit-LE Imperial Palace
  intended: 'Every day I visit/I am now visiting the Imperial Palace with Zhangsan.'

The fact that it is not possible to over-ride the past time interpretation occurring with *le* here would seem to indicate that past time interpretation is not simply a conversational implicature which might arise when *le* occurs as perfective aspect but significantly now actually part of the meaning of *le* in these contexts.

Thirdly, one finds that *le* might sometimes seem to be *necessary* to signal a past time interpretation even though contextually a past time interpretation might appear to be obvious:

(77) Q: ni   zuotian wanshang zuo-le shenme?
       you yesterday evening   do-LE what
       'What did you do last night?'
    A: wo shang*(-le) Fawen ke.
       I attend LE French class
       'I attended French classes.'

There is then simple reason to believe that *le* may be more than just a marker of perfective aspect but also have an association with the higher functional category of tense, instantiating past tense in a way which cannot be cancelled as an implicature. Further plausibility for the contention that *le* instantiates tense comes from a reflection on the likelihood of such an interpretation. If it is supposed that *le* originated as a marker of completive aspect and then grammaticalized to instantiate perfective aspect, it would be a highly natural third development for it to subsequently reanalyze further as an instantiation of (past) tense. Not only do completives and perfectives commonly give rise to past time implicatures which may naturally strengthen over time to become an encoded part of the meaning of a morpheme, formally such a reanalysis would also be very natural from the point of view of the model of grammaticalization proposed here. *Le* as a suffix could simply be re-interpreted as being active in a checking relation not only with $Asp_1^0{}_{perfective}$ but also with the T^0 head which occurs above Asp_1P, i.e., *le* would be interpreted as instantiating an additional higher head in the functional structure which the verb raises to at LF.

Given then the obvious arguments in favor of a past tense analysis of *le*, one might wonder why *le* has been commonly held to be an aspectual marker rather than a tense element. This is largely due to the existence of a number of specific cases and environments where verbal *le* does NOT seem to indicate past time. In order to defend an analysis of *le* as past tense, in sections 6.2.2-6.2.3 I will therefore consider how well-supported these arguments against a past tense analysis actually may be. Before doing this however, I will first

CHAPTER 6

briefly re-examine the notions of tense and aspect, emphasizing that they are formally distinct properties and outline an analysis of *le* as tense.

6.2.1 Tense, Aspect and Perfectivity

Section 6.1.2 presented an overview of Smith's two-tiered view of aspect which justifies the division of aspect into two clear major types—situation aspect and viewpoint aspect. Situation aspect corresponds to Vendler's (1967) notion of Aktionsart and the classification of a predicate according to its telic, durative and dynamic properties. Viewpoint aspect was then argued to apply to a predicate which already has a situation aspect characterization and present it from a particular perspective (viewpoint), essentially either as imperfective and focusing on the internal stages of an event or perfective and focusing on the event as a whole by making both its endpoints visible. These functions of aspect were then shown to be independent of tense. In (78) below the situation type is +telic as the predicate is naturally bounded, and the viewpoint type encoded by the *be...-ing* form is imperfective, this resulting in a focusing of the internal stages of the event. It is also significantly seen that tense is an independent function which can be varied quite separately from both the situation aspect and the imperfective viewpoint—either a present, future or past tense specification can co-occur with imperfective aspect in the sentence:

(78) Mary is/was/will be drawing a circle.

Commenting on the tense/aspect distinction, Smith (1997, p.98) observes that: "Temporal location (i.e., *tense*) and aspect are complementary temporal systems. The former locates a situation in time, while the latter specifies the internal temporal structure of the situation." Assuming therefore that there is indeed good justification for taking tense and viewpoint aspect to correspond to two formally distinct functions, and arguing furthermore that completive aspect is licensed by a discrete functional head potentially encoding situation aspect, the expanded structure in (79) was adopted for a head-initial language such as Chinese. In (79) each distinct function is represented by a distinct functional projection/head. In the course of the analysis, various overt instantiations of both types of aspect heads were argued for, and although tense was not discussed, there are certain free-standing morphemes which might be taken to instantiate tense and relate to the T^0 position, e.g., *hui* 'will':

(79)

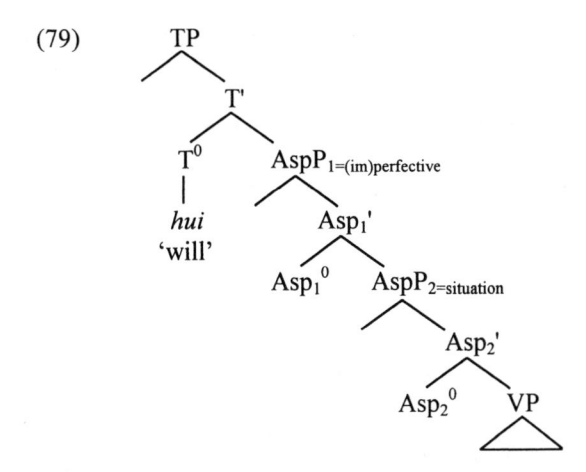

```
           TP
          /  \
         /    T'
        /    /  \
       T⁰   AspP₁ ₌₍ᵢₘ₎perfective
       |    /  \
      hui  Asp₁'
     'will' /  \
          Asp₁⁰  AspP₂₌situation
                 /  \
                Asp₂'
                /  \
             Asp₂⁰  VP
```

Considering perfective aspect now, following Smith (1997) its functional role has indeed been taken to be a focusing of the endpoints of a telic situation, and as with imperfective, such a role is assumed to be formally quite distinct from the addition of tense to a structure. A somewhat different view of perfective is to be found in Bybee, Perkins and Pagliuca (1994). These authors define perfectives as signaling a situation which is temporally bounded (p.54), but also seem to assume that perfective is often a complex category combining both aspect and past tense. Perfective is described as standing in contrast with imperfective aspect, but *not* being distinct from or combining with any simple past tense morpheme. In other words, whereas an imperfective aspect morpheme may combine with a discrete simple past tense morpheme to result in a past imperfective interpretation, commonly it is found that perfective morphemes do not combine with the same past tense morpheme to indicate past perfective; instead they signal past time 'inherently' without other overt support. Cross-linguistically this may perhaps often be true and there may well only be a single overt morpheme resulting in the interpretation of 'past perfective.' However, it is important to recognize that there are nevertheless two distinct formal properties involved here—the property of perfective aspect contrasting with imperfective and the property of past time reference contrasting with present/future. As such properties are semantically quite distinct and also represented by discrete morphemes when the aspectual specification is imperfective, it is only natural to assume that there are indeed two functional heads/projections present in the syntactic structure (as in 79) even when the two properties of past and perfective are phonetically encoded in a single overt morpheme.

The observation which Bybee, Perkins and Pagliuca (1994) make that it is common across languages for there to be a distinct morpheme encoding past tense with imperfective aspect markers, but not so with perfective morphemes is however interesting, and indicates that perfective morphemes potentially may also signal a past time specification *in some way*. Structurally it can be assumed that distinct tense and perfective aspect functional heads and projections must be present, but in terms of overt morphology it is actually a single element (the perfective morpheme) which may encode both the relevant properties. This is in essence what I have already argued in the case with *le* and aspect, namely that the single overt morpheme *le* may sometimes carry the specifications of two functional heads, completive and perfective aspect. In a development of the same theme in this section I will now go on to suggest that *le* may also instantiate past tense in addition to perfective aspect.

First however, I would like to note that a developmental connection between aspect markers such as *le* and the encoding of past time reference is indeed a common cross-linguistic phenomenon. Bybee, Perkins and Pagliuca (1994) observe that both simple past and perfective markers which both signal past time reference frequently derive from completives and resultatives, i.e., elements of the V_2 type in Chinese RVCs and hence also *le* in its origins. Harris (1982) and Bybee and Dahl (1989) similarly discuss how resultative constructions often evolve into perfectives and pure past tense markers, referring to languages such as French, Italian, Dutch, German and Turkish among others. Harris and Campbell (1995) also point to the Mayan language Cakchiquel as another instance in which a completive aspect marker has been reanalyzed as a past tense morpheme. This common process of change is generally assumed to result from a natural increase in the strength of a past time association with resultatives and completives. Use of a resultative to make reference to a result state is most common if the action leading to the result state has already occurred; consequently the use of resultatives often infers a past action (as does the use of completives). Such a natural past time inference may then over time become strengthened to the point of becoming part of the genuine meaning of a morpheme. Writing about Chinese in particular, Smith (1997) observes that:

> Temporal location is often conveyed by a perfective or imperfective viewpoint. There is a conventional association of the imperfective with the Present and the perfective with Past. In the absence of other information, including adverbials, the viewpoints are taken to convey these times. (p.279)

Smith therefore assumes that perfective markers such as *le* also give rise to natural inferences of past time interpretation in Chinese as in other languages.

While the suggestion that resultatives and perfectives frequently infer past time is both natural and easy to accept, it is important to note that there comes a time during language change when a conversational implicature strengthens to the point of becoming a real part of the meaning associated with a morpheme so that this meaning can no longer be denied or over-ridden. Smith explicitly argues that the past time interpretation found with perfective markers in Chinese is still essentially a conversational implicature (a 'conventional association') which is made: '*in the absence of other information, including adverbials.* . . . .' However, as shown in (75) and (76) repeated below, in fact this is not true, and it is actually not possible to use adverbials to over-ride the past time inference with *le*:

(75) *wo mingtian (hui/cai-yao) zai Beijing canguan-le Gugong.
    I tomorrow (will/then-will) in Beijing visit-LE Imperial Palace
    intended: 'Tomorrow I will visit/will have visited the Imperial Palace.'

(76) *wo mei-tian/xianzai gen Zhangsan canguan-le Gugong.
    I every day/now with Zhangsan visit-LE Imperial Palace
    intended: 'Every day I visit/I am now visiting the Imperial Palace with Zhangsan.'

What this then now strongly suggests is that diachronically *le* has indeed followed a very common and natural route of change originating as a completive and later turning into a perfective marker, but that synchronically *le* now also encodes past time not simply as a pragmatic inference but genuinely as an instantiation of tense/T^0.

Considered from the point of view of the more formal model of grammaticalization developed in 6.1.4, such a change to a situation in which tense is taken to be encoded on *le* is also very natural. Attempting to account for the earlier aspectual change where *le* hypothetically instantiated completive aspect with a restricted set of verbs to the present situation where *le* occurs as a general perfective marker it was suggested that this resulted from *le* raising at LF with the rest of the verbal complex and being re-interpreted as instantiating not only the lower Asp_2^0 head (completive aspect) but also as being licensed against the higher Asp_1^0 head (perfective). Here with regard to tense it can be suggested that *le* simply becomes interpreted as being actively engaged in a licensing/checking relation with a higher head still, the T^0 head which selects for the perfective Asp_1P. As noted above, a past time/tense interpretation of a perfective/completive morpheme is a natural pragmatic inference resulting from the inherent meaning of completion/resultatives, and so the re-interpretation of perfective *le* as instantiating not only perfective aspect but also the structurally higher past tense would also be a very normal extension of its original interpretation.

Formally the following stages of reanalysis can be suggested to result in the present synchronic situation. At an initial stage it may be assumed (as in 6.1.4) that *le* is base-generated with completive/perfective aspect features and that tense features are inserted on a phonologically null suffix $\varnothing_{(Tns)}$ as in (80) (or alternatively base-generated on a free-standing phonologically zero morpheme inserted directly into T^0). (80) considers a case where the verb stem attaches both completive and perfective aspect encoded by *le* (raising through the functional structure as indicated at LF):

273

CHAPTER 6

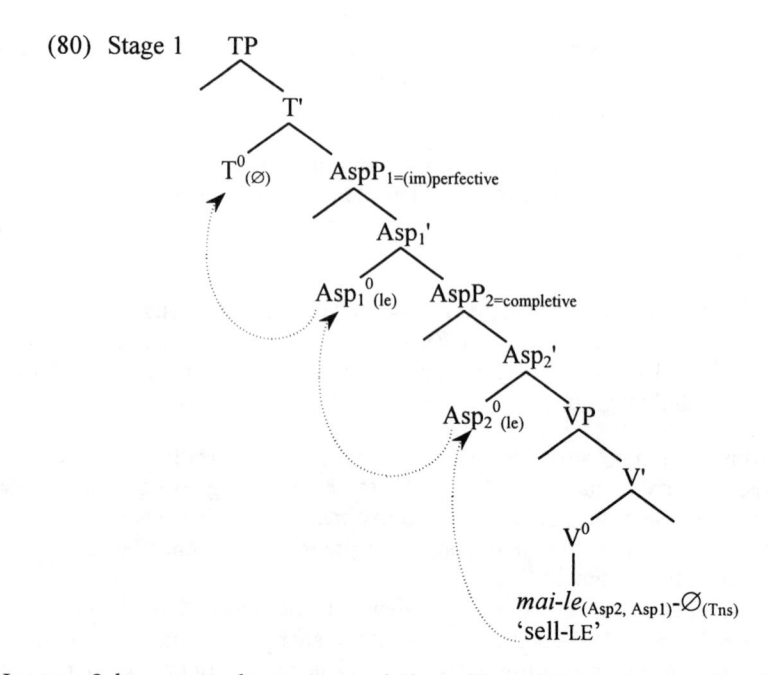

(80) Stage 1

```
           TP
          /  \
             T'
            /  \
          T⁰    AspP₁₌₍ᵢₘ₎ₚₑᵣfₑcₜᵢᵥₑ
          (∅)   /  \
              Asp₁'
              /  \
           Asp₁⁰  AspP₂₌cₒₘₚₗₑₜᵢᵥₑ
            (le)   /  \
                 Asp₂'
                 /  \
              Asp₂⁰  VP
               (le)   |
                      V'
                      |
                      V⁰
                      |
                  mai-le₍Asp2, Asp1₎-∅₍Tns₎
                    'sell-LE'
```

In stage 2 *le* comes to have an association with past time reference, but this has the status of an implicature which can be cancelled given appropriate means (adverbials, etc.). This association of *le* with past time in a way which allows for cancellation can be described somewhat formally as signifying that *le* at such a stage is *optionally* understood as representing past tense. In terms of feature-theory, the 'implicature period' may be suggested to correspond to a stage 2 in which (past) tense features are only optionally added to le and checked against T⁰. If synchronically there is evidence that past tense/past time reference has in fact now become a part of the meaning of *le* which cannot be cancelled by adverbials, this can be taken to indicate that past tense features will now always be added to *le* for subsequent checking against T⁰ as schematically represented in (81) (the 'optional' period Stage 2 simply corresponds to the choice of either the derivation in 80 or 81):

274

VERBAL *LE*

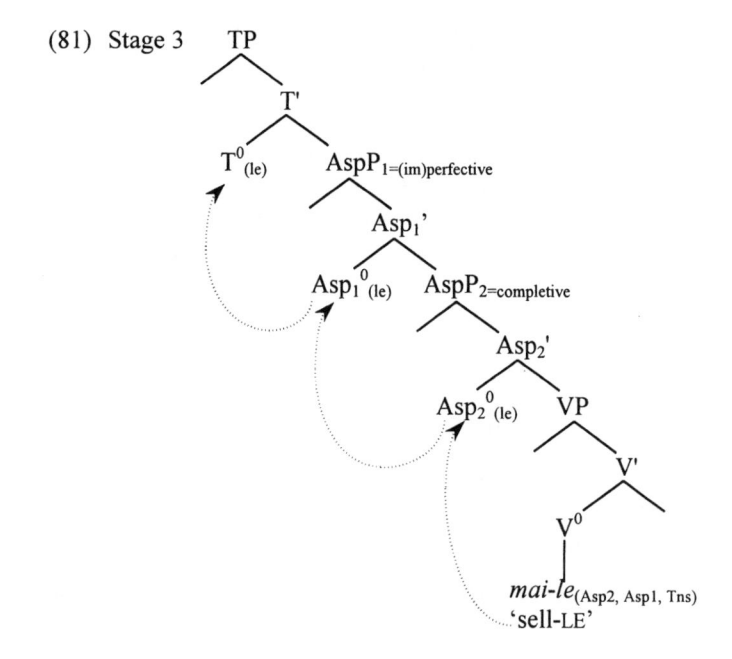

(81) Stage 3

```
            TP
           /  \
              T'
            /    \
        T⁰(le)   AspP₁=(im)perfective
                 /    \
                    Asp₁'
                   /    \
               Asp₁⁰(le)  AspP₂=completive
                          /    \
                             Asp₂'
                            /    \
                        Asp₂⁰(le)  VP
                                  /  \
                                    V'
                                    |
                                    V⁰
                                    |
                              mai-le(Asp2, Asp1, Tns)
                               'sell-LE'
```

Ultimately then, the hypothesis that further grammaticalization of *le* has led to *le* coming to instantiate past tense would seem to have much to support it. First of all, cross-linguistically the reanalysis of resultatives and completives similar to *le* into higher functional types encoding past time reference is well-attested, and such a change is easily understood to be the result of a pragmatic inference naturally available with such elements becoming standardized as part of the inherent meaning of these morphemes over time. Secondly, there is clear synchronic evidence that *le* may often only have a past time interpretation and such an interpretation cannot be over-ridden via the use of any adverbs. Thirdly, the hypothesized development of *le* from perfective into tense is also highly natural in the modeling of grammaticalization argued for here, where categorial reanalysis results from upward movement within a tree. Lower affixal elements come to be reanalyzed as optionally instantiating higher functional heads when raised up to such positions in larger feature-sets. In the case of *le*, it is naturally interpreted as potentially being active in a checking relation not only with the lower heads Asp_2^0 and Asp_1^0 but also with the higher T^0 head which selects for Asp_1P.

In what follows I will now re-examine the classic objections to an analysis of *le* as tense, and argue that in all cases the objections are either misconceived or alternatively allow for other explanations. [13]

6.2.2 *Possible Objections to an Analysis of* Le *as Tense*

CHAPTER 6

In Li and Thompson's (1981) chapter 6: '*Le* Does Not Mean Past Tense', (pp. 213-215) there are four essential arguments against the assumption that *le* instantiates past tense. To these can be added two other obvious reasons why one might not initially assume *le* to be a morpheme encoding tense.

Li and Thompson's claim that *le* does not mean past tense is based on the following observations.[14] First of all, it is noted that if an event is interpreted as having taken place in the past it is sometimes/often not necessary for *le* to occur, as in examples (82) and (83) below. The inference is therefore that if *le* were to be a genuine marker of past tense, one might expect it to be necessary here and in all references to events occurring in the past, contra observation.

(82) wo zao zhidao you yi-dian bu dui.
I early know there-is a-little NEG right
'I knew a long time ago that something was wrong.'

(83) zuotian yeli wo meng-jian wo muqin.
yesterday night I dream-meet I mother
'Last night I dreamed about my mother.'

Secondly, it is noted that *le* need not signal past time in certain subordinate clauses such as (84):

(84) wo chi-le fan zai zou.
I eat-LE rice then go
'I'll go after I eat.'

Thirdly, Li and Thompson point out that *le* does not encode any past time reference when it occurs in imperative sentences such as (85):

(85) he-le ta!
drink-LE it
'Drink it!'

Finally, it is shown that there is even one instance in which *le* may apparently occur in a matrix clause with a non-past meaning:

(86) mingtian wo jiu kaichu-le ta.
tomorrow I then expel-LE him
'I'll expel him tomorrow!'

In addition to Li and Thompson's arguments it can be added that there is a widely-held assumption articulated in Bybee, Perkins and Pagliuca (1994) that for a morpheme to be considered a marker of past tense it should be fully general in its potential application and combine with verbal elements of all types and aspects. With regard to such a criteria, it can be noted that *le* is commonly taken *not* to be able to combine with a whole range of simple verbs such as *shuo* 'say', *jueding* 'decide', *xiwang* 'hope (to)', etc. This might therefore be taken to suggest that it is not in fact a simple marker of past tense:

(87) ta shuo(*-le) Zhangsan mai-le yi-liang xin che le.
he say   LE Zhangsan buy-CL one-CL new car LE
'He said that Zhangsan has bought a new car.'

(88) ta jueding(*-le) mai yi-ge fangzi.
he decide(-LE) buy one-CL house
'He decided to buy a house.'

Finally, as well as not being able to combine with a certain sub-set of quite regular activity and achievement verbs, *le* is also argued (e.g., in Smith 1997 and many other works) to be unavailable as a simple marker of past with all of the stative verb group. It is commonly stated that although *le* may occur with stative verbs, this does not result in a simple interpretation of a past event/state but rather in a special inchoative interpretation. For example, (89) is not interpreted as 'Zhangsan was ill' (a simple past interpretation) but as 'Zhangsan *became* ill' (inchoative). Such a patterning is again seen as a reason not to consider *le* as past tense:

(89) Zhangsan bing-le.
Zhangsan be-sick-LE
'Zhangsan got sick.'

There might therefore seem to be a range of potentially good reasons not to consider verbal *le* as tense, despite the evidence and arguments presented in 6.2.1 supporting such an account. In what follows however, I will argue against these objections one by one, and attempt to show that they can in fact be quite satisfactorily answered while still maintaining the suggestion that *le* has indeed come to be an instantiation of tense.

6.2.3 Arguments against the Objections

6.2.3.1 Optionality of *le*

The first of Li and Thompson's objections I will re-consider is their observation that *le* often need not occur in situations where there is a past time interpretation, as in (82) and (83) above. It is inferred that if *le* were to be a genuine marker of past tense, it should occur in these and all other instances of past time reference. Such a position would seem to be influenced by considerations of the synchronic state of English and various other languages, where past tense must always be marked in past time situations. From a cross-linguistic and a diachronic point of view however, it is certainly *not* true that languages always encode tense explicitly wherever this may be possible. Bybee, Perkins and Pagliuca (1994) note that one common property of grammaticalizing morphemes is "frequency increase", and that from a stage where new functional elements are only used when obligatory in otherwise potentially ambiguous environments, they later come to be simply applied wherever their meaning is compatible with the general context. An example they give is that the English simple past tense *-ed* is (now) used not only where it supplies new information that a situation occurred in the past, but also in contexts where it is very clear from other elements such as adverbs and previous occurrences of past tense that the interpretation must be past time. The use of past tense in Modern English is therefore frequently rather redundant. However, similar obligatory use of functional morphemes in every compatible situation is by no means fully common. Bybee, Perkins and Pagliuca note for example that the past habitual form *used to* need not be used in every case where there is a past habitual interpretation, and that (91) has the same interpretation as (90) even without the overt past habitual form:

(90) When she lived with him, she *used to sing* to him every day.

(91) When she lived with him, she *sang* to him every day.

Bybee, Perkins and Pagliuca also mention Cheyenne as an example of a language where none of the tense markers are obligatory (p.98). It is therefore not true that a functional morpheme must appear in every compatible context in order to be classed as a functional element.[15] Such rather redundant overuse is simply a *possible* stage in the development of grammatical elements, and functional morphemes which are only used when really necessary are by no means any less functional than those which are used wherever possible.

Relevant and interesting here is also the diachronic development of the English past tense form in *-ed* which arguably came into use as an optional encoding of an *emphatic* past tense form (see Bybee, Perkins and Pagliuca p.150). The original assumed source of the *-ed* suffix was in fact the Old English free-standing past-form auxiliary *dyde* (Modern English *did*). Occurrence of this element in the auxiliary position following the main verb is assumed to have caused phonetic reduction of *dyde* and its development into a suffixal element *-ed*, as abstractly diagrammed in (92) (see also section 5.4 in chapter 5 on suffix-creation in SOV languages):

(92) John to London walk did. → John to London walk-ed.

Diachronically then it can be argued that the English past tense element *dyde* and its reduced form *-ed* would have originally occurred when the speaker also intended a certain emphasis and would not have occurred in every past time environment. Something similar (in the sense of there being optionality in the use of a marking of past tense) may quite possibly be true of the use of Chinese *le*. Research has indicated that *le* appears to occur with a high degree of frequency in two particular types of situation. Studies such as Spanos (1979) (reported in Smith 1997) agree with other investigations that *le* is used when the context makes it "necessary to explicitly state the realization of a given action." (p.81), and that speakers use *le* commonly when past time reference is otherwise not clear from the context. *Le* therefore frequently occurs when past time reference must be made clear and explicit—a disambiguating function. Elsewhere it would appear that *le* is often used when the speaker wishes to *emphasize* an action. In Chang's (1986) study reported in Smith (1997) it is argued that *le* occurs predominantly as 'an explicit marker for the peak event in a discourse segment.' (p.265). Smith (1997) also observes that *when*-type clauses in Chinese such as in (93) function to foreground the event in the main clause and that this usually means that the verb in the main clause needs to carry a viewpoint morpheme such as *le*:

(93) ta zai Beijing de shihou xue-le Hanyu.
     he be-in Beijing DE time   study-LE Chinese
     'When he was in Beijing he learned Chinese.'

If the *when*-clause depicts the background of an event/situation, this has the effect that the verb in the main clause carrying the viewpoint morpheme is automatically highlighted and focused. T'ung and Pollard (1997) additionally note that *le* "is not necessary when describing circumstances (i.e., the background to an event) or relating sequences of events (if it is used, it breaks the sequence into separate steps)." (p.144). It therefore might seem that speakers use *le* when the event depicted requires a certain emphasis, and hence that *le* is actually rather similar to (the development of) the English emphatic past *dyde/-ed*. Following the conclusions of other researchers, the distribution of *le* can consequently be suggested to be largely dictated by two main factors: *le* is used when the context requires *disambiguation* as past, and *le* is also used to mark an *emphatic* past event.[16] Given the apparent optionality of *le*, it is rather natural that the use of overt phonetic material should in fact result in an emphasized interpretation. Similar patterns are elsewhere found where a language has both null pronominals (*pro*) and overt pronouns; the overt forms are basically only used when there is either ambiguity or in order to emphasize the referent. Elsewhere where no emphasis or disambiguation is required, overt forms are avoided, this being reflected in Chomsky's (1981) suggestion of an Avoid Pronoun Principle. With optional elements such as *le* one may assume that a parallel and general Avoid Overt Realization Principle also leads speakers to only use *le* when necessary (or for emphasis).

Ultimately then, the optionality of *le* does not argue against its status as a tense element in any convincing way. There are other languages in which tense is clearly only given optional phonetic realization, and there are also simple reasons why one can understand the avoidance of overt forms if this is possible in a language.

CHAPTER 6

6.2.3.2 Lack of generality I: non-occurrence with simple verbs of cognition or communication

In addition to Li and Thompson's arguments concerning optionality of use, it can be added that there is a widely-held assumption articulated in Bybee, Perkins and Pagliuca (1994) that for a morpheme to be considered a marker of past tense it should be fully general in its potential application and combine with verbal elements of all types and aspects. With regard to such a criteria, it can be noted that *le* is commonly taken *not* to be able to combine with a range of simple verbs such as *shuo* "say", *jueding* "decide", and *zhidao* "know" as illustrated in (87-88) repeated below, together with example (94) with *zhidao*. This apparent lack of full generality in its use might therefore be taken as indication that *le* is not in fact a simple marker of past tense.

(87) ta shuo(*-le) Zhangsan mai-le yi-liang xin che le.
he say LE Zhangsan buy-LE one-CL new car LE
'He said that Zhangsan has bought a new car.'

(88) ta jueding(*-le) mai yi-ge fangzi.
he decide(-LE) buy one-CL house
'He decided to buy a house.'

(94) ta zhidao(*-le) Mali yao he Zhangsan jie-hun le.
he know LE Mali want with Zhangsan marry LE
'He knew that Mali was/is getting married with Zhangsan.'

An understanding of the potentially emphatic properties of *le* noted above however allows for an explanation of this lack of generality of *le*. With all of these rather general verbs of cognition and communication it is their following clausal complement which encodes the new and hence focused information in the sentence. This being so it is quite inappropriate for *le* to be used on the embedding verb as *le* is essentially licensed as a means to emphasize and focus a verb. Were the matrix verb to carry an emphatic focus with *le* this would result in two unconnected foci in the sentence—the first being emphasis on the act of saying, deciding, etc., and the second the natural focus encoded by the new information of the complement clause. As a single sentence normally is restricted to encoding a single center of focused information, it is not surprising that the use of *le* would be avoided on verbs whose complement clauses are common foci. The likelihood of such a mode of explanation being correct can in fact also easily be checked. Whereas clausal complements to verbs of saying, knowing and deciding tend to be consistently interpreted as new information, if the complement of these verbs is instead a DP headed by an anaphoric demonstrative such as *zhei/nei* "this/that" it is easily interpretable as old information not in focus. Interestingly, as soon as the objects of *zhidao* and *jueding*, etc. are nominal and old information it is found that *le* is perfectly acceptable on the verb, as shown in (95) and (96):

(95) ta   huran   zhidao-le nei-jian shi.
     he suddenly know-LE that-CL thing
     'Suddenly he knew about that thing/found out about that thing.'

(96) nei-jian-shi   ta jueding-le hen jiu/liang tian le.
     that-Cl-thing he decide-LE very long/two day LE
     'He decided that very long ago/two days ago.'

Furthermore, while *shuo* 'say' is a very general verb of oral communication and hence a verb which will naturally focus its complement clause as new information, if an adverbial is added to *shuo* which allows for emphasis on the verb it is found that *shuo* can occur both with *le* and a clausal complement, as in (97) (note that *you* 'again' is also used to force an interpretation in which the complement clause must be old information and emphasis is on *shuo*):

(97) ta you dashengde shuo-le ta bu qu.
     he again loudly   say-LE he not go
     'He then again *shouted* that he wasn't going.'

Consequently, the apparent 'non-generality' of *le* with certain verbs actually can be explained in a rather simple way and cannot be taken to provide evidence against a past tense analysis of *le* (on the grounds of lack of expected generality). Once certain discourse factors are controlled for it is found that the verbs in question are in fact able to carry *le* signaling past tense and that there is no genuine lack of generality with these predicates.

6.2.3.3 Lack of generality II: *le* with statives

The next potential objection to an analysis of *le* as tense to consider here is another very broad case of lack of generality—the apparent inability of *le* to occur signaling simple past tense/time with the *stative verb* group. Commonly it is argued that only a special inchoative interpretation is available when stative verbs combine with *le* and not an interpretation corresponding to a simple past usage. The example (89) repeated below is consequently not interpreted as 'Zhangsan was ill' (a simple past interpretation) but as 'Zhangsan *became* ill' (inchoative):

(89) Zhangsan bing-le.
     Zhangsan be-sick-LE
     'Zhangsan got sick.'

CHAPTER 6

In order to approach this issue, we need to first understand what is meant by inchoativity as a linguistic term, and whether referring to a particular interpretation as inchaotive would necessarily classify it as anything significantly different from 'regular' past interpretations.

Recall that the hypothesis of the present section is that the morpheme verbal *le* has evolved a dual nature and currently instantiates both past tense and perfective aspect, this being due to the fact that *le* is developing from an aspectual marker and coming to encode interpretations of (past) tense as well. Such a dual specification as past and perfective can now be argued to allow for a natural account of the apparent inchoative restrictions on the interpretation of *le* with stative verbs. First of all it should be noted that despite traditional morphological views (such as the Item and Arrangement approach) that a single morpheme corresponds to just a single function, there are good reasons to believe that a single morpheme may actually fulfill multiple functions (as in fact assumed in the Word and Paradigm approach to morphology).[17] Such dual functionality is also very commonly found in the interaction of tense and aspect functions. Smith (1997), for example, notes the case of English *used to* which encodes both past tense and habitual aspect and can nowadays *only* occur in the past tense—thus a tense and an aspectual specification are bound up inseparably in a single morpheme:

(98) John used to/*uses to like Mary.

The French *Imparfait* verb form is another case given where there is an inseparable combination of tense and (imperfective) aspect. As shown in (99), French *Imparfait* suffix, like English "used to", only occurs in the past tense (Smith 1997). To express a present counterpart of a progressive event, a different strategy is employed as shown in (99b), rather than using an imperfective verb form.

(99) a. Jean lis<u>ait</u> un roman.
 Jean read-past-3rdsg-IMP a novel
 'Jean was reading a novel.'
 b. Jean est en train de lire.
 Jean is in train of read
 'Jean is (in train of) reading a novel.'

Aspectual restrictions on the use of English simple present tense are also noted in Smith. When present tense in English does not occur with imperfective aspect (i.e., *be...-ing*), it receives an automatic interpretation as habitual aspect, indicating again that tense and a type of aspectual interpretation are bound up together in a single overt morpheme (as well as 3rd.sing. agreement):

(100) John plays tennis.

VERBAL *LE*

Consequently it is fairly clear that diachronic change may frequently lead to situations where tense and aspectual properties co-occur in a single overt element.

The assumption that Chinese *le* encodes the dual functions of past tense and perfective aspect (and sometimes also completive aspect) now provides the basis for an explanation of the patterning with *le* and stative verbs. Comrie (1976) points out that there is in fact a common connection between perfective aspect and inchoativity with stative verbs: 'In many languages that have a distinction between perfective and imperfective, the perfective forms of some verbs, in particular of some stative verbs, can in fact be used to indicate the beginning of a situation (ingressive meaning).' (p.19). What needs to be asked now is whether inchoativity really is a primitive type of aspect different from simple perfective, or whether (as Comrie hints) that it is possibly quite a predictable bi-product of perfective aspect combining with a certain class of verbs.

Supposing that inchoative were to be a primitive different type of viewpoint aspect contrasting with perfective and imperfective, one could possibly attempt to explain the inchoative interpretation of *le* with stative verbs in the following way. It could be suggested that because perfective aspect *le* originally derives from a predicate meaning 'to finish' it may still retain something of its earlier meaning and still require/select for a complement which is +dynamic. For example, in English the word 'finished', when used as a perfective marker, still requires an agentive subject and a +dynamic predicate:

(101) a. John finished reading.
 b. *John finished being sleepy.

It is actually quite common cross-linguistically for aspectual verbs derived from predicates having an original interpretation of the 'to finish' type to show similar restrictions to Chinese *le* and give rise to inchoative readings when combined with stative verbs (see here Bybee, Perkins and Pagliuca 1994). If such predicates originally had agentive subjects in control of dynamic actions, then it is possible that they would not readily combine with non-dynamic states.[18] Then a type of aspect different from perfective would have to occur with stative predicates, and inchoative aspect might then be this different type. However, such an approach would seem to require the assumption that *le* could represent two types of different aspect contrasting in the viewpoint category, which seems to be somewhat implausible. Furthermore, *le* is derived from a sentence-final *liao* which takes the whole sentence as its argument, so it is not so obvious that *liao* originally did have anything like an agentive subject and a necessary dynamic complement, unlike other aspectual elements such as English 'finished' in (101).

Smith (1997) seems to suggest that inchoativity is really independent of perfectivity and instead part of situation aspect:

283

CHAPTER 6

> The perfective is not available to statives in Chinese, Russian and Navajo. These languages have no perfective sentences with stative verb constellations and the interpretation of a basic-level stative situation type. Stative verb constellations do allow the perfective viewpoint when they undergo a shift in situation type. They appear as inchoatives in derived telic sentences. As such they present a change into the state which the verb constellation lexically denotes. In situation type they are either Achievements or Accomplishments, depending on the feature of duration. (p.70)

However, this also does not seem to be right for two clear reasons. First of all if stative verb + *le* combinations are intransitive telic achievements or accomplishment predicates, they should be expected to exhibit unaccusative syntax. In Chinese achievement/accomplishment verbs are either inherently unaccusative/telic (for example *si* 'die') or become telic and unaccusative in virtue of a V_2 telic bound. All such unaccusatives allow indefinite subject inversion, whereas unergative intransitives with simple perfective *le* do not. As noted in Sybesma (1999), *ku* 'cry' in (102) is not one of the 28 verbs which allow *le* as a completive V_2 and *le* must therefore be simply perfective when combining with *ku*. Perfectivity alone does not license indefinite subject inversion whereas the telicity encoded by a V_2 corresponding to $Asp_{2completive}$ does (examples (102b) and (103b) are adapted from Sybesma 1999):

(102) a. dangshi henduo ren ku-le.
      that-time many people cry-LE
      'Many people cried then.'
   b. *dangshi ku-le h**e**nduo ren.
       that-time cry-LE many people
      intended: 'Many people cried then.'

(103) a. dangshi henduo ren ku-lei-le.
      that-time many people cry-tired-LE
      'Many people cried themselves tired then.'
   b. dangshi ku-lei-le henduo ren.
      that-time cry-tired-LE many people
      'Many people cried themselves tired then.'

(104) a. dangshi henduo ren si-le.
      that time many people die-LE
      'At that time many people died.'
   b. dang-shi si-le henduo ren.
      that time die-LE many people
      'At that time many people died.'

If *le* occurring with a stative verb resulted in a telic achievement or accomplishment, then it is expected that stative verbs and *le* should allow for indefinite subjects to invert. This is however not the case:

(105) a. dangshi henduo ren bing-le.
 that-time many people be-ill-LE
 intended: 'At that time many people got ill.'
 b. *dang-shi bing-le henduo ren.
 that-time be-ill-LE many people
 intended: 'At that time many people got ill.'

This would seem to indicate both that *le* is not occurring in the V$_2$ position here making the stative verb telic, and that inchoativity does not correspond to any telic shift to an achievement/accomplishment type occurring in the situation aspect.

Secondly, if *le* occurring with stative verbs were to represent some further type of aspectual primitive either in complementary distribution with simple perfectivity or somehow in the completive V$_2$ position, one would expect that it should be able to occur in a sentence with future reference such as (106), but again this is not at all possible:

(106) *wo mingnian yiding hui bing-le san tian.
 I next-year certainly will be-ill-LE three day
 intended: 'Next year I will certainly be sick for three days.'

As shown in the intended gloss, there is a perfectly good anticipated interpretation that should be available if inchoativity were to be an independent type of aspect, and the notion of inchoativity should be in theory compatible with future time reference. The fact that sentences such as (106) are unacceptable can be taken to indicate instead that *le* in fact is simply perfective aspect here combining also with past tense, and it is the past tense specification which is incompatible with the future oriented adverb.

Consequently, if 'inchoative *le*' is not taken to be a primitive independent type of aspect contrasting with perfective, the inchoative interpretation still needs some explanation. I would like to suggest that this can in fact be understood quite naturally when one reflects on what happens when a perfective such as *le* is applied to stative verbs. Following Smith (1997), the role of perfective viewpoint is here taken to be the focusing of endpoints present in a telic predicate. As statives are atelic and clearly have no obvious endpoints, when perfective is combined with a stative verb, it can only signal realization of the state, not completion of the state (which would require a final endpoint). As simple realization logically implies that there must be some beginning point but no explicit end, the realization interpretation comes to be understood as simple inchoativity, resulting in the salient inchoative readings in examples such as (89).

CHAPTER 6

A second, rather different potential explanation of the interpretation of inchoativity found with stative verbs and the morpheme *le* is to question whether the element *le* occurring in such cases really is verbal *le*, and to consider the alternative possibility that it might instead be the homophonous sentence-final particle *le*. In all of the examples commonly given in the literature, *le* with intransitive stative verbs comes in sentence-final position (as in 89) and there has not been any attempt to control for whether this might instead really be sentence *le*. As sentence *le* signals that the general situation of a predicate is ongoing and relevant to the current moment, an interpretation of inchoativity with stative verbs might indeed be rather natural with such an element, indicating that the state of the predicate has begun and is relevant to the speech time and is not yet terminated. In support of such a possibility is the data in (107) and (108) which indicate that when a stative verb is *transitive*, it cannot in fact occur with verbal *le* but instead allows for an interpretation of inchoativity with sentence *le*:

(107) *xianzai ta zai-le Beijing.
now he be-in-LE Beijing
intended: 'Now he is in Beijing.'

(108) xianzai ta zai Beijing le.
now he be-in Beijing LE
'Now he is in Beijing.'

However the inchoative interpretation arises, either as a default via perfective aspect just signaling realization with no indicated endpoint or alternatively through sentence *le* signaling open-ended relevance to the current situation, the conclusion is that inchoativity here does not correspond to any primitive alternative aspectual type necessarily excluding perfective aspect. There is also simple but highly significant evidence indicating that verbal *le* actually can in fact encode a straightforward interpretation of perfectivity and simple past tense with stative verbs, despite the common assumption that only inchoative interpretations are possible. Compare (89) to (109). A durative time phrase is added on to the combination of a stative verb and *le* in (109), whose word order makes it clear that this is a verbal *le* and not a sentence-final *le*. The resulting interpretation is of simple past time:

(89) Zhangsan bing-le. (inchoative)
Zhangsan be-sick-LE
'Zhangsan got sick.'

(109) ta (zai Beijing de shihou) bing-le san tian.
he (in Beijing DE time) be-ill-LE three day
'He was sick for three days (when he was in Beijing).'

It clearly shows that stative verbs do indeed combine quite regularly with verbal *le* to give a basic past time perfective reading, despite the frequent denial that this is possible. Above it was suggested that stative verbs might perhaps not easily combine with perfectivity because the perfective's function is to focus the endpoints of a situation and stative predicates have no inherent endpoints. Functionally what the addition of the duration phrase to a stative verb + *le* does is simply to provide an explicit temporal bound to the predicate. Once this is added in to the structure, the combination of stative verb and *le* is perfectly well-formed with a past perfective interpretation just like other predicate types. What is also interesting is that the 'inchoative' interpretation supposed to result from the particular combination of verbal *le* and stative verbs is actually not restricted just to this class of predicate and also arguably occurs with *activity* verbs when they occur without a telic bound. The interpretation of (110) and (111) with an activity verb occurring alone with *le*, paralleling the common examples of a stative verb alone with *le* (as in 89), would also seem to have primarily an inchoative reading signaling an entry into the activity:[19]

(110) ta   ku-le.
       he cry-LE
       'He started to cry.'

(111) ta   shui-le.
       he sleep-LE
       'He started to sleep (he has gone to bed).'

Again, once some kind of telic bound is added in, the interpretation is of simple past perfective:

(112) ta   pao-le/shui-le   liang-ge zhongtou.
       he run-LE/sleep-LE two-CL   hour
       'He ran/slept for two hours.'

The ultimate conclusion concerning stative verbs and *le* is therefore that there is no fundamental difference between stative verbs and other predicates in the possibility of being combined with past perfective *le*, and that any inchoative reading is simply due to the lack of any telic bound, statives behaving here just like activity verbs which otherwise do combine with past perfective *le*. Consequently, as in the previous cases considered (i.e., the potential combination of *shuo, jueding, zhidao*, etc. with *le*), careful investigation shows that ultimately there is no necessary restriction on the generality of past perfective *le*, and that potential lack of generality can therefore not be used as an objection to the analysis of *le* as instantiating past.

CHAPTER 6

6.2.3.4 Subordinate clauses

I will now move on to consider the three other remaining objections to a past tense analysis of *le* raised by Li and Thompson. The first of these was that verbal *le* regularly occurs embedded in examples such as (84) without necessarily signaling past time:

(84) wo chi-le fan zai zou.
 I eat-LE rice then go
 'I'll go after I eat.'

If *le* here may occur without having a past time interpretation this might seem to falsify the contention that verbal *le* has come to instantiate past tense and suggest that such a claim should be abandoned. However, given the constant past time interpretation arising with *le* in environments other than this subordinate clause case and the two other specific contexts to be re-considered below (imperatives and main clauses with *jiu* 'then') I believe it is worth attempting to see if such cases might perhaps have some alternative explanation.

I believe that a possible solution to the problem here involves focusing on two particular properties of this non-past usage of *le*. The first is that this non-past use of *le* is confined to a certain type of *subordinate* clause/constituent. The second is the general suggestion that *le* is a morpheme undergoing diachronic change and reanalysis, i.e., it is claimed to have developed from a completive to a perfective marker, and now to be an instantiation of past tense. Note now that much diachronic research has shown that morpho-syntactic change and reanalysis is often not effected at the same time in all potentially available environments and that changes very frequently occur in main/matrix clauses before they later spread to other subordinate contexts. Harris and Campbell (1995) attribute this significant 'discovery' originally to Biener (1922a/b) and point out that it is an assumption both widely held among historical linguists and substantiated by much research work. Quite commonly it is believed that:

> ...subordinate clauses are less subject to syntactic change than are main clauses because they exhibit a more restricted range of morpho-syntactic trappings due to their backgrounding function in discourse (Givón 1971, 1984; Hopper and Thompson 1984). The general idea involved is the belief that change starts in main clauses and may or may not ultimately come to affect subordinate clauses, but that it does not begin in subordinate clauses, later reaching main clauses. (p.27)

In a footnote (footnote 8, p.382) it is also added that: ". . . in general, subordinate clauses do contain fewer morphosyntactic contrasts than main clauses."

Making use of this general insight that morpho-syntactic changes occur first in main clauses and then only later spread to subordinate clauses--or possibly even remain confined to main clauses and do not get incorporated into subordinate environments—it could here be quite reasonably suggested that such a main clause/subordinate clause developmental distinction is behind the non-past interpretation of *le* in examples such as (84). Having argued that *le* has undergone reanalysis into an instantiation of past tense as well as perfective, one could now suggest that while this change has indeed occurred in regular main clauses and even many subordinate clause environments, it has not yet spread to the subordinate clause type found in examples such as (84), and consequently *le* simply instantiates perfective in such an environment. Such a suggestion would be fully in line with the view mentioned above that morpho-syntactic changes may only gradually spread from matrix clauses to other subordinate environments. It would also be supported by the assumption made here that *le* instantiates perfective aspect as well as past in most environments. The particular subordinate context found in (84) would simply be a case where *le* has reanalyzed as far as being perfective but not undergone the further change to be interpreted as past tense as well (i.e., has not reached Stage 3 of the process outlined in 81). A similar, highly relevant example of a morpho-syntactic change which has occurred in a language in main clause contexts but not in all subordinate clauses is the diachronic reanalysis of the classical Japanese aspect system into tense. From an earlier stage in which Japanese is taken to have had only a contrastive system of aspect in both main and embedded clauses there arose the Modern Japanese system of tense, created when various of the early aspect markers became re-interpreted as tense elements (see e.g., Takeuchi 1999). What is interesting to note is that while the element -*ta* has clearly grammaticalized as past tense in most main and embedded clause environments, in relative clauses it is still possible for -*ta* to occur with just a perfective aspect interpretation and actually refer to a future context. Example (113) is from Nakamura (1994):

(113) [ashita   ichiban hayaku kita] hito-ni   kore-o   ageru.
       tomorrow most   early   came person-DAT this-ACC give
      'I will give this to the person who comes (*lit.* came) first tomorrow.'

In Japanese it is widely accepted that -*ta* is a past tense marker, but there nevertheless remains this one subordinate context in which it can still be interpreted as perfective aspect. Such a situation is precisely what may be argued to be found also in Chinese—although there has been a general reanalysis of *le* as both past and perfective, in the particular subordinate clause case in examples such as (84) this change has not yet occurred and *le* still remains with a perfective aspect interpretation in such an environment.

A developmental approach such as that outlined above therefore allows one to maintain the claim that *le* has indeed *essentially* undergone reanalysis as past as claimed and is also supported by the occurrence of similar historical changes in other languages. A possible technical interpretation/implementation of such a hypothesis is to suggest that *le* is not necessarily interpreted as instantiating past tense in (84) because there actually is no legitimate tense position in the subordinate clause in (84) which could license *le* as past. It can be suggested that the subordinate clause containing *chi-le* 'eat-LE' is either just an AspP rather than a TP, or that it is a necessarily non-finite TP. In either case, because no potentially finite T^0 occurs, *le* will not be interpreted as (past) tense but instead be licensed as simply perfective aspect. In other words, it can be assumed that verbal *le* will only necessarily be interpreted as past when there is the opportunity for it to be licensed as past tense in the presence of a +finite T^0 position.

In support of the assumption that the subordinate clause in forms such as (84) is essentially without any tense specification, one can note that the temporal orientation of this clause is completely determined by the time/tense interpretation of the main clause predicate. Thus in (114) where the matrix verb *zou* 'to leave' in combination with *hui* 'will' necessarily refers to a point in the future, the subordinate clause action must also be understood as occurring in the future. If, however, the matrix verb *zou* 'to leave' is understood to refer to a past time as in (115), then the verb in the subordinate clause *chi(-le)* 'eat-LE' must also be understood as having past time reference.

(114) ta chi-le fan jiu hui zou.
he eat-LE meal then will leave
'He will leave after he has eaten.'

(115) ta chi-le fan jiu zou-le.
he eat-LE meal then leave-LE
'He left right after he ate.'

The structures of (84)/(114) and (115) therefore have the fully dependent status of English subordinate participle clauses such as (116) and (117) and are best translated into English with clauses of this type:

(116) Having eaten, he will leave.

(117) Having eaten, he left.

In (116/117) just as in (84) the action of the subordinate clause must be interpreted as occurring at the same past or future time as the action of the main clause. This temporal dependency can be suggested to result either from the complete absence of a T^0/TP in the subordinate clause in (84) (and therefore no possibility of an independent time specification), or perhaps from a T^0 head being present but obligatorily filled by some [-finite] specification controlled by the main clause tense specification (i.e., a PRO-like non-finite tense, as e.g., suggested in Stowell 1996).

Consequently the assumption that the subordinate clause in structures such as (84) does not contain a +finite T^0 allows for a straightforward account of why *le* may occur without necessarily causing a past time interpretation. It is suggested that *le* obligatorily instantiates +past only when there is a potentially +finite T^0 in a clause and it is actually possible for *le* to be interpreted as past. If a clause either does not contain any T^0 position at all, or this T^0 can only be interpreted as -finite and necessarily dependent/controlled by a higher clause tense, then there simply is no possibility for *le* to be interpreted as past and it will only be licensed as perfective aspect. It will therefore only be where there is a genuine +finite T^0 present in the structure that the possibility for *le* to be interpreted as past actually arises and is forced as the interpretation of *le*.

Note that an important component of such an explanation of (84) is the suggestion made earlier in section 6.1.4.1 that overt lexical morphemes such as *le* are essentially just lexical hosts for the semantic features which really encode meaning in syntactic structure. There it was suggested that semantic/functional features are critically *added* to elements such as *le* in the lexicon and that the lexical host and the features which it carries are subsequently inserted into syntactic structure together. Such a view essentially assumes that overt lexical morphemes may not *inherently* instantiate a meaning (such as +past for example), but instead acquire this meaning via a compositional process in the lexicon where functional/semantic features are added to the morpheme, which is then effectively just a physical carrier/host for the relevant features. Most frequently this process of combining features and a particular host will be quasi-automatic as the majority of morphemes are understood as having fairly constant meanings. However, during the course of language change there may be periods in which a certain set of features is only optionally added to a particular morpheme in the lexicon and this morpheme may consequently only optionally be understood to instantiate a certain meaning. Here in the case of *le* it has been argued that *le* has come to instantiate not only perfective aspect (and sometimes completive aspect) but also past tense. What this is taken to mean in formal Minimalist terms is that functional-semantic features encoding +perfective and +past are regularly combined with *le* in the lexicon resulting in its +perfective +past interpretation, and the morpheme *le* has been constantly been described as 'instantiating' past/perfective aspect. In such an approach in which functional-semantic features and their physical hosts/carriers are combined together before insertion into syntactic structure and the functional-semantic features are assumed not to be a *fully inherent* part of the lexical host, it can furthermore be argued that the relevant features are combined with their natural specified hosts *only wherever this is possible*. In the case of *le* this means that +past features will be combined with *le* only where there is a possibility for *le* to instantiate a past tense meaning, hence only where there is a genuine +finite T^0 also present in the sub-part of the numeration linked to a particular structure (e.g., a subordinate clause).[20]

CHAPTER 6

Such a view essentially sees overt lexical morphemes as the carriers of certain meanings rather than actually inherently communicating those meanings. Naturally in most cases there will be a very close or even automatic association of a morpheme with a certain meaning, but the approach also allows for change to occur and for a morpheme to only optionally instantiate a certain meaning when it is used. In support of such a general view and as a further clear example of the active combinatorial process suggested to take place between lexical hosts and feature-sets, I would like to mention briefly the interesting case of yes/no question morphemes in Egyptian Arabic.

As noted in Wahba (1984) and Demirdache (1991) in Egyptian Arabic yes/no questions are signaled by the occurrence of a pronoun in sentence-initial Comp position as seen in (118a/b) and (119a/b) taken from Wahba:

(118) a. Mona ablit il-talamiiz.
       Mona met the-students
       'Mona met the students.'
   b. hiyya Mona ablit il-talamiiz?
       she   Mona met the-students
       'Did Mona meet the students?'

(119) a. il-talamiiz   ablu Mona.
       the-students met Mona
       'The students met Mona.'
   b. humma il-talamiiz ablu Mona ?
       they   the-students met Mona
       'Did the students meet Mona.'

As these pronouns clearly specify the interrogative nature of the sentences they occur in, it can be assumed that in question environments they carry a +Q feature specification into Comp/the C^0 position (otherwise the Comp/C^0 position would not be interpreted as +interrogative). Importantly, in other non-question contexts such elements occur as very regular non-clitic pronouns and do not give rise to any +interrogative interpretation. What this can therefore be taken to indicate is that in questions some additional +Q feature specification is *added* to the pronouns as lexical hosts before they are inserted into the syntactic structure, and the pronouns simply serve as specified hosts for the +Q feature set on certain (+interrogative) occasions. Furthermore it can be noted that this combination of +Q features with a pronoun in questions must be a productive and active process. Supposing there were to be just a single pronoun type used to signal a yes/no question, it could be argued that such an element might have been grammaticalized with +Q features as a distinct entry in the lexicon. However, from (118b) and (119b) it can be seen that the pronoun occurring as the +Q morpheme actually varies according to the subject of the sentence. If the subject is feminine singular, the pronoun used will be *hiyya* 'she' (example (118b), whereas if the subject is masculine plural as in (119b) this will trigger a different pronoun question marker *humma* 'they.' This suggests then that there is indeed an active combinatorial process in the lexicon as suggested, and certain specified lexical hosts may have additional functional-semantic features actively added to them when this is required to encode a particular interpretation. In Egyptian Arabic +Q features are optionally added to a pronoun in the lexicon when a +interrogative interpretation is required.

Turning back to *le* now, it can be suggested again that past tense features are formally distinct from the overt morpheme *le* and not an inherent and fully automatic encoding on *le*, but instead combined with *le* as a physical host wherever this is possible. In a numeration in which there is no +Finite T^0 which could license past tense features carried by *le*, the past tense features will simply not be added on to *le* in the lexicon and *le* will just instantiate perfective aspect, giving rise to the interpretations found in (84), (114) and (115). Ultimately then, a principled account of the potential non-past interpretation of *le* in participle-like subordinate clause cases such as (84) is indeed possible, and such an account is significantly fully compatible with the basic assertion that *le* is in other instances a genuine instantiation of past tense.

6.2.3.5 Imperatives

The next of Li and Thompson's objections to an analysis of *le* as tense to be briefly re-considered here is the occurrence of *le* in imperative sentences such as (85). As there is no past time interpretation in (85) it is suggested that *le* cannot be past tense:

(85) he-le   ta.
     drink-LE it
     'Drink it!'

Concerning such cases, I will adopt the basic approach outlined for the subordinate clause case above and suggest that *le* cannot be licensed as past tense here in (85) because imperative sentences are reduced clausal structures and there is no +Finite T^0 present in the structure to license *le* as past tense. In fact, it can be suggested that there is also no (Im)perfective aspect projection present in imperative sentences either. Closer investigation of the occurrence of *le* in imperatives reveals that verbal *le* can only combine with Lü's (1980) 28 verbs (see footnote 9). Recall that these 28 verbs are the only verbs that can combine with *le* to give rise to a purely resultative (completive) interpretation. This then suggests that the verbal *le* which occurs in imperative sentences is in fact only the instantiation of inner completive aspect and not outer perfective aspect, as otherwise *le* should be able to occur with the whole range of verbs which elsewhere allow for perfective *le*. As examples (120) and (121) show, verbs from outside Lü's group of 28, such as *qu* "go" and *xue* "learn" cannot be combined with *le* in imperatives.

CHAPTER 6

(120) *qu-le Beijing.
go-LE Beijing
'Go to Beijing.'

(121) *xue-le zhei-ge zi.
study-LE this-CL character
'Learn this character!'

Consequently, if no T^0 node and no $Asp_{viewpoint}$ node occurs in imperative structures, past tense features will not be added to *le* when taken from the lexicon, and *le* will not be interpreted as past tense (or perfective aspect). Note that such a treatment of the patterns found in Chinese imperatives would seem to be supported by the cross-linguistic observation that tense and finite T^0 positions seem to be absent from a very wide range of languages in imperative sentences.

6.2.3.6 Matrix *jiu* sentences

The final case noted by Li and Thompson where *le* occurs without necessarily resulting in a past time interpretation is (86) repeated below:

(86) mingtian wo jiu kaichu-le ta.
tomorrow I then expel-LE him
'I'll expel/fire him tomorrow!'

Whereas with other cases of matrix clause use *le* seems to automatically result in a past time interpretation, here (86) naturally refers to a future event and so might seem to falsify the hypothesis that *le* encodes +past wherever this is possible. As (86) is obviously a non-imperative matrix clause it must be assumed that a +Finite T^0 is indeed present in the structure and it is not possible to suggest that any subordinate or reduced clausal status is responsible for the possible non-past interpretation. (86) would therefore seem to constitute a serious potential counter-example to the *le*-as-past hypothesis.

Considering rather carefully what allows for the non-past interpretation in (86), I believe that a plausible and interesting explanation can in fact be offered for this otherwise exceptional non-past occurrence of *le* in a non-subordinate clause. Essentially it is the critical addition of the element *jiu* 'then' in (86) which facilitates the non-past interpretation, as a future-oriented adverb such as *mingtian* is otherwise not sufficient to make available a future time interpretation, as was shown earlier in (75):

(75) *wo mingtian (hui) zai Beijing canguan-le Gugong.
    I tomorrow (will) in Beijing visit-LE Imperial Palace
    intended: 'Tomorrow I will visit/will have visited the Imperial Palace.'

There is consequently something in the element *jiu* which is highly relevant here. Focusing on the importance of *jiu* in allowing for the non-past interpretation, I believe that an account of the patterning can now be given which significantly supports the central contention that *le* both commonly instantiates tense and that such an interpretation is formally licensed via LF movement to a higher T^0 position. Quite simply I would like to suggest that (86) is very much like a covert instance of the *do*-support phenomena which occurs in English in the presence of negation, here the blocking element being *jiu* rather than negation however.

In Chomsky (1993), (1995) it is suggested that finite verbs in English are base-generated together with their tense specification/suffix and that tense features present on verbs are licensed/checked only at LF when the verbal complex/its feature-set raises up to T^0. Interacting with this licensing of tense features on verbs is the observation that sentential negation may not co-occur with finite verbs in English, as illustrated in (122), and that *do*-support is necessary to save such structures (123):

(122) *John not walked home/*John walked not home.

(123) John did not walk home.

Structures such as (122) are assumed to be ungrammatical because the presence of negation as an X^0-head intervening between T^0 and V^0 prevents the tensed verb/its tense features from raising up to be checked in T^0 at LF, such a movement hypothetically violating the Head Movement Constraint. In such instances the tense features are therefore base-generated directly on the dummy element *do* in T^0 and no LF movement from V^0 to T^0 occurs/is necessary.

Turning now to Chinese examples such as (86), I would like to suggest that a similar mode of explanation can be offered for the fact that the presence of *le* does not necessarily give rise to an interpretation of past tense in the presence of the adverbial *jiu*. Recall that it has been argued that past tense features are added to *le* wherever possible and licensed/checked against a +finite T^0 via LF raising. If it is now assumed that *jiu* is an X^0 head element occurring between T^0 and V^0, it is expected that *jiu* might indeed block the LF raising of the verb and *le* to tense. I suggest that this is indeed what happens in (86) and that when *le* cannot raise up to T^0 a (phonologically covert) tense specification is independently base-generated in T^0 precisely as in cases of English *do*-support in the presence of negation.[21] Because such a tense specification will not be licensed by *le*, it is therefore possible for this tense to be either past or non-past, accounting for the possible future orientation found in examples such as (86).

Le itself, when it cannot be licensed as past tense, will then only have perfective features added to it prior to insertion and raise up to Asp$_1$P (*jiu* can therefore be assumed to be higher than Asp$_1$P but lower than TP). In this sense *le* will be effectively used and interpreted in the same way as in cases such as (84), i.e., just as perfective.[22]

In further support of such a possibility, there is also interesting evidence from tone sandhi patterns in Taiwanese showing that the direct equivalent morpheme to Mandarin *jiu* syntactically is indeed an X^0-head element rather than an XP in a specifier position. As argued in chapter three, X^0-heads which are followed by tonic elements undergo tone sandhi, whereas elements in specifier positions do not exhibit any tone changes. Regarding the element *toh* (Mandarin *jiu*), critically this element does undergo tone sandhi clearly suggesting that it is a syntactic head rather than a specifier. This is shown in (124) where a bolded dot following a syllable indicates that the syllable undergoes tone sandhi:

(124) Goa bin•-a•-chai toh• khi• chhoe• lin• lau•su.
      I   tomorrow then go look-for your teacher
      'I'll go see your teacher tomorrow.'

Such a patterning would consequently seem to add good support to the hypothesis that Mandarin *jiu* may well block LF verb-raising due to having an X^0-head status.

Example in (124) also has further potentially revealing information. Earlier it was noted that future-oriented adverbs such as *mingtian* 'tomorrow' may not occur with a verb suffixed with *le*, as seen in (125):

(125) *Zhangsan mingtian qu-le Beijing.
      Zhangsan tomorrow go-LE Beijing
      intended: 'Zhangsan will go to Beijing tomorrow.'

The simple explanation for this was that *le* instantiates past tense in such cases and this is incompatible with the future time phrase *mingtian*. Now, supposing that *mingtian* were to be an X^0-head element similar to *jiu* and that *mingtian* could occur located structurally lower than T^0, one might expect that it would also block LF raising of the verb and therefore allow for *le* to occur licensed as simply perfective in the same way that *jiu* does. This would then in theory allow for tense features to be base-generated on a covert *do*-equivalent in T^0 and (125) might be expected to be acceptable with a future time orientation. The fact that examples like (125) are unacceptable suggests that adverbs such as *mingtian* are not X^0 heads in the main functional projection line of the clause (unlike *jiu*), and occur instead in specifier (or adjunct) positions. Such a conclusion is further supported by tone sandhi patterns in Taiwanese. Whereas *toh*, the equivalent to *jiu*, undergoes tone sandhi in the way typical of elements in X^0 head positions (followed by overt complements), the final syllable of the adverb *bin-a-chai* 'tomorrow' in (124) does not, indicating that the adverb occurs in either a specifier or an adjunct position. If the adverb 'tomorrow' in both Mandarin and Taiwanese have a similar adjunct/specifier non-head syntactic status, this accounts of why *jiu* but not *mingtian* allows *le* to co-occur with it and why *le* may have an exceptionally non-past interpretation when in main clauses with *jiu*, a patterning which otherwise is quite mysterious.

This consideration of the blocking effects caused by *jiu* now completes our examination of the range of patterns which have been cited as objections to an analysis of *le* instantiating the meaning of past tense in modern Chinese. Throughout this second major part of the chapter, section 6.2, I have attempted to show that while there is certain variability in the interpretation of verbal *le*, this variation is significantly *not random*, and the non-past interpretations of clauses containing *le* are restricted and confined in very clear ways. Outside of the particular environments identified and considered in sections 6.2.3.4– 6.2.3.6 above, the interpretation of *le* in modern Chinese is strictly that of past tense, even in the presence of future time adverbs as in (75) (hence (75) is unacceptable). The past tense interpretation of *le* is therefore not the result of pragmatic inferencing and a conversational implicature, as such a conversational implicature/enrichment should allow for itself to be over-ridden with appropriate means such as future-time adverbials and modals, yet this is clearly not possible as examples such as (75) show. Consequently, in order to capture the patterns with *le*, what appears to be needed is a more sophisticated formal approach to the linking of lexical items and interpretations which is flexible enough to correctly allow for the range of interpretations found and able to predict exactly when and why these interpretations will occur. Much of the chapter has been an attempt to develop such an approach, and to try to understand how it may be formally possible for lexical elements to undergo apparently gradual shifts in functional-grammatical meaning over time. Here, in approaching this issue an important hypothesis has been the idea that lexical morphemes act as simple physical hosts for functional-semantic features and that lexical morphemes are actively combined with such features in the lexicon. While this combination operation may quite frequently be semi-automatic, the possibility that features and morphemes are formally distinct objects has allowed for the suggestion that, during periods of diachronic change, the combination operation may be either optional or alternatively blocked by other interfering factors, and that this is directly responsible for the kinds of non-uniform patterning attested. Though there is certainly much more to do in formally exploring such an approach, the analysis outlined has attempted to show that an explicit characterization of the synchronic variation with elements such as verbal *le* should indeed be possible, and that the re-grammaticalization of bound morphology as an area of study has the potential to be very informative about synchronic and diachronic relations between meanings and morphology. In section 6.3 now, I close the chapter with a brief summary of some of the main points argued for during the chapter.

CHAPTER 6

6.3 Summary

This chapter began as an attempt to understand the origin and development of verbal *le*. Largely because of the original completive meaning of *liao/le* and its re-positioning adjacent to the verb at a time when other V_2 elements in RVCs also became right-adjacent to the verb, it was concluded that *liao/le* initially instantiated completive aspect (here following work on the development of completive aspect from RVCs described in chapter 5). The chapter then noted that *le* often appears to have a different function in modern Chinese and occurs together with other overt V_2-completive elements. In order to account for this, I adopted Smith's (1997) two-tiered approach to aspect and suggested that since its initial grammaticalization, *le* has developed from being a completive aspect marker to instantiate structurally higher perfective viewpoint aspect, a view which accords with common synchronic perceptions of *le*. I then attempted to provide a formal modeling of this hypothetical change of *le* from completive aspect to perfective aspect and argued for a development of the approach to grammaticalization assumed in chapter 2 for *ge*. Whereas this approach was initially intended to account for the reanalysis of free-standing morphemes, the current chapter has argued that *suffixes* are significantly also subject to highly similar (further) grammaticalization and reanalysis, and that the model of grammaticalization initiated for free morphemes can be naturally developed to account for this. Importantly it was argued that grammaticalization and reanalysis in *both* free *and* bound morpheme cases is critically movement-dependent and results from raising of an element upwards in the functional structure dominating a lexical projection to successively highly positions. In the case of the hypothetical reanalysis of *le* this was argued to have the further significance that it supports the Minimalist view that functional affixes are base-generated together with their lexical host and then licensed via movement to a functional head, such movement furthermore often being covert and taking place at LF (as with *le*).

Following this, in section 6.2.1, the chapter attempted to account for other aspects of the interpretation of *le* and made the more contentious claim that *le* has now developed further to instantiate past tense as well as perfective aspect. While such a possibility has been rejected in the literature, it was argued that this is largely due to the commonly-held view that overt morphemes must stand in a fully rigid one-to-one correspondence relation with a single meaning/function (such as past tense). Here it was suggested instead that functional meanings/interpretations are associated with morphemes as the result of an active combination process linking functional features and lexical hosts. In such a process it is possible both for a single morpheme-host to be combined with more than a single functional interpretation/feature (and therefore instantiate multiple functions), and it is also possible for the association of a particular function with a particular morpheme to be blocked in certain circumstances. Such assumptions and a careful re-consideration of the range of objections to an analysis of *le* as tense then ultimately allowed for a full account of the distribution and interpretation of verbal *le* and a principled defense of the hypothesis that modern Chinese verbal *le* regularly instantiates past tense. The chapter has throughout attempted to emphasize that this emerging past tense interpretation is significantly not random but instead now determined by clear syntactic factors.

Notes

[1] I do not attempt to provide any account of sentence-final *le* here. It is included in many of the examples simply for naturalness.

[2] If a hearer can interpret predicates such as 'recognize X', and 'die' in a non-canonical way and create a special context in which they can be understood as requiring certain time, then sometimes such predicates can be acceptable. Native speakers indicate that this is particularly difficult with 'arrive' and only marginally possible with 'recognize' in a game show type context.

[3] Smith (1997) also argues for a third type of viewpoint aspect which is referred to as 'neutral' viewpoint aspect. As the existence of such a third basic viewpoint type is somewhat open to question, I here concentrate on the more traditional binary contrast of perfective and imperfective (viewpoint) aspects.

[4] The element *ne* is a sentence-final emphatic particle which frequently co-occurs with *(zheng-)zai*. For a partial account of this element, please see Simpson and Wu (2002c).

[5] Stylistically the combination of a V_1-V_2 sequence with *zhengzai* may perhaps be avoided for the reason that both the V_2 and *zhengzai* encode a separate focus—use of a V_2 element focuses the meaning of completion and use of an overt imperfective marker such as *zhengzai* focuses the progressive nature of the action. This may result in two independent foci in a single clause/sentence which may be felt to be somewhat confusing in terms of presentation of the information (and hence avoided). However, such strings are not ungrammatical. What may not occur is the combination of *zhengzai* with a V_1-V_2 sequence where the V_2 is a phase-type V_2 such as *wan*:

(i) *wo zhengzai kan-wan shu ne.
I ASP-PROG look-finish book NE
intended: 'I am finishing reading the book.'

This I believe is because *kan-wan* is taken to be an instantaneous event with no internal or prior stages/extension over time available for modification by *zhengzai*. Being an instance of imperfective aspect describing the progression of an action, *zhengzai* importantly requires an event which does have internal stages potentially available. As V_2s such as *wan* are themselves instantaneous achievement predicates, they may disallow any focusing on any internal stages of an activity depicted by the V_1, instead encoding the single final stage of completion of the event. Note that the instantaneous/durative distinction is one which is standardly assumed to be part of situation aspect/a predicate's Aktionsart rather than relate to higher viewpoint-type aspect, and predicates are distinguished as being either instantaneous (e.g.,

CHAPTER 6

achievements) or durative (e.g., accomplishments, activities). Consequently it is natural that *wan* and other V₂s which might encode instantaneity should be licensed by Asp$_{2\text{-situation}}$ rather than Asp$_{1\text{-viewpoint}}$.

Finally it should be noted that the unacceptability of examples such as (32) with *le* and *zhengzai* cannot be ruled out by any similar considerations. In (32) *le* is clearly not occurring in the V₂ position and it is therefore not possible to suggest that *le* is unacceptable because it makes the predicate +instantaneous (thereby being in conflict with the +durative requirements of *zhengzai*). As pointed out, the +/-instantaneous property is encoded in the situation aspect and consequently by V₂; *le* in V₁-V₂-*le* sequences is however not in the V₂ situation aspect position and therefore effects some other higher function (perfectivity, most obviously).

[6] The situation in Chinese here is similar to ungrammatical English sentences such as (i):

(i) *John did not walked to school.

Parallel to the patterns with aspect in Chinese, it would seem that a single tense position/T⁰ cannot check/ license more than a single set of Tense features.

[7] Note that sentence-final *le* can co-occur with *mei-you* 'have not', as shown in (i):

(i) wo houlai jiu mei-you zai huiqu Beijing le.
    I   later then NEG-have again return Beijing LE
    'I never returned to Beijing after that.'

As with many others, I assume that sentence-final *le* is a morpheme distinct from verbal *le* and not an instantiation of perfect aspect. In many varieties of Chinese, such as Cantonese, the equivalent morphemes to verbal *le* and sentence-final *le* are indeed pronounced in quite different ways, indicating that they are different morphemes.

[8] XP elements may go through a similar route of grammaticalization, as Simpson (1998) suggests for French *pas* (see chapter two).

[9] Those 28 verbs listed in Lü (1980) are: wang 'forget', diu 'throw/get ride of', guan 'close, shut', he 'drink', chi 'eat', yan 'swallow', tun 'swallow', po 'splash', sa 'spill', reng 'throw/get rid of', fang 'release', tu 'scribble', mo 'wipe', ca 'wipe', peng 'bump', za 'break', shuai 'throw', ke 'crack', zhuang 'hit', cai 'step on', shang 'injure', sha 'kill', zai 'kill', qie 'cut', chong 'flush', mai 'sell', huan 'return', hui 'destroy.'

[10] Note that sentences such as (67) are not acceptable with *le* in all dialects of Mandarin, but can nevertheless frequently be found in Mainland Chinese writing. No dialect (to my knowledge) however allows for sentences such as (69b).

[11] Note that there have been certain suggestions that verbal *le* may encode past tense in other works. For example, Chiu (1993) assumes that TP is a universal projection in all languages and in Chinese *le* is a past tense marker that heads this universally projected TP in Chinese. Tsang (1978), Rohsenow (1978), Z. Shi (1990), Ross (1995) and Hsieh (1998) also make suggestions that *le* might be a relative past tense marker. The particular focus and special interest of the present chapter and its analysis are (a) to attempt to show how the development of *le* as a past tense marker is a natural consequence of a certain formal approach to grammaticalization, (b) to show how the development of *le* as a past tense marker can be understood better once

a more explicit analysis of Aspect is assumed (as argued for above), and (c) to provide clear and principled attempted explanations of the wide variety of counter-arguments frequently given against any analysis of *le* as a past tense marker.

[12] For example, Smith (1997) refers to Chang's (1986) investigation of *le*'s occurrences in newspaper articles as noting that *le* was frequently found to be used as a past realis marker. In another experimental study, Spanos (1979) reports that subjects clearly used *le* to signal the explicit realization of an event (p.81).

[13] Note that in addition to *le* there is another verbal suffix in Chinese which may instantiate some kind of past tense, 'experiential' *guo*. This element will not be considered here as the primary goal of the paper is not to examine tense per se as a category in Chinese, but rather to examine the consequences of the development of a particular morpheme (*le*) for the more general theory of diachronic change viewed from a Minimalist perspective. If *guo* is indeed a further instantiation of past tense in Chinese, this would not impinge on the paper's analysis of *le* as past tense. It is quite possible and not uncommon for languages to have more than one past tense marking—as, for example, Bengali, which has three different past tense paradigms (Thompson 2001). In such cases, the different past tense markings will normally be distinguished by additional associated meanings. In Chinese, *le* instantiates the secondary meaning of perfective aspect, and *guo* is associated with rather different 'experiential' readings (see Li and Thompson 1981).

[14] Note that the order of presentation of these points is slightly changed from that in Li and Thompson. This is done simply in order that they can be sequentially addressed as problems in the most natural and logical order.

[15] A further simple example of the non-obligatory use of a functional element is the fully optional occurrence of the English complementizer 'that' in the C^0 head position of embedded declarative clauses:

(i) John said (that) he was leaving.

The status of 'that' as a complementizer is not questioned simply because its use is not obligatory in every appropriate context (i.e., every non-interrogative subordinate C^0 position).

[16] It is commonly noted that verbal *le* must also appear when the object of the verb is quantified and specific. This can be considered to be a sub-case of the focusing use of *le*. If an object is explicitly quantified in object position, then both the quantified object and the predicate are arguably in focus.

[17] For both morphological models, see the discussions in Matthews (1974).

[18] See here Bybee et al (1994, p.76): "In the early stages it would not be normal for constructions with 'finish' or anteriors from *be* or *have* auxiliaries to be used with stative predicates. They are compatible only with dynamic predicates, and it is the meaning they develop with dynamic predicates that is transferred in their use with stative predicates."

[19] Note that informants indicate that the *most salient* interpretation in the combination of past perfective and activity verbs which are not explicitly bounded in English is also that of inchoativity and entry into the activity, as e.g., in:

CHAPTER 6

(i) John ran.

(ii) Mary ate.

This inchoative interpretation is very clear and almost forced when a single time point is added in as in (iii) and (iv):

(iii) When I looked at him, John ran.

(iv) Mary ate at two/Mrs. Smith's command.

Although there would seem to be inchoative interpretations here, it is not obvious that one would want to say that the occurrence of past perfective is any different here from that in non-inchoative readings.

[20] An alternative to the suggestion that functional-semantic features such as [+past] and [+perfective aspect] are actively combined with *le* in the lexicon prior to use of *le* in the syntax would be to assume that there are multiple, fixed lexical entries for *le*, each with a different feature specification. In order to account for the range of patterns found, at least five different *le*'s would need to be assumed in the lexicon, with the following properties: (i) [+past, +perfective], (ii) [+perfective], (iii) [+perfective, +completive], (iv) [+past, +perfective, +completive], (v) [+completive]. Instead of such a proliferation of related lexical items, it might seem more economical to assume the existence of a single lexical item/host to which different combinations of features can be productively added, as suggested here. It can also be noted that the proposal here brings the treatment of multi-functional items such as *le* into line with assumptions made about other alternations taken to be effected in the lexicon, such as (for example) those between active and passive variants of verbs. Rather than assume that each verb is listed in the lexicon in both active and passive form, it is commonly held that one form is productively derived from the other via an operation which affects the meaning of the verb (amongst other things deleting the agent, external argument of the verb). If lexical operations can regularly delete and in other cases add aspects of meaning to a morpheme, such mechanisms can be taken to generalize in the way suggested to actively produce items such as *le*, with its potential for variation in interpretation.

[21] I do not attempt to go into the challenging question of why the base-generation of features directly in T^0 is not always/elsewhere used and only occurs as a means to save a derivation which would otherwise crash. I will simply assume that whatever explanation allows for such a possibility to occur in English with *do*-support may also apply in Chinese with a covert counter-part to *do*.

[22] Such an approach to *jiu/le* interactions leads one to expect that it should be possible for *le* to occur as simple perfective aspect if other X^0 head elements occur lower than tense and higher than $Asp_{viewpoint}$. This is indeed so, and the overt presence of the element *ye* 'also' similarly blocks the possibility for *le* to be licensed as past tense in T^0, consequently allowing it to be interpreted as simply perfective aspect in non-past tense sentences:

(i) women mingtian ye kaichu le ta!
   we   tomorrow also fire LE him
   "We'll also fire him tomorrow."

7

POST-WORD

Having worked through a range of phenomena relating to functional categories and elements which have undergone grammaticalization in Chinese in chapters 2-6, in this final 'post-word' I would like to briefly look back at and highlight certain aspects of the analyses of the main chapters as well as look forward to and signal topics and issues which remain on the research agenda for the future.

Quite generally, the book has tried to offer solutions to a number of interesting puzzles relating to functional categories/grammatical morphemes in Chinese, and see what information these paradigms may reveal about mechanisms of language change and the licensing of synchronic syntax. The method of approach has been to apply the formal model of Minimalist linguistic analysis proposed in Chomsky (1993, 1995) together with insights from more traditional descriptive linguistics and in each case examine the whole of the syntactic construction which contains the grammaticalizing morphs. During the course of the main chapters, a variety of different routes of grammaticalization were attested and formally examined. Chapter 2 highlighted the potential role of *movement* in facilitating categorial reanalysis, a process referred to as 'vertical grammaticalization', as it corresponds to the movement and reanalysis of an element in a higher position in the functional structure dominating a lexical phrase. Such a process was argued to typically take place in a sequence of three stages, leading to the potential renewal of the source category (i.e., new overt instantiations of the original position and syntactic category occupied by the element which has undergone grammaticalization and reanalysis). The chapter also showed that the output of grammaticalization can be considerably nuanced, and in the case under consideration, Mandarin Chinese *ge*, has resulted in the creation of a new unselective, non-specific, weak determiner from a classifier source. Chapter 3 considered the identity and status of an element in the end stages of grammaticalization, relative clause *de*, and saw how clues to its identity and function could be gained from a careful study of related cross-linguistic patterns together with language-internal evidence from acquisition data, phonology, and diachronic predecessors of *de*. The chapter also examined the element *kong* in Taiwanese, and showed how the study of tone sandhi patterns allows for critical insights into the development and present syntactic properties of this new evidential particle and how sentence-final particles may in principle grammaticalize in head-initial languages when bi-clausal forms collapse into structures containing just a single clause.

Chapter 4 took the consideration of relative clause/"nominalizing" *de* one stage further and examined its occurrence in sentence-final position in the *shi-de* construction. This led to an analysis of a rather different type of (re-)grammaticalization, which was called 'lateral grammaticalization', and represents the categorial reanalysis of an element from one kind of functional domain as a corresponding functional head in another domain. In contrast to the 'vertical grammaticalization' process outlined in chapter 2, lateral grammaticalization is not derived via any movement operation, but was argued to result from a critical comparison of parallel functional domains. Chapter 5 then moved on to examine how the grammaticalization of a whole class of elements may result when a functional interpretation associated with the use of lexical elements in a particular construction becomes more highly valued than the lexical, descriptive interpretation provided by such elements. This grammaticalization of a new paradigm of completive aspect markers was shown to have clear associated surface effects over time, including a repositioning of the aspect markers relative to object NPs which was ultimately attributed to forces of directionality of selection imposing themselves in the language. Finally, chapter 6 re-considered the verbal suffix *le* and used the range of complex patterns found with *le* to argue for a development of the movement-based approach to grammaticalization introduced in chapter 2. Whereas this approach was initially intended to account for the reanalysis of free-standing morphemes, chapter 6 suggested that affixes may also be subject to (further) reanalysis in a highly similar way, and that the model of grammaticalization accounting for movement-based reanalysis with free morphemes can be naturally developed to account for this. The chapter also confronted the problem of modeling the apparent gradualness of change and argued for the potential separation of formal interpretative features from their lexical hosts as a means to capture variation in interpretation during periods of grammaticalization. Such an approach then allowed the chapter to show that the different interpretations of an element undergoing change may not be random and unconstrained but can in fact be quite predictable from the structure which is projected in different syntactic environments.

Throughout chapters 2-6 then a wide variety of classic issues relating to grammaticalization were addressed and the attempt was made to see how a formal syntactic approach might be able to offer a different perspective on such problems, as well as raise a set of different theoretical questions. In many cases adopting a formalist approach has resulted in potentially interesting results and possible solutions to many of the puzzles posed by morphemes such as *de*, *le* and *ge* in modern Chinese. If we now however look forward to the future and potential extensions of formalist approaches to grammaticalization both in Chinese and in other languages, it can be suggested that among the many avenues for future research there are four particularly natural areas where further progress can and perhaps should be made.

One very obvious area for future research is simply to extend the consideration of grammaticalization in Chinese to morphemes and constructions not dealt with in the present work. Among the individual morphemes whose grammaticalization history it would certainly be useful to know more about from a formal perspective are verbal -*guo* and -*zhe*, and the directional-aspectual uses of VP/S-final *lai* and *qu*. There are also full constructions which have grammaticalized in Chinese (sometimes around individual morphemes) which it would be very valuable to subject to further formal study from a grammaticalization point of view, e.g., the A-not-A question form, and the often studied *ba*- and *bei* constructions, where original verbs have undergone grammaticalization and de-verbalization in a way which might be useful to compare with the de-verbalization of Taiwanese *kong*.

A second direction for further research relating to the present study may be to look for and examine grammaticalization phenomena in other, typologically similar languages (perhaps from mainland Southeast Asia) which resemble the instances of reanalysis in Chinese studied here. Macro-linguistic, comparative local studies of this type are extremely useful in adding further information about the plausibility of hypotheses established predominantly on the basis of patterns in a single language, and both help correct and expand analyses in very insightful ways.

On a more general, theoretical level, a third future development of the present project might hopefully be to examine more closely certain of the consequences of the formal mechanisms of development and synchronic licensing proposed in chapters 2-6. Both the ideas of 'vertical' movement-driven grammaticalization and 'lateral' reanalysis deserve much more attention and probing from a theoretical point of view, as does the proposal in chapter 6 that interpretative features and physical hosts are actively combined in the lexicon during periods of ongoing change rather than being automatically associated/linked. Much more empirical evidence of instances of cross-domain reanalysis, movement-related reanalysis, and constraints on variation in the interpretation of elements undergoing change will certainly be helpful in developing and fine-tuning these ideas. One particular theoretical question relating to reanalysis which is parasitic on movement concerns how a morpheme which is developing a new meaning as the result of raising higher in a functional structure can apparently avoid taking on the meaning of intervening projections/heads moved through, and 'skip' to adopt the interpretation of a higher functional head. For example, it is frequently assumed that projected above the VP predicate there is an array of verb-related functional projections including different kinds of aspect, mood, negation and tense, simplified as in (1):

CHAPTER 7

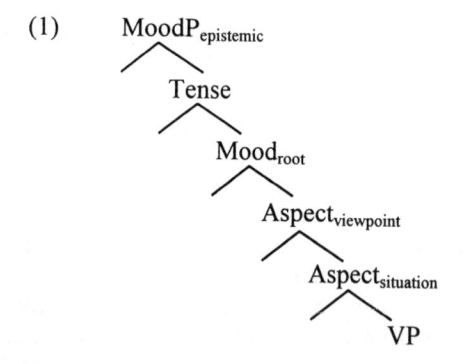

(1) MoodP$_{epistemic}$
    Tense
        Mood$_{root}$
            Aspect$_{viewpoint}$
                Aspect$_{situation}$
                      VP

The movement-driven hypothesis of grammaticalization/reanalysis suggests that an element such as a verb will undergo movement from its base position (the V^0 position for verbs) to a higher X^0-head position in the functional structure and then potentially undergo reanalysis as instantiating this higher position, hence lexical verbs are often found to grammaticalize as new instantiations of Aspect, Tense and Mood. What seems to occur furthermore is that lexical descriptive verbs may often grammaticalize *directly* as instantiations of functional heads which are relatively high in the functional structure and not the most immediately adjacent/higher head. Consequently, it is observed that a descriptive verb such as 'get/obtain' (for example) may grammaticalize as a new root modal verb and does not need to first reanalyze as instantiating the meaning of lower functional heads that are (assumed to be) present, such as Aspect. Similarly, a verb which has grammaticalized as root modal in Mood$_{root}$ may undergo a further reanalysis as instantiating epistemic mood without having to first re-grammaticalize as Tense, the functional head which intervenes between Mood$_{root}$ and Mood$_{epistemic}$. Given the Head Movement Constraint, it is nevertheless assumed that verbs will raise through all of the functional head positions which are projected between their base position and final landing-site. All theories of movement-related reanalysis will therefore somehow have to allow for grammaticalizing elements to move through intervening positions without necessarily being re-interpreted as instantiating these positions, and be able to reanalyze directly in non-adjacent, higher functional positions.

    A constraint on this movement-parasitic re-interpretation process which does seem to hold though is that once an element has come to be re-interpreted as instantiating a position of a certain height in the functional structure (e.g., Tense), it is not possible for it to be subsequently reanalyzed as instantiating a position further down in the functional structure. Hence if a verb has been reanalyzed as a new instantiation of Tense, it will not at any later point re-grammaticalize as a lower functional head such as Aspect. This is essentially the empirical patterning described by the Unidirectionality (of development) Hypothesis noted in chapter one (see also, in particular, Bybee, Perkins and Pagliuca 1994), in which more abstract/less referential meanings are held to develop from more referential/descriptive meanings and not the reverse. The hypothesis of Unidirectionality is a central tenet of traditional grammaticalization theory, and is a patterning which is a natural consequence of a movement-based account of grammaticalization. If an element has (fully) undergone reanalysis in a functional head position such as Tense as the result of movement from a lower verb/V position, it will consequently be base-generated in the Tense position, and as movement is assumed only to be possible in an upwards direction, the only further developmental possibilities open to the new tense element will be to undergo raising to positions higher than Tense and grammaticalize/be reanalyzed as instantiating such higher positions. Re-grammaticalization/reanalysis of a tense element in a lower Aspect position should critically require lowering/movement downwards in the syntactic structure, and so should never occur. This aspect of the Unidirectionality Hypothesis is therefore nicely captured by a movement-based approach to grammaticalization. What may be interesting and revealing to examine in future work though are the few noted apparent *exceptions* to the Unidirectionality Hypothesis, and how to account for these exceptions. A movement-based approach to grammaticalization which assumes that movement must *always* be in an upwards direction (for principled reasons) expects that there should be *no* exceptions to the upwards direction of reanalysis, as movement should never be able to proceed in a downwards direction. The claim that there are exceptions to Unidirectionality therefore requires close consideration and might pose a serious challenge to the movement-driven analyses of grammaticalization. When one considers cases suggested to be exceptions to Unidirectionality however, it is not clear that they are instances of grammaticalization which relate to movement. For example, one often-quoted counter-example to Unidirectionality is the development of English genitive *'s* from a noun-inflection/suffix to an NP clitic [[$_{NP}$ the woman you were talking with]'s son]. This change may be unexpected from the point of view of Unidirectionality as traditionally conceived, because an element which has grammaticalized as far as becoming a bound morpheme attached as a suffix in the morphological component has later become a clitic attached in the syntax, and this is the opposite to the general pattern of development in which clitics (less tightly attached, less selective elements) become affixes (more tightly attached, highly selective elements). However, although such a development might perhaps raise important questions about morphology-syntax interactions, it would not seem to be a case in which an element corresponding to a higher functional head has undergone exceptional lowering and reanalysis in a lower head position, and would therefore not be an exception to Unidirectionality conceived of in terms of upwards movement in a syntactic structure. Whether or not the full array of cases taken to be exceptions to (traditional) Unidirectionality are likewise not challenges to a movement analysis of grammaticalization will be an interesting matter to investigate though, and might perhaps result in some unexpected discoveries.

CHAPTER 7

Finally, a fourth important avenue for future research will be to see how studies of grammaticalization such as the present work may be used to probe the status of the Universal Base Hypothesis/UBH. The Universal Base Hypothesis is a currently influential but also contentious hypothesis about the inventory/types and arrangement of grammatical/functional categories across languages, which suggests that a universal set of functional categories is aligned in a uniform way in all of the world's languages. In Cinque (1999), it is furthermore suggested that all such functional categories and their syntactic projections are present in all languages (and essentially in all sentences too) even where there is no overt morphological evidence for such elements. Such very bold claims have perhaps understandably not been accepted by all linguists, and a frequent question raised about the UBH is how the very sizeable sets of functional categories posited come to be assumed by learners of language when there frequently appears to be no clear morphological evidence for these in a particular language. In the face of such potential criticisms, certain variant forms of the UBH (or alternative ways of approaching the UBH) have recently been suggested, for example in Poletto (2000) and Giorgi and Pianesi (1997), where it is proposed that languages may not all initially have the full range of functional projections described in works such as Cinque (1999), but if languages do develop such functional projections, these will indeed develop in the way of the UBH (i.e., following a fully universal patterning). Given the very nature of the study of grammaticalization, such a field is in a natural position to provide highly valuable theoretical and empirical input into the debate about the status of the UBH, and whether languages really show signs of developing functional categories and projections which did not previously exist in a language, or whether one should assume that all that may develop in a language is new overt instantiations of functional projections which are already in existence. This issue is not at all easy to decide or be sure about, but an increase in careful empirical studies such as Poletto (1999) may perhaps tip the balance in favor of the more conservative and traditional view that languages do in fact *develop* functional categories (an assumption held by the 'father' of modern grammaticalization Antione Meillet, see chapter 1). Concerning the present work, the most relevant chapter for such questions about the UBH is chapter 5 where the diachronic rise of completive aspect has been argued for, resulting in the creation of a functional category and projection/position which did not seem to previously exist in the same clear way, hence suggesting that completive aspect came to be a new functional category present in Chinese some time during the period of the Wei, Jin, and Northern and Southern dynasties. What one now might hope for from future studies of grammaticalization is more information and investigations of a similar kind charting the (apparent) *initial emergence* of new functional categories so that theoretical debate about the UBH and the way that grammar initially develops within language can proceed with a broader stock of relevant, empirical support. The traditional study of grammaticalization with all its

POST-WORD

valuable insights and data is a resource which one can turn to and help understand and adjudicate a range of current theoretical problems relating to synchronic syntax such as the UBH, and is an area of linguistics which appears set to expand significantly both in descriptive and formal fields of linguistics, with hopefully a greater future bridging between the two methods of approach.

BIBLIOGRAPHY

Abney, Steven P. 1987. *The English noun phrase in its sentential aspect*. Doctoral dissertation, MIT.

Abraham, Werner 1997. "The interdependence of case, aspect and referentiality in the history of German: the case of the verbal genitive." *Parameters of Morphosyntactic Change*, eds. Ans van Kemenade and Nigel Vincent, 29-61. Cambridge: Cambridge University Press.

Allen, Robert Livingston 1966. *The verb system of present-day American English*. The Hague: Mouton.

Baker, Carl Lee 1970. "Notes on description of English questions: the role of an abstract question morpheme." *Foundations of Language* 6, 197-219.

Baker, Mark 1985. "The mirror principle and morpho-syntactic explanation." *Linguistic Inquiry* 16, 373-415.

Baker, Mark and Kenneth Hale 1990. "Relativized minimality and pronoun incorporation." *Linguistic Inquiry* 21, 289-297.

Biener, Clemens 1922a. "Zur Methode der Untersuchungen über deutsche Wortstellung [On the methods of inverstigation of word placement in German]." *Zeitschrift für deutsches Altertum und deutsche Literatur [Journal of German Antiquity and German Literature]* 59, 127-44.

Biener, Clemens 1922b. "Wie ist die neuhochdeutsche Regel über die Stellung des Verbums entstanden [How did the new high German rule of verb placement arise]?" *Zeitschrift für deutsches Altertum und deutsche Literatur [Journal of German Antiquity and German Literature]* 59, 165-79

Boskovic, Zeljko 1999. "What is special about multiple wh-fronting?" Paper presented at NELS, Rutgers University.

Borer, Hagit 1994. "The projection of arguments." *University of Massachusetts occasional papers in linguistics* 17, eds. E. Benedicto and J. Runner, 19-48. Amherst: GLSA, University of Massachusetts.

Bresnan, Joan 1971. "Sentence stress and syntactic transformations." *Language* XLVII.2: 257-281. Reprinted in *Syntactic argumentation*, eds. D. J. Napoli and E. Rando (1979), 233-257. Washington: Georgetown University Press.

Bresnan, Joan and Samuel Mchombo 1987. "Topic, pronoun, and agreement in Chichewa." *Language* 63, 741-782.

Brody, Michael 1994. *Lexico-logical form*. Cambridge, Mass.: MIT Press.

Bybee, Joan, Revere Perkins and William Pagliuca 1994. *The evolution of grammar*. Chicago: University of Chicago Press.

BIBLIOGRAPHY

Bybee, Joan, and Östen Dahl 1989. "The creation of tense and aspect systems in the languages of the world." *Studies in Language* 13, 51-103.

Chang, Vincent 1986. *The particle* le *in Chinese narrative discourse: an integrative description.* Doctoral dissertation, University of Florida.

Cao, Guangshun 1987. "Yuqici *Le* yuanliu qianshuo [Preliminary disscussion on the origin of the particle *Le*]." *Yuwen Yanjiu* 2, 10-15.

Chao, Yuen Ren 1968. *A grammar of spoken Chinese.* Berkeley: University of California Press.

Chen, Matthew 1985. "The syntax of Xiamen tone sandhi." *Phonology Yearbook* 2, eds. Colin Ewen and John Anderson, 109-150. New York/Cambridge: Cambridge University Press.

Chen, Matthew 1990. "What must phonology know about syntax?" *The phonology-syntax connection*, eds. Sharon Inkelas and Draga Zec, 19-46. Chicago: University of Chicago Press.

Chen, Matthew 2000. *Tone sandhi.* New York/Cambridge: Cambridge University Press.

Cheng, Lisa Lai-Shen and Rint Sybesma 1999. "Bare and not-so-bare nouns and the structure of NP." *Linguistic Inquiry* 30, 509-542.

Cheng, Robert 1968. "Tone sandhi in Taiwanese." *Linguistics* 41, 19-42.

Cheng, Robert 1973. "Some notes on tone sandhi in Taiwanese." *Linguistics* 100, 5-25.

Chiu, Bonnie 1993. *The inflectional structure of Mandarin Chinese.* Doctoral dissertation, UCLA.

Chiu, Bonnie 1995. "An object clitic projection in Mandarin Chinese." *Journal of East Asian Linguistics* 4.2, 77-117.

Chiu, Bonnie 1998. "Relative clauses in child Chinese." Ms., National Taiwan University.

Chomsky, Noam 1977. "On wh-movement." *Formal syntax*, eds. P. Culicover, T. Wasow and A. Akmajian, 71-132. New York: Academic Press.

Chomsky, Noam 1981. Lectures on government and binding: the Pisa lectures. Dordrecht: Foris.

Chomsky, Noam 1985. Knowledge of language: its nature, origin and use. New York: Praeger.

Chomsky, Noam 1993. "A minimalist program for linguistic theory." *The view from building 20: essays in linguistics in honor of Sylvain Bromberger*, 1-52. Cambridge, Mass.: MIT Press.

Chomsky, Noam 1995a. Bare Phrase Structure. *Government and Binding Theory and the Minimalist Program*, ed. Gert Webelhuth, 383-439. Cambridge, Mass.: Blackwell.

Chomsky, Noam 1995b. *The minimalist program.* Cambridge, Mass.: MIT Press.

Chomsky, Noam 1998. "Minimalist inquiries: the framework." Ms., MIT.

Cinque, Guglielmo 1999. *Adverbs and Functional Heads: A Cross-Linguistic Perspective.* Oxford: Oxford University Press.

Collins, Chris and Hoskuldur Thrainsson 1996. "VP-internal structure and object-shift in Icelandic." *Linguistic Inquiry* 27, 391-444.

Comrie, Bernard 1976. *Aspect.* Cambridge, Mass.: Cambridge University Press.

Comrie, Bernard 1985. *Tense.* Cambridge, Mass.: Cambridge University Press.

Comrie, Bernard 1989. *Language universals and linguistic typology.* Chicago: University of Chicago Press.

BIBLIOGRAPHY

Curme, George 1914. "The development of verbal compounds in Germanic." Beiträge zur Geschichte der deutschen Sprache und Literatur [Research into the history of German language and literature] 39, 320-61.

Davis, Henry and Lisa Matthewson 1997. "Determiners, tense, and the entity/event parallel." Paper presented at NELS, Toronto.

Dayal, Veneeta 1995. "Quantification in correlatives." *Quantification in Natural Language*, eds. Emmon Bach, Eloise Jelinek, Angelika Kratzer and Barbara Partee, 179-205. Dordrecht: Kluwer.

Dayal, Veneeta 1996. Locality in WH quantification: questions and relative clauses in Hindi. Dordrecht: Kluwer.

De Francis Henry 1963. *Beginning Chinese*. New Haven, Connecticut: Yale University Press.

Demirdache, Hamida 1991. Resumptive chains in restrictive relatives, appositives and dislocation structures. Doctoral dissertation, MIT.

Den Dikken, Marcel 1995. *Particles*. Oxford: Oxford University Press.

Dryer, Matthew 1992. "The Greenbergian word order correlations." *Language* 68, 81-138.

Feng, Shengli 1998. "Prosodic structure and compound words in Classical Chinese." *New approaches to Chinese word formation*, ed. Jerome Packard, 197-260. Berlin: Mouton de Gruyer.

Fu, Jingqi 1994. *On deriving Chinese derived nominals: evidence for V-to-N raising*. Doctoral dissertation, U. of Massachusetts, Amherst.

Gamillscheg, Ernst 1957. Historische französische Syntax [Historical French Syntax]. Tübingen: Niemeyer.

Gildea, Spike 1993. "The development of tense markers from demonstrative pronouns in Panare (Cariban)." *Studies in Language* 17-1, 53-73.

Giorgi, Alessandra and Fabio Pianesi 1997. *Tense and Aspect: From Semantics to Morphosyntax*. Oxford: Oxford University Press.

Giusti, Giuliana 1997. "The categorial status of determiners." *The new comparative syntax*, ed. Liliane Haegeman, 95-123. London/New York: Longman.

Givón, Talmy 1971. "Historical syntax and synchronic morphology." *Papers from the 7th Regional Meeting of the Chicago Lingustic Society*, 394-415.

Givón, Talmy 1979. *On Understanding Grammar*. New York: Academic Press.

Givón, Talmy 1984. *Syntax: a functional-typological introduction*, vol.1. Amsterdam: John Benjamins.

Gordon, Lynn 1986. "The development of evidentials in Maricopa." *Evidentiality: the linguistic encoding of epistemology*, ed. Wallace Chafe, 75-88. Norwood, New Jersey: Ablex.

Greenberg, Joseph 1963. "Some universals of language with particular reference to the order of meaningful elements." *Universals of language*, ed. Joseph Greenberg, 73-113. Cambridge, Mass: MIT Press.

Greenberg, Joseph 1978. "How does a language acquire gender markers?" *Universals of human language, vol. 3: Word structure*, ed. Joseph Greenberg, 47-83. Stanford: Stanford University Press.

Grimshaw, Jane 1990. *Argument structure*. Cambridge, Mass.: MIT Press.

Grimshaw, Jane 1991. "Extended projection." Ms., Brandeis University.

Grosu, Alex 1988. "On the distribution of genitive phrases in Roumanian." *Linguistics* 26, 931-949.

BIBLIOGRAPHY

Guasti, Maria Teresa and Ur Shlonsky 1992. "The acquisition of French relative clauses reconsidered." Paper presented at the Annual Boston University Conference on Language Development, Boston.

Hale, Kenneth and Jay Keyser 1993. "On argument structure and the lexical expression of syntactic relations." *The view from building 20*, eds. Kenneth Hale and Jay Keyser, 53-110. Cambridge, Mass.: MIT Press.

Harris, Alice 1982. "Georgian and the unaccusative hypothesis." *Language* 58, 290-306.

Harris, Alice and Lyle Campbell 1995. *Historical syntax in a cross-linguistic perspective*. Cambridge: Cambridge University Press.

Hawkins, John. A. 1979. "Implicational universals as predictors of word order change." *Language* 55, 618-648.

Heine, Bernd and Mechthild Reh 1984. *Grammaticalization and reanalysis in African languages*. Hamburg: Helmut Buske Verlag.

Heine, Bernd, Ulrike Claudi and Friederike Hünnemeyer 1991. *Grammaticalization: A Conceptual Framework*. Chicago: University of Chicago Press.

Heycock, Caroline 1995. "Asymmetries in reconstruction." *Linguistic Inquiry* 26, 547-570.

Hoekstra, Teun 1992. "Aspect and theta theory." *Thematic structure, its role in grammar*, ed. Iggy Roca, 145-174. Berlin: Foris/Mouton.

Hoji, Hajime 1985. *Logical form constraints and configurational structures in Japanese*. Doctoral dissertation, University of Washington.

Hopper, Paul. and Elizabeth Traugott 1993. *Grammaticalization*. Cambridge: Cambridge University Press.

Hopper, Paul. and Sandra Thompson 1984. "The discourse basis for lexical categories in universal grammar." *Language* 60, 703-52

Hsieh, Miao-ling 1998. "Tense interpretations in Chinese and the related issues." *On the formal way to Chinese language*, eds. Chen-sheng Luther Liu and Sze-wing Tang, 3-20. Stanford: Center for the Study of Language and Information.

Huang, Cheng-Teh James 1982. *Logical relations in Chinese and the theory of grammar*. Doctoral dissertation, MIT.

Huang, Cheng-Teh James 1984. "On the distribution and reference of empty pronouns." *Linguistic Inquiry* 15, 531-574.

Huang, Cheng-Teh James 1988. "*Wo pao de kuai* and Chinese phrase structure." *Language* 64, 274-311.

Huang, Cheng-Teh James 1990. "Shuo 'shi' he 'you' [On 'Be' and 'Have' in Chinese]." *The Bulletin of the Institute of History and Philology* 59-1, 43-64. Taipei, Taiwan: Academia Sinica.

Huang, Cheng-Teh James 1993. "Reconstruction and the structure of VP: some theoretical consequences." *Linguistic Inquiry* 24,103-138.

Hwang, Jya-Lin 1998. "A comparative study on the grammaticalization of saying verbs in Chinese." Paper presented at the 7th Annual Meeting of the International Association of Chinese Linguistics/the 10th North American Conference on Chinese Linguistics, Stanford University.

Johnson, Kyle 1991. "Object positions." *Natural Language and Linguistic Theory* 9, 577-636.

Kameshima, Nanako 1989. *The syntax of restrictive and non-restrictive relative clauses in Japanese*. Doctoral dissertation, University of Wisconsin, Madison.

Karlgren, Bernhard 1923. *Analytic dictionary of Chinese and Sino-Japanese.* Paris: Librairie Orientaliste Paul Geunther.

Kayne, Richard S. 1975. *French syntax: the transformational cycle.* Cambridge, Mass.: MIT Press.

Kayne, Richard S. 1985. "Principles of particle constructions." *Grammatical representation*, eds. J. Gueron, H.-G. Obenauer and J.Y. Pollock, 101-140. Dordrecht: Foris.

Kayne, Richard S. 1994. *The antisymmetry of syntax.* Cambridge, Mass.: MIT Press.

Kennedy, Arthur 1920. *The Modern English verb-adverb combination. Language and Literature*, vol.1, no.1. Stanford: Stanford University Publications.

Kim, Soonwon and Joan Maling 1997. "A cross-linguistic perspective on resultative formation." *Texas linguistic forum 38: The syntax and semantics of predication*, eds. Ralph Blight and Michelle Moosally, 189-205. Austin, Texas: Dept. of Linguistics, University of Texas at Austin.

Kim, Young-Kook 1997. "Agreement phrases in DP." *University College London (UCL) working papers in linguistics.* London: UCL.

Kitagawa, Chisato and Claudia Ross 1982. "Prenominal modification in Chinese and Japanese." *Linguistic Analysis* 9, 119-53.

König, Ekkehard 1988. "Concessive connectives and concessive sentences: Cross-linguistic regularities and pragmatic principles." *Explaining language universals*, ed. John A. Hawkins, 146-66. Oxford: Blackwell.

Kuno, Susumu 1973. *The structure of the Japanese language.* Cambridge, Mass.: MIT Press.

Lapointe, Steven and Sarah Nielsen 1996. "A reconsideration of type III gerunds in Korean." *Japanese/Korean Linguistics* 5, eds. Noriko Akatsuka, Shoichi Iwasaki and Susan Strauss, 305-320. Stanford: Center for the Study of Language and Information.

Lecarme, Jacqueline 1996. "Tense in the nominal system: the Somali DP." *Studies in Afroasiatic Grammar*, eds. J. Lecarme, J. Lowenstamm and U. Shlonsky, 150-175. The Hague: Holland Academic Graphics.

Lee, Sookhee 1993. "The syntax of serialization in Korean." *Japanese/Korean Linguistics* 2, ed. Patricia Clancy, 447-463. Stanford: Center for the Study of Language and Information.

Lehmann, Winfred Philipp 1973. *Historical linguistics: an introduction.* New York: Holt, Rinehart & Winston.

Li, Charles and Yuzhi Shi 1997. "Lun Hanyu tibiaoji dansheng de jizhi [On the mechanism of the origin of Chinese aspect markers]." *Zhongwen Yuwen* 14, 83-96.

Li, Charles and Yuzhi Shi 1998. "Hanyu dong-bu jiegou de fazhan yu jufa jiegou de shanbian [Development of the 'V-complement' construction and changes of syntactic structures]." *Studies in Chinese Linguistics* 2, 83-100. Beijing: Beijing Language and Culture University Press.

Li, Charles and Sandra A. Thompson 1974. "An explanation of word order change: SVO→SOV." *Foundations of Language* 12, 201-214.

Li, Charles and Sandra A. Thompson 1981. *Mandarin Chinese: a functional reference grammar.* Berkeley: University of California Press.

Li, Fang. 1993. "Shu+*ge*+bu jiegou de tantao [On the verb-*ge*-complement construction]." Ms., Beijing University.

BIBLIOGRAPHY

Li, Frank. (in prep.) The rise and development of verb compounding in Chinese: A historical and grammaticalization perspective with cross-linguistic implications. LinCom Europa.

Li, Yafei 1990. "On V-V compounds in Chinese." *Natural Language and Linguistic Theory* 8, 177-207.

Li, Yafei 1998. "Chinese resultative constructions and the uniformity of theta assignment hypothesis." *New approaches to Chinese word formation*, ed. Jerome Packard, 285-310. Berlin: Mouton de Gruyer.

Li, Yen-hui Audrey 1990. *Order and constituency in Mandarin Chinese*. Dordrecht: Kluwer.

Li, Yen-hui Audrey 1998. "Nominal projections in Mandarin Chinese." *Proceedings of the 9th North American Conference on Chinese Linguistics*, ed. Hua Lin, 139-155. Los Angeles: GSIL, University of Southern California.

Li, Yen-hui Audrey 1999a. "Plural in a classifier language." *Journal of East Asian Linguistics* 8, 75-99.

Li, Yen-hui Audrey 1999b. "Word order, structure and relativization." Ms., University of Southern California.

Lightfoot, David 1979. *Principles of diachronic syntax*. Cambridge: Cambridge University Press.

Lin, Jo-wang 1993. "Object expletives in Chinese." Paper presented in North American Conference on Chinese Linguistics, University of Delaware.

Lin, Jo-wang 1994. "Noun phrase structure in Mandarin Chinese: DP or NP." Paper presented at the Third International Conference on Linguistics and Language in China. Hsinchu, Taiwan: Ching-hua University.

Liu, Hsiao-Mei 1993. "Fanchou moxing lilun yu Hanyu shuliangci tixi [Categorial model theory and Chinese numeral-measure system]." Ms., Furen University Linguistics Institute, Taipei.

Longobardi, Giuseppe 1994. "Reference and proper names: a theory of N-movement in syntax and logical form." *Linguistic Inquiry* 25, 609-65.

Lord, Carol 1993. *Historical change in serial verb constructions*. Amsterdam: John Benjamins.

Lü, Shu-Xiang 1980. Xiandai Hanyu babai ci [Eight hundred words of Modern Chinese]. Beijing: Shangwu.

Lü, Shu-Xiang 1984. "*Ge* zi de yingyong fanwei, fu lun danweici qian yi zi de tuoluo [The applicable scope of *ge* and the deletion of *yi* before the measure word]." *Hanyu yufa lunwenji [Papers on Chinese grammar]*. Beijing: Shangwu.

Lüdeling, Anke 1997. "Strange resultatives in German: new evidence for a sematnic treatment." *Texas Linguistic Forum 38 The Syntax and Semantics of Predication*, eds. Ralph Blight and Michelle Moosally, 223-235. Austin, Texas: Dept. of Linguistics, University of Texas at Austin.

Mallinson, Graham and Barry Blake 1981. *Language typology*. Amsterdam/New York/Oxford: North Holland Publishing Company.

Matthews, Peter H. 1974. *Morphology: an introduction to the theory of word-structure*. Cambridge: Cambridge University Press.

Matthews, Stephen and Virginia Yip 1994. *Cantonese: a comprehensive grammar*. London: Routledge.

Mei, Tsu-Lin 1981. "Xiandai Hanyu wancheng mao jushi he ciwei 'le' de laiyuan [The origin of the perfective sentences of Modern Chinese and the suffix 'le']." *Yuyan Yanjiu* 1, 65-77.

BIBLIOGRAPHY

Mei, Tsu-Lin 1994. "Tangdai Songdai gongtongyu de yufa he xiandao fangyan de yufa [Syntax of the common language in Tang and Song Dynasties and syntax of Modern dialects]." *Zhongguo Jingnei Yuyan ji Yuyanxue* 2, 61-97.
Meillet, Antoine 1912. "L'evolution des formes grammaticales," *Scienpia* 12.6. Reprinted in Antoine. Meillet 1958, *Linguistique historique et linguistique générale*, Vol. 1, 130-48. Paris: Champion.
Mulder, Rene and Rint Sybesma 1992. "Chinese is a VO language." *Natural Language and Linguistic Theory* 10, 439-476.
Murasugi, Keiko 1991. Noun phrases in Japanese and English: a study in syntax, learnability and acquisition. Doctoral dissertation, University of Connecticut.
Murasugi, Keiko 1998. "An antisymmetry analysis of Japanese relative clauses." Ms., Kinjo Gakuin University.
Nakamura, Akira 1994. "Some aspects of temporal interpretation in Japanese." *Formal approaches to Japanese linguistics 1: MIT working papers in linguistics* 24, eds. Masatoshi Koizumi and Hiroyuki Ura, 231-246. Cambridge, Mass.: MIT Press.
Ning, Chunyan 1993. *The overt syntax of relativization and topicalization*. Doctoral dissertation, University of California at Irvine.
Norman, Jerry 1988. *Chinese*. Cambridge: Cambridge University Press.
Osawa, Fuyu 1998. "The emergence of the D-system and the demise of morphological case in English." *University College London (UCL) working papers in linguistics* 10, eds. John Harris and Corinne Iten, 467-98.
Packard, Jerome 1998. "Introduction." *New approaches to Chinese word formation*, ed. Jerome Packard, 1-34. Berlin: Mouton de Gruyer.
Paris, Marie-Claude 1979. *Nominalization in Mandarin Chinese*. Doctoral dissertation, Paris 7.
Pesetsky, David and Esther Torrego 2001. "T-to-C movement: causes and consequences." *Ken Hale: A Life in Language*, ed. Micheal Kenstowicz, 355-426. Cambridge, Mass.: MIT Press.
Peyraube, Alain 1996. "Recent issues in Chinese historical syntax." *New Horizons in Chinese Linguistics*, eds. C.-T. James Huang and Y.-H. Audrey Li, 161-213. Dordrecht: Kluwer.
Poletto, Cecilia 2000. The higher functional field: evidence from North Italian dialects. Oxford: Oxford University Press.
Pulleyblank, Edward 1995. *Outline of classical Chinese grammar*. Vancouver: UBC Press.
Ramat, Anna Giacalone 1998. "Testing the boundaries of grammaticalization." *The limits of grammaticalization*, eds. Anna Giacalone Ramat and Paul J. Hopper, 107-127. Amsterdam: John Benjamins.
Ritter, Elizabeth 1991. "Two functional categories in noun phrases: evidence from modern Hebrew." *Syntax and Semantics* 26, ed. Susan Rothstein, 37-62. New York: Academic Press.
Rizzi, Luigi 1997. "The fine structure of the left periphery." *Elements of grammar*, ed. Liliane Haegeman, 281-337. Dordrecht: Kluwer.
Roberts, Ian and Anna Roussou 1999. "A formal approach to grammaticalization." Ms., University of Stuttgart and University of Cyprus.
Rohsenow, John 1978. *Syntax and semantics of the perfect in Mandarin Chinese*. Doctoral dissertation, University of Michigan.
Ross, Claudia 1995. "Temporal and aspectual reference in Mandarin Chinese." *Journal of Chinese Linguistics* 23.1, 87-135.

Bibliography

Safir, Ken 1986. "Relative clauses in a theory of binding and levels." *Linguistic Inquiry* 17, 663-90.
Sag, Ivan and Janet Fodor 1995. "Extraction without traces." *WCCFL proceedings*, eds. Raul Aranovich, W. Byrne, S. Preuss and M. Senturia, 365-384. Stanford: Center for the Study of Language and Information.
Selkirk, Elisabeth. and Tong Shen 1990. "Prosodic domains in Shanghai Chinese." *The phonology-syntax connection*, eds. Sharon Inkelas and Draga Zec, 313-338. Chicago: University of Chicago Press.
Shi, Dingxu 1994. "The nature of Chinese emphatic sentences." *Journal of East Asian Linguistics* 3, 81-101.
Shi, Ziqiang 1988. *The present and past of the particle* le *in Mandarin Chinese*. Doctoral dissertation, University of Pennsylvania.
Shi, Ziqiang 1989. "The grammaticalization of the particle *le* in Mandarin Chinese." *Language Variation and Change* 1, 99-114.
Shi, Ziqiang 1990. "Decomposition of perfectivity and inchoativity and the meaning of the particle *le* in Mandarin Chinese." *Journal of Chinese Linguistics* 18, 95-123.
Simpson, Andrew 1998a. "Definiteness agreement and the Chinese DP." *Preceedings of international symposium of Chinese linguistics and language*. Hsinchu, Taiwan: Ching-hua University.
Simpson, Andrew 1998b. "Empty determiners and nominalization in Chinese, Japanese and Korean." Paper presented in Symposium on the Syntax of East Asian Languages, University of Southern California, Los Angeles.
Simpson, Andrew 2001. "Focus, presupposition, and light-predicate raising in East and South-East Asia." *Journal of East Asian Linguistics* 10, 89-128.
Simpson, Andrew 2002. "On the status of 'modifying' *de* and the structure of the Chinese DP." *On the formal way to Chinese language*, eds. Chen-sheng Luther Liu and Sze-wing Tang, 74-101. Stanford: Center for the Study of Language and Information.
Simpson, Andrew and Zoe Wu 2001. "The grammaticalization of formal nouns and nominalizers in Chinese, Japanese and Korean." *Language Change in East Asia*, ed. T.E. McAuley, 250-283. London: Curzon
Simpson, Andrew and Zoe Wu 2002a. "IP-raising, tone sandhi and the creation of S-final particles: evidence for cyclic Spell-Out." *Journal of East Asian Linguistics* 11.1, 67-99.
Simpson, Andrew and Zoe Wu 2002b. "From D to T—determiner incorporation and the creation of tense." *Journal of East Asian Linguistics* 11.2, 169-209.
Simpson, Andrew and Zoe Wu 2002c. "Agreement, shells and focus." *Language* 78.2: 287-313.
Smith, Carlota 1997. *The parameter of aspect*. Dordrecht: Kluwer.
Spanos, George 1979. "Contemporary Chinese use of *le*: a survey and a pragmatic proposal." *Jounral of the Chinese Language Teachers Association* 14.1, 36-70, 14.2, 47-102.
Spencer, Andrew 1991. *Morphological theory*. Cambridge: Blackwell/Cambridge University Press.
Starosta, Stanley, Koenraad Kuiper, Siew-ai Ng and Zhi-qian Wu 1998. "On defining the Chinese compound word: headeness in Chinese compounding and Chinese VR compounds." *New approaches to Chinese word formation*, ed. Jerome Packard, 347-370. Berlin: Mouton de Gruyer.
Stowell, Tim 1996. "The syntax of tense." Ms., UCLA

BIBLIOGRAPHY

Sun, Chaofen 1996. Word order change and grammaticalization in the history of Chinese. Stanford: Stanford University Press.

Sybesma, Rint 1999. *The Mandarin VP*. Dordrecht: Kluwer.

Szabolcsi, Anna 1994. "The noun phrase." *Syntax and Semantics 27: The structure of Hungarian*, ed. K. Kiss, 179-274. New York: Academic Press.

Takeuchi, Lone 1999. The structure and history of Japanese: from Yamatokotoba to Nihongo. London and New York: Longman.

Tang, Chih-chen Jane 1990. *Chinese phrase structure and the extended X'-theory*. Doctoral dissertation, Cornell University.

Tenny, Carol 1987. *Grammaticalizing aspect and affectedness*. Doctoral dissertation, MIT.

Thompson, Hanne-Ruth 2001. *Essential everyday Bengali*. Dhaka: Bangla Academy.

Traugott, Elizabeth and Ekkehard König 1991. "The semantics-pragmatics of grammaticalization revisited." *Approaches to grammaticalization*, eds. Traugott, Elizabeth and Bernd Heine, 189-218. Amsterdam: John Benjamins.

Travis, Lisa 1984. *Parameters and effects on word order variation*. Doctoral dissertation, MIT.

Tsai, Wei-Tien Dylan 1992. "On the absence of island effects." Ms., MIT.

Tsai, Wei-Tien Dylan 1994. *On economizing the theory of A-bar dependencies*. Doctoral dissertation, MIT.

Tsang, Chui Lim 1981. *A semantic study of modal auxiliary verbs in Chinese*. Doctoral dissertation, Stanford University.

T'ung, Ping-cheng and D.E. Pollard 1997. *Colloquial Chinese*. London: Routledge.

Vendler, Zeno 1967. "Verbs and times." *Linguistics in Philosophy*, 97-121. Ithaca: Cornell University Press. Revised from Zeno Vendler 1957, "Verbs and times." *The Philosophical Review* 66, 143-60.

Vennemann, Theo 1974. "Analogy in generative grammar: the origin of word order." *Proceedings of the 11th international congress of linguists* 2, ed. Luigi Heilmann, Societa editrice Il Mulino, 79-83. Bologna: Bologna.

Vergnaud, Jean-Roger 1985. Dependances et niveauxde representation en syntaxe [Dependencies and Levels of Representation in Syntax]. Amsterdam: Benjamins.

Vergnaud, Jean-Roger and Maria Luisa Zubizarreta 1992. "The definite determiner and the inalienable construction in French and English." *Linguistic Inquiry* 23, 595-652.

Vincent, Nigel 1997. "The emergence of the D-system in Romance". *Parameters of morphosyntactic change*, eds. Ans van Kemenade and Nigel Vincent, 149-169. Cambridge: Cambrige University Press.

Visser, Fredericus T. 1963-1973. *A historical syntax of the English language*. 3 vols. Leiden: Brill.

Wahba, Wafaa 1984. *Wh-constructions in Egyptian Arabic*. Doctoral dissertation, University of Illinois at Urbana-Champaign.

Wang, Li. 1980. Hanyu shigao [An outline of Chinese language history]. Beijing: China Book Company.

Wang, Li. 1990. "Hanyu yufa shi [History of Chinese syntax]." *Wang Li Wenji [Collective works of Wang Li]* Qingdao: Shandong Jiaoyu Chubanshe.

Wu, Guo 1999. "The origin of the Mandarin sentence-final particle *le*." Ms., Leiden University.

Yoon, James 1990. "Korean nominalizations, lexicalism, and morphosyntactic interfaces." Ms., University of Illinois, Urbana-Champaign.

Bibliography

Zou, Ke 1994. "Resultative V-V compounds in Chinese." *The morphology-syntax connection: MIT working papers in linguistics* 22, eds. Heidi Harley and Colin Phillips, 271-290. Cambridge: MIT Press.

Zhuangzi, cited according to *Zhuangzi Yinde [A concordance to Chuang-tzu]* 1956. Cambridge, Mass.: Harvard University Press. Reprinted from Harvard-Yenching Institute Sinological Index Series, supplement no. 20, 1947. Peiping: Yenching University Press.

Zubizarreta, Maria Luisa 1998. *Prosody, focus, and word order*. Cambridge, Mass.: MIT Press.

Zwicky, Arnold 1977. *On clitics*. Bloomington: Indiana University Linguistics Club.

INDEX

Abney, Steven P., 31, 153
Abraham, Werner, 65-66
Accomplishment predicate/verb, 20-21, 238, 240-242, 283-284, 299
Achievement predicate/verb, 14, 21-23, 49, 238, 240-241, 244-245, 247, 276, 283-284
Activity predicate/verb, 14-15, 17-18, 20-22, 31-32, 45, 49, 170, 181, 215, 228, 238, 240-242, 276, 286-287, 299, 301
Adjectival reduplication, 24, 26
Adjunct, 78, 87-89, 114-115, 154-155
Adjunction, 52, 61, 184, 227, 296
Adjunt Island, 55
Affix, 91, 124-125, 142, 210-211, 225, 234, 248, 250, 252-257, 259, 264, 266-267, 275, 298, *see also* Suffix; Prefix
Allen, Robert Livingston, 14
Amharic, 63-64, 232
Anaphor, 71, 73
Anaphoric, 133, 280
A-not-A question, 25-26, 31-32, 147-148, 305
Ba in Mandarin Chinese, 35, 46-47, 58, 176, 214, 229, 305
Baker, Carl Lee, 156
Baker, Mark, 143, 221, 247, 256
Bei in Mandarin Chinese, 35, 47, 305
Bengali, 300
Biener, Clemens, 288
Bi-syllabicism, 201-204
Blake, Barry, 206, 218
Bleaching, 38, 65, 69
Borer, Hagit, 20, 31, 48-49, 231
Boskovic, Zeljko, 158

Bound morpheme, 3-4, 242, 297-298, 307
Branching, 90, 207
Bresnan, Joan, 105-117, 119, 142
Brody, Michael, 231
Buginese, 68
Bybee, Joan, 3, 41, 117, 195, 230, 239, 270-271, 276-279, 283, 301, 306
Campbell, Lyle, 99, 203, 222, 233, 271, 288
Cantonese, 30, 37, 46, 60-61, 91, 130, 134, 300
Cao, Guangshun, 125
Category change/shift, 2, 8, 20, 32-33, 38, 78, 91-93, 121, 141-142, 149-150, 152, 186, 250, 252, 271
Causative, 169-170, 218, 233
Chang, Vincent, 278, 300
Chao, Yuen Ren, 14, 129, 132
Chen, Matthew, 114-115, 189
Cheng, Lisa Lai-Shen, 30, 37
Cheng, Robert, 114
Chiu, Bonnie, 53-55, 57, 69-70, 75, 87, 110-112, 120, 153-154, 156, 300
Chomsky, Noam, 1, 5, 90, 103-104, 118, 146, 168, 206, 208, 210, 256, 279, 294, 303
Cinque, Guglielmo, 46, 242, 246
Classifier 8, 13-17, 20-22, 30-34, 37, 41-42, 44-45, 48-49, 189, 194-196, 231, 303
Claudi, Ulrike, 3
Cline 12

INDEX

Cliticization, 3-4, 55, 68-69, 99-101, 107, 121, 124-125, 127-128, 136, 138-139, 142-146, 149, 157-159, 162, 174, 187, 201, 205, 222-223, 235, 292, 307
Collins, Chris, 220, 225, 233
Complementizer, 2, 9, 33, 49, 51, 56, 59-61, 63-64, 87, 90-96, 98-99, 108-109, 142, 151, 158, 216, 301
Completive aspect, 11, 187, 189, 195, 204, 206, 214-215, 221-222, 224-225, 229, 234-239, 244-250, 257-259, 263-274, 282-284, 291, 293, 297, 301, 304, 308
Complex NP/CNP, 54-55, 72-73, 77, 80-83, 113, 121, 132-133, 135-141, 145, 149, 152, 157, 159
Compound, 14-15, 19, 30, 163, 165-167, 173, 200-202, 227, 236
Comrie, Bernard, 232, 240, 282
Connectivity, 69, 71, 73-74, 77, 81, 112
Conversational implicature, 10, 121, 126-127, 135, 137, 156, 268-269, 272, 274, 296, *see also* Pragmatic implicature
Curme, George, 220, 222
Cyclic Spell-Out, 90, 103-107, 118-19
Dahl, Östen, 271
Davis, Henry, 30, 36
Dayal, Veneeta, 85
De Francis, Henry, 133
Definiteness, 36-37, 50, 64-67, 69, 150, 158
Demirdache, Hamida, 292
Demonstrative, 9, 35-36, 53, 65-67, 69, 107-108, 110, 112, 133, 150-151, 157-159, 280
Den Dikken, Marcel, 220
Derived nominal, 78
Descriptive *de* in Mandarin Chinese, 129, 132, 157
Determiner, 2, 8-10, 13, 29-30, 32-37, 41, 44-45, 48-50, 52, 64-69, 80, 107-108, 110, 117, 138, 150, 303
Diachronic information, 1, 5-7, 9, 39, 42, 45, 122, 127, 161-162, 173, 180, 185, 188, 225-226, 233, 236-237, 250, 257, 259, 264, 266, 272, 277-278, 282, 288, 297, 300, 303, 308
Directional resultative verb construction (RVC), 164

Directionality of selection, 51, 58, 69, 78-79, 90-92, 107-109, 111, 163-164, 200, 206-207, 210, 216, 219, 226, 304, 306-307
Di-transitive, 47-48, *see also* Double object construction (DOC)
Double object construction (DOC), 28, 33, 47, 124, 144
Dryer, Matthew, 11, 68, 218
Economy, 206
Egyptian Arabic, 291-292
Empty head, 66, 78, 132-133, 149
Empty operator, 54-55, 70-72, 75, 80-81, 83, 110, 112-113, 115-116, *see also* Null operator
English, 3, 13, 23, 31, 33, 39, 41-42, 45-46, 48-49, 52-53, 55, 57, 59-61, 63-66, 71-73, 81-84, 87, 90-92, 96, 100-101, 105-106, 109-110, 116, 118-119, 120-123, 134-135, 147-149, 151-152, 156, 163, 172, 177, 192, 194, 196, 198, 209, 217-223, 225, 228, 231, 233, 240-242, 244-245, 252, 277-278, 281-283, 290, 294-295, 299, 301-302, 307
Ewe, 92
Expletive, 29, 32, 48-49, 66-67, 141
Expletive-associative chain, 29
Feng, Shengli, 201-203
Focus, 10, 40-41, 100, 102, 106-107, 120-122, 127, 132, 148-149, 153-156, 159, 195, 197-200, 205, 214-215, 226, 241, 280, 299, 301
Fodor, Janet, 115
French, 3, 33, 38-39, 44, 49, 55, 65, 108-110, 113, 233, 252, 254, 271, 281
Frequency increase, 277-278
Fu, Jingqi, 77-78
Functional head, 9-10, 31, 33, 38, 41, 77-78, 87-89, 94, 100, 104, 108, 121, 123, 151-152, 173, 175, 187, 189, 191, 194-196, 204, 210, 212, 216, 222-223, 229, 231, 234, 239, 247-248, 250-255, 257, 267, 270-271, 275, 298, 304-307
Future tense, 3, 5, 126, 134, 136, 150, 152, 270-271, 284-285, 289-290, 294-296
Gamillscheg, Ernst, 39
Generalization phenomenon, 195
Generalized Control Rule (GCR), 55, 75
Genitive case, 26, 32

321

INDEX

Genitive, 129, 307
Georgian, 99, 117
German, 33, 65-66, 122, 156, 196, 224, 230, 271
Gildea, Spike, 150-151
Giorgi, Alessandra, 308
Giusti, Giuliana, 66, 117
Givón, Talmy, 4, 219
Gordon, Lynn, 99
Grammaticalization chain, 3-6
Greek, 66-67
Greenberg, Joseph, 11, 65, 206, 218
Grimshaw, Jane, 77, 175, 217, 262
Grosu, Alex, 38, 66, 68, 117
Guasti, Maria Teresa, 70
Hale, Kenneth, 143, 168, 209
Harris, Alice, 99, 203, 222, 233, 271, 288
Hawkins, John A., 206
Head Movement Constraint (HMC), 224, 295, 306
Head movement, 167, 224, 227
Head-complement relation, 93, 110
Headedness, 11, 51, 93, 163, 210, 216, *see also* Directionality of selection
Head-final, 9, 11, 58, 92-93, 146, 206, 209-210, 212, 218, 226, 232, 236
Head-initial, 9, 11, 58-59, 63-64, 68, 77, 90-94, 138, 146, 163, 206, 210-214, 219, 226, 232, 236, 242, 246, 249, 270, 304
Head-internal relative, 70, 111
Heavy NP Shift, 122-123, 200, 232
Heine, Bernd, 3, 91
Heycock, Caroline, 159
Hindi, 81, 122
Hoekstra, Teun, 170-172, 183, 220, 225, 227
Hoji, Hajime, 72-73
Hopper, Paul, 4, 39, 65, 127, 156, 195, 288
Hsieh, Miao-ling, 300
Huang, Cheng-Teh James, 55, 113, 120, 128, 145, 156-157, 159
Hünnemeyer, Friederike, 3
Hwang, Jya-Lin, 60, 91
Idiom, 14, 21, 26, 30, 36, 62, 69, 71-72
Imperative, 275, 287, 293-294
Imperfective aspect, 21, 31, 240-243, 249, 258-259, 270-271, 281-282, 293, 299
Inchoativity, 31, 276, 281-287, 301

Incorporation, 28, 99, 117, 143-144, 157-158, 209, 216, 288
Indefinite article, 33-34, 45, 68
Intonation, 70, 109
Intransitive, 166-167, 170, 178, 207, 209, 227, 228, 283, 285
Irish, 66
Italian, 114, 271
Japanese, 51, 59-60, 72-75, 77, 79, 83, 108-109, 111-112, 132, 141, 156, 288-289
Johnson, Kyle, 221, 225, 232-233
Kameshima, Nanako, 73
Karlgren, Bernhard, 201
Kayne, Richard S., 47, 55, 61-64, 67, 69, 71-75, 77, 88-90, 107-108, 110-114, 138, 171, 174, 220, 231
Kennedy, Arthur, 220, 222
Keyser, Jay, 168, 209
Kim, Soonwon, 228-229
Kim, Young-Kook, 75, 112
Kitagawa, Chisato, 132-133
König, Ekkehard, 3
Korean, 26, 31, 75, 111-112, 228-229, 235
Kuiper, Koenraad, 232
Kuno, Susumu, 56, 72-73, 111, 113
Lapointe, Steven, 26
Layering, 66, 74
Lecarme, Jacqueline, 159
Lee, Sookhee, 229
Left-branching complement, the puzzle, 57, 61, 87-89, 93, 100, 107, 146, 186, 208, 210, 217
Leftward movement, 51-52, 62, 78, 109, 123-124, 142, 146, 186, 188, 216-217, 230
Lehmann, Winfred Philipp, 206
LF movement 120, 153-156, 239, 256, 294-295
Li, Audrey, 28, 30, 37, 46, 50, 72, 108
Li, Charles, 12, 28, 58, 125, 129, 133, 163-165, 180, 182-183, 190, 192, 200, 214, 226, 239, 245, 249, 267, 275-277, 279, 287, 293-294
Li, Fang, 26
Li, Frank, 202
Li, Yafei, 158, 163-167, 184, 200, 215-216, 227
Light verb, 152

322

INDEX

Lightfoot, David, 49, 252
Lin, Jo-wang, 29, 48, 77
Linear Correspondence Axiom (LCA), 61
Linear order, 1, 61, 64, 89-90, 103-104, 110-111, 115, 125, 154-155, 169, 171, 174-175, 184, 186, 200, 204, 206, 214, 218, 225-226, 241, 246-247
Literal resultative verb construction, (RVC), 164-165, 177, 179-186, 189-194, 196, 215, 219-220, 231-232, 237, 250
Liu, Hsiao-Mei, 16
Longobardi, Giuseppe, 38, 49, 66
Lord, Carol, 91
Lowering, 146, 307
Lü, Shu-Xiang, 25, 33, 259-260, 263, 265, 293, 300
Lüdeling, Anke, 196, 230
Maling, Joan, 228-229
Mallinson, Graham, 206, 218
Maricopa, 99
Matthews, Peter H., 301
Matthews, Stephen, 46
Matthewson, Lisa, 30, 36
Mchombo, Samuel, 143
Mei, Tsu-Lin, 200, 232, 235
Meillet, Antoine, 2, 308
Minimalism, 1, 5-7, 11, 103, 108, 113, 121, 142, 210, 215, 221, 234, 248, 253, 267, 291, 298, 300, 303
Mirror image, 247
Mirror Principle, 221, 247-248, 256
Modifier, 20-21, 24, 132, 138
Mokilese, 68
Mulder, Rene, 58
Murasugi, Keiko, 51, 72-74, 77, 79, 84, 111, 115-116
Nakamura, Akira, 289
Negation, 25-26, 31-32, 38-41, 44, 46, 48-49, 91, 249-250, 252, 254, 260, 294-295, 305
Ng, Siew-ai, 232
Nielsen, Sarah, 26
Ning, Chunyan, 53, 55-57, 75, 77, 80-81, 87, 108, 111-112
Nominalization, 25-26, 31-33, 48, 78, 133-137, 152, 156-157, 304
Nominalizer, 25-26, 30-32, 48, 133, 156, 304

Non-restrictive relative, 108, 112
Norman, Jerry, 201
Null operator, 52-53, 57, 52, 74, 76, *see also* Empty operator
Numeral, 8, 13-15, 17, 21, 30-31, 33-34, 41-42, 44-45, 48-49, 142
Operator-variable chain, 56, 70, 111
Osawa, Fuyu, 41
Packard, Jerome, 203
Pagliuca, William, 3, 41, 117, 195, 230, 239, 270-271, 276-279, 283, 301, 306
Panare, 151-152
Paris, Marie-Claude, 129, 133
Participle, 290, 292
Partitive, 47
Past tense, 10, 12, 23, 121, 125, 127-129, 136-138, 141-143, 145-150, 152-153, 158-159, 204, 234, 241-244, 253, 267-282, 285-289, 291-293, 295-296, 298, 300, 302
Perfective aspect, 6, 11-12, 20-23, 31, 125, 141, 144, 240, 242-247, 250-251, 258-260, 263-300
Perkins, Revere, 3, 41, 117, 195, 230, 239, 270-271, 276-279, 283, 301, 306
Pesetsky, David, 118, 151
Peyraube, Alain, 58
PF movement, 101-103, 110, 115, 118
Phase (constituent), 103-107, 118
Phase resultative verb construction (RVC), 164-165, 179-183, 185-194, 198, 200-201, 215, 219, 226, 231-232, 235-237, 257, 261, 299
Phonetic reduction, 3, 48, 110, 117-118, 125, 195, 201, 218, 235, 278
Phonological dependency/deficiency, 68, 99-100, 107, 110, 117, 124, 138, 142, 144-145, 159, 162, 174, 187, 195, 201-203, 205, 218, 235, 252-253, *see also* Phonetic reduction
Phonological rule, 101-105, 114-115
Pianesi, Fabio, 308
Poletto, Cecilia, 308
Polish, 142
Pollard, D.E., 181, 278
Possessive, 110, 113
Potential *de* in Mandarin Chinese, 129, 132

323

INDEX

Pragmatic implicature, 3, 172, *see also* Conversational implicature
Predicational reduplication, 24, 26, 31-32
Prefix, 91, 99, 222-225
Principle of Cross-Category Harmony, 206
Principle of Natural Serialization, 206
pro, 54-55, 70, 74-75, 111-112, 117-118, 126, 169, 184-185, 206, 214, 221, 228-229, 279
Prosodic attachment, 124, 128, 202
Prosodic structure, 202-203, 216, 227
Pulleyblank, Edward, 69, 110
Quantifier, 36, 52-53, 66-67
Question particle, 57-60, 92, 109-110, 117, *see also* Sentence-final particle
Ramat, Anna Giacalone, 2
Reconstruction, 146
Reh, Mechthild, 92
Remnant, 78, 138
Restrictive relative, 112-113
Resultative *de* in Mandarin Chinese, 45-46, 129, 132, 157
Resultative particle, 163, 170, 177, 198, 219-225, 227, 229, 231-233
resumptive pronoun, 54-55, 70, 75, 81, 112-114
Right-branching complement, 51, 58-61, 78-79, 82, 90, 110, 138-139, 146, 154, 212, 216-217, 230
Rightward movement, 78, 122-124, 186
Ritter, Elizabeth, 41
Rizzi, Luigi, 119
Roberts, Ian, 151, 250
Rohsenow, John, 300
Romanian, 67-69, 118
Ross, Claudia, 132
Roussou, Anna, 151, 250
Russian, 283
Safir, Ken, 109
Sag, Ivan, 116
Salish, 30, 36
Scrambling, 26
Secondary predicate, 45, 170, 177, 192, 197, 199, 228
Selkirk, Elisabeth, 189
Sentence-final particle, 9, 51, 59-60, 91-92, 100-101, 109-111, 118, 285, 299, 304, *see also* Question particle
Shanghainese, 85, 130-132, 189

Shen, Tong, 189
Shi, Dingxu, 120, 153-154, 156
Shi, Yuzhi, 125, 180, 182-183, 190, 200, 214, 226
Shi, Ziqiang, 125, 235, 300
Shlonsky, Ur, 70
Simpson, Andrew, 36-41, 49, 64-65, 68, 78
Situational aspect, 180, 234, 239, 248
Small clause, 36, 47, 170-172, 175-185, 190, 227-228, 231, 261-263
Smith, Carlota, 11, 21, 180, 232, 234, 239, 242, 244-245, 269-270, 272, 276, 278, 281-283, 285, 297-298, 300-301
SOV, 278, 218, 219, 226
Spanish, 66-67
Spanos, George, 278, 300
Specifier, 52, 57, 63, 68, 80, 86, 88-89, 96, 103-104, 106-107, 113-115, 118-119, 145, 146, 151, 170, 187, 188, 200, 205, 207-210, 216, 217, 295, 296
Spencer, Andrew, 113, 124, 142, 158
Split complementizer, 108-109
Starosta, Stanley, 232
Stative predicate/verb, 14, 22, 31, 49, 166, 227, 240, 276, 281-287, 301
Stowell, Tim, 146-148, 159, 290
Stress, 99, 105-107, 195, 216, 229-230
Subjacency, 52, 54-55, 73-74, 77, 111-112, 116-117, 227
Suffix, 11-12, 92, 99, 125, 127, 142-145, 162-163, 175, 180, 187, 188, 204-206, 212-215, 218-219, 221, 226, 234, 236-238, 242, 244-250, 253-259, 263-264, 266-267, 269, 273, 278, 281, 294, 296-297, 300, 307
Sun, Chaofen, 58
Suo in Mandarin Chinese, 53-55, 75, 108
SVO, 59, 91-92, 100, 210, 218, 219
Sybesma, Rint, 30, 37, 58, 162-163, 170-176, 178, 183, 227-228, 231, 235, 239, 245, 259-261, 263, 265, 283
Syllable structure, 202-204
Synchronic property, 1, 5-8, 10-11, 39, 41, 44, 99, 107, 151, 234, 237, 250, 257, 263, 265-266, 273-274, 277, 297, 303, 305, 309
Szabolcsi, Anna, 33, 49, 66, 152

INDEX

Taiwanese, 9, 51, 60-61, 84-90, 92-94, 99, 101, 104-110, 114-119, 130-132, 216, 303, 305
Takeuchi, Lone, 289
Tang, Chih-chen Jane, 77, 158
Telicity 11, 15, 20-23, 31, 37, 45, 48-49, 162, 170-173, 179-180, 185-187, 189-194, 197, 199, 215, 226, 230-232, 239-240, 242-244, 246, 264, 269-270, 283-287
Tenny, Carol, 20, 31
Thai, 34, 49, 59-60, 91-92, 156, 194, 223
Theta grid, 166-167
Theta position, 225
Theta-role, 166-167, 169, 176, 184
Thompson, Hanne-Ruth, 300
Thompson, Sandra, 12, 28, 58, 129, 133, 163-165, 180, 192, 214, 239, 245, 249, 267, 275-277, 279, 287-288, 293-294, 301
Thrainsson, Hoskuldur, 220, 225, 233
Tone sandhi, 9, 51, 84-90, 92-94, 97, 100-108, 114-118, 190, 295-296, 303
Topicalization, 9, 71, 76, 106-107, 118, 214, 221, 230
Torrego, Esther, 152
Transitive, 39, 45, 158, 166-167, 170, 226-229, 234, 285
Traugott, Elizabeth, 3-4, 39, 65, 127, 156, 195
Travis, Lisa, 109
Tsai, Wei-Tien Dylan, 55, 156
Tsang, Chui Lim, 300
T'ung, Ping-cheng, 181, 278
Twi, 92
Unaccusative, 31, 45, 283
Unergative, 189, 207, 209, 216, 283
Unidirectionality, 4
Vendler, Zeno, 239, 269
Vennemann, Theo, 206
Vergnaud, Jean-Roger, 49, 62, 64, 66, 69, 71, 75, 107, 110, 115
Vietnamese, 223
Viewpoint aspect, 11, 234, 239-249, 257, 266, 269-270, 282, 297-298
Vincent, Nigel, 110
Visser, Fredericus T., 220, 222
Wahba, Wafaa, 291
Wang, Li, 201, 232

Wh adjunct, 54, 73, 134-137, 145-146, 149, 157
Wu, Guo, 125, 179, 183, 200, 235
Wu, Zhi-qian, 232
Wu, Zoe, 116, 151, 156, 299
Yip, Virginia, 46
Yoon, James, 26
Zou, Ke, 162-163, 167-170, 173-175
Zubizarreta, Maria Luisa, 49, 66, 101
Zwicky, Arnold, 46